"Packed full of insight, colour and impressive detail, this book will be studied for years to come by civil servants, politicians and anyone who wants to understand what makes good governments succeed and why they sometimes fail to deliver."

ED BALLS, FORMER CABINET MINISTER

"This is a special book. Not only does Michelle Clement possess a rare gift for making the entrails of government fascinating; she has another precious talent: for persuading key players to tell her everything and to hand over their documents. As long as there are people interested in the Blair years, this book will keep both its inherent vitality and its importance for future governments striving to reform Whitehall."

PETER HENNESSY, ATTLEE PROFESSOR OF CONTEMPORARY BRITISH HISTORY AT QUEEN MARY UNIVERSITY OF LONDON

"A compelling and clear analysis. Combining sharp insight and subtle nuance, Michelle Clement chronicles how the Blair government sought to galvanise the machine to modernise public services that had fallen into disrepair. The story Michelle tells is often close to the bone. She paints a picture of how that government painstakingly acquired the know-how to make transformation possible. This book is required reading for those interested in effecting change today."

ALAN MILBURN, FORMER HEALTH SECRETARY

"Understanding public service reform is the key to understanding the Blair government, and this book is the key to both. Michelle Clement writes with flair and clarity about the creation of the Prime Minister's Delivery Unit and its work, capturing the uncertainty, wrong turnings and political tensions of the period. The result is a superb account of the development of a new way of thinking about public services and its maturing into a successful method of service improvement. This book is absolutely essential reading for anyone who wants to understand how to make public services work better."

JOHN RENTOUL, CHIEF POLITICAL COMMENTATOR, *THE INDEPENDENT*

"Michelle Clement's book is both timely and insightful. Tony Blair's New Labour government, though ambitious and eager to make progress, ultimately learnt through trial and error. Michelle's book, based on new research, reveals the unvarnished story of how we learnt the art of delivery and transformed the quality of public services. I highly recommend this book to those at the sharp end now."

SALLY MORGAN, FORMER POLITICAL SECRETARY TO PRIME MINISTER TONY BLAIR

"'Deliver or die', as Tony Blair put it. Michelle Clement has given us the definitive account of how Blair and his guru of deliverology, Michael Barber, revolutionised modern government. With fascinating insider detail and valuable insights, Michelle shows us the ups and downs of refocusing the government machinery and bending it to the Prime Minister's will."

SIMON CASE, FORMER CABINET SECRETARY

THE ART OF DELIVERY

THE INSIDE STORY OF HOW THE BLAIR GOVERNMENT TRANSFORMED BRITAIN'S PUBLIC SERVICES

MICHELLE CLEMENT

Biteback Publishing

First published in Great Britain in 2025 by
Biteback Publishing Ltd, London
Copyright © Michelle Clement 2025

ISBN 978-1-78590-851-4

10 9 8 7 6 5 4 3 2 1

A CIP catalogue record for this book is available from the British Library.

Set in Adobe Caslon Pro and Futura

Printed and bound in Great Britain by
CPI Group (UK) Ltd, Croydon CR0 4YY

FSC
www.fsc.org
MIX
Paper | Supporting
responsible forestry
FSC® C013604

For my mum and dad, who devoted themselves to our family and in doing so left their own motherlands (in Scotland and Pakistan). They instilled in me a deep curiosity for life. For my husband, whose creativity and capacity to listen inspire me every day. For my five siblings, the first 'decision makers' I sought to understand, who remind me of the whole of which I am part. Thank you.

CONTENTS

FOREWORD
BY SIR MICHAEL BARBER

Michelle Clement has written a book which is an important contribution to contemporary history – well-written, well-researched and fascinating. As a character in the story, I am obviously biased, but, given the numerous attempts to replicate the story Michelle tells, I think the 'fascinating' is justified.

Immediately after his 2001 landslide election victory, Tony Blair asked me to set up for him a Delivery Unit that would bring real discipline to implementation and delivery of his domestic policy priorities. He had learnt from his first term and the campaign he had just been through that the public liked the agenda he had set out but were frustrated that so little had changed on the ground. Where were the results?

He said the electorate had given him 'an instruction to deliver' and passed the instruction on to me.

In education there had been some progress in the first term and the challenge Blair set me was: could we apply the discipline of delivery we had shown in education to other domestic policy priorities, such as health, crime reduction and transport?

Working closely with Blair – he was totally committed to delivery throughout his second term – that is what the Prime Minister's Delivery Unit did over the next four years.

Neither Tony Blair nor I knew at the time that what we developed was a significant innovation in how governments could work. Over the years that followed, numerous governments across the globe sought to emulate what we had done. Some did so in a shallow way: the organisation chart included a delivery unit, but it lacked the focus, the rigour, the processes and the persistence to make any real difference. Often, too, a so-called delivery unit didn't understand the culture needed to succeed. And sometimes the leader didn't make the commitment to delivery that Tony Blair so clearly did. But there have also been many governments that learnt deeply from our experience and succeeded. These governments learnt both the science and the art of delivery.

This is what makes Michelle Clement's book so important. She has told the story of the original PMDU and explained how it developed both the science and the art of getting things done. In order to do so with such depth of insight, she has, like all great contemporary historians, interviewed all the key players involved, including the PM, Cabinet ministers and top civil servants. She has also interviewed some of the PMDU team. In addition, Michelle was able to draw on many available documents. She also had access to one unique source.

Over the four years in which I set up and led the PMDU, I kept a diary: at the end of each busy week, I spent hours writing up what had happened and what I had learnt, often drawing on scribbled notes I had made during meetings. When Michelle embarked on this project I lent the diaries to her, hundreds of thousands of hand-written words, completely uncensored.

I personally have never read my diaries (though I have used them to check the accuracy of my own memory when writing my own books). What that means is that, while I wrote them, Michelle is the only person who has actually read my diaries She alone has decided what to include from them and what not to.

I should add, as Michelle will testify, that while I was interviewed for her book like everyone else, at no point have I sought to influence how she tells the story or the judgements she reaches. It's her book and hers alone.

There has never been a time in history when the need for governments to deliver on their promises has been more important than now. Cynicism about politics, politicians and government has grown, is growing and needs to be diminished because it is dangerous. If people lose faith in the whole political system, inevitably they will turn to populist propositions which, while they sound plausible and attractive, are in fact unworkable and destructive. We see exactly this occurring in many places around the world.

Effective delivery alone cannot reverse these disturbing trends – but it is equally clear that they cannot be reversed in the absence of delivery.

Michelle's book, in addition to being an excellent contribution to contemporary history and a good story, is an instructive text for anyone who wants governments in future to deliver results that citizens see, feel, benefit from and perhaps even appreciate! In short, here you will find a great read and a foundation for optimism.

Sir Michael Barber
Author of How to Run a Government
January 2025

CHAPTER ONE

AN INSTRUCTION TO DELIVER: REFORMING BRITAIN'S PUBLIC SERVICES

It is June 2001, you are the Prime Minister, Tony Blair, and you have just won a historic second landslide victory at the polls but the growing rivalry with your second in command, the Chancellor of the Exchequer, Gordon Brown, threatens to derail your ambitious domestic plans for government. What do you do? You decide to create the first ever Prime Minister's Delivery Unit. But what difference can it possibly make, given the fraying tightrope between the Prime Minister and the Chancellor?

Fast forward six months: Prime Minister Tony Blair's right hand official, Jeremy Heywood, tells the head of the Prime Minister's Delivery Unit: 'You've massively increased the power of the Prime Minister without damaging any relationships.'

This is a book about how Sir Michael Barber, who designed and led the Prime Minister's Delivery Unit, crafted an *art of delivery* which transformed the quality of our public services. Whether you are a citizen, policymaker, public servant or politician, the NHS, schools, crime prevention and public transport systems are the public services we use every day. This book offers a story that is yet to be told, one that gives us an understanding of our own shared history. It seeks to unveil what it really takes to govern from No. 10, in a way that makes a real difference to citizens who use and fund public services.

Since the turn of the century, the British government, and increasingly governments around the world, have sought to develop new frameworks to pursue the implementation of their reform agendas. Despite the fact that previous governments and Prime Ministers have long had programmes to 'deliver', there was a step change during Tony Blair's premiership when the Prime Minister's Delivery Unit (PMDU) was created, in June 2001. Sir Michael Barber was made Blair's chief adviser on delivery. The decision to create such a role, and an accompanying unit, was only taken after much prime ministerial anxiety during Blair's first term in office.

The Labour Party won the 1997 general election with the biggest parliamentary majority since the Second World War. Nevertheless, two years into his first term, Blair had become dissatisfied with the slow pace of progress on delivering public service reform – which was central to his mission. Despite the major success of constitutional changes such as the partial reform of the House of Lords and the Good Friday Agreement in Northern Ireland, Blair later suggested that he 'largely wasted his first term'.[1] In 1999, speaking to the Venture Capital Association, he complained of having 'scars on my back' as a result of trying to modernise public services.[2] Blair's rhetoric was arguably a reflection of his own frustration at the challenge of learning how to govern both effectively and boldly. Prime Ministers really do have to learn on the job! During Blair's first couple of years as Prime Minister, he was still deciding how to make his public service reform agenda more radical. By 2000, he had recognised that in relation to ambitious public service reform 'he had to deliver or die'.[3] In the 2001 general election, New Labour won a second big victory, which gave Blair a renewed mandate to govern. Shortly afterwards, Blair told the British people that he took the result as a 'mandate for reform … an instruction to deliver'.[4]

Towards the end of the first term Blair and his advisers looked to the progress being made in education reform, and a key individual delivering this change was Michael Barber. From 1997 to 2001, Barber was chief adviser on school standards to David Blunkett, the Secretary of State for Education and Employment. On taking up his position in the (then) Department for Education and Employment (DfEE), Barber set up and headed the Standards and Effectiveness Unit (SEU). The Permanent Secretary of the DfEE, Michael Bichard, accepted that his department 'as then constituted, could never deliver what the new government would require'.[5] Through the new unit, Barber's aim was therefore to 'change the culture of the department as well as implement the schools reforms'.[6] His approach to implementing these reforms won him respect and good relations with many ministers and civil servants – a hard task for any political appointee working in Whitehall. Indeed, Blair told Barber and the SEU team that they were 'true pioneers'.[7]

By the beginning of 2001, Barber had made the unusual transition from special adviser to civil servant, with a view to pursuing further roles within the department. As a direct result of making progress in education, Barber was asked by Blair's team to propose a design for a 'delivery unit'. After discussion with Blair's closest political advisers and civil servants, Barber was formally asked to establish the Prime Minister's Delivery Unit shortly after the 2001 election. As historian Anthony Seldon noted, 'Blair decided to import his [Barber's] unit and its methodology wholesale into his own empire.'[8] From 2001 to 2005, Barber led the PMDU.

The PMDU was created with the aim of monitoring and

accelerating the delivery of the Prime Minister's public service reform priorities in major policy areas including education, health, transport, crime and asylum. These policy areas encompassed many of the key public services that citizens used regularly and which needed improving after decades of underinvestment and too little focus on raising the standards of services provided. Thus Blair and his government chose to ensure that over the course of the parliament they would focus on targets that made a difference to the daily lives of citizens. These included reducing waiting times in Accident & Emergency and for elective operations, improving the numeracy and literacy skills of school pupils, reducing crime and getting trains to run on time as well as increasing the numbers of nurses, doctors and teachers.

The Delivery Unit mainly worked with four 'delivery departments': the Department for Education and Skills, the Department of Health, the Department for Transport and the Home Office. Throughout Blair's government, there was a second centre of power to the Prime Minister – the Treasury under the Chancellor of the Exchequer, Gordon Brown. A significant source of growing tension between Blair and Brown was the very policy areas where the new Delivery Unit was tasked with building consensus and achieving progress. To be effective, the PMDU had to develop and maintain good relations with No. 10, the Treasury under Brown, Cabinet ministers, special advisers and senior civil servants in the relevant departments. No other prime ministerial unit had such a challenging mission. Under Barber's leadership, the Unit was broadly able to do this. This resulted in the PMDU being institutionally part of No. 10 and the Cabinet Office and physically based (for the most part) within the Treasury, working closely with Treasury officials to align the Unit's targets with the Treasury's own performance measurement framework – public service agreements (PSAs).

Three key elements of Barber's original design brief proved useful throughout his tenure. First, there would be 'rigorous and relentless focus on a relatively small number of the Prime Minister's key priorities'.[9] This meant that Blair and his government were required to identify and adhere to a clear set of domestic objectives – something that had not happened in the first term. Second, Barber decided to keep the Unit small, which allowed it to be agile when developing a delivery method and culture. He was also keen to avoid it becoming a large bureaucratic unit overseeing an even larger bureaucracy, which some Whitehall units had tended to do, leaving them vulnerable to budget cuts and making them more cumbersome to manage. Third, the initial design tied in the Prime Minister's time, the most valued resource in Whitehall, to the delivery of priorities by introducing stocktake meetings. Every two to three months for each priority area, the Prime Minister would meet with the relevant Cabinet minister and Permanent Secretary, the Chief Secretary to the Treasury, Treasury officials and the PMDU team led by Barber to discuss the delivery status of each target. This ensured that the Prime Minister was regularly engaged with the work of his Delivery Unit. The stocktake proved to be a powerful forum for collective discussion and accountability, chaired by the Prime Minister.

The Delivery Unit introduced a new level of accountability within the Civil Service for the delivery of specific targets such as requiring hospitals to treat 98 per cent of A&E patients within four hours. Whitehall civil servants had not previously been held accountable for such specific delivery targets, supported by a delivery framework led by the Prime Minister. Successive Cabinet

Secretaries and Permanent Secretaries accepted and advocated the need to focus on delivery, especially given the huge increase in funding for public services such as the NHS. The PMDU approach to delivery was seen as controversial by some who thought it exacerbated top-down policymaking from No. 10 to departments and contributed to a target-led culture – the journalist Simon Jenkins argued that the Unit disempowered departments.[10] Peter Hyman, a key strategist to Blair from 1994 to 2003 and head of the Prime Minister's Strategic Communications Unit from 2001 to 2003, has written on the 'delivery pains' of Blair's first years in government. He explained that 'focusing on "delivery" – with the introduction of numerous targets – was controversial' but that it was intended to improve Labour's reputation on spending.[11] A further reason for Blair's explicit focus on delivery was 'to change the culture of the Civil Service away from just policy formation ... and instead [to focus] on tangible results'.[12] Hyman characterised Barber as 'one of the most impressive and talented people I worked with in government. Quietly spoken but authoritative and reflective.'[13] Yet Hyman still questioned whether this would be enough.

> [I was] sceptical at first that he [Barber] would be the man to bang heads together in Whitehall and drive through delivery, but his relentless focus on outcomes and his collegiate way of working with departments, as well as his close working relationship with Tony, ensured that he was just about our most effective operator.[14]

In four years, as head of the PMDU, Barber developed an approach which the then managing director of public services in HM Treasury, Nicholas Macpherson, named 'deliverology'.[15] Deliverology has become a tool valued by central and local governments and global organisations. The former president of the World Bank Jim Yong Kim began his tenure (2012–19) by discussing the 'emerging science of delivery' aimed at better understanding not 'what to deliver' but 'how to deliver'.[16] Since leaving government, Barber has further developed his science of delivery – the processes and structures to accelerate results.[17] This book examines what the present author has identified as the 'art of delivery'.[18] The art of delivery is the other side of the proverbial delivery coin: in short it is the shared history, deep understanding of political context and ability to build cooperative relationships which lubricates the machinery of government. Without an understanding of the art, the science of delivery is ineffective. One could loosely compare the science and the art of delivery to the established foreign policy concepts of 'hard power' and 'soft power' developed by Joseph Nye, American political scientist and former Assistant Secretary of Defense in the Clinton administration. Hard power can manifest as military capability, that is, using explicit force to achieve a result; whereas Nye's definition of 'soft power' is 'the ability to get what you want through attraction rather than coercion or payments'.[19] Through the course of this book, Barber and the Delivery Unit's ability to accumulate and apply a version of 'soft power' will be shown to be essential in sculpting the art of delivery.

In 2005, after Barber left government, the PMDU was remoulded and its workload diversified and expanded, eventually being absorbed into the Treasury during Brown's premiership. Yet Barber's legacy can be traced beyond his departure. After the formation of the coalition government in 2010, Conservative Prime Minister David Cameron abolished what remained of the Delivery

Unit, seeing it as too associated with New Labour and a tool of big government. Looking back, Cameron's former Chancellor of the Exchequer George Osborne questioned Cameron about 'drinking' the Conservative Party's 'own Kool-Aid that No. 10 was too big, that Tony Blair had made it too presidential. We got rid of the Delivery Unit ... and then essentially have to recreate it.' In response, Cameron admitted, 'That was a mistake. We did believe our own propaganda about an inflated No. 10.'[20] In 2011, Cameron set up a similar body called the Implementation Group, which later became known as the Implementation Unit (IU). It had the task of ensuring the implementation of the Prime Minister's and deputy Prime Minister's policy priorities. Barber's legacy had once again become a valued resource for a new government. Efforts to support and stabilise working in coalition resulted in the dilution of power and depoliticisation of the centre of government, which meant that the IU operated on the basis of reduced authoritative power. In 2011 Michael Gove, then Conservative Secretary of State for Education, sought to appoint Barber as Permanent Secretary in the Department for Education but he was unsuccessful.[21] This demonstrated the value of Barber's expertise across the political spectrum. Twenty years after the original PMDU was set up, Conservative Prime Minister Boris Johnson commissioned a review from Barber on his government's capacity to deliver. Subsequently a new Prime Minister's Delivery Unit was formed in early 2021 to manage the post-Covid pandemic domestic priorities of the government.[22] The Johnson Delivery Unit continued to be utilised by his successors after he resigned in 2023. But the advent of four Conservative Prime Ministers between 2016 and 2024, each with their own priorities, created instability in the system of government. On 4 July 2024,

Labour won a general election for the first time in nineteen years. The new Labour government under Sir Keir Starmer ran their campaign on a plan to galvanise government around five long-term 'missions'. As part of this mission-driven government, Prime Minister Starmer quickly created a new Mission Delivery Unit, with career civil servant Clara Swinson as its head. Swinson had been a pivotal member of the original Delivery Unit under Barber, and in the intervening years had remained in the Civil Service taking on senior roles in the Department of Health. Alongside the new unit, Starmer appointed Liz Lloyd as Director of Policy, Delivery and Innovation. Lloyd had been Blair's longest-serving adviser (1993 to 2007), rising to deputy chief of staff in 2005. After leaving government in 2007, she built a successful career in finance and global development, most recently at British International Investment. Completing the delivery triangle, Michael Barber was appointed as the Prime Minister's Adviser on Effective Delivery (on a part-time basis). More than two decades after it was established, the Delivery Unit model remains instructive for governments of the day.

In June 2015, speaking to the Strand Group at King's College London, Blair explained that Barber's approach with the PMDU was 'quite revolutionary, more so than we realised at the time'.[23] Since leaving government, Barber has advised more than fifty countries on delivery of domestic policy priorities, including Canada, Pakistan and Malaysia, as well as global institutions and companies.[24] In doing so he has tested and adapted 'deliverology'. Beyond his book *Instruction to Deliver: Fighting to Transform Britain's Public Services*, there has yet to be a comprehensive, independent and rigorous study of the PMDU from 2001 to 2005. This book represents the first study of Barber and the PMDU with the added and crucial dimension of first-hand access to Barber's private and extensive unpublished, handwritten diaries. That resource provides lessons on how the PMDU worked in practice – it enables one to garner new and detailed insights into how and why the PMDU was created, what challenges Barber encountered, and how he and the Unit responded to them. This book is also a lens through which to view wider themes related to how government really works in practice – the power of the Prime Minister, the role of the Civil Service in public service delivery, and media spin versus substance.

During New Labour's second term, the Delivery Unit under Barber began the huge task of shifting the psychology of government towards innovative methods for effective delivery. This book offers new insights into how a government can improve results across the most important areas of public service provision.

BARBER THE MAN

As Prime Minister, Tony Blair set the scope and detail of his public service reform agenda alongside key Cabinet ministers but it was Michael Barber whom Blair entrusted to build an effective unit to ensure it actually happened. To make sense of the approach Barber developed, it is helpful to look back at his life and experiences prior to 1997.

Michael Barber was born into a Quaker family. His father, Christopher Barber, was a pacifist who spent much of the Second World War driving medical supplies across China. He was an accountant by training and chairman of Oxfam from 1983 to 1989.[25] Barber's mother, Anne, read medicine at the University of Oxford, and was one of the first women admitted to Barts Hospital as a clinical student.[26] Barber recalled that as a child his mother taught him about equality.[27] He would later draw 'deeply' on his Quaker upbringing during his time in government.[28] Britain's public services and public sector embody many Quaker principles – challenging injustice through peaceful means and speaking truth to power – and thus Barber's choice of career aligned with his family background. He attended an independent Quaker school, Bootham in York, where he developed a passion for history and, incidentally, was taught by the father of his future colleague Jeremy Heywood.

The popular and political culture of the era in which Barber grew up shaped him. He characterised himself as a 'student radical of the 60s/70s grown up to be hard-edged because positive change depends on it'.[29] The late 1960s and 1970s were decades in which Britain experienced the deepest lows of relative economic decline, and successive governments of both political hues tried (and largely failed) to lift the country out of this intractable economic quagmire. The country was beset by energy crises, sterling crises, debt crises and major trade union strikes – immortalised in the collective memory by the three-day week and the Winter of Discontent. In the decade that followed, Margaret Thatcher's Conservative government launched an economic strategy which helped to put the economy on an upward trajectory, though this came at the cost of high unemployment. Her industrial policies had a damaging impact on communities which relied on manufacturing and mining. In 1974, Barber went on to read history at the University of Oxford where he developed an admiration for historic Labour Party 'heroes', including Aneurin Bevan, who as minister of health (1945–51) played a central role in creating the National Health Service.[30] Barber was active in college politics and was elected president of the Queen's College Student Union.[31] He trained as a teacher in the late 1970s, and taught history and English in secondary schools in London and then Zimbabwe.

By the mid-1980s, Barber began to see 'active politics as a way to change the world'; he became a Labour councillor in Hackney (where he lived) from 1986 to 1990.[32] As a councillor, Barber found that his weekly surgeries were regularly focused on housing complaints. But he was largely 'unable to get the bureaucracy' to resolve these issues.[33] He also joined the National Union of Teachers (NUT), where he worked on policy and research and engaged with the Conservative government of the day.[34] In the late 1980s, he was elected chair of education for Hackney; in this role he engaged with Labour shadow ministers including Jack Straw, who at the time led on education.[35] During the 1987 general election, Barber unsuccessfully ran as the Labour Party parliamentary candidate against incumbent Conservative MP Michael Heseltine in Henley-on-Thames. In 1993, he began working at Keele University where he was made professor of education before moving to the Institute of Education at the University of London two years later. Barber described his career up to this point as in the 'borderlands' of various roles within the education sector.[36]

During the summer of 1994, Barber was asked to advise on a speech on education that Tony Blair was due to make as part of his campaign to lead the Labour Party.[37] Blair won the leadership election in July 1994. As an education expert, Barber was then invited by Blair's head of policy, David Miliband (whom he had known for a couple of years), to advise on Labour's education policy. Barber met Blair for the first time in January 1995, and he was struck by how open the agenda was and how committed the new leader was to making education his top priority.[38] In a paper for this meeting, Barber set out two principles which underpinned his professional approach then and now: one, 'intervention should be in inverse proportion to success'; two, 'standards matter more than structures'.[39] The following year, Barber was asked to write a paper on what Labour's agenda for a second term might be. He argued for 'a radical shift of power and direction from producer to consumer'.[40] This was in line with the emerging New Labour ethos. From this point onwards, Barber became regularly involved in advising Miliband, David Blunkett and Blunkett's chief policy and press adviser Conor Ryan.[41] During this time he continued to give speeches on the education sector. In one lecture at Greenwich Town Hall, he challenged the complacent culture that he believed had developed within the teaching profession, whereby failure was accepted:

> For too long, it has been a powerful strand of the culture of this country that failure in education is inevitable and, like the poor, it will always be with us ... We, as educators, might be expected to be in the vanguard of a campaign to challenge this poverty-stricken culture. In fact, all too often we reinforce it.[42]

This blend of Quaker upbringing, 1970s student radicalism, political experience as an inner London Labour councillor dealing with local and often intractable issues, and diverse roles in the education sector on the frontline and in devising policy, as well as an appreciation of historic Labour Party figures who had helped build the welfare state, came together to produce the Michael Barber who helped to craft the education strategy for a first-term Labour government. Andrew Adonis, special adviser to Blair and later minister for schools, described Barber at the beginning of the Blair government as a 'brilliantly can-do and insightful London university education professor' with experience that meant 'he knew every crevice of the political as well as educational mountain he was climbing'.[43] Clara Swinson, a civil servant who worked for Barber in the Delivery

Unit, noted the impact Barber's educationalist background had: 'Fundamentally, his background was as an educationalist. It was about learning, it was about "What's the current position? What can we do better? What can we learn from that kind of learning as an organisation?"'[44]

Once New Labour was elected in May 1997, Barber found himself 'taking responsibility for the implementation of the policy strategy' which he partly developed.[45] In 1997, Blunkett as Secretary of State for Education appointed Barber to become head of the Standards and Effectiveness Unit (SEU) in the DfEE. The SEU became a sizeable unit, focused on school standards reform, particularly numeracy and literacy. The implementation of the National Literacy Strategy was one of the main successes achieved in the first term.[46] Leading the SEU was a formative experience for Barber: 'I found myself learning how to manage not just officials, but also the system as a whole.'[47] He encountered civil servants who lacked a belief in their ability to achieve 'visible change'.[48] The SEU taught Barber lessons that he would be mindful of when it came to the PMDU. For instance, by the end of 2000, the SEU became 'too large' (around 300 people) and the 'widening span of responsibility' meant that he was 'no longer on top of the detail'.[49]

In early 2001, Barber formally became a senior civil servant, an uncommon move for a political appointee.[50] This perhaps demonstrated his dedication to education reform and indicated his intended career path after the election. Barber, however, was not a career civil servant. He believed that the New Labour education policies had 'brought a new set of values to education reform in which diversity, co-operation, equity and commitment to tackling disadvantage were given priority alongside the market values of the previous government'.[51] In 2000, he outlined his commitment to delivery in the first term and beyond:

> Having set high profile national targets and established clear objectives for the end of the present Parliament, the government has to ensure it will be held to account by the people for the delivery of those outcomes. Politically, this is either bold or foolhardy, depending on your perspective. Our view is that the risk is worth taking because it helps to create a performance culture and ensures sustained focus … People are impatient for change and suspicious of politicians who cannot demonstrate that they are delivering what they promised.[52]

The following statement, also from 2000, on the components of successful education reform was indicative of Barber's later approach with the PMDU:

> Whether we succeed will, in the end, depend on whether we are able to sustain our focus and maintain the drive for change, whether we are capable of resolving the dilemmas that arise regularly in any process of complex change and whether we are able to convince teachers and the wider public that much higher standards than have ever been achieved before are not only possible in theory but also achievable in practice.[53]

These insights into Barber 'the man' provide an indication as to why he was supportive of public service reform, his own ambitions, why delivery mattered to him and his personal experience of what it takes to deliver domestic reform in government. When it comes down to it, government is run by the people for the people, and so in seeking to understand how it works it is crucial to understand the protagonists and their relationships with one another.

THE DELIVERY UNIT IN HISTORICAL CONTEXT

The Prime Minister's Delivery Unit was in many ways a distinctly new invention. But several prime ministerial units were created in the twentieth century to improve the effectiveness of government which resonate with the PMDU. One can go further back, as academics Andrew Blick and George Jones have. They note that in December 1873, Prime Minister William Gladstone asked his private secretary, Algernon West, for evidence of the India Office's poor performance.[54]

LLOYD GEORGE – GARDEN SUBURB, CREATION OF CABINET OFFICE AND SECRETARY TO THE CABINET

Upon becoming Prime Minister in December 1916 during the Great War emergency, David Lloyd George introduced reforms that transformed the machinery of central government. He created the Cabinet Office, the position of Secretary to the Cabinet and his own Prime Minister's Secretariat. The Cabinet Office originally emerged out of the War Cabinet Secretariat, which was formed to provide administrative support to the War Cabinet and later to the Cabinet. The modern-day Cabinet Office is now the overall coordinating department of central government, primarily providing administrative support to the Prime Minister, the Cabinet and Cabinet committees.

The powerful Civil Service role of Secretary to the War Cabinet, which became Secretary to the Cabinet (commonly known as Cabinet Secretary), was established and the position has continued thereafter. The holder not only takes the minutes of Cabinet meetings but is also one of the most senior advisers to the Prime Minister. The first holder of the post was Sir Maurice Hankey, who held the position for twenty-two years, until 1938. In the words of Sir Robert Vansittart, a senior British diplomat, Hankey 'progressively became secretary of everything that mattered'.[55] Since the 1980s, the position has often been fused with the role of head of the Home Civil Service.

The Prime Minister's Secretariat, known as the Garden Suburb (due to initially being housed in temporary huts in the garden of 10 Downing Street), was staffed by a small group of advisers to Lloyd George, each with their own policy area. Its role was never clearly defined.[56] The note announcing its establishment on 5 January 1917 explained: 'The Prime Minister has decided, with a view to keeping himself in close touch with the several Departments, to establish a Department in connection with the Office of the First Lord of the Treasury.'[57] It formed part of a new highly centralised machine organised around the Prime Minister, rather than the Cabinet, which helped Lloyd George bridge policy and politics in wartime. Though the Garden Suburb was described as a department, it operated as a secretariat and at its peak was made up of six members of staff.

In March 1918 the head of the Garden Suburb, political scientist W. G. S. Adams, noted the role and impact of the secretariat. The staff created 'free and informal' relationships with departments 'to help the departments in getting matters to the attention of the Prime Minister when they were of urgency, and, as far as possible to arrange and prevent matters from pressing upon the Prime

Minister'.[58] Adams explained that it had been 'possible to do a great deal in the way of securing settlement on points upon which there was doubt, if not dispute, and of helping to bring people and bodies together who would benefit by closer relationship with one another in their work'.[59] The Garden Suburb provided a channel for the Prime Minister to communicate and loosely monitor priorities, and to assist in joining up departments to create common goals. After the war ended in 1918, the Garden Suburb was scaled down and eventually abolished; the purpose of the secretariat would, however, re-emerge in future premierships.

WINSTON CHURCHILL – STATISTICAL SECTION

When Winston Churchill became Prime Minister in 1940, he brought with him a unit known as the Statistical Branch which he had set up a year earlier as First Lord of the Admiralty. The unit became known as the Statistical Section and was headed by Churchill's good friend the physicist Professor Frederick Linde-mann (later Lord Cherwell). Again, this prime ministerial unit was created during war, when efficient monitoring and coordination of outputs was essential. The Statistical Section was staffed by around twenty people, including economists and civil servants. Churchill found it helpful that complex questions could be resolved in quantitative terms; moreover, he was suspicious of the statistics produced by departments of their own activities and so wanted independent appraisal.[60] Weekly charts were produced which showed the state of aircraft production, the losses and new building of ships, the output of tanks and guns and the availability of coal stocks.[61] The main channel of power between the unit and the Prime Minister was through notes from Lindemann to Churchill, roughly once a day.[62] The Statistical Section did not survive the change of government in

July 1945 but like the PMDU, it provided the Prime Minister of the day with reliable information and data about the implementation of policy decisions. Both units, sixty years apart, faced struggles in obtaining data from departments and both were aided by the Cabinet Secretary (of the day).

EDWARD HEATH – CENTRAL POLICY REVIEW STAFF

In 1971, Edward Heath's government created the Central Policy Review Staff (CPRS), known as the 'Think Tank', to fill a gap at the centre of government. It performed three main functions: early warning of major issues affecting the government's objectives, 'keeper of government strategy and scrutineer of selective policy'.[63] The latter two functions were where it had most success. Heath retrospectively defined its mission as 'If not think the unthinkable, then at least express the uncomfortable.'[64] It was located in the Cabinet Office and the formidable businessman and scientist Lord Rothschild was appointed as its first chairman. It was later led by economist Kenneth Berrill, then businessman Robin Ibbs and finally by merchant banker John Sparrow. Like the PMDU, it was staffed by a small team. The CPRS had around twenty people at any one time, consisting of a mix of civil servants, academics and businesspeople. This was similar to Barber's later approach with the PMDU. Heath, who was often hostile to the Treasury, created the CPRS in part as a challenge to the Treasury's monopoly; its relations with the Treasury were not harmonious.[65]

Despite being a relatively small unit, the CPRS focused on broad and disparate issues which changed from year to year. In 1972, its portfolio included 'unemployment and inflation, energy and raw materials, resource allocation, growth and declining industries'.[66] It did not initially consider intelligence or foreign affairs issues. The

CPRS strengthened the power of the Prime Minister, not least through the 'clarity of information' it provided.[67] The PMDU's expertise in gathering data to assess performance echoes this. Heath's successors, Harold Wilson and James Callaghan, kept the CPRS in place and found it useful, but Margaret Thatcher disbanded it in 1983. Interestingly Sir Richard Wilson, Cabinet Secretary from 1998 to 2002, compared the CPRS, which he called an 'intellectual powerhouse', to the PMDU.[68] The CPRS was, however, more functionally akin to the Strategy Unit that was set up during Blair's second term. In 1970, Heath also set up the Programme and Analysis Review initiative, which operated outside the Treasury to review existing government programmes, with a view to cutting unnecessary functions and bureaucracy. There was, however, a lack of political will among ministers to cut any major functions of government.[69]

HAROLD WILSON – POLICY UNIT

In his first period in government, from 1964 to 1970, Harold Wilson brought in the first modern-era peacetime paid special advisers. Since then they have been a permanent feature of government. In 1974, when he became Prime Minister again, Wilson set up his own Policy Unit within No. 10 to provide more politically attuned policy advice on short- to medium-term issues. This too has continued to be a model for all Prime Ministers to the present day. It has typically been headed by a special adviser and staffed by a mix of special advisers and civil servants. Prior to 1974, the Civil Service had been the main supplier of policy advice, certainly since the First World War. The innovation marked the desire of a Prime Minister who wanted to engage 'much more deeply' in departments.[70] For example, Wilson used the 'fledgling but quickly influential Policy Unit to combat Tony Benn's interventionist industrial strategy'.[71] This was demonstrably true for Blair too. The Policy Unit did not have a set methodology, and each Prime Minister subsequently shaped it to match their agenda. The Policy Unit strengthened the centre of government, particularly the office of the Prime Minister. Though both the Policy Unit and the Delivery Unit had to command the confidence of the Prime Minister through effectiveness, there are no clear parallels between the ways in which they operated.

MARGARET THATCHER – EFFICIENCY UNIT

In 1979, Margaret Thatcher appointed Derek Rayner to advise her on efficiency and he quickly created the Efficiency Unit. Rayner had been joint managing director of Marks & Spencer and had advised Heath's government on defence procurement. The unit was staffed by civil servants and Rayner purposely kept it small because a larger organisation would 'add to bureaucracy rather than lessen it'.[72] This is a principle from which Barber learnt. The Efficiency Unit produced 'scrutinies', whereby it conducted in-depth studies of specific aspects of government and then suggested solutions to issues that it had identified, with the aim of improving efficiency. Thatcher made it clear that she supported the scrutinies, which carried weight in Whitehall.[73] Rayner said 'the purpose of scrutinies is action, not study'.[74] Again, this is a distinction that Barber later made with the PMDU priority reviews.

Rayner left the Efficiency Unit in 1982 and was succeeded by Robin Ibbs. Ibbs wrote the 1988 report 'Improving Management in Government: The Next Steps', which led to far-reaching changes within the Civil Service. It suggested the creation of a multitude of executive agencies with responsibility for operational delivery, which would have significant powers related to budgets and hiring.

These agencies would perform executive functions that were then managed within Whitehall, and this would result in a slimmed-down Civil Service. Thatcher accepted the Next Steps recommendations and within a few years dozens of agencies had been created, employing tens of thousands of people. Early agencies included the Vehicle Inspectorate, HM Stationery Office and Companies House.[75] Next Steps did not, however, resolve the issue of operational delivery capacity within Whitehall departments. Such capacity would become important as taxpayers, citizens and politicians increasingly came to expect higher standards of public services. Meeting these expectations and addressing the gaps in capacity would become the focus for the Delivery Unit.

JOHN MAJOR – CITIZEN'S CHARTER

In 1991, John Major launched the Citizen's Charter to improve public services and make them more responsive to the service user. It was the focus on the citizen as the customer of public services that was most radical. The scheme established individual charters for public services which set out standards that the user should expect to receive. The charters would act effectively as a contract between service providers and service users.[76] The implementation of the Citizen's Charter was poor and the initiative was not accompanied by investment in public services. Despite this, it did ignite a shift in thinking whereby citizens had the right to expect improved standards of public service delivery.[77]

This brief history of prime ministerial units provides a basis for understanding how the Delivery Unit fits into a range of twentieth-century prime ministerial changes to central machinery of government. With hindsight, one can see that elements of these reforms were also present in Blair's Delivery Unit: the centralising approach of Lloyd George's Cabinet Office and the explicitly prime ministerial focus of the Garden Suburb, the independent data-gathering of Churchill's Statistical Section, the early warning system that Heath sought through the CPRS, the politically attuned nature of Wilson's Policy Unit, the effective scrutiny of policy provided to Thatcher by the Efficiency Unit and the citizen's right to high-quality public services proposed by the Citizen's Charter.

THE DELIVERY METHOD OF THIS BOOK

The approach taken for creating this book builds on a foundation forged by pioneering historians of British government. My former lecturer at Queen Mary University of London, Professor Peter Hennessy, a journalist turned academic, has been developing an approach to the study of British government since the late 1980s. Both *Whitehall* and *The Prime Minister: The Office and Its Holders since 1945* have been instructive books in unearthing how British government – both its political and its civil servant components – work in practice. Secondly Professor Jon Davis, also my former lecturer down the Mile End Road, has built on the Hennessy style of contemporary history using dozens of interviews with prominent politicians, civil servants and special advisers to piece together a comprehensive and balanced account of Blair's premiership. His *Heroes or Villains? The Blair Government Reconsidered* was co-written with John Rentoul, chief political commentator for *The Independent* and visiting professor at King's College London, who though very much still an active journalist has been teaching students about 'The Blair Years' for fifteen years.

The following three factors have guided the formation of this book – policy, process and personality. In seeking to evaluate Barber and the Delivery Unit's art of delivery one must understand the policy that was being pursued, the process by which the decisions were taken and policy implementation was tracked, and the personalities of those who were undertaking the policy development and delivery – their working style and how they engaged with each other. This book focuses on the critical points of uncertainty where policy and process decisions and events arose, which were of fundamental importance to the success or failure of the Delivery Unit. In the words of Peter Hennessy, 'The job of the historian is to put back into the past the same uncertainty we feel today about the future – an indispensable requirement.'[78]

This book has benefited from an invaluable resource, not yet in the public domain: Michael Barber's private diaries. Barber handwrote his diary each week during his time as head of the PMDU. He kept the diary because he recognised the value in the vantage point he would have during a critical period – trying to deliver major public service reform – and this would be of historical importance, at the very least for his own record. Moreover, Barber is a historian by undergraduate training and an author of books that are based upon his own professional experiences. As part of conducting the research for this book, Barber's diaries from 2001 to 2005 have been transcribed by the present author and total almost 600,000 words. This project therefore represents a unique opportunity to conduct research with a new, rich in-depth resource. In utilising Barber's diaries an appropriately critical perspective has been maintained. Findings from the diaries have been cross-checked where possible and multiple viewpoints have been considered. The diaries also contain hard copies of some documents such as email exchanges and delivery updates.

In his diary entries, Barber would consider the events of each week with particular attention paid to his relations with senior politicians, advisers and civil servants, significant meetings or conversations that took place between himself and the aforementioned individuals, issues that had arisen or that he thought might arise, and potential solutions that he was contemplating. There were also regular reflections of his own standing with key individuals within government, and throughout much of the period Barber worried about being sufficiently 'in the loop' so as to maintain the importance of his own role and the effectiveness of the PMDU. From his viewpoint, he would often comment on the conduct of government and the state of relationships between the main protagonists of the Blair government. The Barber diaries thus provide an unprecedented week-by-week insight into how the Blair government developed, debated and delivered major public service reform.

The government papers from Blair's premiership have begun to be released at The National Archives, but given that they are not yet fully released they have not been used for this book. Reports by House of Commons select committees provide a wealth of analysis and primary sources, as do the minutes of evidence, which are publicly available (and often understudied). Media articles from the time inform the story, and help to identify uncertainties that are often lost with the passage of time. Published memoirs from central figures offer crucial detail and analysis from the time that may not be recorded in official documents; nevertheless they are subjective and present only one part of the story.

Interviews have been conducted by the author with several relevant senior civil servants, Cabinet ministers and special advisers,[79] to establish how events transpired, who was involved and what factors were significant in success or failure. The overall interview process was conducted based on an assessment of what is missing from existing publications in terms of content and perspective. There is a gap in the published literature on the Treasury vis-à-vis the Delivery Unit, despite the huge uncertainty as to whether a close working relationship could be formed and sustained. Securing interviews with prominent Treasury figures was therefore of fundamental importance in providing a new and balanced picture of how Barber and the Delivery Unit worked with the Treasury.

WHAT WE ALREADY KNOW

To date many prominent New Labour figures have published their recollections and reflections on all or some of their time in government. They include Andrew Adonis, Ed Balls, Michael Barber, Tony Blair, David Blunkett, Gordon Brown, Alastair Campbell, Alistair Darling, Peter Hyman, Peter Mandelson and Jonathan Powell. These books of New Labour politicians and advisers are immensely beneficial in cross-referencing important decisions, policies, personalities and crises as well as providing some insight into Barber and the Delivery Unit throughout the period.

In his autobiography, *A Journey*, Blair did not discuss the PMDU in detail though he did mention its creation, its ethos and its success. On the Delivery Unit's style of working, Blair wrote: 'It would focus like a laser on an issue, draw up a plan to resolve it, working with the department concerned, and then performance-manage it to solution.'[80] He explained that 'the concept of the Delivery Unit was Michael's idea'; 'it was an innovation that was much resisted, but utterly invaluable and proved its worth time and time again'.[81] In his role as Prime Minister, Blair reflected that 'in domestic policy, changing public service systems inevitably meant getting into the details of delivery and performance management in a radically more granular way'.[82] From his viewpoint, the 'problem with the traditional Civil Service was not obstruction, but inertia'.[83] He did, however, identify the strengths of the Civil Service: 'It was and is impartial. It is, properly directed, a formidable machine.'[84]

We now know something about the beginning, middle and end of the story of how the Blair government created a delivery unit to transform the quality of public services that we use each day, but much still remains a mystery. The forthcoming story will be about how it was done in real time, not a glossy overview devoid of uncertainty, challenge and failure. To my mind, this is the value of history, to feel something of what it was actually like to be there.

CHAPTER TWO

BLAIR'S FIRST TERM, 1997 TO 2001: UNDERPREPARED FOR GOVERNMENT

On 1 May 1997, after eighteen years out of government, the Labour Party won a landslide victory at the general election. Such a feat had been many years in the making. The huge majority, however, heightened public expectations. On becoming leader of the Labour Party in 1994, Tony Blair and his team set about making their party an election-winning machine. Blair's two predecessors, Neil Kinnock and John Smith, had begun the modernising process; indeed under Smith's leadership, Labour was 22 per cent ahead of the Conservatives in the polls by 1993.[1] Blair began developing the New Labour approach to reforming the party's principles, policies and message discipline. At his first party conference as leader, the 77-year-old Clause IV was removed from the party's charter, ending Labour's formal commitment to the nationalisation of industry. These major public-facing changes were underpinned by new and centralised party machinery.

Blair was the leader of the party but he was effectively the senior half of a duopoly with the shadow Chancellor, Gordon Brown. Along with Peter Mandelson they founded the approach which made the party electable, ended the Conservative Party's political hegemony and ushered in thirteen years of Labour government. Labour won a 179-seat majority, the biggest parliamentary majority of the post-war era. Domestic reform was a cornerstone of New Labour's offering, and the scale of the victory brought with it high public expectations. At the 1996 Labour Party conference, Blair said, 'Ask me my three main priorities for government and I will tell you: education, education, education.'[2] But, in opposition, establishing economic credibility was prioritised above all else.

The transition from opposition to government was not smooth. New Labour's overarching strategy directed the broad aims of policy, but how much detailed preparation had there been? A successful party political machine had been created, but how would it integrate into the established machinery of government and work with the impartial, permanent Civil Service? And how would the powerful duopoly adjust to government, where there is one leader – the Prime Minister – and an established convention of collective decision-making through a Cabinet comprising ministers with individual responsibility? In practice, one can argue that the convention of Cabinet as the most powerful central decision-making body was weakened further, as the concentration of power in the hands of the Prime Minister and the Chancellor increased. First, Blair and Brown and their respective teams reordered the conduct of government and in doing so reinforced the dominance of the centre (No. 10, Cabinet Office and HM Treasury). Second, the Prime Minister and the Chancellor pursued dual-track domestic policies; arguably this twin approach drew some power away from departmental autonomy. The use of special advisers across government grew significantly from 1997 to 2001.[3] Special advisers are politically appointed, temporary civil servants employed to assist ministers and the Prime Minister on areas where it would be politically improper for permanent civil servants to be involved, *or* because they provide specialist skills.[4] As mentioned, the first peacetime special advisers were appointed by Labour Prime Minister Harold Wilson in 1964. During the Blair premiership special advisers were generally either policy experts or media strategy specialists. They helped to lubricate the machinery of government by communicating the government's political strategy to the impartial, permanent Civil Service.

During the second half of Blair's first term, his desire to spend political capital grew as he recognised the potential impact of structural reform of public services. As his zeal increased and the intellectual underpinning for it advanced, so too did his frustration with the pace of delivery. At the forefront of Blair's mind was the all-important second election victory. Indeed, on 29 May 1997, just weeks after the landslide, Blair and members of his Cabinet met with the President of the United States, Bill Clinton, and Blair stated, 'Parliament is in recess; we are having a hell of a time getting underway – the honeymoon doesn't last long. The second term is what we need; to take nothing for granted and not rely on the other side's unpopularity.'[5]

1994 TO 1997: A PARTY OF PROTEST BECOMES AN ELECTION-WINNING MACHINE

As Labour supporters and then as MPs from 1983, Blair and Brown had witnessed Labour's descent into a party incapable of winning successive general elections during the 1980s and early 1990s. They shared an office in Parliament and quickly formed a close working relationship. Blair had been the junior partner, having turned to politics relatively late, with Brown a seasoned campaigner for a decade. When the then leader of the Labour Party, John Smith, died suddenly in May 1994, Blair was shadow Secretary of State for Employment and Brown was shadow Chancellor of the Exchequer. After Smith's death, it quickly became clear that Blair was favourite to win the leadership election.[6] Blair swiftly embraced his popularity and decided to run for the leadership, while Brown contemplated standing as a candidate but eventually decided not to.

The decision was allegedly agreed on 31 May 1994, at a meeting at the Granita restaurant in Islington. The meeting has attained a near-mythical status but there does seem to be some limited agreement on what happened from advisers in the Blair and Brown camps. Firstly, both Peter Mandelson and Ed Balls have stated separately that Brown had decided not to stand in the leadership election in the days prior to the Granita meeting. Secondly, both have revealed that the primary objective of the Granita meeting was for Brown to exact his price for standing aside: control of the social and economic agenda.[7] Blair has said that Brown 'wanted free rein on economic policy' but Blair's own opinion was 'close interaction, yes. Partnership, yes. Dual leadership, absolutely not.'[8] Brown's ambition was to become the next leader of the Labour Party after Blair stood down. It is unclear whether Blair agreed to support Brown as his successor and, crucially, provide a date as to when he would stand down as leader.

The ambiguities around succession became problematic in the second and third terms of government but the extent to which Brown could exert control over the domestic agenda began to be tested almost immediately. This rivalry also resulted in a proxy war between the respective teams. Blair alluded to this as early as 1994: 'Every time we met, there was a ripple of anxiety that spread out among the camp followers (already self-identifying fairly robustly) at what concessions either of us may have made.'[9] Despite Brown and Blair's undoubted closeness, Blair remarked that 'the root of the problem was that he [Brown] thought I could be an empty vessel into which the liquid that was poured was manufactured and processed by him.'[10] The nuances played out in the Granita episode are the basis for understanding the relationships and mode of working that would underlie Blair's premiership. They also represent a volatile fault line that Michael Barber and the Delivery Unit would later have to traverse.

After Blair won the leadership election, he quickly began to implement further changes to professionalise and modernise the party. His predecessors Kinnock and Smith had started the work to make Labour electable once again. In 1994, beyond Blair, Brown and the shadow Cabinet, the New Labour inner circle of advisers included Mandelson, by then an MP, on communications and strategy; Anji Hunter, Blair's longstanding alliance-builder and trusted long-term friend, heading the leader's office; Sally Morgan, Blair's political secretary; Alastair Campbell, on media presentation and providing close counsel; Liz Lloyd, policy adviser; David Miliband, head of policy; Jonathan Powell, Blair's chief of staff; Kate Garvey, Blair's personal assistant; Peter Hyman, speechwriter and adviser; Philip Gould, on polling and strategy; Hilary Coffman, press officer; Pat McFadden, policy adviser; Tim Allan, policy adviser; James Purnell, policy adviser; Brown's economic adviser, Ed Balls; Sue Nye, Brown's trusted, longstanding adviser, head of office and Labour Party stalwart; Ed Miliband, Brown's policy adviser; and Charlie Whelan, Brown's press spokesperson.[11] Meanwhile the Conservative government was in disarray: divided over Europe, beset by scandals and crises, weakly led by John Major and tired after nearly two decades in power. The 1997 Labour manifesto was not a detailed policy document but a broad agenda for modernising education, law and order, health and the economy. With hindsight one can argue that

New Labour's lack of detailed policy preparation (with the exceptions of education policy and economic policy) was a significant oversight and would quickly affect their actions in government. For Blair and Brown, however, there were first-order issues to contend with: for example, they worked hard to rebuild Labour's reputation on the economy. For Blair, education was the key to unlocking unrealised potential in society.[12] But after being out of power for eighteen years, what experience and understanding of government could New Labour draw on? As Blair later recognised, 'it was the business of Opposition which we were adept at'.[13] There were very few ministers in Blair's Cabinet who had prior experience in government and thus Blair concluded that he and most of his Cabinet 'were going to come to power as utter novices'.[14] Furthermore, on election night as the exit polls came in Blair realised the magnitude of the task ahead. 'Now we would enter a new and foreign land. I was afraid because I felt instinctively that its obstacles and challenges were of an altogether different order of complexity and difficulty … I realised I knew nothing about … how government really works.'[15] As the size and historic nature of the victory was confirmed Blair's frustration grew. 'I became more and more weighed down by the burden of responsibility that was about to fall on me.'[16]

1997 TO 1998: THE TRANSITION FROM OPPOSITION TO GOVERNMENT

In winning the 1997 general election, New Labour had achieved success as a political party but now the huge task of governing lay before it. To begin with, it implemented pre-election plans and largely continued operating as it had done in Opposition. Jonathan Powell came under criticism in the media before the election for suggesting (in an off-the-record seminar) that in government New Labour 'wanted to move from a feudal to a Napoleonic system'.[17] This set the tone for the way in which he would seek to work from within No. 10. On 6 May, Gordon Brown announced his first major policy decision – to grant operational independence to the Bank of England to set interest rates. In doing so, Brown wanted to bolster his economic credentials; indeed Ed Balls (Brown's economic adviser from 1997, then chief economic adviser from 1999) was an architect of the policy and claims it was an 'institutional way of entrenching credible discretion'.[18] Within the Treasury, it quickly became clear that Brown would operate through his inner circle including Balls, Charlie Whelan, Ed Miliband, Sue Nye and Labour MP and businessman Geoffrey Robinson (Paymaster General until December 1998). The Permanent Secretary to the Treasury, Sir Terry Burns, was not part of Brown's inner circle. In June 1998, Burns took early retirement from the Civil Service and was ennobled. His successor was Sir Andrew Turnbull, who also found difficulty in gaining traction with Brown and his team.

The lack of a strong working relationship between Brown and his first two Permanent Secretaries did not limit his ability to capture the Treasury and make it work for him; it perhaps made it easier. On a visit to the Treasury on 6 May 1997, Campbell noted that Brown 'was making very clear, in word and deed, who was in charge'.[19] For example, Brown set up a new Council of Economic Advisers in which a group of academics, economists and special advisers provided specialist advice on specific policy areas, coordinated by Balls.[20] One could argue that this was tantamount to a policy unit for the Chancellor. The Treasury gave Brown intellectual firepower as well as departmental 'purse strings' that the Prime Minister did not have at his immediate disposal.

In No. 10, Blair relied on many of the same people as he had in opposition. Alastair Campbell became the Prime Minister's chief press secretary and official spokesman, Sally Morgan continued as political secretary, Anji Hunter was Blair's 'gatekeeper' and became director of government relations (initially known as special assistant for presentation and planning), Jonathan Powell was chief of staff, Peter Mandelson became a minister without portfolio, which gave him seniority but flexibility, David Miliband became head of the Policy Unit, which was mostly staffed by political appointments, Liz Lloyd joined the unit to cover home affairs, and Kate Garvey became the Prime Minister's diary secretary.[21] Gould continued independently to advise Blair on polling and strategy and remained a core member of the Prime Minister's team throughout his premiership.[22] Key advisers to Blair, including Campbell and Powell, attended Cabinet meetings, which arguably acted as a deterrent against leaks to the media.[23] Campbell claims that from the outset Blair made it clear to the Civil Service that he 'would not allow his political team to be undermined, let alone broken up'.[24] This defensive 'us and them' mentality would quickly make an impact in the media. Within a month Blair was facing accusations of sleaze; he was accused of trying to appoint Powell to the post of principal private secretary – a role traditionally fulfilled by a career civil servant.[25] Campbell was also coming under increasing attack for his media communications strategy, or 'spin' as it later became known.[26]

After the Mountfield review into the capabilities of the Government Information and Communication Service, set up by Sir Robin Butler, Cabinet Secretary since 1988 (and of which Campbell was a member), there was an overhaul of the associated machinery to bring it up to date with the 24/7 media news cycle. In January

1998, Campbell set up the Strategic Communications Unit (SCU) to coordinate the government's communications strategy, headed by career official Alun Evans until 2000, when Campbell himself took over.[27] Ministers and departments would now receive clear guidance on media interactions and interviews from the SCU, before making commitments. This illustrated one way in which Blair bolstered his control and power over the rest of the government. Unlike his ministers and especially his Chancellor, Blair did not have an official Prime Minister's Department at his disposal. But he did have special advisers who offered professional expertise; and he created new units based in No. 10 and the Cabinet Office to enhance his capacity at the centre. In 1997, Blair spoke of the need for 'joined-up government' to resolve intractable societal issues that are cross-departmental in nature.[28] As part of this drive for 'joined-up government', there was effectively a deeper fusion between No. 10 and the Cabinet Office. For example, Blair set up the Social Exclusion Unit in December 1997. It was based in the Cabinet Office, headed by a civil servant, Moira Wallace, and sought to unpick the multitude of issues that led to social exclusion, particularly among young people in poverty. The unit worked across multiple departments to make recommendations in the way of a think tank but had no formal powers.[29]

In No. 10, Blair was getting to grips with his senior civil servants. On entering Downing Street, Blair met with Sir Robin Butler in the Cabinet Room, where Butler explained that he and his colleagues had 'studied the manifesto and we are ready to get to work on it for you'.[30] Blair did not expect this; he commented that Butler's words 'irrationally disturbed me'.[31] Powell was suspicious of the Cabinet Secretary; he claimed Butler was 'anxious to assert control over a new and inexperienced Prime Minister', which could have challenged Powell's role as chief of staff.[32] There was a cultural and generational gap between New Labour and the very top of the Civil Service, which, in part, was to be expected after almost two decades out of power. The Cabinet Secretary has traditionally been one of the Prime Minister's most influential and trusted policy advisers. The role has also encompassed crisis management, coordinating Cabinet business and Cabinet committees, supervising the security and intelligence services until 2002, when the position of security and intelligence coordinator was created (since remerged), and overall management of the Civil Service.[33] They are the most powerful unelected official most people have never heard of. Prior to the Blair premiership, Cabinet Secretaries often served more than one Prime Minister. Butler retired at the end of 1997 and later criticised Blair's bilateral, 'sofa' style of governing, which Blair preferred over traditional, formal Cabinet government whereby collective decision-making takes place in Cabinet.[34] Commenting, with hindsight, on the way in which New Labour operated in government, Butler observed:

> New Labour was definitely a sort of rather revolutionary cell within the Labour Party ... They were used to keeping their cards very close to their chest, so it wasn't at all a collective operation when it came in, they weren't used to operating with a Cabinet with whom they discussed everything. What they wanted to do was to reach a view and then take the Cabinet along with them and that was the way that they operated. Now, this ran rather counter to the way in which traditionally Cabinet government had worked.[35]

The extent to which Blair's predecessors upheld the principle of

Cabinet government is certainly debatable. Blair reflected on the traditional processes of government after leaving office: 'The old infrastructure of policy papers submitted by civil servants to Cabinet, who then debate and decide with the Prime Minister as the benevolent chairman, is not suitable in responding to the demands of a fast-changing world or an even faster-changing political landscape.'[36] Blair saw himself as more of a chief executive – the person who took decisions and ensured that they were implemented; not as the chairman of a Cabinet which took decisions collectively.[37] The United Kingdom's uncodified constitution coupled with a large parliamentary majority gave Blair a great deal of flexibility with regard to how his own position and those of ministers and the wider government worked. Historian Jon Davis and journalist John Rentoul describe Cabinet under Blair as 'quiet' and 'quiescent'; there was a mutual hunger for governing, after being out of power for a generation.[38] Indeed it can be argued that the traditional concept of Cabinet government is more of an ethic, rather than a practical method for running modern government.

On his relationship with Butler, Blair later said that although there was 'quite a vigorous disagreement about the nature of decision-making in my government … I found Robin thoroughly professional, courteous and supportive. He didn't like some of the innovations, but he did his best to make them work.'[39] One such innovation that caused controversy was Blair's decision to give politically appointed special advisers unprecedented executive authority over impartial civil servants. Special advisers are not formally allowed to direct civil servants and so, at the suggestion of the Cabinet Secretary, an Order in Council was granted to Campbell and Powell, although it allowed for up to three individuals. Blair admits that 'for the first year or so … we did tend to operate as a pretty tight unit, from which some of the senior civil servants felt excluded. From our perspective, we were working flat out to deliver an enormous series of commitments to change.'[40]

In January 1998, Blair appointed a new Cabinet Secretary and head of the Home Civil Service, Sir Richard Wilson. Like his predecessor, Wilson had joined the Civil Service in the 1960s. Wilson, who generally had a good working relationship with Blair, recalled that 'we talked a lot about himself [and] his current problems with Gordon'.[41] This showed a degree of trust between the Prime Minister and the Cabinet Secretary. Like Butler, Wilson noted the contrast between New Labour's expertise as an opposition party and its lack of experience of how to govern:

> Early on his [Blair's] main objective had been to win power and his objective having won power was to win power again at the next election. In a sense, the first Blair Parliament was about continuous campaigning and Mr Blair now feels he didn't make full use of it … Campbell said to me in the early years that he'd always thought that government would be like Opposition except that things would happen. So, there was an unexpected element of naivety.[42]

Wilson typically spent between one-third and half of his time working on Civil Service reform.[43] Blair believed that Wilson 'got behind' reforms to modernise the Civil Service 'thoroughly', that the reforms spoke 'the right language' but the measures themselves were not 'radical' enough, although Blair does hold himself partially responsible for this.[44] Wilson's role and experience began to change from 1999 onwards. While Blair to some extent sidelined his Cabinet Secretaries, he placed growing interest and faith in one senior civil servant: Jeremy Heywood. Heywood had joined the Treasury in 1992 and advised two Conservative Chancellors, Norman Lamont and Kenneth Clarke, and began working for Blair in autumn 1997 as a private secretary focused on economic and domestic affairs.[45] In his diary on 30 January 1998, Campbell observed how Heywood 'was clearly making an impression on TB [Blair], who said he wished he had two or three like him'.[46] Blair and Brown's initial reaction to the most senior civil servants is perhaps not unexpected; it was a continuation of the way they worked within their own party while in opposition. In addition, New Labour's lack of ministerial experience and preparation for government was exemplified with Blair himself: being Prime Minister was his first and last job in government.

The strategy for the domestic agenda, particularly education and health, during 1997 and 1998 was to focus on 'standards not structures' and 'modernisation', which Blair explained meant leaving out 'complex, institutional structural reforms; what counts is what works and by that we meant outputs'.[47] To build economic credibility, Labour had also fought the 1997 election on the basis that it would adhere to Conservative spending plans for the first two years in government, which constrained its ability to reform and invest. Yet Blair quickly began to see structural reform as the next stage. He reflected, 'I was learning rapidly, and what I learned was fascinating but also daunting. The problems were deep, and systemic.'[48] In the winter of 1998, Blair reread the 1997 manifesto pledges and commented, 'I laughed at their modesty.'[49] Even with the relatively limited programme prepared before the election, Blair admitted that within a year, 'we were very quickly appreciating the daunting revelation of the gap between saying and doing'.[50] Philip Gould was receiving focus group results which pointed to 'non-delivery' and 'incompetence'.[51] Ed Balls reflected on this growing gap between public expectations and what was being delivered:

> Probably the mistake we made in the first term was that in 1999–2000, after the two-year freeze, in some areas (but not the economy), we gave the impression that, having established discipline, it was all going to happen quickly. We talked about this being the year of delivery. We raised expectations more than we could deliver them in terms of time. We should have said more about decades of [under]investment that had to be tackled ... In retrospect, everyone feels there should have been a more careful shaping of expectations in the second half of the Parliament.[52]

Soon after the election, Brown introduced flagship domestic reforms from the Treasury. He used a windfall tax on privatised utilities, which was expected to raise £5.2 billion in 1997–99, to fund part of his welfare-to-work programme – the New Deal for young people, the long-term unemployed and lone parents.[53] In March 1998, the Welfare Reform Green Paper brought in working families tax credit, founded the Sure Start programme for young families and introduced the minimum wage.[54] Late that summer, Brown announced the results of the Comprehensive Spending Review, (CSR) which set spending for the period 1999–2002. Prior to this, departmental expenditure was planned on an annual basis. One of the main changes was the announcement of public service agreements (PSAs). PSAs were a new three-year contract between the Treasury and each government department, which linked departmental budgets with performance targets. The concept of PSAs was created shortly before the publication of the spending review at the suggestion of Balls.[55] They would show, as Brown put it to Parliament, 'reform in return for investment'.[56]

Unusually, the targets would be decided *after* the funding had already been allocated in the spending review. John Gieve, who was then managing director of public services in the Treasury and responsible for planning PSAs, explained that 'that first batch was literally cobbled together; the money had already been allocated without agreeing these new requirements'.[57] In December 1998, the government published 600 PSAs. Many of them were based on 1997 manifesto pledges on education, health and law and order.[58] The PSAs would be monitored by the Cabinet Committee on Public Services and Public Expenditure (known as PSX), chaired by Brown. At the time, this was the primary mechanism for holding ministers and their departments to account to deliver the PSAs.[59] The PSAs expanded and entrenched Brown's influence on domestic policy.

The 1998 CSR stated that PSX would monitor performance against 'individual' PSAs and provide 'support and advice' to departments to enable them to meet targets.[60] As a junior minister Charles Clarke sat in on PSX Cabinet committee meetings during the first term. From this vantage point Clarke casts doubt on the usefulness of PSX: 'a bizarre process, not at all effective', adding that it reflected the 'complete dislocation between No. 10 and No. 11 … it wasn't providing accountability for what was happening.'[61] This perhaps showed the limitations of Cabinet committees on their own as mechanisms for delivery. PSAs undoubtedly strengthened Brown's hand. To an extent, they were a bridging method, as Blair outlined: 'To bridge the gap between reform and aspiration, we set alongside these piecemeal reforms a swathe of performance targets to eliminate the longest hospital waiting times, raise school literacy and numeracy and GCSE scores.'[62] PSAs were designed to close the gap between saying and doing. One can argue that the considerable number of PSAs began what would later be criticised as 'target culture'.[63] So large a number of performance targets represented a blunt instrument for change. Moreover PSAs were not underpinned by new, responsive machinery of government to regularly track progress and intervene where necessary.

1999 TO 2001: THE SEARCH FOR DELIVERY, A REFORMING ZEAL EMERGES

By all accounts, 1999 was the year when New Labour began to devote significant attention to better understanding the delivery of public service reform. It was the mid-term stage of the parliament, the shackles of sticking to Conservative spending plans were released and economic growth meant that funds were burning a hole in the country's collective pocket. But Philip Gould's focus groups showed public opinion was starting to turn and the next election was fast approaching. Blair now had experience of how to govern, bold policy ideas were emerging and the issue of delivery was becoming more important.

After broadly keeping to tight Conservative public spending plans, Brown continued to reduce spending in 1999 followed by an increase of 0.7 per cent of GDP in 2000/01, ahead of the 2001 general election.[64] As public spending rose modestly, revenues increased markedly, by 2.2 per cent of national income during the first term.[65] On a fiscal year basis this resulted in a total budget surplus every year from 1998/99 to 2000/01,[66] reaching 1.9 per cent of national income by 2000/01.[67] The auctioning of the 3G mobile phone licences brought in £22.5 billion, which was much higher than expected and helped the public sector net debt to fall from 42.5 per cent (of national income) in 1996/97 to 30.7 per cent in 2000/01.[68] The marked increase in revenue was not expected, even by senior Treasury officials. Nicholas Macpherson, who was principal private secretary to Brown and then director of welfare reform during the first term, remarked that 'we were almost embarrassed' by the huge amount of revenue flooding in.[69] The historic increases in revenue meant that Brown's economic prudence could be loosened. Brown sought to solidify his grip on the domestic agenda and expand his sphere of influence. In May 1999, he gave a speech on 'The New Mission for the Treasury' where he made clear that 'a Labour Treasury would need to be not just a ministry of finance, but also a ministry of working with other departments to deliver long-term economic and social renewal'.[70]

During the two years of tight spending, Powell claimed that Blair had to convince Brown to commit money to health in order to avert a winter crisis.[71] Moreover Powell stated that 'Tony told me it was the most important battle of his prime ministership. If he couldn't get more money into the public services, we couldn't improve delivery by the time of the next election.'[72] The NHS experienced a serious crisis in the winter of 1999–2000 after an outbreak of flu; the vast majority of non-emergency operations were cancelled and at one stage there were only two intensive care beds available in the country.[73] The emergency had a notable impact on Blair's understanding of 'how complex the institutions of public service were'.[74] As a result the Prime Minister concluded that 'profound' structural reforms were needed, though he admits to not being 'entirely sure what the answer was' at the time.[75]

The standout Budget of the first term was in 2000, as it was the first to focus on significant investment in public services. Brown declared that the NHS would see a real-term budget increase in the next five years of 35 per cent, an immediate £2 billion increase in spending for the NHS, £1 billion for education and £4 billion for transport.[76] But crucially, investment for reform did not guarantee delivery. Cabinet Secretary Wilson explained the government's thinking at the time, from his vantage point:

> There was a pretty optimistic view that if you started spending more money at the beginning of April [1999], you would start to see results at the end of April, which is not how the public sector works; these are huge supertankers which take a long time to turn around.[77]

AN EMERGING PUBLIC SERVICE REFORM AGENDA

The period from 1999 to 2001 was a turning point for Blair's approach to public service reform, specifically the development of a bold 'choice agenda'. By 1999, Blair had started to depart from the 1997 mantra, 'standards not structures'.[78] The Prime Minister's private frustration became public when in 2000 a memo he had written in April of that year was leaked. In it, Blair discussed 'touchstone issues' including crime, asylum and family issues where the government was 'perceived as weak ... and insufficiently assertive'.[79] He wanted thorough strategies, policies and messaging developed in these areas; and he finished by stating, 'I should be personally associated with as much of this as possible.'[80] These anxieties led to the drive for a bold public service reform agenda and an accompanying delivery mechanism in the Prime Minister's name.

By 2001, Blair realised, 'I hadn't by any means worked out all the right policy answers, but I had worked out the crucial failing of the first term: the mistaken view that raising standards and performance could be separated from structural reform.'[81] Furthermore, he admitted that he had 'hoarded ... political capital in the first term'.[82] He explained the intention that underpinned his choice agenda: 'We had to divest power away from the dominant interest groups, unions and associations and put it back into the hands of people, the consumer, the parent, the patient, the user.'[83] As Secretary of State for Health from 1999, Alan Milburn was also recognising the need to modernise public services. Looking back on this period, Milburn reflected:

> Public services were a product of the right values, but they were a product of a particular era, when people didn't have choice, they weren't consumers ... Suddenly you are living in a world where people have choice, they don't leave that at the hospital gate. They want to be able to exercise it.[84]

But Milburn also saw the choice agenda as a tool of social justice: 'I hated the idea that if you were poor, you never got a choice, and if you were rich you did. And that didn't seem right to me.' He felt this viscerally from his own childhood experience:

> If you grew up (like I did) on a council estate you get no choice. I could remember as a kid, this is seared on my memory as a child, we grew up in this old mining town, Tow Law in County Durham, and our front door was painted yellow and I went off to school, I was nine, and I came back and that evening the front door had been painted red. I was completely confused ... Who had decided? Not my Mum. I was brought up by a single mum. The council had decided. I hated it ... It was our house, not their house.[85]

Blair had also been influenced by the research of a London School of Economics academic, Professor Julian Le Grand, who argued that in the early post-war period policymakers assumed that public service professionals (such as teachers and doctors) were public-spirited, altruistic 'knights' and citizens who used public services were treated as passive 'pawns'.[86] He believed, however, that since the 1980s policymakers had come to view these professionals as self-interested 'knaves' who provided services in a way that worked for the producer, rather than for the consumer. The introduction of quasi-market reforms since the 1980s demonstrated this view of service providers as operating from a self-interested perspective. These reforms included the privatisation of huge swathes of Britain's nationalised industries such as British Rail. A quasi-market was introduced into the NHS, which split the purchasing of healthcare from the provision of healthcare, with the aim of making the service more efficient. Using a mix of public and private sector providers for the delivery of public services and decentralising choice of provider to the consumer formed the foundation of the choice agenda. This philosophy for reform was not, however, transferred into policy and delivery until Blair's second and third terms.

THE SEARCH FOR DELIVERY

In January 1999, Blair declared to Sir Richard Wilson, 'This is to be the year of delivery.'[87] In March 1999, the government published the Modernising Government White Paper, which listed principles and general aims that would underpin the approach to modernisation: joined-up government to tackle issues that cut across multiple departments, an evidence-based approach to policy using expert advice centred around the citizen, and opening up the Civil Service to external talent so as to resolve capability gaps.[88] The paper stipulated new responsibilities for Permanent Secretaries, beyond policy formulation: 'Within Whitehall, a new focus on delivery – asking every Permanent Secretary to ensure that their Department has the capacity to drive through achievement of the key government targets and to take a personal responsibility for ensuring that this happens.'[89]

Yet this attempt to refocus the senior Civil Service on delivery was not bolstered by new government machinery to monitor progress. Later that year, in June, Philip Gould, Blair's trusted pollster and strategist, informed him that focus groups believed the government had 'failed to deliver'.[90] In July, Blair vented his frustration. In a candid question and answer session after giving a speech to the Venture Capital Association he said:

> You try getting change in the public sector and public services. I bear the scars on my back after two years in government and heaven knows what it will be like after a bit longer. People in the public sector [are] more rooted in the concept that 'if it has always been done this way, it must always be done this way' than any group of people I have come across.[91]

Although the Civil Service may have been too slow to respond to the new priorities set by the Blair government, that is delivery, it is fair to say that the New Labour leadership was underprepared for the task of governing. The Prime Minister, Cabinet ministers and special advisers were still in the process of working out the scale and detail of the next stage of public service reform, for the first half of their first term in government. For example, health was a priority policy area for New Labour, yet Blair chose a Secretary of State who was not of his New Labour reformist ilk, Frank Dobson.

Moreover, Dobson had not even performed the role in opposition, Chris Smith having been shadow Secretary of State for Health during 1996–97. This sharply contrasted with other key policy areas where there had been continuity and planning from opposition into government – education and the economy. Two and a half years into government, Blair began to comprehend the sheer complexity of public services. Looking back, he reflected:

> I was learning how complex the institutions of public service were, how multiple their pressures, how vast their demands and how great the expectations were of what could be done and in what period of time … At the helm of the NHS, I had put Frank Dobson. This, in itself, indicated how little I understood when first in office.[92]

A close adviser to Blair from the mid-1990s and influential special adviser (later minister and baroness) in government, Sally Morgan explained that during this period New Labour 'didn't have any of the bigger reform work' on public services clearly planned out.[93] That was partly because Labour had 'been so long out of government and partly because we were relatively conservative in the scope of what we did in the 1997 election manifesto because we wanted to make sure that we would have a manifesto that we would get elected on, and we could deliver'.[94] The necessity of navigating Labour's perceived weakness on economic issues and winning an election versus preparing an ambitious programme for government can evidently be at odds with one another.

In October 1999, Blair replaced Dobson with Milburn, who had been appointed a junior health minister in 1997, before becoming Chief Secretary to the Treasury from December 1998 to October

1999. Milburn was a reformer and together he and Blair set about formulating substantial reforms to the NHS. On his initial appointment in 1997, Milburn had asked Blair what he wanted him to focus on. Blair's reply: 'We need a health policy.'[95] Milburn acknowledged the lack of preparation: 'In Opposition we didn't have a health policy. We had a slogan, we had a pledge card, we had a sort of rough idea, but we didn't have a policy.'[96] As Secretary of State, Milburn recognised the scale of the challenge ahead:

> I basically worked out that the [Health] department, if not quite
> a force for conservatism, was definitely not at the radical end of
> the spectrum. My analysis was that if this thing [the NHS] was
> going to survive and be sustainable then it had to go through quite
> a fundamental, and sometimes quite brutal, transformation.[97]

What followed was a 'messy process' in which Milburn and his team sought to learn best practice from other industries, as well as high-performing NHS hospitals and international health services, 'to understand what the levers were that you needed to pull in order to make change happen'.[98]

Blair received advice on delivery from Richard Wilson, Jeremy Heywood, Peter Hyman and the head of the Performance and Innovation Unit, Geoff Mulgan (special adviser, later civil servant). Wilson witnessed the Prime Minister's attention move to delivery early on. He reflected that with hindsight he would have taken time to better understand and prepare for the focus on reform and delivery that his role as Cabinet Secretary would entail. Discussions before he took up the post and in his early months had not been particularly concerned with delivery, although there had been a lot of unspecific talk about 'modernisation'.[99] Blair had asked Wilson to draft his own proposals for reshaping the Cabinet Office 'without specifying this concentration on delivery issues'; he submitted his recommendations around Easter 1998 and they were accepted.[100] Evidently there was a lack of clear prioritisation and communication of said priorities, let alone working out how to deliver them. Blair's move to task his most senior civil servant with delivery is substantiated by Alastair Campbell, who noted in his diary on 22 February 1999 that Blair 'raised again the need to involve Richard Wilson more if we're to get the machine focused properly on delivery'.[101] Wilson's predecessor, Robin Butler, explained how he would have reacted had he been given a new delivery brief when he was Cabinet Secretary.

> I would have said, 'Look, there's no way in which somebody sitting in the Cabinet Secretary's room in the centre of Whitehall can deliver your policies for individual hospitals and schools and police forces and so on.' You can't, Whitehall can't control in that way, you've really got to set your policies and then you've got to expect people to do them.[102]

Butler's view underlines the decisive shift that New Labour were introducing to make delivery an explicit function. There was, however, another senior civil servant on whom Blair was relying. Jeremy Heywood was becoming indispensable to Blair and in 1999 he became his principal private secretary. Wilson observed that 'the person who was much the most important player in No. 10 in the debates about delivery and reform was Jeremy Heywood'.[103] Heywood described the reality of his role for the Prime Minister as 'principal adviser as it were'.[104] It can be argued that Blair utilised Heywood in the way that previous Prime Ministers had relied on their Cabinet Secretaries. Heywood also played a pivotal role in managing the conduct of government business between Blair and Brown: for instance, by opening 'a channel of communications through Ed Balls when things were difficult'.[105] Wilson explained that Blair's 'relationship with Gordon [Brown] sometimes became a kind of rock around which we had to navigate the conduct of business'.[106]

Blair and Brown had regular bilateral meetings but the majority of detailed brokering was undertaken by Balls and Heywood (from 1999) acting on behalf of their principals.[107] Jonathan Powell had carried out this role for Blair up until 1999 but had a difficult relationship with Brown.[108] He credits Heywood with carrying out the negotiating role for six years 'brilliantly ... without poisoning his relations with either Brown or Balls'.[109] The Blair–Brown relationship was also actively held together by Anji Hunter for Blair and Sue Nye for Brown. These two powerful women on opposite sides of the duopoly were close friends, having worked together for many years. Each was deeply trusted by her principal, Blair or Brown. This achievement was rare and later Barber would have to walk a tightrope between the two centres of power.

Peter Hyman had worked for Blair since 1994, and in the first term was a special adviser in No. 10 with a roving policy, strategy and communications brief.[110] From Hyman's perspective, 'focusing on delivery – with the introduction of numerous targets – was controversial' but it came about in part because of 'sensitivities about Labour's past reputation' on efficiency and spending.[111] He admitted that 'delivery proved harder than any of us imagined' and was made no easier by the size of the majority or the rhetoric, which 'often made things worse' because it led to high public expectations, all of which did not make it any quicker 'to train the doctors or easier to repair the railways'.[112] Hyman wrote a note to Blair in January 1999 that outlined the delivery problem and potential solutions:

Why is delivery so hard to get across?
Our problem on delivery is deep-seated:

- A media that is not interested.
- A 179-majority leads people to believe that there is nothing to stop us delivering more quickly.
- Turning round huge bureaucracies takes time e.g. we are short of cancer surgeons. They take thirteen years to train.
- Raw data often fails to translate into anecdotal evidence.
- The public act as consumers of public services, no longer as passive recipients.
- We have convinced ourselves that we have allocated historic sums of money. We have not. Over the Parliament (1997–2001) the money going into education and health is not a quantum leap.[113]

He explained that in meetings, Blair would exasperatedly ask his ministers policy questions which he thought needed 'immediate attention'.[114] His ministers would sometimes 'wince at the crudeness with which Tony wanted to act'.[115] Hyman quoted Blair as saying in February 1999:

The basic problem, which is not new for prime ministers, is control. How do we drive our will down through the system, monitor progress and then achieve delivery? A stronger centre could give more direction and keep on the job until we are sure people are moving in the way we want.[116]

Blair was slowly realising the need for delivery machinery at the centre of government because the existing machinery lacked an explicit delivery function. But how would it work and who would run it? Geoff Mulgan was based in the Policy Unit from 1997 to 2000 and then became head of the Performance and Innovation Unit (PIU). The PIU looked at long-term strategic cross-departmental issues and was based in the Cabinet Office.[117] It also proposed 'policy innovations to improve the delivery of the Government's objectives'.[118] In January 2001, Mulgan co-authored a paper entitled 'Better Policy Delivery and Design'. It was created as a discussion paper for a government seminar and explored many issues around delivery through contemporary case studies which 'illustrate the varied experience of delivery in practice'.[119] One recommendation was:

> To develop a challenge function in the centre of government through the creation of a 'Challenge Team', largely made up of people with proven experience of delivery, to test and probe departmental plans and report to the Prime Minister on deliverability and potential risks. At present the main challenge functions focus either on money inputs, or are retrospective audits. A more formal challenge team, focusing on a relatively small number of major initiatives, might encourage departments to raise their game without undermining departments' ownership of the policy.[120]

This represented an incisive identification of the issues and broad solutions. The paper was written in the run-up to the 2001 election when the post-election reorganisation of the centre was under consideration and is therefore indicative of the thinking at the time. A month later, the Public Administration Select Committee (PASC) published a report on the role of special advisers entitled 'Special Advisers: Boon or Bane?'[121] The government's increasing use of special advisers had received great criticism from political commentators and thus necessitated the committee's interest. The report stated that the number of special advisers had risen from thirty-eight under John Major in 1997 to seventy-eight under Blair in January 2001.[122] There was some discussion on the distinction between political advisers and specialist advisers. Richard Wilson advocated taking a more nuanced view that avoided 'lumping them all together'.[123] PASC concluded that overall special advisers had a positive impact on the machinery of government: 'In particular, they broaden the range of policy advice upon which Ministers can draw. None of this need be threatening to the traditional role of the Civil Service.'[124]

LEARNING THROUGH CRISES

During the first term Blair learnt the value of the established machinery of government through crises. He also got to grips with the structural strengths and limitations of public services, as they were then configured. The flu epidemic of 1999–2000 stretched hospitals to breaking point. Hospitals struggled to deal with the influx of flu patients, leading to an acute shortage of intensive care beds, and the cancellation of thousands of operations. The crisis led both Blair and his new Secretary of State for Health, Milburn, to recognise the need for systemic change in the NHS, as well as investment. Looking back, Milburn reflected:

In 1997 for Tony and the government, health wasn't really a sort of number one priority. It really only became such as a consequence of the winter of 1999/2000 and the flu epidemic. And at which point, the system was obviously crashing and burning ... So, there was an increasing political focus on how do we turn the ship of state around and get it pointing in the right direction? Tony then became much more personally animated about health, to try to understand it, but we didn't really have mechanisms to ensure that No. 10 and the Department of Health were working in sync.[125]

Blair, with hindsight, says that 'it is hard now to look back and realise just how inevitable such crises appeared'.[126] Nigel Crisp, Permanent Secretary at the Department of Health and chief executive of the NHS from 2000 to 2006, viewed Blair's first term as a make-or-break point for the NHS:

> There was a real question about whether ... this organisation, which offers free health care for every citizen regardless of their ability to pay, [would] be able to survive and prosper in the 21st century[.] ... This was a crucial issue at the end of the 20th century. The NHS had been in decline for some years with falling standards and failing public support ... Its friends were beginning to question its viability.[127]

On 8 September 2000, a fuel crisis began when a group mainly made up of farmers and hauliers began to blockade oil refining plants. Filling stations began to run out of petrol, panic buying ensued and the emergency services were affected.[128] In No. 10, Powell, who had been charged by the Prime Minister to 'deal with the crisis', was pulling 'every lever available' but 'none of them seemed to be connected to anything'.[129] On returning to No. 10, Blair observed that Campbell was 'in full crisis mode but the rest of the machine seemed curiously paralysed'.[130] Blair tried to take charge himself, he assembled his ministers but 'no one seemed to have much of an answer.'[131] Wilson convened an established emergency response committee for dealing with crises, known as the Cabinet Office Briefing Room (COBR). Through COBR, Wilson said they 'began to nail the problem'.[132] Blair, however, doubted this mechanism and said to Wilson, 'Your COBR is hopeless.' Wilson suggested that the Prime Minister attend a meeting, which he did.[133] Blair soon recognised COBR's value in 'getting a handle on the machine and making things happen'.[134] The fuel protests ended on 14 September and a major crisis was narrowly averted.

In February 2001, a foot-and-mouth epidemic began among livestock. The disease spread at an alarming rate and subsequently the European Commission imposed a ban on all British meat, milk and livestock exports. Eventually this led Blair to postpone the 2001 general election by a month.[135] The Ministry of Agriculture, Fisheries and Food proved unable to get a grip on the emergency. Blair, having learnt from the experience of the fuel crisis, called in Wilson 'to take charge' using COBR.[136] Wilson gathered experts including the chief scientific adviser, Sir David King, a 'masterstroke' for which Blair credits Wilson.[137] King's advice was successfully implemented. Blair said that in resolving the crisis it was necessary for him to undergo a 'deep immersion in every detail' and in doing so he 'learned more about crisis management and the utter incapacity of the normal system to deal with abnormal challenges'.[138]

THE PATH TO THE DELIVERY UNIT

Throughout the first term Michael Barber was based in the Department for Education and Employment (DfEE). During this time, he maintained good relations with No. 10 staff including Peter Hyman, Jeremy Heywood, Andrew Adonis (senior adviser in the Policy Unit) and David Miliband.[139] In a conversation with Barber in March 2001 about the forthcoming manifesto, Miliband, who was writing it, said, 'I still think of you as one of us,' to which Barber, by then a civil servant, replied, 'I am, spiritually.'[140] Barber had also developed good relations with senior civil servants in the DfEE including Permanent Secretary Michael Bichard (in post until 2001) and David Norming-ton, director general for schools from 1998 to 2001.[141] Normington stated that Barber 'was not a problem for us, he was a help'.[142] Barber understood that Blair remained committed to radical reform. In 1995, Blair had told him that he planned for 'a quantum leap' in the second term.[143] In late March 2001, Barber recorded in his diary that David Pitt-Watson, former assistant general secretary to the Labour Party (1997–99), called to discuss the reorganisation of No. 10 after the election, which he was connected to through his Labour Party role. Barber and Pitt-Watson were close friends, the latter having served as vice-president and treasurer of Queen's College Student Union while the former was president.[144] Pitt-Watson asked if Barber wanted to work in No. 10 after the 2001 election.

Barber: It would depend on [as] what.
Pitt-Watson: Head of the Policy Unit.
Barber: I'd be very interested, I wouldn't do it the way they do it now. I'd focus on delivery.[145]

This was a pivotal moment and one that would set Barber on the path leading to the Delivery Unit, though at this stage it was not a done deal. In early May, Barber began to expand his thinking on a potential new role as head of the Policy Unit. He told Miliband that he 'was interested in doing his job when he left' to stand as a Labour candidate in the 2001 election.[146] In response, Miliband said that he thought Barber would be 'excellent' and he had recently spoken to Powell about him.[147] They ended the conversation by agreeing that it 'would be worthwhile' for Barber to see Powell, so that Barber could set out his 'thinking on the Policy Unit'.[148] Previously, on 30 April, Barber had attended a No. 10 seminar chaired by Miliband, to discuss a paper authored by several Labour backbench MPs on the theme of delivery.[149] Miliband had invited a range of people from across Whitehall to debate the issue, including John Gieve (the new Permanent Secretary at the Home Office), Geoff Mulgan, Moira Wallace (head of the Social Exclusion Unit), Ed Miliband (special adviser to the Chancellor of the Exchequer), Simon Stevens (special adviser to the Secretary of State for Health), Nicholas Macpherson (senior Treasury official) and Heywood.[150] David Miliband asked Barber to respond to the paper. Barber's comments included the need for policies which were both universal and targeted; the need to deliver short-term results in order to have a long-term strategy; and the need for policies of high priority to be centrally driven.[151] He said that he received a positive reaction from those in attendance.[152] In early May, Barber met with Pitt-Watson and discussed his view that 'the functions of the Policy Unit needed separating out. One was about ideas and maybe speeches; the other was the relentless pursuit of implementation of Blair's priorities across government. This was the job I could do and [I] knew how I would do [it].'[153] On 11 May, Barber met Powell at a café in the Millbank Tower Complex and the discussion was as follows:

I went through with Jonathan what I thought about the Policy Unit … It needed to focus on delivery relentlessly. Tony [Blair] should set out the six big things he wanted each Cabinet minister to deliver. This should be the agenda for the Policy Unit which should pursue those things with each of the departments. The process should revolve around Blair's stocktakes, in which Blair and the Head of the Unit should really put ministers under pressure on the 'how' of delivery. The six things in each case should be Tony's personal priorities ... Being frank, I added No. 10 needed to be much stronger in relation to No. 11.[154]

Barber's counsel that Blair needed to contend with Brown and the strength of the Treasury through this mechanism was perceptive. It reflected the institutional asymmetry between the role of the Prime Minister and No. 10 and that of the Chancellor and the Treasury. Indeed, the limited capacity of No. 10's levers of power, as then constituted, was an issue which Blair's first principal private secretary, Alex Allan, identified.

It became quite clear early on that No. 10 was not geared up to driving forward the New Labour agenda in the ways that they had hoped. John Major had been a far more passive Prime Minister. He cared deeply about a few things but was not trying to drive the whole agenda across government. The machinery was simply not set up to support Blair in driving the whole of his agenda forward at once.[155]

Though the necessity for change can often be clear, adapting the machinery of government is a delicate art, and easy to get wrong. There is an understated power in quietly effective machinery of government changes. Barber continued to reflect on the conversation with Powell.

Jonathan kept asking questions which sharpened my own thinking. In particular, I realised that this delivery function didn't need to cover the whole Whitehall waterfront. It could just concentrate on the top priorities – education, health, crime, prisons, immigration and maybe not much more. In return – and being equally open and trusting – Jonathan told me about the thinking they had done about reorganising inside No. 10. They had a plan to split the No. 10 Policy Unit into three functions – a think tank/blue skies function; a day-to-day marking function (he was using a football metaphor) in relation to each department and a delivery unit. What I was describing he could see was the delivery unit ... As we drew to a close he said, 'You've obviously thought this through in much more depth than we have.' ... I was struck by how little they had thought it through with just four weeks to go until the second term began.[156]

During an interview with the author, Powell confirmed how the meeting unfolded. In particular he said that he 'loved' Barber's proposal for how a 'delivery unit' would work in practice.[157] Powell informed Barber that within No. 10 they had been considering 'a successful business person' to lead on the delivery function of the Policy Unit.[158] Barber, however, suggested to Powell that the issue for such a person would be 'knowing how Whitehall worked – being able to get to the right place, whether at political or official level, in the machine to shift things along'.[159] It was at this point that Powell asked if Barber would be interested in undertaking such a role; he would. Barber wrote, 'He studiously avoided offering me the job.'[160] This exchange demonstrated that, as in 1997, there was still a degree of unpreparedness on Blair and his team's part but this time around they were planning for change, and listening to those with proven experience of delivering domestic reform.

Powell explained that he was not the chief thinker on the reorganisation of No. 10, Heywood was, and he would brief Heywood on their discussion.[161] Heywood had written a paper for Powell in November 2000 which captured their ideas about how to track delivery.[162] In the paper, Heywood proposed setting up a delivery unit based on the Standards and Effectiveness Unit (SEU), which Barber had led in the DfEE. Heywood's delivery unit would be part of the Cabinet Office and report to a minister – a Chief Secretary to the Cabinet – who would sit alongside the Chief Secretary to the Treasury and the Prime Minister during regular stocktakes between the centre and departments.[163] Powell had agreed with Heywood's idea and suggested they come back to it in the New Year when the planning for a second term would intensify.

Barber met Heywood on 16 May 2001 at (the now defunct) Churchill's Café on Whitehall. Barber explained his thinking from the beginning.[164] The SEU, which Barber had created, had been 'very formative' in his thinking about a delivery unit.[165] Heywood informed Barber that 'he'd prepared a paper last year proposing a delivery unit' and that 'Blair was broadly signed up to the idea'.[166] There were remarkable similarities between Heywood and Barber in their respective planning for a delivery unit. Heywood, like Powell, asked Barber if he would 'really do this' job, to which Barber responded that 'I'd be very interested if the conditions were right but that I was about to apply for the Director-General for Schools post in DfEE and I loved what I did'.[167] Heywood said that Barber should 'go ahead' and apply as 'he didn't know whether any of this would happen'.[168] He divulged the current wider plans for the reorganisation of No. 10: 'He became really enthusiastic. He explained how the "marking" function of the Policy Unit would be merged with the private office and managed by him ... He concluded with real enthusiasm, "I think we can do this."'[169] Barber agreed to prepare a paper for Heywood that would note their discussion and explain who would staff the unit. Shortly after this, Heywood discussed the plan for a delivery unit with the Permanent Secretary to the Treasury, Andrew Turnbull. Turnbull was somewhat 'less enthusiastic' and was concerned that such a unit would challenge the Treasury's responsibility for holding departments to account.[170]

In mid-May, Barber met with Pitt-Watson to test out his ideas for a delivery unit. Pitt-Watson said that he knew a businessman, Nick Butler of BP, who was 'interested' in the job.[171] Together they considered the potential disadvantages of taking a role at No. 10:

> We both agreed working at the court of King Blair could be a nightmare; the intrigues around the King; the competition for influence; Blair's obsession with presentation; his weakness in wanting always to be liked; his lack of interest in or understanding of systems and organisations; his unwillingness to choose between people; his indecision and all that before you even consider the war with Gordon.[172]

This was a critical statement on the limitations of Blair's governing style and personality, as Barber saw them in May 2001. Barber submitted his 'No. 10 Policy Delivery Unit' paper to Heywood and a couple of days later, Heywood informed Barber that the Cabinet Secretary was 'signed up to the concept' and had said to Heywood that he thought Barber was the 'ideal person' to run it.[173] But

Heywood cautioned that Blair 'might prefer' Barber to stay in education.[174] He said that he thought Barber's paper was 'compelling' and that he had shared it with Powell.[175]

Barber met with Wilson in the Cabinet Secretary's grand office to discuss what a delivery unit would look like.[176] Rather surprisingly, Wilson informed Barber that he was 'preparing to receive John Prescott as the Deputy Prime Minister in charge of delivery'; Barber responded frankly that he 'couldn't do this [delivery unit job] working for him'.[177] Wilson agreed with Barber; he thought the delivery adviser needed to report directly to the Prime Minister – and that Blair himself agreed with this.[178] As the conversation ended, Wilson clarified that he did not have the authority to offer Barber the job.

Although the conversations of the past week had gone well, Barber was still unclear as to whether Blair would want to move him from education.[179] In the final days before the 2001 general election, he noted an interview with Blair in *The Times* which described a new 'Policy Delivery Unit' as part of a wider No. 10 reorganisation but claimed that the head was likely to be a 'top businessman'.[180] The article mentioned Barber by name, as head of another unit (the SEU) that had been successful in the first term. Barber contemplated the likely outcome:

> I still sense the chances of me going to head the unit are no more than 50–50. I really want to do that job now … I believe I can do the job I've described in the paper and very well. Of course there are risks but that only adds to the challenge.[181]

For Barber, the future was one of uncertainty but also huge potential.

THE FIRST TERM IN RETROSPECT

In the years 1994–97 Blair, Brown and the New Labour team transformed the party into an election-winning machine, with highly professionalised media communications and political strategy. This machine continued to perform effectively in government, on these areas. But as Barber has reflected, while 'spin really does matter[,] the danger comes when it is divorced from substance'.[182] While Brown and his advisers managed to get the Treasury machine working to implement their policy agenda relatively quickly, the challenges in creating an effective No. 10 were of a different magnitude. Nevertheless, Blair and his team had evidently not done enough in their planning to ensure an efficient transition to government, where steering and engaging the Civil Service machine is what turns policy from rhetoric into reality. Instead they largely believed that their way of working in opposition would be sufficient. Once in office, the overarching aim was to win a second election so they could entrench their evolving programme, which led to the first term being conducted in continuous campaign mode.

The period 1997–98 was when New Labour put its manifesto plans to the test. In places, it was able to use its mandate to jolt the machine into action. By 1999, its pre-election plans, particularly Brown's, were taking root but it now realised how modest the 1997 manifesto was. There was a gap between rhetoric and strategy, and between policy and delivery. Even with new public funding coming on tap, it could not quantify its delivery problem without a coherent strategy on public service reform. This oversight had a negative impact on public opinion and the government's standing in the media.

The final two and a half years of the parliament, the period from 1999 to 2001, was dominated by the search for a radical public service reform plan and a mechanism for delivery. Blair went into the 2001 election with plans for a reorganisation of No. 10 in preparation for an ambitious second term focused on the delivery of public service reform. The blueprint of a delivery unit was ready. Yet going into the election Michael Barber did not know whether he would be the one to lead it; therefore tracking this pivotal period is important in understanding the origins of the Prime Minister's Delivery Unit and the subsequent 'art'. The tricky issue remained that a delivery unit would impinge on Brown's domain and so, if it was to be effective, there would need to be a deal struck with the Treasury. By its own admission, New Labour was underprepared for how to govern and so the first term was to an extent a missed opportunity.

CHAPTER THREE

2001 GENERAL ELECTION TO 9/11: THE CREATION OF THE PRIME MINISTER'S DELIVERY UNIT

On 7 June 2001, New Labour won a second general election, with another huge working majority in Parliament, this time of 166. The campaign had been fought under the banner of 'a lot done and a lot more to do' with a focus on 'radical' public service reform, investment and a strong role for Britain in Europe.[1] This win was pivotal for New Labour; indeed much of the first term had been spent in perpetual campaigning mode to ensure a second victory at the polls and allow for a 'quantum leap' in ambitious reform during a second term.[2] To put this in context, at the time it was the second largest majority of the post-war era; the last successive election victory for the Labour Party had been a generation before, in October 1974 when Labour under Harold Wilson went from a minority government to a three-seat majority. It was now highly likely that there would be, for the first time in history, at least two successive full terms for Labour.

The three months following the 2001 election were, in part, characterised by disquiet about the scale of the challenge ahead. Tony Blair was undoubtedly emboldened and recent appointments at the centre of government provided much-needed energy and tenacity. This chapter captures the creation of the Prime Minister's Delivery Unit, headed by Michael Barber; it begins after the 2001 election and ends just before the watershed of the 9/11 terrorist attacks in America a few short months later.

In government 'process' is one of the political battlegrounds for warring factions. Yet the in-depth story of how organisational change unfolded within No. 10 during this period is largely absent from publications on the Blair government. Such changes in government can be slow, arduous and susceptible to attrition. At the start of the second term, there was uncertainty with regard to policy, process and personality. Barber's diary throughout provides new details on how the transition transpired. He usually wrote weekly diary entries but often during this period there are several entries per week. The growing power of the Treasury under Gordon Brown is well documented, but the Treasury's perspective and actions during the emergence of the Delivery Unit were heretofore largely unknown. Unearthing the challenges in launching the PMDU will reveal how the Unit managed to cut through and gain prominence. It will also track how Blair, in his own words, would need to metamorphose as a leader from 'the Great Persuader' to 'the Great CEO'.[3]

THE AFTERMATH OF THE 2001 GENERAL ELECTION

On winning the 2001 general election, Blair declared that he took the election victory as 'an instruction to deliver'.[4] During much of the first term, domestic reform and investment had largely been dominated by the Chancellor of the Exchequer, Gordon Brown, and the resurgent Treasury. From 1999, Blair's rhetoric became bolder, but this presented a 'problem' as identified by his director of government relations (2001–05), Sally Morgan: the rhetoric 'was way ahead of delivery'.[5] Meanwhile, Barber went into the election having contributed to the planning for a delivery unit but not knowing whether he would lead it. Shortly after the election he reflected: 'The time for excuses has passed … The public is impatient for change … [Blair's] interpretation of the election result reflected this and is exactly what I hoped for.'[6] Tapping into the internal mood Barber observed that there was 'no euphoria, just a sense of the task ahead; the need for a relentless drive for delivery. The question is, can his [Blair's] government think in a way and organise itself in a way that makes successful delivery possible?'[7]

In the days immediately following the election, Barber received little clarity on his own position. Jeremy Heywood, the principal private secretary to the Prime Minister, informed Barber that he, Richard Wilson (Cabinet Secretary) and Jonathan Powell (Blair's chief of staff) had all recommended him for the position but that currently the Prime Minister 'wouldn't want to move' Barber from his role in developing and delivering education policy.[8] Heywood suggested that they could appoint Barber on a three-month basis and then work to persuade Blair that education was 'alright' without him but Barber was 'sceptical'.[9] Barber listed newspaper reports which suggested alternative external candidates to lead the new unit but Heywood reassured him that these were 'not a serious prospect'.[10] The *Sunday Telegraph* claimed that Nick Butler, a former Labour Party parliamentary candidate and senior executive at BP, was expected to be appointed.[11] Heywood agreed to share and take comments from Barber on the Prime Minister's letters to incoming Secretaries of State.[12] Barber believed that the 'most serious problem was a failure to prioritise' especially in the health and transport letters; Heywood said the letter had several purposes but Barber stated that 'this made a clear separate delivery section all the more important'.[13]

Barber continued to carry out his role in the Department for Education and Skills (DfES, formerly DfEE). He maintained contact with David Blunkett, who had moved from education to become Home Secretary. Barber agreed to advise Blunkett on setting up a Police Standards Unit, based on his experience in education with the Standards and Effectiveness Unit (SEU).[14] Blunkett knew Barber's approach involved more than merely setting targets and demanding delivery from departments. Speaking to the present author, he explained the view which he and Barber shared: 'There's got to be some understanding of what the barriers are to delivery, including psychological, ingrained inertia as well as practical barriers to delivery, and then work on them.'[15] Six days after the election, Barber had resorted to trying to work out what was happening to the 'Policy Delivery Unit' through the press and threw himself into the education reform agenda, 'on the assumption that the Delivery Unit option had somehow gone'.[16]

On the evening of 13 June, Barber received a telephone call from Jeremy Heywood.

'It looks as though the Prime Minister has decided to appoint you,' he said. 'Sorry it's taken so long … It took much longer than we expected to get through the Cabinet and all the other appointments.' … In response to the appointment, I said, 'On the conditions we agreed?' He said, stiffening, 'What conditions?' I said, 'Not pay and conditions … an office in No. 10, and answering to Blair, not Prescott.' He relaxed. This was fine.[17]

The following day, Barber informed the newly appointed Permanent

Secretary to the DfES, David Normington, and the new Secretary of State for Education, Estelle Morris, about the delivery role he would be moving to. He then met with Heywood to discuss practicalities.

> Most problematic, we talked about the Treasury. There was an article in *The Times* that morning containing a very obvious Treasury counter-briefing against the Delivery Unit. Jeremy [Heywood] had been in discussion with Ed Balls. He also said the Treasury officials Nicholas Macpherson and Adam Sharples [director of public spending] ... were in a state of excitement about it. Jeremy concluded: 'We should have announced it a week ago ... the rats have got at it.' This all sounded rather alarming.[18]

In the *Times* article, the negative tone was explicit.

> The Chancellor of the Exchequer had been infuriated by Downing Street plans to establish a new unit within the Cabinet Office to monitor how Whitehall departments deliver ... Treasury sources said that the planned Delivery Unit in the Cabinet Office would provide 'secretariat support' for the PSX committee and help to progress chase.[19]

Safe passage would need to be identified sooner rather than later, otherwise the Delivery Unit would be born with a noose around its neck. Barber met with Normington and summarised the perilous pressures under which the Delivery Unit might struggle to operate.

> The new Unit could find itself shunned by the Treasury, separated from Blair by the Policy Unit, and institutionally resisted

by departments. It would be buried. On the other hand, it was a huge compliment, the government had a huge majority, the Prime Minister had staked its future on delivery of improved public services and I was being asked to lead his work on this ... How could I turn him down?[20]

In response, Normington advised Barber:

'As a friend, rather than as Permanent Secretary, I'd advise you to take the job in Downing Street.' I asked him quite a lot about how the PDU [Policy Delivery Unit] might work in relation to the DfES. He said, 'It worries me when I hear you describe it ... but at least it'll be you.' He added that even the proposal had already had its effect on him.[21]

Barber secured a small office in No. 10 close to Blair's. Later that week, he met with Blair, Powell, Heywood and Wilson in Blair's study.[22] Barber had a list of points to raise:

The first was access to him [Blair]: 'You'll certainly have that,' he said matter-of-factly. My main point, though, was that the Delivery Unit would need Blair's ongoing personal commitment ... I quoted the example of the Rayner [efficiency] reviews in the early 80s which David [Normington] said had made a real difference because Margaret Thatcher had given them her continuing high profile attention – people knew she was on the case. I said he would need to do the same. He understood.[23]

The conversation moved onto the policy areas that the Delivery Unit would focus on and effective process.

I said [the policy areas] should be the ones that mattered most to the electorate. Blair agreed strongly. Indeed, this is what he believes the DU is for. I asked which areas it should cover and listed health, education, crime and transport … Blair wanted prioritisation. He wanted to know how it would work and we discussed that too. When he directed a question to Jonathan [Powell], he replied by saying that 'Michael did most of the thinking.' He was keen on the integration of the DU with his stocktake meetings which will form the centrepiece of the process.[24]

At this early stage, it was clear that the Prime Minister was engaging deeply with his nascent unit. They moved on to discuss the potential challenges that could impede the Delivery Unit.

I wanted to know how the DU would relate to the Comprehensive Spending Review/PSX process [Cabinet committee on public services and public expenditure, chaired by Brown]. It was agreed that as Delivery Adviser, I would attend the meetings of PSX. Blair was pretty contemptuous about the process though and suggested it had become meaningless. He clearly considers his stocktakes to be more the key to holding people to account. On the four key ministers [Blunkett, Byers, Milburn, Morris], Blair clearly thinks they'll do a good job and agreed that my role largely was to help them ensure that their departments actually delivered.[25]

There had been a form of stocktakes in the first term whereby Secretaries of State and senior civil servants would meet with Blair. But they were not underpinned by a regular delivery framework and as Sally Morgan observed, they lacked 'an honest broker role', a vital function which she explained Barber and the PMDU fulfilled be-tween No. 10 and departments.[26] In the meeting, Barber described what delivery meant to him: 'I stressed that in my view it was not just about meeting numerical targets valuable though they might be: it was about bringing big visible change that people noticed and felt ... "That's absolutely right, Michael," he [Blair] said.'[27]

After giving a final speaking engagement in the DfES, Barber reflected on what motivated him: 'As I left I wondered if I was right to be changing jobs – the depth of my knowledge and my interac-tion with and responsiveness to participants gave me real pleasure – the pleasure of being on the frontline advocating change.'[28] Inter-estingly, Alastair Campbell's diary entry around this time shows the contrast between what Barber was experiencing as a new appoint-ment to the No. 10 team with a forward-looking brief and the flat sentiment among some of those who had worked closely with Blair for many years. Campbell wrote:

> TB asked if I was depressed and I said I was ... He faced real challenges and real issues ... I had done what I was best at, during the period it was most needed and now he needed those skills less than he used to ... [Anji Hunter] said she felt exactly the same ... She felt surer than ever that she wanted and needed to leave.[29]

Moreover, Campbell commented on the troubling divergence be-tween Blair and Brown:

> TB said he was more than happy for GB to be seen as a big figure because that was good for the government ... I said we had to really watch the potential fault line running through everything as a result of GB putting himself in slightly different positions.[30]

GETTING STARTED

In mid-June Barber met with Wilson, Heywood, Suma Chakra-barti (head of Economic and Domestic Affairs Secretariat, Cabinet Office) and Mavis McDonald (Permanent Secretary to the Cabinet Office) in Wilson's office. They worked through the descriptions of the Delivery Unit, using the short document drafted by Wilson and the five-page paper drafted by Barber and Heywood prior to the election, and made minor amendments.[31] The Cabinet Secretary was enthusiastic about the idea that Barber had got from Chris Wormald (a DfES civil servant, part of the SEU under Barber) that every six months the Delivery Unit should look at delivery perfor-mance on each delivery objective and put them in a league table form.* Wilson said that he would use these 'to determine perma-nent secretaries' performance'.[32] Wilson encouraged Barber: 'This is your moment of power.'[33] The potential impact of the PMDU was quickly becoming clear. Heywood's 'concern throughout was to ensure the right relationship with the Treasury, he knew this would be extremely difficult and his instinct was to unfold the role to them slowly and involve them wherever possible.'[34] Barber noted that Blair 'had said he didn't want the Treasury involved in his stock-takes. Apparently in the last Parliament they had been – though not for some reason in the education ones ... Wilson was clear this had to report to Blair.'[35] After the meeting ended, Barber considered how he would approach the delivery role:

As we left this heart of Cabinet government, I said to Richard [Wilson] that I would make this work. I liked the fact that earlier

---

* Chris Wormald was appointed Cabinet Secretary in December 2024.

he had said that in setting up this unit and carrying out this role we should nail our colours to the mast. If we seriously want delivery, we have to go for it.[36]

The Cabinet Secretary's support for Barber and the new Delivery Unit was marked. Later that day, Barber viewed the offices where the PMDU would be based in 53 Parliament Street, close to Downing Street.[37] The two meetings chaired by Blair and Wilson indicated that Barber had overcome his first potential challenges; he had been well received and taken seriously by the key figures in No. 10 and the most senior civil servants in the Cabinet Office. The next tasks were to decide the specific issues that the Delivery Unit would concentrate on; build working relationships with departments at ministerial and official levels; and, crucially, work out how to handle the Treasury under Brown – each of these presented opportunities for considerable challenge.

Barber met with Gus Macdonald (Lord Macdonald of Tradeston), the new minister for the Cabinet Office who would have day-to-day ministerial oversight of the Delivery Unit.[38] They discussed the 'characteristics of delivery ... beyond numerical targets'; however, Macdonald 'was keen to assert his role as the political head of this operation'.[39] As a result, Barber affirmed, 'I wanted to ensure that while being respectful and allowing him this political role, I didn't concede too much authority. I took several opportunities to point out that I knew the leading politicians well.'[40] These existing relationships provided fertile soil for Barber in which to grow the Delivery Unit; they also formed part of the emerging art of delivery. After the election, it was confirmed that Blair's private office and the Policy Unit would be merged to form the Policy Directorate, jointly led by Jeremy Heywood and special adviser

Andrew Adonis.[41] Barber met with Heywood and Adonis to talk about the Delivery Unit and the Policy Directorate.

> I introduced my early thinking about the Delivery Unit to them ... There are some dangerous grey areas between policy development where they lead and policy delivery where I lead. It will depend on the quality of the relationships, in the end ... I thought in a low-key way we had established a good foundation.[42]

Barber then saw Blair to discuss the delivery letters which would be sent to the four key Secretaries of State. They were joined by Heywood, Adonis, Powell, Liz Lloyd (special adviser, No. 10 Policy Unit), Simon Stevens (Blair's health policy adviser) and Brian Hackland (civil servant).[43] They started on the transport letter. Blair said, 'I want the Delivery Unit focused on issues of real salience ... I only want Michael to sort out the railways and the tube.'[44] The focus then shifted to health, education and crime.

> We had a long conversation about health in which I thought Blair muddled means and ends but nevertheless we arrived at a clearer agenda. We had to rush education and crime (he wanted to include asylum). On education again he wanted the agenda for the Unit sharply focused. The result is that we will have about ten or a dozen major policies to track. This seems a stronger approach than I'd originally envisaged, though it's still clear that the achievement of these goals depends on wider reform issues which span the policies.

These major policies revolved principally around four departments: the DfES, the Home Office, the Department of Health and the

Department for Transport, Local Government and the Regions. Barber observed the way in which the Prime Minister engaged with his No. 10 team.

> I had been interested, riveted even, to watch how Blair works with a circle of staff around him – people chipped in thoughts, argued to a point but didn't really take him on. Jeremy [Heywood] and Andrew [Adonis] appear to have most weight but what was most encouraging in the end was that Blair was decisive.[45]

With Blair's support and attention, Barber was able to make rapid progress. On the evening of 21 June, he went to his first meeting with the Treasury as head of the Prime Minister's Delivery Unit. The meeting was held in Ed Balls's office and attended by Heywood, Adonis, Balls, Macpherson, Ed Miliband (special adviser to Brown) and Andrew Smith (Chief Secretary to the Treasury). Balls began the meeting: 'Reading the press over recent weeks you'd get the impression that this meeting was to be the beginning of a war. Actually … we're delighted by your appointment and looking forward to working with you.'[46] For context, the *Sunday Times* journalist Martin Ivens had earlier used his newspaper column to query how the PMDU would 'mesh' with the Chancellor. Ivens had mused, 'The Treasury has hitherto enforced its targets on departments through public service agreements, using its grip on their finances as a lever. Now two centres of power are proposed at the centre of government. Are two progress-chasing departments better than one?'[47] This final question was pertinent. In the Treasury meeting, Barber responded positively to Balls's welcome, and the discussion then moved onto the potential areas of tension between the Treasury and the PMDU.

We discussed PSX and DELs [the Treasury's departmental expenditure limits] and agreed existing targets would not be changed or challenged. The nub of the debate, again, was the definition of delivery. They thought the Unit might concentrate on some things within the PSX context; I agreed but thought also it might look at larger broader things beyond the PSX targets such as 'secondary education transformed' ...

We agreed we'd consider doing some joint projects which PSX could commission. They wanted to do one on the definition of delivery in health. I suggested a couple of topics but Ed [Balls] didn't seem to like them much ... The meeting had gone alright and we had not said what we knew Blair believed – that he didn't want the Treasury involved in his stocktakes.

As the three of us left, I said to Jeremy I didn't want the new Unit getting bogged down with too many joint projects with the Treasury – we'd need to keep our focus. He agreed and suggested, with his urbane cynicism, that I could just appoint two extra people to do joint studies while the rest of us got on with the core task.[48]

Though this formative meeting seemed to go reasonably well there were unresolved conflicts under the surface, although Barber had a significant advantage in having Heywood on side, who was able to deploy effective tactics in response to Treasury interventions. That evening Barber spoke with Heywood, who explained that Gordon Brown was unconvinced about the creation of the Delivery Unit. From Barber's recollections, the exchange went as follows:

'We've got terrible problems with Gordon,' he said. 'Ed [Balls] described the proposal to him and he completely lost his temper.' ... He said that Gordon had demanded to see the Prime Minister about it but that Blair had refused. Blair in fact was gung ho about the Unit and would not countenance changing it.

After dinner, I caught up with Jeremy again ... Blair was in no mood to concede. It wasn't that he wanted war, it was simply that he didn't think Gordon had any right to tell him how to run his affairs. The announcement would go ahead. Minor amendments to the DU brief, which I had cleared, would be made. Beyond that, no concessions.[49]

Jonathan Powell later confirmed this: 'There was of course a subsequent clash with Gordon who had thousands of targets for departments whereas the Delivery Unit was focused on a limited number of measurable priorities.'[50] It is clear that the fractious nature of relations between Blair and Brown was already impinging on the Delivery Unit's ability to do its job. History tells us that there is often tension between a Prime Minister and a Chancellor because the latter tends to act as a check on the former's costly policy programmes. This was true for Blair and Brown. Unusually, Brown also had his own separate and substantial policy priorities for public spending. Blair had less of a check on his Chancellor's policy agenda, partly because a Prime Minister institutionally lacks such fine tools, though they always have a proverbial axe by their side. Moreover, Blair largely trusted his Chancellor to get on with the job! The fluctuating state of Blair and Brown's personal relationship was, however, more impactful to those working with them than the institutional friction which was inherent between their roles.

At this stage, Brown appeared to be against the idea of the PMDU as it was a challenge to the expanded domestic policymaking and accountability role of the Treasury under his leadership. Powell, however, claimed, when interviewed by the author, that the PMDU was not set up as a buffer to the power of Gordon Brown.[51] The desire for a 'lever on the machine' emerged from Blair's 'constant frustration' with delivery in the first term; thus the focus for the PMDU was 'how to actually make things happen in government'.[52] Despite the Chancellor's objections, Blair was resolute about the vision for the Delivery Unit and his response demonstrated the strength of his conviction. The Treasury's view of the Delivery Unit may have been informed by a concern about wider machinations. Speaking to the author, Balls recounted how the Treasury was informed about the PMDU and its initial reaction:

> In 2001 after the election, Jeremy [Heywood] delivered the intention to have a Delivery Unit as a sort of *fait accompli*. There was a lot of scepticism from us and a lot of pushback and there was then an extended negotiation between me, Tom Scholar [principal private secretary to the Chancellor of the Exchequer] and Jeremy about how this was to work ... We didn't like it because we didn't know what it was going to be and we wanted it to be clear [that] there was going to be a partnership.[53]

Balls explained that there was a worry that the PMDU would conflict with both the Treasury's traditional and recently established roles: 'The Treasury was worried that its role in both controlling spending but also its new role in delivering outputs and the whole PSA [public service agreements] process was going to be undermined if it looked as though responsibility was moving somewhere else instead.'[54]

Critically, Balls stated that the Treasury perceived the creation of the PMDU as part of a broader plan to recalibrate the role of the Treasury, with the aim of restricting Brown's influence over domestic policy.

The context of this [time] was continual speculation. There were clearly some people, John Birt for example,[55] who thought that the Treasury should be split. That the Cabinet Office ought to be the place that was doing public spending, not the Treasury; the Treasury should become a more narrow finance ministry in charge of taxation and forecasts but that the whole spending process should happen outside of the Treasury.

I think that in the run-up to [the] 2001 [general election] … there would always be a kind of question around, was there going to be a new Chancellor? And was there going to be a change of Chancellor with machinery of government changes also, to change the relationship between the Treasury and the Cabinet Office on spending?[56]

Balls described the Treasury perspective of Blair's inner circle; of note is his distinction between Blair's personal view and Blair's tendency to encourage his team to come up with radical plans to combat the perceived threat posed by Brown.

There would be some people pressing Tony Blair to do that [split the Treasury]. Tony Blair was always more cautious about that because in the end he wasn't sure it was a good idea and didn't really want to try and break up the Treasury. I think he'd seen [Harold] Wilson try that and fail [with the Department of Economic Affairs, 1964–69], and he didn't think Gordon would accept it. But there would always be people pressing and because we knew this, any proposal we would see in that context.[57]

Balls's recollections are critical in understanding the Treasury's initially hostile reaction to the PMDU. Nicholas Macpherson led the

Public Services Directorate in HM Treasury from 2001 to 2004, and worked closely with Brown throughout Blair's government (later rising to become Permanent Secretary). He witnessed Brown and the Treasury's early reaction to the Prime Minister's new unit.

> One of the Treasury's original concerns was obviously that the Delivery Unit would become a source for more public spending and would weaken the Treasury's grip on public finances. There was also concern about how the PMDU activities would align with the broader framework of public service agreements, which had been agreed quite painfully in the 1998 and 2000 spending reviews.[58]

But Macpherson also recalled that a 'critical' factor in forming good relations was 'some quite early engagement where Michael [Barber] came to the Treasury and explained to the spending teams what he was doing, how he wanted to work'.[59]

On 22 June 2001, Barber's appointment as head of the Delivery Unit was publicly announced.[60] Other changes at the centre of government were released: the creation of the Policy Directorate, jointly led by Heywood and Adonis; a new Forward Strategy Unit (FSU) in No. 10, focused on 'blue skies policy thinking for the Prime Minister' and headed by Geoff Mulgan; and a new Office of Public Service Reform (OPSR) in the Cabinet Office, led by Wendy Thomson, a former director of the Audit Commission, reporting to the Prime Minister through the Cabinet Secretary. The OPSR was tasked with advising on how the government's commitment to 'radical reform of the Civil Service and public services' could be taken forward.[61] There was a possibility that the OPSR's brief could clash with that of the PMDU. Barber, however, reported directly to the Prime Minister while Thomson did not, and the PMDU brief had clear short- to medium-term objectives whereas the OPSR had a broader medium-term outlook.

This major reorganisation of No. 10 and the Cabinet Office was designed to bolster the Prime Minister's support across the board. It had taken two and a half years to create a mechanism which sought to address the challenge of delivery, which Blair had identified. The year 1999 did not turn out to be 'the year of delivery'. The question remained as to whether the delivery conundrum could be solved in the second term. After the 2001 victory, Blair also made changes to the departmental borders within Whitehall, some of which impacted the remit of the PMDU: the Department for Education and Employment became the Department for Education and Skills; and the Department for Environment, Transport and the Regions became the Department for Transport, Local Government and the Regions. The Department of Health and the Home Office remained unchanged.

On the same day as his appointment was announced, Barber spoke at an awayday for Permanent Secretaries across Whitehall departments. The assembled cadre of the most senior civil servants in each department seemed interested and eager to contribute to the PMDU's work.[62] Barber took the opportunity to speak with the Permanent Secretary to the Treasury, Sir Andrew Turnbull. 'We wrestled with targets and goals but I assured him that the PSX targets and existing DELs [departmental expenditure limits] were sacrosanct from my point of view.'[63] Barber was already carefully positioning the Delivery Unit from the outset. On 25 June, Barber's first official day in his new role, he 'set out to create an urgent, positive, can-do culture in the new Delivery Unit' and to 'make an impact within Whitehall' within a week![64] He had three

staff seconded from the Cabinet Office – William Jordan, Liz Law-
rence and Roger Wilshaw.[65] During this first week Barber met with
Blair, deputy Prime Minister John Prescott (who wanted to be kept
informed of the Delivery Unit progress), Home Secretary David
Blunkett, education secretary Estelle Morris, transport secretary
Stephen Byers, Cabinet Office minister Gus Macdonald, minister
without portfolio Charles Clarke and the heads of the other No.
10 and Cabinet Office units.[66] Forming good relationships early on
would be important for establishing the new Delivery Unit in the
rivalrous centre.

Blunkett recalled his initial reaction to the Delivery Unit: 'I think
that's fine so long as it's understood that you've got to engage, in-
corporate and mobilise the departments. You can't do it from the
centre, all you'll get is pushback.'[67] Blunkett knew that Barber had
experienced the 'antagonism at being told what to do by No. 10'
during the first term in the DfEE and so would be mindful of that
in his new role.[68] Though he had yet to meet with the Secretary
of State for Health, Barber had been involved in meetings with
the four delivery Permanent Secretaries and the Cabinet Secretary.
John Gieve, Permanent Secretary to the Home Office, was already
sharpening his department's 'capacity to deliver'.[69] Barber had a
one-to-one meeting with the Treasury's Nicholas Macpherson,
whom he characterised as a 'highly intelligent, grown up '60s radical' and they 'hit it off'.[70]

By his second week, Barber quickly realised the all-consuming
nature of working at the centre and was wary of becoming 'absorbed' by it.[71] He had his first one-to-one meeting with Blair on
the terrace outside the Cabinet Room. He said to Blair that he
wanted to 'avoid the quagmire' of the centre and 'focus firmly' on
the delivery agenda.[72] Blair agreed. 'That's absolutely right … You

must, Michael.'[73] Barber moved onto his next issue: 'in order to be successful' people he spoke to needed to know that he spoke 'with the authority of the Prime Minister' and to do that he 'needed to know his mind'.[74] He continued, 'I think I'll know that instinctively because I've been a Blairite since the beginning,' to which Blair smiled.[75] Barber was nailing his colours to the mast in a manner that would have been difficult for a traditional career civil servant (which he was not), given that the Civil Service is politically impartial. He was, however, a civil servant at this point, having transitioned from special adviser, though any senior civil servant working very closely with a Prime Minister is more political (with a small 'p') than a typical departmental civil servant.

Barber and Blair agreed that 'any tough unpopular [policy] decisions' should be taken 'as early as possible'.[76] Moving onto the methods he was developing for the PMDU, Barber explained the concept of delivery contracts – a concise brief, with 'each goal described in a sentence and then supported by a series of bullet points describing what delivery would look like'.[77] Here Blair pushed Barber: targets needed to be 'measurable' and have 'definable products'; the Prime Minister wanted to see 'big, visible change … and some quick early wins'.[78] The meeting finished with Blair enthusiastically agreeing to speak at Barber's first delivery seminar later in July. 'It's really important that people see that I'm absolutely behind what you're doing.'[79] In this first one-to-one, Blair had been decisive in urging Barber to understand the need to achieve definable short-term wins as well as broader change. Such a conversation reflects a competency in government that is often understated and undervalued. Reflecting on the week, Barber wrote, 'My power and the power of the Delivery Unit will flow from being evidently close to him [Blair]; able to speak for him and able to speak to him and influence him.'[80]

Barber's relationship with the Prime Minister would be the single most important factor in the PMDU's success, and his own.

Later that week, the first two PMDU stocktakes, on health and transport, took place. The stocktakes were to be a forum where the Prime Minister would meet with the relevant Cabinet minister and Permanent Secretary, the Chief Secretary to the Treasury, Treasury officials and the PMDU team led by Barber to discuss the delivery progress on each target. They would allow the Prime Minister to hold Cabinet ministers to account and they were to be held every two to three months for each priority area. The concept of a stocktake both suited and enhanced Blair's style of working; whether they would be effective remained to be seen. Barber reflected on the first round of stocktakes, and the early signs of aptitude:

> Alan [Milburn, Secretary of State for Health] was the most impressive of the four different secretaries of state … especially in the way he dealt with Blair. He was very respectful but also lively in debate … combative, sharp and clear-thinking. He had the advantage over the others of having held his office for almost two years before the election so he's completely on top of his brief.[81]

The transport stocktake took place on 5 July. From the Treasury, Chief Secretary Andrew Smith and Shriti Vadera, a special adviser to Brown, were in attendance. Blair had accepted Treasury attendance at stocktakes but the Chief Secretary would attend, not the Chancellor of the Exchequer or the chief economic adviser, then Ed Balls. There was discussion on the use of public–private partnerships to modernise the London Underground. The stocktake gave the Treasury an opportunity to contribute to the policy discussion. For Barber 'the most striking contribution to the meeting came from Shriti Vadera … who argued with Steve Byers and John Spellar [minister of state for transport] and kept talking about "the transfer of risk'".[82] Blair concluded the stocktake with an eyeball-to-eyeball look at Byers and the statement 'Well, as they say, you've got a lot to do'.[83]

In these episodes, stocktakes are shown to have been a useful accountability tool for the Prime Minister and the Treasury, enhanced by the emerging PMDU framework for delivery. They also provided an environment where multiple stakeholders could collectively discuss and debate public service reform. Perhaps the stocktake was becoming a nascent forum where the traditional conventions of Cabinet government were exercised. Barber's personality and style was also proving to be an integral ingredient for success. Sally Morgan, who was a senior special adviser to Blair and director of political and government relations for most of the second term, recalled the impact of Barber's character.

> It wouldn't have worked with a different personality, if we'd sent in someone very aggressive … but he [Barber] was always really clear that he was doing it for the right reasons … [We thought,] we trust you politically, you're not going to play games here with us. You felt, even though he was a civil servant, he really wanted the government to succeed. And his great skill was then to engage the civil servants in that.[84]

Evidently Barber was able to maximise his hybrid role as special adviser turned civil servant alongside his expertise and belief in New Labour's mission to convince and motivate both special advisers and civil servants. Jonathan Powell also highlighted the importance of personal disposition in establishing the Delivery Unit: 'The reason the Delivery Unit worked so well was in part because of Michael's non-threatening and extremely pleasant personality.'[85]

In early July, Barber and Macdonald met with Milburn and his team to go through the Department of Health's delivery contract. Milburn was 'very cooperative' and 'said he'd welcome advice and thinking on ways of measuring the performance of something as complex as a hospital and ways of rewarding success and inter-vening in cases of failure'.[86] He asserted that he 'wasn't prepared to have conflicting targets' from No. 10 and the Treasury; instead the PMDU should 'ensure' that he worked to a delivery contract and not Treasury PSAs.[87] The Secretary of State for Health was seemingly seeking to use the PMDU as a buffer to Treasury control over his department. In response Barber argued that, as Milburn himself had earlier stated, 'every part of the health service, not just Blair's priorities, was entitled to targets'.[88] Later that week, Barber contemplated this exchange. 'It was the first with a minister that had real edge. Milburn knows of course that in the clash between Tony and Gordon none of us can bring about resolution. On the other hand, in terms of systems and ministerial accountability his basic point is right.'[89]

This meeting showed the friction between the Treasury's PSAs and the PMDU's delivery contracts – each represented the respec-tive domestic ambitions of the Chancellor and the Prime Minister. The discussion displayed Barber's conviction in challenging minis-ters, as well as the nuances of his working relationship with them. Looking back, Milburn reflected on the complexity of the account-ability framework he was facing:

When you're sitting in a delivery department your accountabili-ties are already quite varied and quite ambiguous because you've got accountability to the public, you've got accountability to Parliament, you've got accountability to the system, in this case, the healthcare system. You've got accountability to the Treasury, because they're giving you the money and the PSA agreements, and it's all about benefits against costs. You've got accountability to No. 10. You've got accountability to Cabinet committees ... The concern would be, are we just sort of making the accountability framework even more complex and ambiguous than it already is? So, I can see why it would be that I was saying, 'Hold on a minute, where does this end?'[90]

BEGINNING TO EMBED THE PMDU

Barber experienced 'extraordinary drama' when he started to try to embed new processes and agree a paper on how the PMDU would work in practice, especially with the Treasury.[91] He met with Adam Sharples and Nicholas Macpherson to discuss the issue, the latter being part of Brown's 'inner circle'.[92] Sharples and Macpherson were happy with the paper, but it turned out that Brown was not persuaded.[93] Tom Scholar, Brown's principal private secretary, informed Barber that the Chancellor's 'problems with the paper' were firstly that 'it hung too much on the year 2005 (which was not 2004, the end of the spending review period)' and secondly that 'it suggested an over bureaucratic process'.[94] Barber was content to change the target end dates but highlighted that the Treasury's PSA targets did not all end in 2004, and there were now ten-year plans in health and transport to consider. The following day, Scholar informed Barber that Brown still took issue with the paper, particularly the 'concept of "contracts", which he said he'd never heard of'; Barber inwardly complained that 'this was an outrage'.[95] Barber and Heywood informed Blair that Brown 'was blocking progress by refusing to allow the four-pager on the Delivery Unit to go out [to departments]. Blair was firm, "Just send it out. Send it out, I'll talk to Gordon later."'[96] Blair had reinforced his commitment to the PMDU, even at the expense of increased tensions with the Chancellor. The PMDU represented an extension of Blair's own personal authority.

When Barber advised his ministerial sponsor Gus Macdonald that he had been given permission by the Prime Minister to send out the PMDU paper, Macdonald erupted and told him that if he 'carried on like this he'd fire' him.[97] Barber was 'taken aback' but did not lose his 'concentration or temper ... At no time did I point [out] the crucial fact here which was that he didn't appoint me – the Prime Minister did – and therefore he had no power to fire me.'[98] It is clear that Barber saw Blair as his boss rather than Macdonald, who had after all been given responsibility for day-to-day oversight of the PMDU. Nevertheless Barber was taken aback by the incident, and he emailed Heywood: 'I'm beginning to wonder if this is a doable job.'[99] Heywood and Barber agreed it made sense to show Blair a draft delivery contract to make sure they were fighting for something he definitely wanted. They met with Blair that afternoon, before his meeting with Brown, relayed Macdonald's reaction and then showed him a delivery contract, to which Blair responded, 'That's exactly what I want.'[100]

Heywood updated Barber on Blair's meeting with Brown, which Balls had also attended. Again, Blair appeared to be steadfast: 'The meeting was a difficult one. Blair was absolutely uncompromising. He wanted to keep the contract concept. Brown apparently left the meeting "in a bit of a huff".'[101] That evening Barber updated Macdonald on the latest development. Macdonald asked what 'we had to contribute that the Treasury process did not'; Barber was 'emphatic – in four years at education no one from the Treasury had ever asked me how we were implementing any policy. The Treasury just didn't do that.'[102]

MAKING PROGRESS

Negotiations on the PMDU paper began to move forwards. It was crucial to get it right, and to secure buy-in, as it would set the foundation for how the Unit would work with Whitehall. Macdonald suggested amendments that Barber accepted and Heywood agreed a redraft of a key paragraph with Balls, which he cleared with Barber.[103] Meanwhile, the Prime Minister called Barber regarding the delivery contracts: 'He said he'd cut them a lot and wanted them [to be] much simpler ... He said he wanted to avoid the mistake of the last Parliament and separated out primary education as the exception ... [Blair said,] "We don't want to bury the services in too many targets."'[104]

Blair's caution with regard to numerous targets at this early stage is notable – he was aware of the dangers that excessive targets posed for public servants trying to deliver on the ground. Barber went through Blair's amendments to the delivery contracts: 'He hadn't just cut it, he cut swathes through it. But, as Jeremy [Heywood] said, it was superb to get so much of his attention for it. We could be sure now of what he really wanted.'[105] Barber studied Blair's comments and replied with some of his own. Meanwhile the PMDU paper was faxed to the Permanent Secretaries of the four delivery departments. Soon afterwards a minor issue emerged as Heywood had not realised that the paper had been circulated and he was still negotiating with his opposite number in the Treasury, Scholar. They faxed a second copy to the Permanent Secretaries noting that they had done some 'tidying up' and hoping that 'no one, least of all the Treasury, would ever know that the previous draft had gone before Gordon conceded' on the concept of delivery contracts.[106] Heywood remarked, 'It's a great triumph, Michael. It's a huge difference. This is Gordon saying he's not going to take it any further.'[107] According to Balls, the four-page PMDU paper represented a protocol which established the rules of engagement with the Treasury as well as with departments.

> We ended up with a whole negotiation protocol ... It was essentially a dual partnership between the Treasury team and the Delivery Unit team about how this process was going to work and it was quite difficult. And there was a lot of suspicion to begin with. The whole protocol of who wrote the papers and who submitted them, for PSX and for stocktake. The establishing of the protocol ... took a few weeks.[108]

Brown's acceptance of the PMDU was hard won. Arguably the agreement to involve the Treasury in the Delivery Unit processes, including stocktakes, had persuaded Brown and Balls to view it as a 'dual partnership'. Barber found that the experience 'really tested my patience, there were moments of total exasperation'.[109] While this was going on Barber had also been proceeding with his delivery brief; 'I learned a lot about transport and the DTLR – intelligent, urbane officials who believed they were in no position to deliver anything'.[110] The Delivery Unit would evidently have to persuade transport officials that they could in fact improve outcomes.

Blair instructed Barber to send out the delivery contracts in mid-July. He sent them 'simultaneously to the four departments and to the Treasury', even though Barber had 'promised a week before to share them with the Treasury first'.[111] He reneged on this because first, the Prime Minister had instructed them to be sent out, and second, Barber did not want another delay, as there had been with the PMDU protocol paper.[112]

Barber was in a meeting with Macdonald when a call came through from Balls to Macdonald. Macdonald's private office urged Barber to listen in. 'I listened to a sentence or two of the Ed Balls whinge, "Michael promised to share them with us first but now he's sent them out at the same time as giving them to us, which is hardly in the interests of partnership."'[113] Barber explained his reasoning for doing so to Macdonald.[114] Later that day, in passing, Heywood informed Macdonald and Barber that 'he too had been Edballsed'.[115] At this stage, it is apparent that Barber was willing to work with the Treasury but he was stringently following the Prime Minister's lead in allowing as few concessions as possible. The PMDU was a fledgling unit at this point and Barber was focused on building momentum and acutely aware of the threat posed by inertia in government. Balls later described the Treasury's view of Barber and the PMDU at this early stage:

[Barber] arrived into this clearly having been part of the pre-election discussions but quite keen for it to be this sort of partnership, but always slightly wary that, were we trying to have a genuine partnership or were we trying to kill it at birth? Because actually it would have been quite easy to do that if we wanted to. And I'm not sure at the beginning whether the Treasury quite knew which one it was doing. When the Delivery Unit came on the scene, we start[ed] off thinking, is this an attempt to subvert the PSA process by instead moving the discussion of money and targets to a separate place, the stocktake? The protocol was about stopping that happening.[116]

Balls's recollections are crucial in understanding the power of the Treasury and the hurdles that the PMDU faced in establishing itself. His admission that the Treasury was not quite sure whether its goal was to form a partnership with the PMDU or destroy it is striking. This ambiguous aim corresponds with the experience of Barber and Heywood in their negotiations with the Treasury.

Completing and disseminating the initial versions of the delivery contracts had been an arduous task but it was not the end of Barber's negotiations with the Treasury and the delivery departments. He now experienced difficulties with the Treasury spending teams; familiar issues arose.

> The Treasury officials [are] … wholly unwilling to alter targets even when it is already clear they are unachievable. For them, the PSA targets agreed in July 2000 have taken on biblical proportions. I had to keep pointing out that since their 'Bible' was published, there had been ten-year plans for health and transport published … A bit of common sense should be applied.[117]

Back in Blair's court, Barber had a conversation with the head of the OPSR, Wendy Thomson, about their overlapping areas of focus: '[She] appeared to be trying to carve out a role for herself doing large parts of what I considered to be my job. I didn't give in but we had an uncomfortable discussion as I defended my role.'[118] A Home Office stocktake took place on 17 July; good progress had been made on negotiating the delivery contract. Later, Barber met with Milburn and his Permanent Secretary in Health, Nigel

Crisp, to discuss health priorities. A big topic for discussion was how the bed-blocking issue in hospitals (delayed discharging of patients, which reduces the number of hospital beds available) was increasing waiting times.[119] Barber reflected, 'Whenever I actually get into the real issues I enjoy the role. Much depends on whether I can establish my position and the Delivery Unit in such a way that I can do this.'[120] Barber was not just chasing the delivery of existing targets, he was attempting to understand intractable issues and problem-solve.

The Treasury had not given up on making alterations to the delivery contracts. Barber and Sharples met with representatives from the four delivery departments, and Sharples came with his own redrafted version of all the contracts. Barber refused to let him distribute them, and felt that in doing so he 'had prevented a Treasury coup'.[121] That evening, Barber met with Treasury officials in the PMDU office to reconcile the two versions of the delivery contracts. He noted that they made concessions, particularly when Barber was able to show that the PMDU targets were directly related to 2001 election manifesto pledges. He had fought for 'the status and influence' of the PMDU and left the meeting with a 'sense of progress' but awaited Brown's reaction.[122] The following day, after being briefed by Barber, Macdonald met with Brown and Balls, and then updated Barber. The meeting had gone well; Macdonald reassured Brown on the issue of 'possible rival goals for departments and about departments using the Delivery Unit as a means of securing extra resources'.[123] Macdonald would attend the next meeting of PSX and outline how the PMDU and the Treasury would work together.[124] Barber and Balls would draft a speaking note for Macdonald which gave the Treasury 'an equal role in the process on which the Delivery Unit should lead'; Barber redrafted it to 'loosen the tying of the Delivery Unit to the Treasury'.[125] Balls approved it unchanged.[126]

On 23 July, Macdonald and Barber attended PSX for the first time. The terms of reference for the Cabinet committee were: 'To review public expenditure allocations and to make recommendations, including on Public Service Agreements, to the Cabinet; and to review progress in delivering the Government's programme of investment and reform to renew the public services.' The regular composition of PSX was as follows:

- Chancellor of the Exchequer (Chair)
- Deputy Prime Minister and First Secretary of State
- Secretary of State for Environment, Food and Rural Affairs
- Secretary of State for Transport
- Secretary of State for Work and Pensions
- Leader of the House of Lords
- Lord President of the Council
- Chief Secretary to the Treasury
- Leader of the House of Commons
- Lord Privy Seal
- Secretary of State for Wales
- Secretary of State for Constitutional Affairs
- Minister for the Cabinet Office and Chancellor of the Duchy of Lancaster
- The Prime Minister's Chief Adviser on Delivery (Michael Barber) is invited to attend.[127]

Barber's paper on the PMDU had become a Cabinet committee paper. Brown introduced the PMDU to PSX and Macdonald spoke at length; there was no further debate. The Delivery Unit and its role now had the approval of what Barber considered the Cabinet's 'most important committee and its Chair, Gordon Brown'.[128] This was a significant milestone for the PMDU. It made a material difference to their relationship with the delivery departments.

> To their [Byers's and Milburn's] view that PSX and the Delivery Unit were rival systems of accountability, I was able to point out that they were now integrated; to their view that Gordon and Tony were divided, I can now answer that I had Gordon's backing as Chair of PSX.[129]

The PSX meeting had revealed the gaps in the Treasury's existing delivery mechanism. Two members of the Treasury's Public Services Productivity Panel presented their findings on how departments were responding to the PSA regime:

> Their findings showed precisely why a Delivery Unit was necessary. They said the departments they looked at had no plan, a lack of clarity about leadership ... a muddled chain of command ... These messages were surely not lost on Gordon Brown, Andrew Smith and the Treasury officials. In fact, Robin Cook and the other ministers who spoke thought it was worrying but not surprising. That's how Whitehall seemed to them.[130]

Later that day Barber had a 'friendly' meeting with Smith, the Chief Secretary to the Treasury, where they discussed the PMDU–Treasury relationship.[131] After a month or so working with the Treasury in his new role, Barber commented on its power dynamic under Brown as he had witnessed it:

[Smith] is a sound thoughtful decent man. The problem is that he has so little power. Gordon rules. Ed Balls is his deputy in effect and the others, including Andrew, kowtow. In the row which raged and which was, after all, over a core piece of Andrew's responsibility his name was never mentioned. The description of the Unit and the Contracts went via Ed to Gordon. Essentially, Andrew has accepted that the price of a place at the heart of government and in the Cabinet is to give up the power that should go with the job.[132]

This was a candid observation, particularly on the power of Balls as de facto 'deputy' to Brown.

Barber attended the Prime Minister's awayday at Chequers on 25 July. In attendance were Blair's closest officials and advisers. Barber said that it was 'by far the most significant [day] for me personally'.[133] Alastair Campbell set out the strategy for the parliament to those assembled:

We needed to learn the lessons of the last Parliament ... Reduce the number of targets ... these needed to be joined in a 'clear compelling political narrative' ... The row over private sector involvement was overshadowing delivery. The story needed to be different – investment plus reform equals delivery ... [Campbell] urged Blair himself to rethink his role as PM. He should adopt the tone of the campaign – PM as an agent of change ... The government should not chase every headline, instead it should engage only in the big arguments.[134]

Peter Hyman spoke next and argued for a 'quantum leap in

investment'.[135] Campbell believed that on public service reform 'a lot of the big questions were still being ducked'.[136] Barber set out the emerging agenda in the delivery contracts and was quizzed by Blair and others on what difference he thought these would make. Barber 'was positive – simply by improving the capacity to deliver we could have a difference'.[137] Campbell described Barber's input as 'impressive'.[138] The Prime Minister's principal private secretary, Jeremy Heywood, 'set out with immense clarity the financial parameters for the next spending review'.[139]

> It was not just that the economic circumstances were less favourable than last time; it was also that Gordon's beloved tax credits … were eating up a larger and larger slice of the government's available resources. Moreover, as he tactfully put it, 'your next-door neighbour' also makes all the rules.
>
> Not only has expenditure on tax credits of various sorts already increased by a staggering 56 per cent since 1997 but as these are part of Annually Managed Expenditure (AME) and not Departmental Expenditure Limits (DEL), Gordon can adjust them, always upwards, in every budget. Whereas, DEL is fixed for three years and held there. So while Gordon's playground is wide open, Blair's, which is all about public services, is tightly constrained.[140]

Barber wrote that he 'had never before understood that the Blair–Brown rivalry was played out across macroeconomic policy in such a vivid way … Blair and everyone expressed huge frustration at this account of the public finances.'[141] It demonstrated to him how Brown used the power of the Treasury to promote his agenda. After the presentations, Blair questioned the group on whether they had 'the right programme' for public service reform that would 'really bring delivery'.[142] Blair set out his 'core script for reform ... we're building public services around the consumer'.[143] He was not interested in 'cautious government'.[144] The four principles for public service reform were clearly drawn out at this awayday:

> One, set standards. Two, devolve power, authority and budgets as far to the front line as you can. Three, do away with demarcations between professions where they are not needed, such as between nurses and doctors or teaching assistants and teachers. Four, which was added during the course of the away day, was choice.[145]

Blair told Adonis and Barber that they 'had not yet done an adequate job'; he wanted two or three timetabled outputs in each domestic policy area so that he was fully informed ahead of negotiating the next Budget.[146] Summing up, Blair said, 'I have no doubt that there will be far more involvement of the private sector in the end ... It's going to be hell for a large part of the time we are doing this.'[147] This account showed that Blair was prepared to spend political capital on his ambitious public service agenda. After the awayday, Blair called Campbell and said that 'he [Blair] would be fighting for his political life quite soon, and that GB was limbering up'.[148] The underlying political rivalry of the New Labour era was never far from the surface.

Barber focused his attention on getting delivery ministers to sign off their delivery contracts. Milburn in particular was 'playing tough'; if he signed the delivery contract he wanted to be 'accountable through the stocktakes to Blair for delivery and therefore not to PSX'.[149] Barber argued that Milburn needed to attend PSX ahead of the spending review, which he agreed with. But Milburn 'wasn't convinced' when Barber explained that 'he'd still be accountable to PSX for delivery across those things outside the Contract'.[150] Milburn said, 'In the real world priorities were priorities and these things in the Contracts would suck resources from elsewhere so the Treasury pretence that all PSAs were equal was a farce.'[151] Barber concluded, 'I had no room to manoeuvre and he didn't want to give ground. As the call finished I thought this is precisely the kind of tough conversation with a secretary of state I hankered after when I took the job.'[152] Barber had a similar conversation with Byers on transport, who 'put his points more mildly'.[153] Charles Clarke, then minister without portfolio, viewed these concerns as 'completely justified'.[154] Barber drafted letters to Permanent Secretaries to explain how the PMDU would work with them. He reflected that these letters and the final versions of the delivery contracts were a 'major symbolic step': the Delivery Unit had, 'in extremely difficult circumstances, met its first major deadline'.[155] Although it remained to be seen whether the delivery ministers would sign up to the contracts.

The first Delivery Unit seminar took place on 26 July in No. 10 and each department sent a minister and senior officials. Blair opened the seminar and Macdonald chaired it. Barber gave a presentation on delivery: 'What is it? Is there an architecture of it? What is the sequence over four years?'[156] He regarded it as a 'huge success' that also helped to improve relations with Macdonald.[157] In mid-August, Barber began to receive replies from Permanent Secretaries to the letters he sent at the end of July. The response from his former colleague in the DfES David Normington struck a chord and helped him to refine future communications.

He complained that I seemed to be suggesting 'micro-managing' his staff ... He ended up apologising for 'an end of term whinge'

and saying, with a tone of resignation, 'We will do our best.'
I wrote him a cheerful, robust reply ... saying that we had no
intention of micro-managing and that to attempt it would be
counter-productive.

His letter helps me think hard about the tone I wanted to strike
and the content of the letter I had promised to send permanent
secretaries on the delivery planning process.[158]

Blair strongly endorsed Barber's letters to delivery Permanent Secretaries; the next step would be for the Prime Minister to meet the
senior team from each department to make clear that 'I'm right
behind this'.[159] Blair asked Barber to ensure that Richard Wilson
was 'consulted' before he met with civil servants, but Barber had
not sent Wilson a copy of his letter to the Permanent Secretaries.[160] Heywood intervened to smooth out this oversight. Barber
remarked, 'This was another example of Jeremy's mastery of the
small details of process which can have such a substantial effect on
government.'[161]

Ahead of the next Prime Minister's awayday at Chequers in early
September, Barber prepared a 'quick wins' paper which he sent to
Heywood and Adonis for comment. Normington expressed his
discontent at being asked for 'quick wins', telling Barber that they
'risked distracting him and the DfES from the central task of implementation and delivery'.[162] Barber replied, acknowledging that
quick wins could be a distraction if the wrong ones were chosen.
'The key is to choose the right ones. If you do, they are the key to
creating momentum, building credibility, rewarding change agents
and undermining the cynics.'[163]

By the end of August, Byers and Morris had signed up to their
delivery contracts; there was 'silence' from Milburn, and Barber was

negotiating with Blunkett due to issues with the Treasury.[164] On 6 September, the next Prime Minister's awayday took place and while travelling to Chequers Barber spoke with Anji Hunter about the health reforms. He thought some improvements could be made but overall he 'didn't think our reforms were enough'.[165] In Campbell's diary entry of 6 September, Blair's comments echoed those of Barber's.

> His [Blair's] main fear was whether we really had the structures and the changes planned that would actually deliver the better public services. He was still worried that even if Michael Barber's changes went through, and even if all the targets were met, would that actually deliver the first-class public services we had talked of.[166]

Blair was anxious to ensure that the rhetoric matched outcomes. In attendance at the awayday were those who had been present at the previous one plus Wendy Thomson, Charles Clarke, Stephen Wall (adviser to the Prime Minister on Europe) and other civil servants. Blair presented a strategy paper for the parliament, and emphasised getting the 'structures' of public service reforms right.[167] Campbell responded:

> Gordon had carved out a very clear definition of who he was: Mr Prudence, Mr Anti-Poverty (especially child poverty) ... What ... was Tony's profile in this context? ... Too many people either thought of Blair as purely pragmatic and/or technocratic or didn't know anymore what he believed.[168]

As at the previous Chequers awayday, Heywood gave a paper on tax and spending which made it clear that the planned domestic reforms would likely make it necessary to raise taxes.[169] The second awayday had indicated the big policy decisions still to be taken that could potentially inflame the Chancellor but without these an emboldened Blair, with a renewed mandate, would not be satisfied.

THE END OF THE BEGINNING

During this period of early June to early September 2001, Barber's transition from highly regarded education expert with a track record of delivery in education to chief adviser on delivery to the Prime Minister took place. He had been entrusted with ensuring the delivery of Blair's public service priorities.

Barber understood that his and the Unit's success depended on 'the quality of the relationships' that he could form and deepen.[170] As such he quickly sought to engage with major partners. Vanessa Nicholls, a civil servant in the PMDU working on the Home Office brief, saw its effective working relationships as 'absolutely fundamental' to its success.[171] Barber was accepted by and formed a strong foundation with the Prime Minister, the Cabinet Secretary and Blair's closest operators in No. 10. He was developing good relations with the Secretaries of State and Permanent Secretaries in delivery departments and he was forging a largely civil relationship with Gus Macdonald, his departmental minister. Crucially, requiring much perseverance, the PMDU was creating a tentative working relationship with the Treasury under Brown. Barber credits Heywood for expertly managing this challenge: 'I had no idea how difficult that first few months was going to be in the relationship with the Treasury. Jeremy involved me a bit but he also protected me from a lot and did it himself.'[172]

Once the Treasury wrangle was resolved, Barber got started on the emerging processes of the PMDU – stocktakes, delivery contracts and delivery seminars. Barber himself had started to act as a conduit between the fragmented centre and departments. Yet important factors to his success remained partially outside of his control. The foundations that Barber formed during this period would be tested when the major international emergency on 11 September 2001 started to disrupt the government's strategy for the second term.

CHAPTER FOUR

9/11 TO THE 2002 BUDGET: DELIVEROLOGY IN DEVELOPMENT

INTRODUCTION

The 11 September 2001 terrorist attacks in the United States ir-revocably changed the course of Tony Blair's premiership. He had been due to give a speech to the Trades Union Congress on public service reform and Europe, but the speech was never deliv-ered. Instead he announced that Britain stood 'shoulder to shoulder' with America, viewing the atrocity as 'a battle ... between the free and democratic world and terrorism'.[1] In the aftermath of 9/11, Blair created a War Cabinet which held 'daily meetings for a month'[2] and by November 2001, Britain had deployed troops in Afghanistan in pursuit of the al-Qaeda network, as part of a US-led coalition.

This chapter will examine the Prime Minister's Delivery Unit during the period from 9/11 until the 2002 Budget, in which Gordon Brown announced a major investment and reform programme for key public services. It will consider the immediate impact of 9/11 and the progress which Michael Barber and the Delivery Unit were able to make during this period. The new focus Blair put on foreign policy after 9/11 would inevitably have an impact on his attention and time – but how would this manifest itself? How adaptable would Barber be? Would the PMDU be able to build momentum in the changing political climate?

9/11 TO OCTOBER 2001

THE IMMEDIATE AFTERMATH – DELIVERY NEVER SLEEPS

Barber quickly anticipated that the new foreign focus for Blair could be 'overwhelming in the next few months and even beyond'.[3] Both the then Home Secretary, David Blunkett, and the Home Office Permanent Secretary, John Gieve, have commented on the huge impact that 9/11 had on the Home Office as a department.[4] Gieve recalled, 'After 9/11, you've got to understand that the Home Office found itself at the centre of the security, legislative and immigration implications of this new strand of terrorism and that was a huge rock in our pool.'[5] Stocktakes (on health, transport and the Home Office) that were due to take place on 12 September were postponed until the following week. Instead there was a meeting of the government's COBR emergency response committee, in which Blair became 'entirely absorbed'.[6] Barber meanwhile sought to get on with what delivery business he could. He spoke with Jeremy Heywood, who explained the current state of affairs: 'He didn't think we'd see much of Blair in the next few weeks. I said we'd have to try to keep the business moving in Blair's absence. He sort of shrugged. There are some things … where you have to have the Prime Minister's personal involvement.'[7] There was uncertainty about how much time the Prime Minister would now be able to commit. Heywood later added that he thought the PMDU had got off to 'a brilliant start'.[8] The first potential impact on the PMDU had surfaced and in response Barber and the Unit would aim to keep building momentum. Later in the week, Barber met with the Secretary of State for Health, Alan Milburn, Cabinet Office minister Gus Macdonald and John Birt (Lord Birt), a strategy adviser to Blair. They believed that with the post-election machinery changes 'the "IQ" of the centre had been increased'.[9] Heywood told Barber that Blair had 'not forgotten about delivery in spite of his leading role in creating a "global coalition"'; in fact he was 'worried that people were taking their "eye off the ball" while he was distracted'.[10] But this did not assuage Barber's worries, he wrote in his diary:

> I was irritated about this process. As head of the Delivery Unit, I only found out incidentally that the PM was concerned about delivery. If he's worried about delivery, I should be the first to know. The pattern of Blair's work and the way his mind works doesn't seem to have adapted to take account of the existence of the Delivery Unit. What happened in the last Parliament was that Blair had spasms of concern about various aspects of reform but never had any means of ensuring that it was being consistently pursued. This was the whole point of setting up the Delivery Unit … On Wednesday morning I told him [Blair] that he should know that whatever he was doing, we'd be consistently pursuing delivery. My motto, I told Jeremy, is that 'Delivery never sleeps'.[11]

With the media focused on Blair and the emerging 'war on terror', the PMDU continued its work.[12] The delivery contracts which Barber had been negotiating since August were settled; Milburn accepted his 'grudgingly' though he remained concerned about 'dual accountability' to the stocktakes and PSX.[13] The contracts would allow the PMDU to monitor a set of targets agreed between the Prime Minister and the relevant Secretary of State. This duplication perhaps revealed Blair's lack of concern for the pressure on delivery ministers. In the week following 9/11, much time 'in the engine room of the Delivery Unit' was spent on assessing the plans that the four delivery departments had submitted on how they would deliver the Prime Minister's top priorities.[14] Barber recorded the tiresome task of evaluating these delivery plans.

> [It was] hard, thankless work and the truth is we're not quite sure what we're doing. We need to get through this phase still working focused, fast-paced and challenging to the outside world. The very fact of asking for plans and now interrogating departments about them, will have had a beneficial impact … We don't have to approve their plans if we don't like them. It's clear that they have a huge challenge simply putting effective plans in place.[15]

The contrast between the PMDU's emerging reputation and the reality that the Unit was learning as it went is notable.

The postponed stocktake meetings took place in the week after 9/11, in Blair's office in No. 10 rather than the Cabinet Room.[16] In the health stocktake, bed-blocking in NHS hospitals came up as a significant issue.[17] This was an early sign that despite the time-consuming, fast-moving foreign crisis, Blair was committed to delivery and the PMDU routines. By late September, Barber noted 'real effective progress on the core delivery task; involvement at the highest/deepest level on major issues. Some effective problem-solving with the Delivery Unit playing a key part.'[18] He was now integrated into Blair's No. 10 machine and was attending regular 'round-up' meetings chaired by Jonathan Powell in the Cabinet Room, with 'crucial people' – David Manning (Blair's foreign affairs and defence adviser), Anji Hunter, Alastair Campbell, Geoff Mulgan (head of the Performance and Innovation Unit and the Forward Strategy Unit) and Jeremy Heywood.[19]

In one such meeting, Campbell referred to a dinner that Blair had arranged with the four delivery ministers. Blair 'had urged them to be more radical but this caused anxiety and rightly, they weren't even delivering on the agendas that they already had'.[20] Barber discussed the progress that the PMDU was making, the 'poor' state of the departmental delivery plans and the intention to assess the 'capacity to deliver' in departments.[21] Being a part of these meetings allowed Barber to strengthen relationships and keep abreast of the wider issues on which the Prime Minister was focused; the PMDU could not operate in a vacuum. Two prominent domestic issues which concerned Blair during this period were anti-terror measures and asylum. On asylum, Barber became increasingly involved in problem-solving and the consideration of policy options. In late September, he attended a high-level meeting in the Cabinet Room, with senior Cabinet ministers, senior officials and advisers including the Prime Minister, Home Secretary and Chancellor. The Home Secretary, David Blunkett, was bringing forward a new law to 'prevent suspected terrorists from claiming asylum' as well as seeking to reform the UK's asylum system.[22] There was a 43,000-case backlog and cases were piling up in the appeal system; 'just establishing the facts had been a nightmare'.[23] Blunkett exclaimed, 'I've never seen a bigger mess in all my life.'[24]

Blunkett said that the budget 'was out of control – £700 million overspend on a £450 million budget' and so 'postponing decisions or mere refinement or tinkering were simply not options'.[25] He outlined his plans to set up 'accommodation centres' to house asylum seekers, which were expensive but, he exclaimed, 'If somebody has a better idea, let's hear it.'[26] Blunkett's accommodation centres (alongside ID cards for asylum seekers) were designed to enable the government to provide health and education support, to allow free movement but also to monitor people who were applying for asylum. The existing system was fragmented, with some asylum seekers being held in prisons and detention centres and others being dispersed across the country into council housing. Collective debate ensued. The Lord Chancellor, Derry Irvine (Lord Irvine), and Gordon Brown had doubts about the reform programme. Barber recorded that Brown was 'angry' about Blunkett's attempt 'to bounce him by going straight to the PM and not sending proposals to the Treasury'.[27] Brown insisted that 'detailed work was essential'; Blair agreed more work needed to be done but wanted it done 'urgently'.[28] 'Blair weighed in' on Blunkett's side and 'against Gordon'; the need to send a strong signal was crucial for Blair and as he kept saying to Brown, 'I've been dealing with this for four years now ... If we could get a system that worked, we would save money.'[29] He became quite animated and continued to 'contest the issue' with the Chancellor.[30]

This intervention by the Prime Minister was noted by Blair's team in No. 10: 'In the Blair camp there was a scarcely concealed glee that Tony had really taken on Gordon and held his position.'[31] This indicated the rarity with which Blair challenged Brown in front of others. It also showed the rivalry between the courts. Campbell confirmed that on the same day as this meeting, Blair and Brown were quarrelling over when Blair would step down as leader of the party. Blair was reluctant to give a date despite Brown's insistence. Blair declared to Brown: 'You say I have a choice about when to go. It's you that has a choice, about whether you work with me or against me, and get it into your head that if you work against me, you'll get no help from me.'[32] This volatile political dimension is important to consider; Barber had to navigate the duopoly in order to be successful.

The following day Barber attended a meeting to discuss Blunkett's asylum proposals with civil servants from the Home Office, the Treasury and No. 10. Barber was essentially advocating Blunkett's reforms on accommodation centres for asylum seekers.[33] Blunkett reflected that Barber had been 'extremely helpful' in the asylum policy debate.[34]

An indication that Barber was slowly cementing his position in No. 10 came when he was invited to a meeting in Blair's Downing Street flat, along with Heywood and Andrew Adonis. Barber had rarely visited the flat and so this was a significant invitation. He observed that 'Blair looked exhausted' as they ran through the current issues on domestic policy – 'education (basically okay); health (serious concern in general and about bed-blocking in particular); crime (worry about progress and police reform); asylum (worry about the chaos which Jeremy and I reported)'.[35] Barber saw it as a 'huge opportunity' and on bed-blocking he said they had to 'break the culture in the NHS which allowed it to be taken by surprise by winter every year and to come back with the begging bowl to be assisted through it'.[36] Blair said, 'Yes, that's absolutely right, we do have to break the culture.'[37] The meeting showed Blair's growing confidence in Barber. Barber took the opportunity to reiterate to Blair that 'whatever you are doing, whatever the distractions, you can still be sure that we [the PMDU] are driving delivery on your behalf'.[38] This was an attempt by Barber both to reassure the

Prime Minister and to remind him that concerns regarding delivery should be directed to the Delivery Unit. He reflected on his role in engaging with divisive domestic issues: 'I'm riding several horses at once here: loyal to Blair, first and foremost ... committed advocate of the Blunkett scheme ... opponent of the Treasury, therefore, though in agreement with them on the crass inefficiency of the present scheme. Out-on-a-limb in other words.'[39]

DELIVEROLOGY IN DEVELOPMENT

By the end of September 2001, the PMDU team had assessed the delivery plans which the four departments had drawn up themselves and now had to make judgements about each department's 'preparations for delivery'.[40] They had graded the priorities using a traffic light system on the capacity to deliver. In Barber's view, the chart made 'depressing reading – acres of amber and red and the odd patch of green'.[41] Barber recognised, however, that this was 'a crucial piece of work' and he thought his 'talented young team had done a good job'.[42]

In early October, a team from each delivery department gave presentations to the PMDU in No. 10, on their respective plans for the Prime Minister's top seventeen targets. The PMDU and a group of 'associates' posed questions to the assembled departmental teams.[43] The associates were individuals from outside Whitehall with experience of delivery in both business and the public sector. The health presentation revealed to Barber that they had a 'lack of confidence ... that they would ever really do anything other than manage crisis'; he felt they lacked a 'vision of, at some stage, achieving a recognisably quality system'.[44] The education presentation revealed 'flaws' in plans to 'transform' secondary education.[45] The Home Office civil servants were 'more effective' than Barber had expected in relation to tackling robbery; by contrast, in relation to the criminal justice system (CJS) they were 'dire'.[46] John Gieve said to Barber, 'We're not even at first base on this (the CJS), are we?'[47] Barber agreed. This candid question about the Home Office's capacity to deliver indicated the seriousness with which the delivery agenda was taken. The transport presentation was postponed until early November.

Within the PMDU, the team were 'assessing systematically the progress being made on each of the seventeen delivery priorities', grading them on ambition of the targets, quality of planning, capacity to drive progress, and stage of delivery.[48] Then they put them in rank order on 'likelihood of delivery' – adult basic skills came top and asylum bottom.[49] The PMDU team were 'gloomy' about the task ahead, 'in part because once this data goes back to departments they, as relatively junior civil servants, will have the task of justifying and sustaining some tough judgments and partly because we are as yet uncertain as to how we will follow up, especially where departments are weak'.[50] This was deliverology in development.[51] This approach was not without risks: Barber updated Blair on the delivery picture, to which the Prime Minister replied, 'That sounds pretty bad.'[52] Barber discussed the letter he was planning to send to the four Permanent Secretaries on the assessments of the delivery plans. Blair was wary of leaks but Barber reassured him that the letters needed to be tough and he would take care in drafting them.[53]

In early October, Blair addressed the Labour Party conference, in which he linked the relationship between the foreign and domestic agendas: 'Ninety per cent of the heroin on British streets originates in Afghanistan. The arms the Taliban are buying today are paid for with the lives of young British people buying their drugs on British streets.'[54] On public services he set out the principles for reform.

Public services are the power of community in action. They are social justice made real ... There is a simple truth we all know. For decades, there has been chronic underinvestment in British public services. Our historic mission is to put that right ... There has to be choice for the user of public services and the ability, where provision of the service fails, to have an alternative provider.[55]

Blair continued to be influenced by Julian Le Grand's research on choice and competition in structural public service reform. Le Grand would become a senior policy adviser to Blair from 2003 to 2005, and his book *Motivation, Agency and Public Policy* stressed 'the importance of having a responsive system for users'.[56] Le Grand's view that, however committed public service professionals are, 'they can never have the degree of concern for users that users have for themselves', was influential in No. 10 and underpinned the choice agenda.[57]

Barber had an update meeting with Richard Wilson on 4 October, to check that he supported Barber's 'tough approach' towards delivery at this early stage; he did.[58] Moreover, the Cabinet Secretary remarked on the 'whiff of success' about Barber and the PMDU – a significant indication that they were making an impact in Whitehall.[59]

During this period Barber and Blunkett's relationship evolved; they had worked closely together during the first term and cared deeply about education reform. Barber was keen to strengthen his relationship with a senior delivery minister and Blunkett wanted Barber to assist him in improving the Home Office's ability to deliver. In early October, Barber recorded that he and Blunkett were regularly in touch. Blunkett was under 'huge pressure' but was 'thriving on it'; he had asked Barber for help on police and asylum reforms.[60] Blunkett reflected on his frustration with the civil servants in his new department in his diary: 'They really do think that they run the show, and we ministers are just passing flotsam and jetsam.'[61] Not only was this relationship-building important to both Barber and Blunkett's own success, it also demonstrated that the Delivery Unit may have been originally a tool of the Prime Minister's but in practice it was becoming a resource for delivery ministers too.

ASSESSING CAPACITY TO DELIVER

On 9 October, Barber gave the Prime Minister the first PMDU delivery report on the likelihood of delivery, including a league table of key priorities. The report was created by the PMDU based on the departmental delivery plans and presentations. With the Prime Minister worried about leaks to the media, Barber also gave a copy to Wilson and Campbell. Campbell looked at the league table and said, 'Bloody hell.' Barber replied, 'You told me to keep things shifting on the domestic front.' 'Absolutely,' said Campbell.[62] A copy of the report was sent to the four departments in mid-October, with requested amendments.[63] The league table was a powerful tool; it had the potential to motivate but it was not welcomed by all. For Barber, the use of league tables became 'the centrepiece of deliverology', as they made performance transparent and comparable.[64] The delivery report explained the areas of progress and issues that needed attention. In summary:

- 'In all key departments delivery is undoubtedly top of the agenda'; however, the shift to delivery had only just begun, and it needed to be developed and embedded.
- There was more clarity about what the priorities were and an openness to learn from best practice elsewhere.

- Delivery plans were 'in many cases weak ... there is a lack of clarity about the critical steps to take, about which levers are available and how they can be pulled.'
- There was a lack of urgency. Delivery successes of the last parliament were based on policy that had already been developed before the 1997 election. 'Yet in relation to many of the current priorities, either policy is still being developed ... or the necessary capacity to deliver is not yet in place.'
- Overall the key priorities could be 'delivered "on time, on standard" but only if: the lessons of successful delivery, wherever it occurs, are learnt and applied; urgent, decisive action is taken to tackle the problems this first phase of our work identified; and there is a sustained focus on their effective implementation from now until 2004–05'.[65]

Ahead of wider dissemination, Barber spoke with three of the Permanent Secretaries affected by the content of the report – David Normington (education), Nigel Crisp (health) and John Gieve (crime and asylum).[66] He does not record having a discussion with the Department for Transport, Local Government and the Regions (DTLR). Barber found his conversation with Crisp 'the most difficult' he had had so far in this role; Crisp was 'furious' that Barber had sent the report to Blair before discussing it with him, to which Barber said it was his job to do that.[67] Barber would need to resolve this oversight and limit the damage to his relationship with Crisp, and he said that he would 'reflect on the process' in light of Crisp's 'remarks'.[68] As Barber explained, Crisp exclaimed, 'Bloody hell, you've even traffic-lighted it' and stated that 'he'd now want to reflect on whether they should continue to be open with us in future'.[69] Barber recorded in his diary that 'any honeymoon is now certainly over'.[70] Normington later commented that 'we, as civil servants, were being invited to be partners in a great endeavour to modernise public services'.[71]

On his conversation with Gieve, Barber noted that the 'contrast with Nigel couldn't have been greater: the news for him was much worse, the challenge much greater, but his response much more positive'.[72] Gieve did not seem to share Crisp's concerns about viewing the delivery report before it was submitted to Blair. Rather, he asked Barber 'to tell it like it is'.[73] Barber advised him that he needed 'three really good people at second-tier [management] on whom he could rely'.[74] This episode illustrated the tough conversations that Barber had while building relationships. It also marked the beginning of bespoke support provided by the PMDU to departments on their capacity to deliver. What is more, Barber's delivery report evinced a difference of opinion between a Secretary of State and Permanent Secretary. Crisp was frustrated with the report but Alan Milburn was pleased and thought the analysis was right.[75] Retrospectively, Milburn said that he too was applying pressure on the Department of Health, including his Permanent Secretary, and so there was already existing 'tension' between him and Crisp. Milburn believed that 'the effort that was needed to transform the [health] system was, of course, being helped by the Civil Service, but couldn't be exclusively delivered by the Civil Service'.[76] He sought to find 'agents of change' both within and outside the department. The PMDU was permeating the key power relationships; however, it was doing so in a way that sought to resolve conflict and reach a solution. Conflict resolution had been a part of Barber's family life growing up as well as his professional career; his Quaker upbringing had been 'really important' and his father had chaired a Quaker-established international conflict resolution organisation.[77] Barber had read and understood the theories of conflict resolution and he had been 'very conscious' of them in his mind during the first term in the DfEE.[78] Furthermore, Barber ensured that the whole PMDU team had 'systematic' conflict resolution training.[79]

On 7 October, the US-led military action in Afghanistan began, with UK involvement. In mid-October, there was a crisis developing in the DTLR over the decision to put Railtrack into administration. Railtrack was a private company created during the privatisation of British Rail in 1994, which owned the rail infrastructure in the UK. The crisis was worsened by a leak from within government and as a result the shareholders discussed taking legal action. Barber was not involved in the Railtrack decision but the media associated him with Treasury talks on how to resolve the crisis.[80] Almost simultaneously, there was arguably one of the most infamous leaked emails ever, which caused a furore. The Secretary of State for Transport's special adviser Jo Moore had written an email on 11 September which suggested, 'It is now a very good day to get out anything we want to bury.'[81] This became widely quoted as 'a good day to bury bad news'.[82] From Barber's viewpoint, this 'undermined' the Railtrack decision because although No. 10 and Byers defended Moore, it 'took Byers out of commission' and by the end of the week there were calls for Byers to resign.[83] For Barber it showed 'how fragile a political career is'.[84]

Barber attended a meeting with Blair and Andrew Adonis on a public service reform speech which Blair was drafting. During the course of the meeting Blair took the opportunity to give feedback on the PMDU's progress. 'I just wanted to tell you that I think the Delivery Unit's got off to a very good start. You're doing very well.'[85] This was an important sign of confidence from the Prime Minister. Blair's public service reform speech was delivered on 16 October;

Barber noted that it was 'designed to show he was still focused on that in spite of the war and his leading role in building the global coalition'.[86] In the speech, Blair stated this himself:

Despite current events, we continue to focus rigorously on this agenda ... I am passionate about this ... If we don't get the systems and structures right, we will never grip the roots of the problem, only prune its visible branches ... We are making the public services user led, not producer or bureaucracy led.[87]

He outlined several of the specific pledges – 'We will cut maximum waiting times by two-thirds, from eighteen to six months, over four years' – but he explained that these 'will take time to deliver' and described the work of the PMDU.[88] Blair's public statement on his commitment to the delivery of public service reform was an important signal inside and outside government.

Barber held meetings with the Permanent Secretaries on the delivery contracts to discuss the next steps. Normington said that he and the Secretary of State for Education 'would take an even closer degree of interest in delivery and that he would personally work on the combination of issues' raised.[89] Towards the end of the meeting, Normington said, revealingly, 'It's our careers at stake here ... and yours too I suppose.'[90] Delivery was being taken seriously. Barber's meeting with Gieve followed on from their earlier conversation. Gieve 'knew how problematic the Home Office was' and wanted 'help'.[91] They seemed to have developed a good initial working relationship. Nevertheless, Barber felt that overall in terms of valuing delivery in career progression 'the system still has no respect at all for delivery'.[92] During Barber's meeting with Crisp, it became clear that the Permanent Secretary was frustrated.

He said I had to choose between treating the Health Service as a complex system and join him in solving problems and, on the other hand, trying to impose top-down solutions. He also said I had to choose between being supportive and an ally of his or reporting on him. I said these were false dichotomies ... The difference between my approach and what had gone before was that I was telling the permanent secretaries what I was saying to Blair.[93]

Later that week, Barber met with Milburn's special adviser Paul Corrigan, whom he had known for many years, and they discussed the tension with Crisp. Corrigan agreed to help bring Crisp, Milburn and Barber 'together'.[94] Milburn himself saw Corrigan as 'very instrumental' in delivering the health reform agenda.[95] Barber's longstanding relationships with those in the New Labour circle were proving useful. Meanwhile, the focus on asylum steadily increased. Barber attended a three-hour asylum summit on 18 October with Blunkett, Irvine, Blair, Brown, Wilson, Heywood, Balls, Macpherson, Andrew Smith and Home Office officials in the Cabinet Room to discuss the various (competing) proposals.[96] Barber walked over to the pre-meeting with Heywood and told him that his 'ambition was to work the Delivery Unit out of a job', to which Heywood said, 'We need you to stay for four years'; Barber concurred, seeing it as a 'four-year task'.[97] Regarding the asylum meeting, Barber remarked that from the official minute you would think it was an 'ordered, rational event' but 'in fact what happened was an unholy row'.[98] In short, it was Irvine and Brown versus Blunkett, with Blair chairing and questioning where necessary in order to 'make a judgment'.[99]

Blair expressed his preference for Blunkett's proposal for accommodation centres. Blair prefaced his request for Blunkett to set out his ideas by saying, 'I insisted on getting this right in the last parliament and we didn't deliver … This time, set out whatever you need … Let's have your perfect system.'[100] Blair recognised a failing of his first term and demonstrated his resolve to get it right in his second. The asylum wrangle was resolved on 22 October, when Heywood and Balls negotiated a compromise.[101] Blunkett got his 'minimum condition' to trial 3,000 accommodation centre places while the Treasury wanted 'hard evidence before proceeding to the full rollout of the proposals' and funding would not become available until the 2004 spending review.[102] Barber was not satisfied with this compromise. Blunkett said Blair thought he had given him what he wanted[103] but in fact Blunkett felt the deal had been 'lost' for him, although he was still 'grateful' to Barber for helping.[104] The result may not have gone in Blunkett and Barber's favour but the process had allowed Barber to test and extend his remit, make himself valuable to a senior delivery minister and gain access to the top table of decision-making.

Relations between the PMDU and Barber's former home department were not as collaborative. The PMDU encountered pushback from the DfES when Barber sought to get information on trends in data on failing schools. When asked by one of the PMDU staff members, the DfES officials initially refused to share the data. This irritated Barber. 'It's a tiny thing but I hate everything that this episode represents about the Civil Service … The closing of the ranks; the absence of trust; the concentration on institutional protection to the exclusion of a real-world outcome.'[105] This showed that the PMDU encountered obstacles even with a department with which its head had close ties. On 23 October, there was an awayday with the Prime Minister, all Cabinet ministers, Permanent Secretaries and the Cabinet Secretary at the Commonwealth Club – Alastair

Campbell called it a 'big bonding session'.[106] Blair told the attendees that delivering on promises was the 'challenge of our time'.[107] Barber and Brown debated delivery in a 'challenging' but 'not hostile' way; Barber felt Brown was 'testing' him.[108]

On the evening of 5 November, Barber received an unexpected call from the Prime Minister. Blair wanted to check in with Barber on delivery and explained that he was 'most' worried about the Health Service.[109] For Barber, this call was significant because in spite of all of Blair's international commitments 'he was still focused on delivery'.[110] This was a mark of progress: Blair had addressed his concerns to Barber directly in a way that he had not done in the immediate aftermath of 9/11. During early November, multiple stocktakes took place with Blair attending all of them despite his burgeoning foreign policy agenda. In the eight weeks after 9/11, Blair had held fifty-four meetings with foreign leaders, which had meant taking thirty-one flights covering 40,000 miles.[111] This had to have some impact.

Barber felt the education stocktake on 6 November did not go well. Blair was present, but he 'wasn't properly prepared', nor were Estelle Morris and David Normington; the paper submitted by the department was 'muddled'.[112] Barber later had a meeting with Normington, who recognised that he and Morris had 'not done well'.[113] They discussed the impact of the PMDU. Normington said the 'urgency and pressure' applied by the Unit was making a difference but that he wanted to get to the stage when the PMDU 'wasn't necessary'.[114] He explained that another 'major impact' was that the department was 'organising itself around the delivery priorities', which was not always 'easy to achieve' but Normington was 'determined'.[115] This showed the gradual impact that the PMDU was having on Whitehall. Normington noted regretfully, however, that the department had 'forgotten all the things' Barber taught them during the first term.[116] This highlighted Barber's strong reputation as an education adviser in the first term but also indicated the limited capacity for institutional memory in the DfES. Normington reflected on stocktakes: 'These occasions were nerve-wracking and demanding ... but ultimately they were energising and empowering.'[117]

The crime and asylum stocktake took place after education, on 6 November. The contrast was 'stark'; Blair 'had read the briefing' that Barber and Justin Russell (home affairs special adviser to Blair) prepared and 'decided what issues he wanted to raise'.[118] Blunkett was 'confident' and made a point of stating how 'helpful' the PMDU had been; Gieve was 'open about the problems' his department faced and 'impressive' in describing solutions.[119] Blunkett later noted the effectiveness of stocktakes during autumn 2001:

> This was not one of the 'chats on the sofa' referred to some years later but formal meetings that were much more useful than traditional cabinet committees ... Stocktakes were very much more about investigating what had gone right or wrong and determining the next steps to be taken while ensuring both prime ministerial and Treasury support.[120]

This supports the idea that stocktakes represented a new formal collective forum for decision-making, under the New Labour government.

The transport team gave their delivery presentation which had been postponed the previous month. The director general for railways, David Rowlands, was unable to attend so the presentation was given by the Permanent Secretary of the DTLR, Sir Richard

Mottram.[121] Barber stated that the presentation provided 'a lot of information' but he did not think Mottram took 'the challenge of running Britain's railways' seriously, which could breed 'cynicism' within the department.[122] Moreover, what came through most strongly to Barber was that the levers of power available to the department were limited yet those that were at their disposal were not being sufficiently utilised. Barber urged the officials to devise a 'plan of how the eight or nine levers' could be used.[123] He believed that Rowlands was 'the one person' who truly understood the issues.[124]

In mid-November, a health stocktake was held but Barber felt that Blair was 'distracted' by the pace of events in Afghanistan – 'the Taliban regime was falling apart faster than anyone could imagine.'[125] The focal point of the stocktake was the likelihood of the waiting times target being met in 2002. Barber wrote that the 'most encouraging developments' in the NHS were 'the increasing use of the private sector to extend capacity flexibility and progress with cancer and coronary heart disease'.[126] From Milburn's perspective, the use of the private sector to bring down waiting lists was implemented 'in a very, very precise way … to deal with particular bottlenecks, in particular parts of the country'.[127] Milburn sought 'to get the public sector to respond because if it didn't respond to the competition from the private sector, for the first time was going to lose the money' (if patients chose an alternative provider because of shorter waiting times),[128] 'which is where the choice the patient makes having an impact on who gets the money was so critical … The changes that I made, they were a managed market mechanism. It wasn't a free-for-all. It was deeply planned.'[129]

As the new units that were formed after the 2001 election started to get to work some tension arose, particularly where territory overlapped. Throughout this period there was a strained relationship between the Office of Public Service Reform (OPSR) and the PMDU. Barber recounted an 'unhappy meeting' with the head of the OPSR, Wendy Thomson; Thomson explained that she thought they differed 'philosophically' and suggested that Barber was moving too fast.[130] Barber was resolute; he would 'pursue delivery of the priorities with all the urgency and passion I could muster, until someone stopped me'.[131] Eventually the Cabinet Secretary negotiated a deal to placate both parties which protected the PMDU's relationship with the four delivery departments. The 'Wilson deal' was backed by Gus Macdonald, who was 'proving to be a remarkable ally' for Barber.[132] With hindsight, the conflict between the PMDU and the OPSR may seem somewhat parochial. Sally Morgan, director of government relations in No. 10, commented on the difference that shared history and established relationships made: 'Michael was of us and [Thomson] wasn't and that made a real difference.'[133]

On 20 November, a meeting of PSX focused on health took place. Milburn was cross-examined by a Cabinet committee of his colleagues including Robin Cook (leader of the House of Commons), Alistair Darling (Secretary of State for Work and Pensions), Andrew Smith and Derry Irvine. It was an opportunity for ministers to hold one another to account but also for Gordon Brown to exert his power; for Barber it was 'an impressive and a sobering occasion'.[134] Barber observed that Milburn was 'humiliated' by Brown and 'poorly assisted by his officials'.[135] With such intense pressure one can understand why, during earlier negotiations with the PMDU, Milburn had been keen to cease reporting to PSX. From a Treasury perspective, and in relation to the PMDU protocol, Ed Balls explained that the two forms of reporting had distinct purposes: '

It was accepted that they would have two different processes; the

PSX process was about making sure that the Treasury had a grip on how the money was being spent but thinking about the next spending review, and the stocktake was much more micro-delivery.'[136]

The PMDU received the updated delivery plans from departments in mid-November. The DfES and the Home Office submitted 'significantly improved' plans; whereas the Health plan had 'barely changed'.[137] Barber subsequently had another difficult call with Crisp, and afterwards he reflected on their working relationship: 'I do not want to destroy our relationship with Nigel; nor do I want to drive him to despair ... I want a productive working relationship with him.'[138] Barber decided to send the Education and Home Office delivery plans to Crisp in a bid to share best practice. Whitehall departments were largely siloed, distinct institutions with their own cultures and practices, with little impetus for them to share best practice; Barber was acting as a conduit. The PMDU's staunch but collegiate approach was a notable contrast to the sharp tone of PSX. This example illustrated the challenge function of the PMDU and its role in seeking better operational planning in departments.

NOVEMBER TO DECEMBER 2001

A NEW PHASE IN PMDU–TREASURY RELATIONS – A TOOL FOR THE TREASURY

Barber met with senior Treasury official Adam Sharples to discuss the PMDU and the forthcoming spending review. They made initial agreements whereby the PMDU would have a role in assessing the 'deliverability' of proposals relating to the PMDU priorities.[139] Barber offered to assess 'deliverability' on other policies at the Treasury's request; he saw this as an olive branch from him to them.[140] Barber gave the Treasury 'this thinking free of conditions … to build trust and, not least to gain influence in the Spending Review'.[141] This was an important milestone: Barber, the head of a prime ministerial unit, had secured an agreement with the Treasury whereby the Delivery Unit would have a role in the spending review – which itself would fund and determine domestic policy for the remainder of Blair's second term. Nicholas Macpherson recalled that Balls and the Treasury 'got quite involved in the Delivery Unit as part of the 2002 and 2004 spending reviews – getting an understanding of what money would buy and what the government could say would happen as a result of putting more resources in these programmes'.[142]

Brown delivered the Pre-Budget Report on 27 November 2001. The Chancellor committed an extra £1 billion for health, linked to the results of the interim report of the Wanless review on the NHS's long-term financial needs.[143] Brown naturally concurred that the 'best way to fund the health service was out of general taxation'.[144] The decision on how the £1 billion would be spent to reduce waiting times was a matter of contention between Blair and Milburn on the one hand, who were keen to involve the private sector in NHS delivery and learn from private sector practices, and Brown on the other, who favoured public sector health provision and solutions.

In late November, Barber met with Milburn, who spoke about the danger of tensions between Blair and Brown: 'It'll destroy us in the end.'[145] Barber told Milburn that he hoped he would stay as Secretary of State for Health through the parliament. 'Oh God,' Milburn laughed, 'if I did I'd end up as grey as you, my friend.'[146] This was of significance because Cabinet reshuffles would have an impact on Barber and the PMDU. Milburn was the longest-serving of the existing delivery ministers, having been in post since 1999, and was playing a pivotal role in leading the health reforms. Brown had written to Milburn regarding the £1 billion for health 'telling him not to spend it on the private sector, which the choice policy would'; Milburn thought this letter was 'outrageous'.[147] Blair told Brown that he 'didn't agree with this letter at all'.[148] Barber advised Milburn that he thought the choice policy was a good idea but that they should test it through a 'pilot' because the 'risks both administratively and politically of doing it all at once were too high … Once the guarantee was made there could be no question of failing to deliver.'[149] Milburn's special adviser Paul Corrigan informed Barber that they planned a pilot focused on coronary heart disease in London.[150] Barber told Milburn, Corrigan and Simon Stevens, Blair's health policy adviser, that 'the value of the private sector was that it created capacity quickly and flexibly' and so could be sold to the Treasury on 'value for money grounds'.[151] In providing a rationale that might be acceptable to the Treasury, Barber was fulfilling a new and integral bridging function which was essential to delivery.

Barber met with Brown and Balls, and they debated health reforms at length. Balls and Brown were 'very critical' of the health reforms as they stood.[152] Barber boldly told them, 'The reality is … that if you want to deliver seriously improved outcomes by 2004 or 2005 you will have to do so through the current structures which are only just coming into place.'[153] Balls was 'enthusiastic' when Barber explained his offer of assessing 'deliverability' during the spending review; he advised that they could 'apply intervention in inverse proportion to success'.[154] Balls said he had been 'impressed that the Delivery Unit had so effectively avoided becoming a lobbyist for departments with the Treasury'.[155] Brown decided that Balls and Barber should work together on the spending review.[156] From his perspective, Balls recognised the strengths that Barber and the PMDU methods provided.

> Michael had done a lot of delivery in education, he was quite technocratic about it all. He didn't really seek to insert himself into the difficult political debates. He was much more about, how do you get this traffic light from red to amber to green? And we all thought it would be good to have traffic lights that weren't red, so get on with it.[157]

This was a notable moment in the relationship between the Treasury and the PMDU and specifically between Brown and Barber. It also marked significant progress since the creation of the PMDU in June 2001. Barber had been open and bold, focused on outcomes and carefully positioned himself so that he was not seen as a threat. The PMDU was beginning to have an influence on the Treasury and this would likely be noticed more widely in Whitehall. Barber himself felt that 'if we can succeed in the next phase of our work, we might just have brought about a significant innovation in the nature of government'.[158] In early December Barber spoke with Macpherson, who informed him of a letter that he was drafting for Brown to be sent to Milburn to discuss the terms under which the extra £1 billion of funding for health would be released. Macpherson agreed to share a copy of the letter once Brown had signed it. He summed up, indicating the notable cooperation between the Treasury and the PMDU, 'Once a sum of money has been agreed our interests and yours are identical … we're allies.'[159]

Remarkably, Brown stated that the Treasury would release funds to the department subject to joint Treasury–PMDU approval. (A copy of the letter, signed by Brown, was included in Barber's diary.)

No other prime ministerial unit worked with the Treasury in this way. Brown said that he would now approve the £120 million coronary heart disease (CHD) choice pilot* as he had been 'assured' by his Treasury officials that 'this scheme is underpinned by robust analysis and delivery plans are … consistent with the NHS Plan'.[160] But 'a more ambitious scheme for greater choice for inpatients in London and the South East' would need more work between officials from both departments and the Delivery Unit, 'to develop options which are deliverable, affordable and consistent with the NHS Plan'.[161] The PMDU was becoming a tool for the Treasury in its decisions to release or withhold funding to a major department. Barber saw this as 'a major breakthrough in the influence of the Delivery Unit'.[162]

In No. 10, it appeared as though Blair's view of media presentation and delivery was developing. In early December, Barber attended a meeting in Blair's office to discuss spending the £1 billion on improving NHS waiting times. Blair urged Milburn and Crisp to make progress with the CHD pilot. Barber noted its importance – 'in a statement which represents the difference between the first and second terms, he [Blair] said: "We don't get credit for announcement anymore; we only get credit for results."'[163] Blair's focus had shifted decisively. In mid-December, however, Barber privately considered Blair's long-term dedication to delivery. He reflected in his diary:

There is an issue … about the extent to which Blair will really stick with the delivery agenda as I see it. I don't mind if it bores

---

* According to the Chancellor's letter, the CHD scheme proposal was as follows: from mid-2002, 'every patient in England who has waited for a heart operation for six months will be able to choose between hospitals which can do the operation more quickly than their local trust'.

him as long as he lets me get on with it and makes clear, wherever necessary, that he supports me getting on with it.[164]

Barber provided Blair with an 'end of term' delivery report and sent copies to Macdonald, Wilson and Heywood. Barber had negotiated the PMDU's traffic light ratings with two Permanent Secretaries, Gieve and Crisp.[165] This showed his responsive approach; based on the reaction to the first delivery report, he had compromised on discussing ratings with Permanent Secretaries before submitting them to the Prime Minister. Gieve and Barber had not known each other prior to the PMDU, yet they swiftly formed a productive working relationship. Gieve was 'open, vigorous, funny and willing to accept an argument that stood up'; he persuaded Barber to change a couple of rankings where Barber thought he had 'the better case'.[166] Indeed in Gieve's view, 'there was an alignment' between his agenda for the Home Office and the PMDU's role but the Unit still represented 'another bit of pressure'.[167] Gieve saw the PMDU as an 'ally for me in setting my department clear measures of success which went beyond the immediate political agenda and getting it to focus on making progress over the medium term'.[168] This correlates with Jonathan Powell's view on why the Delivery Unit worked: 'First, it had the complete authority of the Prime Minister ... Second, Michael made it collaborative rather than a direct challenge to departments. It helped them meet their targets rather than criticising them for failing to do so.'[169] In contrast, the call with Crisp was 'edgy'; he was 'more defensive and altogether unwilling to accept the weaknesses which seemed highly visible' to the Delivery Unit and the Treasury.[170] Barber admitted there was 'much more to do to build this relationship'.[171]

The second delivery report showed marked improvements overall.

In addition to the letter, there was an updated league table and 'commentary explaining briefly and very personally' what Barber thought about each of the priorities.[172] Barber spoke to Balls about the health reforms. He saw that his newfound influence was a 'poisoned chalice' if the Treasury meant to use the PMDU as a means of blocking the extension of the pilot – 'it is easy to see how the Delivery Unit could be shot down in the flames of a cross-fire between No. 10 and No. 11'.[173] There was a balance which Barber had to find between engaging a pivotal stakeholder – the Treasury – and avoiding becoming used as a device against No. 10. Similarly, Balls has indicated that progress, though tangible, was still subject to friction: 'There's no doubt in the first year of the Delivery Unit there would have been tension and scepticism from both sides about the other's processes, even though it was cooperative.'[174]

Barber called the four delivery ministers to brief them on the contents of the delivery report. Estelle Morris 'was relaxed'; Barber attributed this partly to the fact that she knew Barber 'so well' and partly because education had made progress. Morris also 'knew she had more of a grip on delivery than back in October'.[175] She asked Barber if he 'thought her giving her personal attention to delivery made a difference. "Of course it does,"' Barber replied.[176] In their call, Barber told David Blunkett that the Home Office-related priorities were the 'fastest improving part of my brief'.[177] Blunkett noted that Gieve was 'trying very hard' and encouraged Barber 'to keep the pressure on'.[178] Barber's call with Stephen Byers was 'cool but not unfriendly'.[179] Byers asked Barber about the red traffic light classification attributed by the PMDU to one of the transport targets. Barber said 'there was so much risk involved … that predicting successful delivery was not possible'.[180] He explained why and Byers said, 'I'm sure your judgments are right, as ever, Michael.'[181] The call with Alan Milburn went 'okay'; health was the area with the most focus and 'worries' and of the four delivery ministers Barber knew Milburn the least well.[182] Milburn thought Barber might be being 'a bit harsh' with his judgements on the likelihood of meeting the waiting times target.[183]

This overall approach had numerous benefits for Barber: it put the PMDU 'firmly on their [the Secretaries of State's] map', it reinforced 'the sense of openness – no surprises' from the Delivery Unit, and it enabled Barber to speak to Permanent Secretaries and other officials with the knowledge that he had 'the backing of the key politicians'.[184] After this, the PMDU produced delivery reports twice a year, in July and December.[185]

In his final diary entry of 2001, Barber evaluated the highs and lows of the year. The highlights included 'creating the Delivery Unit concept and then being asked to set it up' by Blair; 'realising in the last six weeks that the Delivery Unit has really made a difference'; and 'the Chequers away days, the first league table, the meeting with Gordon Brown'.[186] The low points of the year were the 'rows with the Treasury at the beginning' and 'coming to terms with letting go of education policy'.[187]

JANUARY 2002

BEGINNING TO EMBED THE MECHANICS OF DELIVERY

As the New Year began, Barber took the opportunity to refine the stocktake meetings. The main change was that each stocktake would now begin with a five-minute presentation from Barber himself, first implemented in the crime and asylum stocktake in mid-January.[188] For this first one Barber 'spent a great deal of time honing and refining'.[189] In Barber's view, if he could get these right he could have 'a huge impact on each policy area and perhaps more importantly, on how the Prime Minister and his senior ministers think about delivery'.[190] For the crime and asylum stocktake Barber used graphs to show two 'worrying trends' – the 'rapid rise in street robbery and the equally rapid fall in the number of cases being brought to justice'.[191] Blair subsequently gave Blunkett and Gieve a 'hard time' on this and it was agreed that the PMDU and the Home Office would conduct a 'joint investigation'.[192] The street crime issue, like asylum reform and reducing waiting times, showed clearly that the PMDU had a role in helping to formulate policy solutions. Barber himself explained the importance of this to his vision for the Delivery Unit: 'This is exactly what I always wanted the Delivery Unit to do: identifying a problem, putting it firmly on the agenda and then making sure something happens to solve it.'[193]

Problems emerged with the planning for the Department of Health's London patient choice pilot (for treating CHD), which the PMDU had been charged with assessing. The pilot was designed to improve choices for patients who were clinically eligible for treatment but had been waiting for six months at an NHS hospital in London. The new plan would give these patients a choice of alternative providers who could offer earlier treatment. PMDU staff member Adrian Masters reported back to Barber that 'there was no project plan, no detail on the likely numbers involved, the costs, the capacity or the staffing'; for Barber this was 'deeply depressing' as the pilot was due to go live in October 2002.[194] Barber got in touch with the PMDU's assigned 'key contact' in the Department of Health, senior civil servant Hugh Taylor, and said he was 'willing to fight hard for the pilot with the Treasury but it was up to them' to give him the 'ammunition'.[195] This careful, mutually beneficial positioning was becoming a hallmark of Barber's approach – the emerging art of delivery. In mid-January, Barber had dinner with Andrew Adonis and Jeremy Heywood. Heywood remarked to Barber, 'You've massively increased the power of the Prime Minister without damaging any relationships.'[196] This was a major statement from the person who, along with Ed Balls, was charged with negotiating much of the business of government between Blair and Brown. By the end of the month, Barber was surprised and pleased to see that planning for the London patient choice pilot had gone from 'nowhere to almost credible in three weeks'.[197]

On 22 January, a stocktake took place in which Barber was seen by a Cabinet minister as a potential threat to their relationship with the Prime Minister. At the education stocktake Barber gave an introductory five-minute presentation, despite the fact that the Secretary of State, Estelle Morris, had 'doubts' about the necessity of such a presentation as 'she thought it was an intrusion on her time with Blair'.[198] To allay these fears, Barber had told David Normington that he would stick to his assigned time, but by proceeding he was asserting his position. Barber thought the stocktake was 'flat' and regretted that some of the points he had made for 'some new policy work on behaviour management were not picked up'.[199] Evidently the progress and influence of the Delivery Unit was not linear.

FEBRUARY TO APRIL 2002

ADDRESSING GAPS IN CAPABILITY

In early February, in No. 10, there was a meeting of the civil servants responsible for the seventeen delivery priorities. Barber discussed the 'difficult' challenges but also their 'collective capacity to deliver'.[200] Blair spoke frankly to the civil servants responsible for delivering his government's domestic agenda for the second term: 'You've probably got used to the idea that your career depends on me … I'm just coming to terms with the idea that my career depends on you.'[201] This was a revealing comment from Blair, for it showed an acceptance that his success depended on the Civil Service and in order to elevate the conditions for success, he sought to embolden them. It was also a marked departure from his comment three years earlier when he complained about the 'scars on my back' from trying to get change in the public sector.[202]

Barber had a meeting with the Cabinet Secretary, Richard Wilson, in which part of the agenda was to discuss future Cabinet Secretary candidates.[203] Wilson wanted to know if Barber could suggest any candidates 'inside or outside Whitehall', adding, 'You might be interested yourself.'[204] It remained to seen whether this notable comment was serious. At this stage, Barber 'made no reference to any personal interest in the post'.[205] Wilson went on to explain 'that many of the duties of the post including those relating to honours and security were to be delegated out so that his successor could concentrate on the crucial issues of "delivery and public service reform"'.[206] Barber told Wilson of an anxiety he had:

> To his credit he [Wilson] had let me get on with the job, watched and offered occasional advice. I have really appreciated the space this has given me. Since Blair is really only interested in the outcomes not the process and Jeremy and Jonathan trust me, I've been given space by them too. But if Wilson's successor has delivery as perhaps his/her main responsibility then it's unlikely I'll continue to have the same room for manoeuvre.[207]

Wilson recognised this potential conflict 'immediately' and said that he would raise it with Blair.[208] They discussed potential candidates, Barber suggested Michael Bichard, who he said had been 'a rock' when they worked together on education reform.[209] They also considered David Normington, and Barber said, 'If he got the job I'd be interested in following him [as Permanent Secretary] at the DfES'; Wilson 'didn't react'.[210] Barber's continued passion for education reform had been confirmed. After the meeting, Barber reflected that perhaps he should have given more consideration to Wilson's point about putting himself forward for the post of Cabinet Secretary: 'If the job is refocused as is suggested, then I surely have a case to make. Also, I believe I could do the job.'[211] As a result, he arranged to have a meeting with Wilson the following week to 'tell him that I was indeed interested in being considered'.[212] This was of importance (and to date, not recorded in published literature): the head of a new prime ministerial unit, now technically a civil servant, but who had recently been a politically appointed special adviser, sought to put himself forward for the most senior position in the UK Civil Service, which had always been held by a career civil servant.

In the meantime, a PMDU seminar for eighty Treasury officials on how the Unit 'measured deliverability and thought about targets and trajectories' took place in early February.[213] Barber recorded that the attendees responded positively.[214] Sharing best practice was important for building the Delivery Unit's reputation in Whitehall and in starting to reposition the culture within the Civil Service towards delivery. As planned, a week after their last meeting Barber met Wilson to ask to be considered as a possible successor but 'the conversation did not go as planned'.[215] Wilson did not recall mentioning to Barber that he could consider applying for the role of Cabinet Secretary. Nevertheless, Barber said, 'If the post is to be refocused on delivery and public service reform, I would like to be considered.'[216] In response, Wilson stressed the Cabinet Secretary's responsibility to Permanent Secretaries 'when they needed confidential advice' and in part, he believed fulfilling this function depended on 'age and experience'.[217] Barber felt that Wilson thought he was 'too young' (Barber was forty-six, Wilson was fifty-nine) but remained outwardly unflustered and gave a 'brief rundown' of his career.[218] Wilson began to consider the idea aloud – 'the job was about delivery' and 'no one knows more about delivery than you do … and you have extraordinary diplomatic skills', and so Wilson agreed to take Barber's interest 'seriously'.[219]

A series of stocktakes took place, the first on transport. Barber had missed the previous one which meant it had been six months since he last attended. His five-minute presentation focused on railway performance in London. Stephen Byers said they would take forward the improvement programme Barber set out.[220] Barber noted that Byers was relaxed and 'supported' by minister of state John Spellar; there was 'no sign of the furore about Martin Sixsmith and Jo Moore' scandals* which dominated headlines later that week.[221] Then Blair asked 'suddenly and precisely when they would do something about the small number of places that caused a large proportion of delay'.[222] Byers said, 'Right away,' and offered to

---

* After various leaks and briefings from individuals within the DTLR and No. 10, there was an announcement made that Sixsmith and Moore had both resigned their positions. But Sixsmith (head of communications, DTLR) stated that he had not resigned and it appeared that he was being forced out. In May, the DTLR eventually admitted 'incorrect understandings' of a discussion between senior officials and Sixsmith; he subsequently received a sizeable financial settlement. Leader, 'Sixsmith to quit government post', *Daily Telegraph*, 7 May 2002, http://www.telegraph.co.uk/news/1393421/Sixsmith-to-quit-Government-post.html accessed 26 February 2017.

provide a timetable.[223] Eoin Daly from the Delivery Unit informed Barber that Byers had 'put pressure on DTLR officials to respond on this agenda'.[224] Ahead of the Home Office stocktake Barber bumped into Blair, who having already read the PMDU stocktake briefing said, 'I'm worried about crime.'[225] During the meeting itself Kevin Bond, head of the new Police Standards Unit (in the Home Office), outlined his plan for addressing the sharp rise in street robbery; Blair supported the plan.[226] John Gieve explained that there was value in 'having the Prime Minister and his Unit looking systematically at trends and results of our work'; indeed, he saw it as 'absolutely vital'.[227]

Barber conveyed how the PMDU worked to a meeting of special advisers from across Whitehall. Blair's political secretary, Robert Hill, had invited special advisers with whom the PMDU worked to comment on whether the Unit was 'a pain in the neck or helpful'.[228] Paul Corrigan from the Department of Health said it was 'helpful' and Will Cavendish from the DfES agreed but said a lot of this was down to the way that Barber led it: 'In the wrong hands, it would be a disaster.'[229] Barber told the group that 'the key is to do the simple stuff thoroughly and consistently'.[230] Special advisers were important to Barber in the same way that they were of growing importance to government as a whole. They lubricated the joints between the elected politicians with a mandate but who were temporary and the permanent, politically impartial officials.

In late February, Barber provided Blair with a delivery update on robbery, which showed Blair the 'startling statistics on the increase in numbers of 11–15-year-olds involved in street robbery (500 per cent in eight years!)'. Barber 'promised him a detailed report in two weeks'.[231] Blair later replied stating that he wanted 'something done now'.[232] Barber's reputation was growing in the media. An article in

The Guardian claimed that Barber was one of a 'new breed' of advisers in Whitehall and that he had 'won widespread praise for his skilful leadership' of the Delivery Unit.[233] It did, however, include some conceivable areas of tension.

> Traditionalists are uneasy, believing that Professor Barber is usurping the roles played by individual secretaries of state. One old Whitehall hand complained: 'It is wrong to work around secretaries of state. If Downing Street is unhappy, it should follow the example of Margaret Thatcher and put the fear of god into secretaries of state, rather than set up new structures.'[234]

At the beginning of March, Barber observed that 'the politics of the 2002 Spending Review' were becoming the 'dominant issue in Whitehall'.[235] He considered areas on which the Blair premiership, thus far, could be criticised:

- A belief, in Blair's head, that things are just simple ('Why don't you just do it?' being the classic question that represents this).
- A failure to reform the Civil Service sufficiently fast or far enough.
- The failure to build early enough a core team of politicians capable of driving collectively the domestic reform agenda.
- Too much fear of how things will look and reacting to press comment.
- An odd combination of a No. 10 that looks too powerful but is in fact too weak. Too often, contrary to Teddy Roosevelt's advice it speaks loudly and carries a small stick.[236]
- Blair's niceness, which creates a good atmosphere among his staff and a remarkable degree of harmony among Cabinet members,

is also a weakness sometimes. Perhaps he doesn't induce enough fear.

- The extent to which on critical issues he allows Gordon to control events (e.g. the Euro; public expenditure).[237]

This assessment of the Blair premiership adds nuance to the often simplistic debates on Blair's style of governing. Barber received feedback on his own working style and that of the PMDU from the Civil Service Management Board (which was composed of the Cabinet Secretary, Permanent Secretaries and other senior civil servants). David Normington said that it was 'irritating' sometimes but mainly when 'Michael gets ahead of us, when in fact we like to be ahead of him'.[238] The work of the PMDU and Barber's approach was evidently subject to some scrutiny and there were opportunities for senior civil servants to give feedback.

On 5 March, Barber and Wilson met again to discuss Barber's request to be considered as a candidate for the role of Cabinet Secretary. Wilson said, 'You asked to be considered as a possible successor … I've spoken to some permanent secretaries and your name is not running strongly … I've spoken to the PM too.'[239] Barber said to Wilson that he 'understood'.[240] He later wrote to Wilson, 'You've got an amazing opportunity to appoint someone who can really drive reform in the next 18 months. After that, prospects are much more murky.'[241] Wilson replied thanking him for the 'marvellous minute'.[242] Evidently Barber saw the reshaped role of Cabinet Secretary as an axis for change focused on delivery.

HOW TO TURN PRIME MINISTERIAL ANXIETY INTO A FORCE FOR CHANGE

Blair was agitating for urgent action on street crime and on 11

March, Barber attended a meeting which Blair had scheduled with his core team. The Prime Minister 'quizzed' him on plans for tackling street robbery and said, 'I've been going on about this for three years.'[243] Barber informed him that the preparations made with the Home Office would be ready to launch in 'late April and early May' but Blair 'wasn't happy' with that or with the progress on asylum.[244] On asylum, Barber explained that 'the system was becoming more efficient [but] we seemed powerless to stop the flow of asylum seekers into the country'.[245] He noticed that Blair was 'restless and uncomfortable about the state of politics and delivery'.[246]

The PMDU and the Home Office completed a joint 'priority review' into robbery and street crime.[247] The priority review was an innovation whereby the PMDU and the relevant department conducted a 'rapid analysis of the state of delivery of a high priority strategy and identification of the action needed to strengthen delivery'; the review would result in a report for the Prime Minister, ministers and Permanent Secretary.[248] The reviews, which usually took six weeks to complete, were designed to generate 'pace and urgency'; the PMDU would 'stress-test departmental strategies' as well as conduct 'field visits and interviews' with stakeholders and frontline staff.[249] PMDU staff member Richard Page-Jones and Barber designed the process. From Barber's perspective the priority reviews became an 'immensely powerful tool in the delivery toolkit', although when they first tested the concept on street crime they had 'yet to learn' this.[250] Blunkett endorsed the joint PMDU–Home Office robbery priority review.[251]

Blair arranged a meeting with Blunkett and Barber to follow up his concerns about street crime. Blair stated that the street robbery priority review recommendations were focused on the medium to long term, whereas he wanted 'something much more vigorous' in the short term.[252] He questioned why when a crisis happened like foot-and-mouth or the fuel blockade they were able to 'get it done'.[253] He suggested, 'Perhaps we should call COBR and deal with robbery through that mechanism?'[254] Blunkett responded positively with one caveat, and it was agreed that as Home Secretary he wanted to be seen as 'leading this'.[255] Blair's decision to use COBR to tackle a domestic policy priority was significant. Previously COBR had been used for domestic crises, therefore this indicated the importance of the issue to an increasingly proactive Prime Minister. What role would Barber and the Delivery Unit play, if any? Later that evening Barber received a call from a worried John Gieve, who thought that this was 'getting out of hand'.[256] Barber sought to reassure him and framed it diplomatically: 'We have to see this as an epidemic ... It's a real opportunity for you. We can get Whitehall lined up behind you.'[257]

The PMDU was starting to give support on cross-departmental issues for the mutual benefit of the Prime Minister and Cabinet ministers. Ahead of an education stocktake, Barber and Blunkett assisted Estelle Morris in preparing for a cross-departmental focus on street robbery and schools. Around the same time, Alastair Campbell noted in his diary that Blair 'said all that mattered was that we delivered, he was frustrated at the lack of delivery, at departmental slowness and the poor quality of cross-cutting work'.[258] In the meeting, Barber's graph showed the sharp rise in 11–15-year-olds' involvement in street robbery, which 'drew a genuine intake of breath'.[259] Barber recognised an emerging specialism: 'If the Delivery Unit has a unique selling point other than its focus on delivery, it's our growing capacity to present data with clarity, power and simplicity.'[260]

A health stocktake took place on 19 March; there had been

marked progress. The waiting times and bed-blocking data had 'improved dramatically in the last two months', beyond Barber's expectations.[261] He noted 'a new sense of confidence' in the Department of Health from Milburn and Crisp.[262] Barber was pleased for them and for his Unit – 'the stress and the sensitivity of the autumn is behind us', the PMDU's 'persistence and focus' and emphasis on strategy had 'borne fruit'.[263] Milburn, however, said that the recent progress had been achieved by 'deeply micromanaging' the NHS and that they now needed to 'move on'.[264] This was a significant criticism that both the department and the PMDU would need to continually examine and work to alleviate.

The crucial crime summit took place in the COBR rooms in the Cabinet Office on 20 March.[265] Members of the Delivery Unit were in attendance to hear a presentation by the Home Office. Other prominent attendees included Blair, Barber, Morris, Tessa Jowell (Secretary of State for Culture, Media and Sport), Derry Irvine, Alistair Darling, Andrew Smith, Metropolitan Police commissioner Sir John Stevens, and Sir David Phillips, head of the Association of Chief Police Officers.[266] Despite Barber's earlier criticisms of Blair's tendency to offer simplistic solutions, when the Prime Minister decided to put his personal attention on an issue he could focus on the detail, chair the debate effectively and demand action. Blair 'dominated' the meeting and showed 'a good combination of real passion and determination on the one hand and perception and attention to detail on the other'.[267] The Prime Minister insisted on going through the whole process start to finish, from catching offenders to prosecution.[268] Barber contemplated this episode in his diary: 'There are times when you think he's too shallow or too indecisive and then you see him dominate a meeting like this and you see the leadership quality that makes a potentially great

Prime Minister.'[269] This statement shows the complexity one must be aware of when considering Blair's prime ministerial style. Afterwards, Barber attended a meeting as Blair's representative, to operationalise decisions made at the crime summit.

Barber began a new week with a single challenge – 'to turn prime ministerial anxiety into a force for change'.[270] He had pushed for a check-in meeting with Blair first thing on 25 March. Heywood joined the meeting, in which Barber outlined the PMDU's impact so far: 'It's improved planning; clarified priorities, provided sharp feedback, tracked the data … and departments want more … it's making a difference.'[271] Blair said his worry was that recent progress on bed-blocking and waiting times had been done by 'flogging the system harder'.[272] Barber acknowledged that that was true but explained that the PMDU was developing 'sustainable approaches to delivery' with departments.[273] Barber asked Blair if he was happy with the stocktake process, which included the Delivery Unit briefing, the presentation by Barber and the agenda. Blair replied, 'I think I am actually.'[274] They then broached the topic of Blair's anxiety about delivery and prioritisation, which was apparent at an earlier awayday. Barber explained the PMDU's 'four levels of intensity' for dealing with delivery issues:

1. 'Our standard approach'
2. 'Our problem-solving approach'
3. 'Intensive' – 'more powerful than problem-solving but not as demanding' on the Prime Minister's time as the COBR street crime approach
4. 'The emergency approach' – COBR-style for street crime.[275]

Blair said he understood and they agreed that the only other policy they should 'consider' for level four intervention was asylum.[276] Barber was pleased to have 'rationalised the anxiety' and created a framework to use; he felt he had further established the position of the Delivery Unit.[277]

Gieve chaired a second meeting to implement the crime summit decisions which Barber attended to advocate the Prime Minister's view, that there must be 'urgency and rigour'.[278] The following day, Blair chaired a second COBR meeting. Eoin Daly from the Delivery Unit had worked out a plan which Blair used as a checklist; for Barber this was 'another impact' for the Unit.[279] There appeared to be progress and momentum was building.[280] Barber and Daly were closely monitoring the Home Office capacity to respond to the street crime initiative. Daly spotted gaps in planning. Barber got in touch with Gieve, who called a meeting with his officials and Daly; they agreed on a course of action 'mapped out' by the PMDU.[281] Barber believed that this was the kind of situation the PMDU had been 'invented for'.[282]

In late March a problem arose ahead of the next transport stocktake. DTLR officials informed the PMDU that they were 'too busy' to produce a paper for the stocktake due in two weeks and said that there 'was not much they could do' about short- to medium-term train time reliability.[283] As a result Barber rang Byers's special adviser Dan Corry and Permanent Secretary Richard Mottram. He told them both in 'different ways that this was unacceptable, they risked [sending the Secretary of State] naked into the stocktake chamber' on an issue that the Prime Minister was 'deeply exercised about – rail delay'.[284] The result: 'Whitehall began to jump.'[285] This validated Barber's astute approach to dealing with resistance from departments. He reflected, 'it's important that the Delivery Unit gets taken seriously.'[286]

Simon Stevens chaired a meeting in No. 10 on the choice agenda with Barber, Balls, Ed Miliband (Brown's special adviser) and health officials. Ahead of the meeting, Adrian Masters from the Delivery Unit worked with the Department of Health to prepare for questioning from Balls and others. Barber claimed that Balls's opposition to choice dissolved 'once it became clear that the key issues were building up capacity, creating the right incentives and managing choice'.[287] At one point, Balls 'embarked on a line of questioning which was designed to demonstrate that you could get the benefits of choice in terms of matching demand to supply without the offer of choice'.[288] But Barber pointed out that it 'must have dawned on him [Balls] ... that if you didn't offer choice you'd have to direct patients to other parts of the country which was obviously impossible in the 21st century. So, he reached for a term that wasn't "choice" – opt.'[289] There would be many more battles on the emerging choice agenda.

The third street crime meeting for officials took place on 3 April. Ten police forces from within England and Wales had been selected to be part of the street crime initiative. There appeared to be some early signs of progress. For the second successive week, the Metropolitan Police figures suggested 'a real fall in street crime compared to a year earlier', which was seen as 'very good news'.[290] In performing his 'commissar role', Barber challenged the police representatives on how they would 'disseminate best practice' to the other nine police forces.[291]

A STEP CHANGE IN DELIVERY UNIT–TREASURY RELATIONS

The PMDU's relationship with the Treasury was of fundamental importance to the success of Barber and his Unit. Barber reflected,

'As a result of the burgeoning strength of my relationship with Ed Balls, my relationship with the Treasury is stronger than ever. The potential for the Delivery Unit, if I can maintain the excellent relations with both the Policy Directorate and the Treasury, is high.'[292] A turning point in Barber's relationship with the Treasury took place in spring 2002. Barber met with Balls, Ed Miliband and Nicholas Macpherson to discuss progress on health and the major area of debate, which had dominated since the pre-Budget announcement, of how best to spend extra funding to reduce hospital waiting times. Barber 'felt no hostile edge' that he might have felt six months before.[293] They discussed choice and the London patient choice pilot and agreed next steps for the pilot. Balls and Barber would meet with the Chief Secretary to the Treasury and suggest that he should write to Alan Milburn 'expressing his support' for the pilot.[294] Barber gave a round-up of progress across the Delivery Unit's priorities. On health, he stated that Nigel Crisp had 'sorted out the strategic management weaknesses' that they had identified in early 2002.[295] On the Home Office, Barber felt it was 'too early to reach judgment' on the impact of new policies and new management.[296] Balls said this was why he was 'so hostile to funding' the Blunkett street crime initiative – 'he saw it as a Home Office idea to get more clout in the Spending Review'.[297] Barber said he 'didn't think that was fair' as the street crime initiative was 'a Blair initiative prompted by the Delivery Unit pointing out the dreadful trends in the data'.[298] On education, Barber reported progress but also 'a lack of edge'.[299] On transport, he defended Stephen Byers's record but agreed with the group that the DTLR seemed 'hopeless'.[300]

As agreed, on 10 April, Barber and Balls met with Andrew Smith to advance the London patient choice pilot. Smith questioned Barber, and Balls explained 'with fluency and urgency' that the work on the pilot was a 'really good example of collaboration between' the Delivery Unit and the Treasury.[301] Balls said he thought the PMDU was a 'major benefit and said he wished "we'd had a Delivery Unit at the time of the 2000 Spending Review"'.[302] This was a significant acknowledgement of the PMDU's value to the Treasury. Smith agreed to approve the pilot and to share a draft letter stating this with Barber. Barber was 'euphoric'.[303]

> Several months of hard work and thought had gone into this and the result was a stronger more organic relationship with the Treasury and increasingly effective relationship with Health – a real appreciation in both of the Delivery Unit's value and crucially of course, a pilot that is much more likely to work as a result of our efforts.[304]

Barber's distinction between the formal protocol negotiated the previous summer, which set out the working relationship between the PMDU and the Treasury, and the 'organic' PMDU–Treasury working relationship is important. Balls said that after the written protocol was agreed, 'the establishing of the relationship … took quite a few months … I think the Treasury would have been cautious about the Delivery Unit for a year, even after we'd drawn up the agreement.'[305] Barber was making progress in embedding the Delivery Unit, while navigating the major rock around which the business of government had to be conducted – the rivalry between Blair and Brown. Furthermore, this showed the way in which Barber carefully balanced stakeholders – No. 10, the Department of Health and the Treasury.

Blair chaired another COBR meeting in early April and was on 'good decisive form'.[306] Barber had briefed him on the issues he thought needed to be concentrated on: police outside London, schools and exclusions, bail and the courts.[307] The Prime Minister pursued these and in doing so he illustrated the Delivery Unit's role in advising him during the COBR process. On the same day as the COBR meeting, Barber attended the PSX Cabinet committee meeting on health. The main debate was about choice; Brown was worried 'about creating a legally enforceable entitlement'.[308] Barber felt Milburn and Crisp had been 'effective'.[309]

During this period the Treasury was preparing the forthcoming Budget. As Budget Day approached, Alastair Campbell complained that Brown was not sharing enough information on the Budget with Blair.[310] At a Cabinet meeting, Blair explained the context of the Budget – enterprise, 'big battle on investment and tax, the need to get up delivery and reform'.[311] He 'slipped a note to GB saying he should say something, he said nothing'.[312] It took until two days before the Budget for Blair and Brown to be in 'constant dialogue' on the details.[313]

In the run-up to the annual Budget speech, Barber experienced first-hand the tempo of last-minute negotiations between No. 10 and the Treasury. On the Sunday prior to the Budget, Barber received a call from Jeremy Heywood. The draft delivery contract for health had been settled on Friday 'but the Treasury were now pursuing the detail' in areas which Barber thought were going to be decided after the Budget.[314] Barber had a series of calls with Heywood, Simon Stevens and the No. 10 duty clerk to settle various aspects including on 'how choice is represented in the contract'.[315] Later that evening Barber took part in a conference call with Blair, Heywood and Stevens. Blair 'generally approved' of where they had got to and was 'most concerned with the reform message that would accompany the Budget and especially with promoting the Choice Agenda'.[316] Heywood said that the Treasury was 'ideologically opposed' to the choice agenda; Blair asked to see the delivery contract the following morning.[317] Heywood sent the updated delivery contract for health to Barber on Sunday night and informed him that Brown and Blair had had 'a long very difficult phone call, arguing mainly about health inequalities' and then left Balls and Heywood 'to sort out the issues'.[318] This insight into the way in which the human machinery of government worked in practice is revealing. The anecdote also shows the role that Barber played – one of the three key No. 10 advisers to the Prime Minister on health policy negotiations with the Treasury.

In mid-April, Barber met with Blair, Stevens and Heywood in Blair's Downing Street flat to discuss the health reform package, due to be announced the day after the Budget.[319] Stevens said he thought that he and Barber had 'slightly different views' on rolling out the choice agenda.[320] Barber acknowledged 'that was true' but they 'were agreed about the goal'.[321] He was keen to see 'choice introduced carefully and all the processes tested', as with the London patient choice pilot, whereas Stevens wanted to introduce 'choice fully in 2003–04 rather than in a phased way'.[322] Barber felt Blair 'sympathised' with Stevens, and Blair unsurprisingly pushed for urgency, to really 'emphasise choice publicly'.[323] Barber was focused on operationalising 'choice' based on an iterative approach while the Prime Minister saw the necessity of getting an understanding (and thus public expectation) of 'choice' into the public domain, in order to push for a more ambitious choice agenda with the Treasury.

A Home Office stocktake took place on crime and asylum. The discussion centred on the early progress of the 'Safer Streets' initiative but both Barber and Blair emphasised the need for the other nine police forces outside London to aim for a 'similar impact in eight weeks'.[324] Barber said that this 'made a strong impression on Gieve and the following day, he and I really did push the police at the Street Crime round-up'.[325] On asylum there had been 'progress on processing applications; no real progress on removals and the rapid rise in the number of applications since Christmas'.[326] Barber thought Blair was on 'good form – clear where he knew what he wanted and stating his instinct but urging David [Blunkett] to decide, taking account of discussion'.[327] Blair was being collegiate, while Barber and Gieve were working collaboratively to accelerate the government's agenda on street crime.

By the end of April 2002, across the country 2,000 police officers had been refocused onto street crime.[328] By August 2002, there was a fall in street crime of 14 per cent across the ten targeted police forces, though the initiative continued.[329] Blunkett viewed the street crime initiative as one of the PMDU's biggest successes in his policy area – 'I think that was a great success and it was helped not just by Michael's Delivery Unit with us but Michael's ability to persuade Tony.'[330] He clearly saw the value in the PMDU's technical approach and in Barber's art of delivery. When interviewed, Gieve provided his evaluation of the initiative in retrospect.

The street crime initiative went quite well … Some felt it was disproportionate because it was a relatively small issue but it seeded an approach, a results-based approach that had a big impact on the Home Office and on the police. I felt that by the time I left the Home Office, if you asked a chief constable or chief inspector what their local crime figures were, and how they were using the data to direct their resources, they knew. That wasn't normal before.[331]

In mid-April, a meeting took place which marked a further strengthening of PMDU–Treasury relations. As part of Budget preparations, Barber attended a high-level meeting in Balls's office with Heywood and Adonis where they met with Balls, Macpherson and Adam Sharples to discuss 'Delivery Contracts/PSAs, the redefined role of the Delivery Unit and the timing of the next Delivery Report'.[332] They all agreed that the delivery contracts and PSAs 'needed merging' and 'discussed how they should be monitored; some targets would get Delivery Unit treatment; and others PSA plus and others still the routine Treasury treatment'.[333] This was a critical moment: the Treasury and No. 10 accepted the need for Blair's delivery contracts and Brown's PSAs to be reconciled. Barber said the No. 10 representatives pushed for fewer targets while Balls argued for 'continuity'.[334] This, however, was not the only mark of rapprochement.

The group 'discussed redrafting and recirculating' the four-page protocol which 'had caused so much stress' after the 2001 election.[335] By the following day they had 'agreed a shortened version and a revised longer version' of the protocol.[336] They also agreed that Barber would present a report on delivery to PSX. This was a remarkable meeting of both symbolic and material importance. A group of the most senior people in No. 10 and the Treasury had in one meeting: agreed to merge the PSAs and delivery contracts – which thus far had ostensibly been two rival methods for setting and tracking targets as well as holding departments to account; renegotiated the formal protocol on which the PMDU–Treasury relationship was based; and agreed that Barber would present at the powerful PSX Cabinet committee, which the Chancellor chaired.[337] It showed the fundamental importance of building relationships and the value of the PMDU approach.

THE 2002 BUDGET

The 2002 Budget represented the peak of annual increases for public services during Blair's premiership and indeed for the preceding two decades.[338] The Chancellor gave his Budget Statement in the House of Commons on 17 April. Barber commented on Brown's performance:

> One word sprang to mind … awesome. The pace and clarity of his argument, the direct relationship of philosophy, idea and action which is only possible on this scale in a Budget, the sensational economic performance of this country compared to others and above all the sheer scale of the funding now to be injected into the Health Service over the next five years.[339]

The 2002 Budget was arguably the most significant of Blair's premiership. Brown set the tone in his speech: 'Money must be matched with modernisation leading to results.'[340] The headline announcements were: 1p in the pound increase in National Insurance contributions; a 43 per cent rise in the NHS budget in real terms over the next five years, the equivalent of £40 billion; and the introduction of two new tax credits in 2003 – the child tax credit and the working tax credit.[341]

The decision to countenance raising National Insurance contributions by 1p to ensure the NHS was 'properly funded' had not been taken lightly.[342] According to Balls, Blair was 'incredibly anxious about it' and 'scarred by the impact that the threat of an NI increase had had when Neil Kinnock announced it before the 1992 election' (which the Conservatives won).[343] Balls explained the heightened pressure of delivering on the government's promises.

We had won the 2001 election on 'A lot done, a lot more to do' with a sense that we weren't delivering enough yet. Then we raised taxes for the Health Service; in that context whether or not we actually delivered these outputs was a really big deal and a particularly big deal for Tony and Gordon's credibility.[344]

Brown cited an announcement that Alan Milburn would make the following day which included a mention of the choice agenda:

And, in furtherance of the NHS Plan, the Secretary of State for Health will tomorrow announce for England: new financial incentives for hospital performance; greater freedoms for high performing hospitals and trusts; powers and resources devolved to front-line staff in primary care trusts; reform of social services care for the elderly; and a series of measures increasing choice for patients.[345]

Both Brown and Milburn's announcements echoed the final report of the independent Wanless review, which was released that week: 'The Review has concluded that the UK must expect to devote a significantly larger share of its national income to health care over the next 20 years ... The scope for greater future cooperation between the NHS and the private sector in the delivery of services should be explored.'[346]

On the evening of the Budget announcement, Barber watched the BBC *Six O'Clock News* in Blair's outer office with Jonathan Powell, Sally Morgan, Heywood and Stevens. They discussed the huge funding for the NHS, and Heywood said this was 'the last throw of the dice'. Barber agreed.[347] As the news report came to an end, Morgan and the others turned to Barber and said, 'Gordon's provided the money; now Michael's got to go and deliver.'[348] Barber wrote in his diary, 'We will.'[349]

CONCLUSION

The period from 9/11 to the 2002 Budget was a critical phase for Barber and the PMDU. As the head of a unit still in its infancy, Barber adroitly navigated the highly strung political climate which was taxing on the Prime Minister's attention and time – but this was not achieved without anxiety.

The Unit quickly set about driving delivery and introduced numerous processes: delivery plans, stocktakes, planning presentations, delivery reports, league tables, priority reviews, delivery updates, delivery seminars. These processes included preparing progress reports, presentations and regular data-tracking and the 'four levels of intensity' framework for dealing with delivery issues. The Delivery Unit pursued compliance and sought to resolve any subsequent tensions. Departments responded to the PMDU's instruction to deliver. Capacity to deliver may have varied but the response of departments – from both ministers and Permanent Secretaries, who could have chosen to resist – was generally to try to work with the Unit. The PMDU learnt as it went, there were occasional oversights. The fulcrum of the Delivery Unit was Barber's investment in building resilient working relationships – a key facet of the emerging art of delivery because this built up a store of soft power.

The Delivery Unit was able to gain an understanding of the capacity to deliver in each department, identify gaps in capability and assist ministers and Permanent Secretaries in addressing these. Simultaneously Barber was embedding the Unit in the established processes of power – No. 10 inner circle meetings and PSX Cabinet committee meetings. He expanded the PMDU's remit to advise on forthcoming policy challenges and supported the use of domestic crisis machinery (COBR); in doing so Barber was beginning to make the PMDU a valuable tool not only for the Prime Minister but for delivery departments and the Treasury.

During this period Barber made marked progress in strengthening the Delivery Unit's relationship with the Treasury, by building trust with Brown, Balls and Macpherson and offering PMDU expertise to assist the Treasury in the forthcoming spending review. The result was not only the fulfilment of the initial Delivery Unit–Treasury protocol, which formally set relations, but also a degree of trust and mutual respect which could foster deeper collaboration. In managing these stakeholder relationships Barber had to maintain balance and be aware of being used in a way that could cause damage.

CHAPTER FIVE

APRIL 2002 TO THE 2003 BUDGET: WHEN THE FOREIGN BECOMES DOMESTIC – ADAPTING THE ART OF DELIVERY

The 2002 Budget had shown New Labour's commitment to investing in public service reform; indeed, Ed Balls saw it as the 'high point' of the New Labour governments as a whole.[1] The July 2002 spending review would align the broad spending increases to departmental budgets and a set of updated public service agreements (PSAs). After building a good foundation with the Treasury, what role would the PMDU have in the spending review? During this period there were several changes at Cabinet and Permanent Secretary level; some were planned, others were not. Given that relationships were proving to be the hidden wiring of deliverology, how would this affect the PMDU? How would the choice agenda manifest itself in terms of policy and would the PMDU contribute to its development? And how would the growing prime ministerial focus on the invasion of Iraq impact the PMDU's ability to do its job?

APRIL TO SEPTEMBER 2002

A DANGER OF DUPLICATION AND FRICTION
On the day after the 2002 Budget, Barber was told by Blair's chief

of staff, Jonathan Powell, that the successor to Sir Richard Wilson as Cabinet Secretary would be Sir Andrew Turnbull, who had been Permanent Secretary to the Treasury since 1998.[2] Turnbull formally took over from Wilson in September 2002. During his tenure, Wilson had played a role in enabling the PMDU to succeed; however, a new Cabinet Secretary with a focus on delivery might seek to prune the early shoots of success that the Unit had produced. The day prior to the 2002 Budget, journalist Larry Elliott quoted Turnbull, still as Permanent Secretary, referring to the ongoing prospect of tension between the Delivery Unit and the Treasury:

> There is a danger of duplication and friction, but we manage it. Will the Delivery Unit undermine the PSA process? There is a certain nervousness, but we are working actively with Gus Macdonald in the Cabinet Office and Michael Barber. We will use the process to reinforce the PSA. It requires active management to make that happen.[3]

Barber and Turnbull would now need to develop a more trusting relationship. The PMDU and Barber also had to respond to unplanned ministerial changes. On 28 May, Stephen Byers resigned as Secretary of State for Transport, which led to a reshuffle of ministers and departmental responsibilities. Alistair Darling moved from Work and Pensions to become Secretary of State for Transport; responsibility for local government was absorbed by John Prescott in his role as deputy Prime Minister. Andrew Smith, Chief Secretary to the Treasury, became Secretary of State for Work and Pensions, Paul Boateng took over as Chief Secretary to the Treasury, and David Miliband became minister of state for schools in the DfES.

There were also changes at Permanent Secretary level: Rachel

Lomax moved from the Department of Work and Pensions (DWP) to the Department for Transport (DfT), and Richard Mottram moved from Transport to the DWP. These changes brought potential challenges for the Delivery Unit as important relationships would have to be re-established. Yet it also provided an opportunity for a new start. Barber himself noted that he had 'major relationship-building to do'.[4] He was shocked at Byers's resignation but understood the pressure (largely from the media[5]) which Byers had been under due to the Jo Moore and Martin Sixsmith affairs.[6] Barber wrote to him and expressed his gratitude for the work they had accomplished together in government.[7] In response, Byers indicated that he remained supportive of the government's reform agenda. He wrote, 'The only way we can fight back is to deliver high quality public services – over to you!'[8] Darling and Lomax's first transport stocktake took place on 25 June. The recent data on the performance of the railways was 'damning'; nevertheless Darling was 'respectful, intelligent and calm' whereas Barber felt Blair 'was too tired and insufficiently focused, so there was no real follow-through'.[9] Despite this, Barber was pleased that his pre-meeting briefing for Lomax and the stocktake meeting itself indicated a secure 'foundation for the Delivery Unit's relationship with the new Transport team'.[10]

Data was a fundamental element of PMDU stocktakes, as Barber explained later: 'The critical element of it was that the data was agreed in advance.'[11] Barber outlined a further three critical factors. First, 'there was a proper discussion about whether things were working or not. It was holding people to account but it was not about blaming or yelling at people.'[12] Second, 'I didn't realise this until we got going. It meant there was always a deadline coming up.'[13] Third, 'not least importantly, given the crisis that unfolded, the stocktakes build a routine, they keep the show on the road'.[14] What underpinned all of this was the continuing commitment from the Prime Minister to the work of his Delivery Unit and the reform agenda.

THE 2002 SPENDING REVIEW

The use of targets by government was beginning to come under question. In an interview in April 2002, Nicholas Macpherson defended the Treasury's PSA system – it had initially brought in hundreds of targets which were routinely revised in successive spending reviews.

> PSAs are a big innovation. The first set were developed pretty quickly ... Some were good, some were pretty crap. There were too many of them. Departments couldn't use them to focus resources and cascade resources down to the front line. In 2000 [spending review], it was better. There were fewer targets and they were better focused. They are likely to stand the test of time.[15]

Macpherson's frank comments indicate that there was a recognition within the Treasury that targets needed to be refined and reduced further in the forthcoming spending review. Barber attended a meeting with the Treasury in early May to discuss the review and the PSA targets.

> The meeting, dominated as ever by Ed Balls, began with a general exchange about targets. Adam [Sharples] and I said that real progress was being made and there were no major issues of principle. I added that the major issue was whether there were too many targets in total and we should see whether we could weed some out or at least prioritise.[16]

Balls asked if 'in principle the Delivery Unit might take on targets from outside the four departments'.[17] To this request, it was Heywood who said that 'in principle that might be possible, it would be a matter for the Prime Minister'.[18] Heywood's retort asserted prime ministerial authority over the Delivery Unit. This episode indicated an acknowledgement that the PMDU provided valuable machinery for monitoring the implementation of PSAs in the round. This was a mechanism which the Treasury had not developed in the four years since PSAs had been created. On 27 June, Andrew Adonis and Barber met with Balls and a group of Treasury civil servants to go through each PSA target individually. Barber reflected on the tension in such meetings and the different approaches of the Prime Minister and the Chancellor.

> There is an edge to these meetings – Blair wants fewer targets; Brown doesn't mind whether we have more or fewer, he just wants them to be better. He wants there to be an explanation for any dropped targets. I worked hard on proposing targets to be dropped – but Ed fought most of them.[19]

An hour and a half later, Barber felt that they had 'sharpened quite a few targets, agreed on many and cut out a few but not a lot ... Ed won the renegotiation.'[20] The Treasury arguably wanted to ensure fewer targets were dropped as funding had been assigned to achieve specific targets in the last spending review; and they would not want to give the impression to departments that targets would be dropped in this way going forward. These meetings showed the status that Barber and the PMDU had reached. Barber took part in a series of meetings with the Prime Minister to 'go through the departments' proposed settlements, targets, reforms and money, one-by-one'.[21]

Barber's 'main role' in the spending review was to 'negotiate the targets'[22] and provide what Macpherson called 'granularity' on what could be delivered with new investment.[23] Meanwhile, Adonis and Heywood handled 'the numbers'.[24] The Treasury also utilised 'the PMDU toolkit' as a framework 'to encourage departments to set out how they were going to deliver'.[25]

In the first week of July 2002, Barber attended three evening meetings with the Treasury in Balls's office to go through targets; afterwards a further meeting on 'the numbers' would take place without Barber.[26] At each meeting the targets were sharpened, at least in relation to the four departments Barber dealt with.[27] He characterised the negotiation with the Treasury as 'vigorous and sharp but mostly good-humoured'.[28] In his view Balls was 'completely dominant on the Treasury side, with Nicholas Macpherson the only other [person] likely to make a contribution'.[29] In negotiating the Home Office targets with the Treasury officials Barber 'used all the skills' he had acquired: 'getting people to focus on the real issues, redrafting, moving on to something else and then coming back to a thorny issue'.[30] But what was crucially important in Barber's view was trust: 'The Treasury officials trust me which helps, they don't think I'm trying to bamboozle them.'[31] It is clear that, in this instance at least, Barber was able to work effectively with both No. 10 and the Treasury because he had developed a degree of trust and expertise that was valued by both. An example of the art of delivery bearing fruit. But not everyone was happy with the process.

Barber was contacted by an aggravated John Gieve, Permanent Secretary at the Home Office, who complained that 'we were agreeing his targets, reforms and money without even involving him: it was, he said, "the centre at its worst"'.[32] From Barber's perspective, he could not help agreeing on one level; on another, though, he reminded Gieve that he himself had 'invented the [PSA] process and, what's more, unlike other departments the Home Office hadn't proposed any targets earlier so we'd had nothing to go on'.[33]

With ten days to go until the Chancellor announced the spending review, Barber and Heywood put their list of targets to Blair in two meetings. Barber noted that the Prime Minister 'accepted generally that you couldn't get out of existing targets but he didn't want to add new ones or make them too tough'.[34] 'We're just making rods for our own backs,' he commented.[35]

> [Blair's] experience over the last few years had changed his thinking. Now that the Labour [structural] reforms were coming into place, targets were not so necessary as a means of getting things done. Of course, you needed some on a few key priorities – but too many and you generated bureaucracy and absorbed people's energy in hitting the targets, even if perversely, rather than making the fundamental changes.[36]

Barber agreed to an extent.

> While I accept that having fewer targets ... is absolutely right and while I want to ensure that those targets we do have are smarter, I also wanted to challenge his view that simply making structural reforms would bring about the necessary changes. The question, I suggested, wasn't a choice between reform or targets; it was one of motivation and incentives.[37]

Barber described the forum in which he, Heywood, and Blair debated targets: 'Blair listened carefully, engaged with the debate and the whole discussion took place in an atmosphere of complete respect and trust.'[38] This episode provides nuanced insights into Blair's changing view on targets and the way in which he, as Prime Minister, engaged in debate with civil servants. Alongside Blair, Alan Milburn was another advocate for recognising the range of tools needed beyond targets. At this point in the story, he had already commented on some health target progress being achieved by micromanagement. But looking back, he reflected on his own learning:

> I went through a journey of starting out as a pretty deep performance management guy – if I told them what to do, if I named and shamed enough, if we did enough transparency, etc, then that will get you the result – to understanding, fundamentally, that unless you have got the right incentives in place, and unless you have got the right accountability and responsibility in place, unless you've got the right level of competition in place, all of this performance management stuff in the end would run into the sand … I think they [the PMDU] were operating in a different part of the spectrum, yes. But was it incompatible? No, because you needed all of these things.[39]

Over the following weekend, departmental settlement letters came through from the Treasury for Barber to view. They were 'enormous, detailed documents' which represented 'visibly Gordon's sweeping influence over domestic policy'.[40] To Barber's surprise, the Delivery Unit had been 'pretty well written out of the script'; so, he 'wrote a paragraph about the Delivery Unit and delivery planning for insertion in each of the settlement letters'.[41] Balls accepted this. On 8 July, Brown and Blair met to make 'pragmatic decisions' on the spending review and later that day Barber and Balls 'cleared up the remaining issues ... at least on targets'.[42] In the week prior to the spending review statement, Barber continued to be involved in planning the PSA targets. At a meeting with Balls he was given the opportunity to make it known that he, Barber, had been 'there at the beginning' of the New Labour project; Balls acknowledged this.[43] He wanted Balls to see him 'as a fellow member of the political project and trust' him because of this.[44] This desire to be explicitly trusted politically as part of the New Labour project is arguably incompatible with the impartial nature of a civil servant, though the line is often necessarily less clear-cut for senior civil servants working closely with politicians and special advisers.

The spending review was announced by the Chancellor on 15 July 2002. The headlines included: an increase in the proportion of national income devoted to public spending from 39.8 per cent in the current year to 41.8 per cent in 2005/6;[45] education spending in England to grow by 6 per cent a year until 2005/6; 'building on the Budget announcement of real terms growth of 7.3 per cent a year in UK health spending'; the setting of 'challenging new targets for health and social services'; and 'the largest increase in defence spending for 20 years', whereby resources would grow by 1.2 per cent per year until 2005/6.[46] For Barber, Brown's statement, along with the Budget, was 'one of two decisive moments of the Parliament'.[47] In his view, 'the job of the Delivery Unit, with the relevant parts of the Treasury' was to translate the 'huge increases in public expenditure levels ... into real improvements in outcomes'.[48]

A new feature of this spending review was the publication of a paper which compared changes to departmental targets between the 2000 and 2002 spending reviews.[49] This was identified in the media as a 'big step in the government's efforts to build an identifiable and credible checklist of progress'.[50] Yet there remained a lack of performance management data for a third of PSAs set in the 2000 spending review, which showed the continued need for the PMDU to urge departments to improve data collection.[51] Balls explained how the Delivery Unit and Barber had become involved in the spending review process. Balls said that it was conducted in a 'very cooperative way and in a very intense way': in the 1998–2000 spending reviews 'the whole process of drawing up the numbers would have basically happened between me and the Treasury people and Jeremy [Heywood] and some Downing Street people'.[52] In the 2002 spending review, the Delivery Unit was integrated into the exercise.

> We were working out the processes ... What outputs ... should we ask them to deliver and what resource would they need to make that happen? And that became a discussion which was very cooperatively informed by the Delivery Unit and Treasury working together ... My view would be that in the spending review of 2002 it would have been the Treasury talking to us, and the Delivery Unit talking to the No. 10 people, and then we would come together and argue it out.[53]

Balls also acknowledged the role that the PMDU played in implementing spending reviews:

> The Treasury has all the clout and know-how on tax policy. But when it comes to public spending and delivery issues, and influencing other Cabinet members to take ownership of changes in their departments, the influence of No. 10 ... is hugely important. In particular, having a Delivery Unit outside the Treasury, close to the prime minister ... worked incredibly well. It was a process

which could never have been managed solely from within the Treasury.[54]

Balls's frank analysis corresponds with the process that Barber outlined in his diary during this period. One year on from the creation of the PMDU, the spending review marked a (new) peak in the Unit's influence and incorporation into one of the most important processes of government. The alignment of PMDU priorities and PSA targets was complete.[55]

SUBSTANCE OVER SPIN

Barber marked a watershed in his role as head of the Delivery Unit when on 25 July 2002 he spoke at the Prime Minister's televised monthly press conference in No. 10. He prepared heavily for the presentation, which included a selection of PowerPoint slides to explain the work of the PMDU.[56] It was a 'high point' for Barber, and his slides showed the progress that had been made in priority areas as well as the impact of the PMDU mechanisms in hastening this.[57] On returning to Blair's Downing Street office, Alastair Campbell said, 'Michael was a star.' Blair 'looked quizzically' at Barber and said, 'He was actually.'[58] In his diaries, Campbell wrote, 'Michael Barber did well and it was interesting.'[59] Barber's appearance was covered in many media articles. The intended impact which he and Blair had sought was symbolised in a *Times* article by Peter Riddell. Riddell 'conveyed the message' that the Prime Minister gave 'detailed personal attention to delivery'[60] – 'Blair has assumed responsibilities which none of his predecessors as Prime Minister … has ever sought. He has become chief problem-solver for the public sector.'[61] Vanessa Nicholls, a civil servant working in the Delivery Unit, reflected on Blair's personal involvement in delivery:

'Tony Blair actually understood that it was necessary ... Unless he did that, it wasn't going to work, the relentless grind that Michael describes is actually true.'[62] This is an important point. Blair was pioneering a new standard for the way in which a Prime Minister publicly holds themselves accountable in setting and delivering vast public service reforms.

ONE YEAR IN

At the end of July, Barber and Blair met for a round-up meeting one year on from the creation of the PMDU. Barber went through key issues and reviewed the progress made; he emphasised the 'need to ensure delivery of hard outcomes within twelve months, if the government's credibility was not to be undermined'.[63] He took the opportunity in the meeting to explain two issues to Blair where he had 'always felt his own analysis was insufficiently sharp: his contrast between "flogging the system" and "structural reform" is too crude; so too is his analysis of bureaucracy and its causes'.[64] Blair showed that he 'fully understood' Barber's analysis, though he was perhaps not persuaded.[65]

From August to September 2002, the PMDU team conducted a priority review on A&E waiting times. The monthly data had shown little change since the target had been announced; 80 per cent of hospitals were dealing with patients within four hours, but 20 per cent were not and some patients were waiting much longer.[66] During August, the Delivery Unit team carried out the fieldwork, visiting good and poor-performing A&E departments – 'the data showed the way, but the field visits discovered the solutions'.[67] In hospitals that were not improving, the team observed poor relation-ships between NHS chief executives and hospital management – 'hospital politics' – whereas in high-performing A&E departments management was 'excellent' and they had created approaches to speed up the process for patients.[68] By September, the team had evidence of the problem, and clear solutions to share with the Department of Health (DH) where the ministers and Permanent Secretary could affect change; action was critical as 'the report itself solved nothing'.[69] The DH decided to include A&E performance in the public star ratings awarded to hospitals and to implement a national rollout of the successful A&E approach ('See and Treat') that had been identified in the field visits to hospitals.[70] Alan Milburn saw significant value in the PMDU's priority review as a tool for affecting change, alongside other levers.

> What I needed as delivery minister, was … the facts and not fiction. I needed objectivity, not subjectivity. And critically, I needed a path to progress. And so, there were a variety of ways of eliciting all of that. One of the ways was having people working in the system who could actually tell you the truth – chief executives of trusts … Second tool, the clinical directors, who I appointed for cancer, heart disease, mental health etc. because they were out in the field. They knew their area of expertise incredibly well, and they were very credible with the system … And the third sense check was the Delivery Unit. That was focused unambiguously on data. And that was just fantastic. So that was a gift. And again, it allowed me to do that body language pivot of being able to say to the department themselves, people charged with delivery, 'Well, hold on a minute. So why isn't XYZ happening? Why are we getting this result when we are supposed to be getting a different result?' In terms of an accountability mechanism for me, it was a huge bonus to have … We were concerned about A&E waiting times; clearly being able to actually get a credible source

of information and data, and proof points was part of the arsenal when you are trying to do these changes.[71]

SEPTEMBER TO DECEMBER 2002

CHOICE AGENDA IN ACTION: FOUNDATION HOSPITALS

A central development in this period was the application of the choice agenda in health, chiefly the creation of foundation hospitals. The concept of choice and diversity in health provision had attracted interest in government in 2001, particularly the idea of creating more capacity in the NHS to bring down waiting lists for routine or high-priority procedures. The use of private sector providers could create more capacity, and this strategy was initially translated into policy with the London choice pilot. To this point there had been some resistance from the Treasury but it had been resolved, to an extent. In April 2002, the DH published a White Paper entitled 'Delivering the NHS Plan' (the NHS Plan itself had been published in 2000). In short, new hospitals or existing hospitals with an approved track record could become foundation hospitals. An incentive for this transition was for foundation hospitals to be financially independent. The motivation for Milburn was the introduction of measures which would unleash the capability of already excellent hospitals, echoing Barber's 'intervention in inverse proportion to success' motto. Milburn's inspiration had come from his consultations with domestic and international healthcare professionals.

[Foundation hospitals] came about as a consequence of an afternoon meeting that I had with the twelve or thirteen best performing CEOs of local NHS Trusts in the country. I wanted to go and meet them to do two things. One, to recognise them and say, 'Well done guys, fantastic job', because we have got these new league tables and you are at the top. And then to ask them a very basic question, which is, what can I do for you? I thought the answer was going to be, 'Give me more money.' The answer from them was, 'Give me more freedom.' What they wanted was me off their backs, they did not want me running their local services, they wanted them running their local services. And that's really how it happened. And then coincidentally I went to Spain on a visit … They had just created a class of new Spanish hospitals … (run at a regional level rather than a national level) … called *fundacións* (foundations) …

My view was that you had to break this notion, that the people who got most of the money were the people who were doing worst rather than the people who were doing best, which I thought was a perverse incentive. So, every time a hospital ran into trouble, they came to me and asked me for more money and what do you do? You give them more money. But that means that the pot of money available for the ones who are doing really well is less. There is no other walk of life where that works as an incentive. I wanted to change that. I wanted to give them the ability to fail.[72]

The proposed new borrowing powers for foundation hospitals would add to the public sector borrowing requirement (PSBR), which the Treasury was responsible for.* Barber recognised the potential impact of this: the policy 'blows a hole in the Treasury's capacity to control public borrowing. So the conflict is over an

---

* The PSBR is the amount that a government borrows to cover the budget deficit.

issue at the head of the Chancellor's business.'[73] And as Permanent Secretary of the DH, Nigel Crisp explained that 'there were fears that this represented a step towards privatisation of the hospitals'.[74] In late September 2002, Milburn's special adviser Paul Corrigan told Barber that 'the latest battle between Gordon and Tony' was over foundation hospitals.[75] Crisp described it as 'one of the most significant internal government battles about health'.[76] In his memoir, Ed Balls acknowledged that after the 2002 Budget 'the NHS became one of the big sources of friction between No. 10 and No. 11'.[77] Brown himself resented the judgement he felt had been placed on him as a 'consolidator', as opposed to Blair and Milburn, the 'transformers' of public services.[78] Milburn felt that part of the disagreement over the scope of foundation hospitals was political as well as ideological.

> The truth of it is that there was an ideological piece of it as well that Gordon was just less comfortable about these market mechanisms than Tony or I were. And there was definitely a political element to it in that Gordon thought I was going to run against him to be the next prime minister … In the end, I concluded that I was not going to run but Gordon didn't think that. Gordon thought everything I was doing was about positioning in a way to create a dividing line with him. There was a very strong personal element to it.[79]

Brown's ideological perspective was partly shaped by his view of modernisation and the way in which the public sector could continue to contribute to that. In his memoirs, he reflected:

> I was against a definition of modernisation that implied the

private sector was somehow better than the public sector and that the way forward for the NHS lay in deregulation and privatisation. There were, and are, real limits to the capacity of markets to deliver public services like healthcare, and limits to the desirability of them doing so. The test had always to be the public interest.[80]

When asked whether the NHS should have remained the ultimate monopoly provider of healthcare Milburn said, 'Well, de facto, it always was going to be because 90-plus per cent of the capacity in the UK in the healthcare system is owned by the NHS. So, there isn't an alternative that's available.'[81] The policy debate was evidently somewhat motivated by differing visions of what constituted public interest and modernisation.

The challenge to reform had been set out in August 2002 when Milburn wrote an article in *The Times* outlining his ambitions: 'I believe we must ... choose transformation ... Existing NHS hospitals should be able to become NHS foundation hospitals established as not-for-profit, public interest companies with more freedom from centralised state control.'[82] Milburn was using the media to stimulate public debate and propel his strategy. Milburn's own intellectual and political position had developed over time. In 1999, as a new Secretary of State for Health, he told NHS executives that he would 'come down like a ton of bricks on anyone who has anything to do with the private sector' and again in 2001 he described the NHS as 'thankfully' a 'monopoly provider'.[83] His view changed significantly as he delved deeper into understanding the state of the NHS as it was, and as he began to identify existing and new levers for producing change. For Milburn, it was about maintaining the same values but adapting the system to modern ways of working, and modern public expectations. Blair 'very firmly urged' Milburn to carry on with the foundation hospitals concept.[84] The dispute came to a head publicly during the party conference at the beginning of October. In his 2002 party conference speech Blair set an ambitious tone that echoed Milburn's *Times* article:

> We are at a crossroads: party, government, country.
> Do we take modest though important steps of improvement?
> Or do we make the great push forward for transformation?
> I believe we're at our best when at our boldest …
> [We] require an end to the one-size-fits-all mass production public services …
> Why shouldn't our best hospitals be free to develop their services within the NHS as foundation hospitals?[85]

During the party conference, Milburn reiterated his intention. Brown, Balls and the Treasury had a different perspective on the necessity and use of choice in health policy. Balls outlined this:

> There was a whole issue around choice and managed choice … where the health department were wanting to use a very [political] market, almost pricing, view of choice in the Health Service. We were very sceptical that this was going to be value for money or sensible. But there was a Treasury–Delivery Unit discussion about managed choice; it wasn't about markets/prices, it was about the better, more efficient use of the capacity.[86]

Brown shared his concerns regarding the issue in his memoir: 'My main and specific concern … was that while the new hospitals would be permitted to borrow money against their assets, the government would remain ultimately liable for their deficits and debts ... The foundation hospital scheme meant government accepting all the liability while ceding almost all control.'[87]

Milburn recognised the Treasury's concern if a foundation hospital failed. He reflected:

From a Treasury point of view, there was a quite legitimate concern that if that happened the Treasury would end up picking up the public expenditure tab. It was a bit more nuanced even than that. We were not going to allow the hospital to fail, we were going to allow the management team to fail ... That was a very reasonable Treasury concern to have, discharging its role as the finance department.[88]

In Balls's view, the original Milburn proposal would have meant that hospitals were 'cut loose ... as if they were private entities ... knowing the government would bail them out if things got difficult'.[89] The myriad of concerns from all sides resulted in counter-briefing at the party conference. Barber explained that his 'only small direct involvement' came in response to Nicholas Macpherson's 'innocent question: "Are foundation hospitals crucial to delivery?" Answer: "No."'[90] This was significant. Barber was stating that in the short to medium term, on which the PMDU was focused, Blair and Milburn's major new policy would not have an impact on delivery. The Treasury was aware of Barber's position on the tightrope, as Balls explained when asked later about this policy dispute.

We tried to be sensitive to the fact that he was head of the Prime Minister's Delivery Unit and that he couldn't be put in an impossible position but the reality was [that] he was at times. But it was good to have meetings where we would have people from the Treasury, him, as well as some of the No. 10 policy people because he was sometimes a bit of a check.[91]

THE OCTOBER COMPROMISE

Later that month a compromise was reached at a meeting which was attended by Blair, Brown, Milburn, Jeremy Heywood and Simon Stevens, where both sides claimed relative victory. A *Guardian* article reported that Milburn had 'won the battle, but perhaps not the war'.[92] A No. 10 spokesperson said that foundation hospitals would be able to borrow 'at their own discretion, not that of the government'; they would have 'quick and flexible access to borrowing … [but] any loans will be marked on the DH's balance sheet'.[93] This ensured that they would remain part of conventional public sector borrowing, thus reducing the risk to the PSBR. Balls claimed victory; at the crucial meeting he quoted Blair as saying: 'Of course we can't have public hospitals borrowing off the books. We want them to have more freedom and flexibility, but they're not private institutions.'[94] Milburn told Barber that he was 'pleased with the outcome', as high-performing hospitals would have more independence.[95] The October compromise would make foundation hospital status less attractive but still allowed it to go ahead. For reforming ministers, it arguably showed that though the Prime Minister encouraged radical policy, they could not rely on his unconditional support in tense negotiations with the Chancellor. With hindsight, Blair told Peter Mandelson that 'he regretted not standing by Alan Milburn in seeing through those reforms'.[96]

The row over foundation hospitals also impacted the PMDU in that it affected the broader relationship between the Treasury and No. 10. Barber wrote in his diary, 'The Treasury has a policy position on everything, which is as it should be. It also has a culture of slapping departments down; and arrogance, which it doesn't always merit. Then there's the tense relations Gordon has with Alan [Milburn] and David [Blunkett] for starters, which colours things.'[97] The PMDU was oiling the wheels of these relationships to keep them moving. The Treasury was using the Unit as an extra layer of analysis and accountability between it and departments, but this additional layer also worked to provide some insulation for departments.

A GENUINELY IMPORTANT INNOVATION?

Blair commented that he thought the Delivery Unit was 'a really good innovation' at a meeting with Barber and Heywood in early October.[98] Barber was 'more cautious' and replied, 'We had a good first year but it'll be in the next year that we discover whether it's a genuinely important innovation.'[99] They discussed the progress on delivery department by department: 'school test results flat, A Levels up, but in chaos; rail delays as bad as ever; August figures on health waiting times disappointing; crime other than street crime up. All in all, as Blair put it, "Not a great month for delivery."'[100] For Barber this distinction was critical: 'It's all very well seeing it as a success but if the outcomes are poor, what good is that?'[101] They also discussed the tension between the idea of devolving power (as part of the choice agenda) and central government retaining the levers to monitor and hasten delivery.

Blair was committing a substantial amount of time to delivery; they talked about 'the pressure of 38 stocktakes ("How many have I got?" he asked incredulously)' and about the need for Barber to focus his time on the key priorities.[102] Part of this increase in stocktakes was due to the PMDU's involvement in new policy areas because of the perceived success in the four delivery departments. For example, the PMDU now covered all targets in the four delivery departments[103] plus a selection of targets from the Department for Culture, Media and Sport, the Office of the Deputy Prime Minister, the Department for the Environment, Food and Rural Affairs, the Department of Trade and Industry and drugs policy (cross-departmental).[104] Would this widening of responsibility and commitment of prime ministerial time be sustainable? It went against the principle on which Barber founded the PMDU – consistent focus on a small number of priorities.

Asylum was a priority policy area for Blair, and as such Barber regularly attended meetings with him to monitor and drive progress. At a meeting with the Immigration and Nationality Directorate (IND) 'Blair spelt out clearly' that he wanted the IND to 'produce an effective delivery plan'.[105] Barber 'inadvertently asked a killer question, what had happened ... to the decision we'd taken a year ago, to deliver appeal decisions to rejected asylum seekers in person rather than by post?'[106] In response the IND and representatives from the Lord Chancellor's Department 'were flummoxed – they had never liked this proposal and were forced to admit to Blair that they had never really implemented it. There had just been a tiny and largely ineffective pilot.'[107] Blair was 'outraged and though he didn't lose his temper he was pretty blunt: he said there was no policy area on which he felt more like Jim Hacker;* decisions were made but nothing ever happened.'[108]

A QUESTION OF LEADERSHIP

On 23 October, Estelle Morris resigned as Secretary of State for

---

*   Jim Hacker is the (fictitious) title character in the satirical television programmes *Yes Minister* and *Yes, Prime Minister*. Hacker often noticed that the Civil Service prevented his policy changes from actually being put into practice.

Education. She did not feel that she was able to fulfil the role to the level which she believed it needed; Blair 'accepted her resignation with regret'.[109] During a select committee hearing (after she resigned) Morris explained her experience of the Delivery Unit: '

My personal relationships with Michael and the PMDU are very, very good. I found them a source of irritation when they demanded too much of me but great comfort when they gave me help in trying to achieve something. It was a proper, purposeful, professional relationship.'[110]

Morris's resignation prompted a reshuffle. Barber spoke to Sally Morgan and Jonathan Powell about potential successors and was told later that week that Charles Clarke would succeed Morris.[111] Clarke had been minister without portfolio and Labour Party chairman. Barber was professionally and personally committed to education reform and delivery; he would have to build an effective working relationship with Clarke. He believed Clarke had 'wanted a role like this so much … and he's Tony's, not Gordon's man'.[112] From Blair's perspective, 'for the first time' he felt that with Clarke, Milburn and Blunkett he had the people alongside him 'fully in tune with what' he wanted to 'do and why'.[113]

BARBER DELIVEROLOGY

In the week that Morris resigned there were two stocktakes, on transport and crime. From Barber's perspective, the transport stocktake 'turned out well' though '[Alistair] Darling had been anxious about it'; to reassure him Barber and Gus Macdonald met Darling and Rachel Lomax, Permanent Secretary at the DfT, the evening before.[114] They ran through the stocktake agenda and to Barber's relief Darling was pleased with the PMDU's approach to road congestion. He agreed that his department's 'data was suspect, the assumptions untested and the targets unchallenging'.[115] Bizarrely the congestion data relied on 'thirteen people driving around in cars [which] seemed pretty daft!'[116] During the pre-meeting, Darling and Lomax emphasised their view that 'it would be hard to bring about visible improvement [on the railways] in the next eighteen months – and they wanted my help in communicating that to Blair'.[117] They saw Barber as influential and as this was an important meeting for him he could have acquiesced, but he did not; instead he sought to persuade them of their own ability to deliver. Barber felt they had begun to establish their relationship 'on a very sound footing – which hadn't been inevitable'.[118]

Barber had his first meeting with the new Secretary of State for Education. Clarke asked him to give an 'overview of delivery across the department' and they debated some of the immediate policy decisions including on how to measure progress.[119] Barber found Clarke 'refreshingly open' to giving good schools freedom over pay and conditions and the National Curriculum.[120] As he left Clarke said, 'I told Tony when he appointed me that you and I would get on well.'[121]

The PMDU's 'Driving Delivery' conference was a notable moment in the development of the Unit. Barber, Blair, Brown and Cabinet Secretary Turnbull spoke at the conference. Barber observed that the Prime Minister was 'on good form ... in answer to a question about whether delivery was his top priority, he was unhesitating in saying it was.'[122] The term which would become synonymous with Barber and the Delivery Unit for many years to come was coined at this event. During the event Nicholas Macpherson 'conveyed unequivocally his support for and collaboration with the Delivery Unit' and at one point referred to what he called 'Barber deliverology'.[123] Brown made an 'emotive as well as rational case for delivering', making 'a point of referring back to what Blair had said' and to what Barber had said; 'this ensured that there was a combined, simple message from the day'.[124] The conference was symbolic of the progress achieved; Barber and the PMDU had been praised for their progress so far and the Chancellor and the Prime Minister had given a united message on the need to deliver.

THE POLITICAL BRIDGE

Later that week, Barber met Brown along with Macpherson and Balls. Barber engaged with Brown in a way that few of Blair's close advisers did, which was a significant strength. It allowed the PMDU to work more effectively and collaboratively with the Treasury, and with delivery departments. It indicated his skill in relationship-building, and an absence of the acutely tribal inclination that was present in both courts. At the meeting, Brown 'expressed major doubt about the market elements of the health reforms'; Barber 'told him that as far as delivery by 2005 was concerned … the work on financial flows and incentives was crucial; the DTCs [diagnosis and treatment centres, which utilised private sector capacity] were important and foundation hospitals, while maybe important for other reasons, not crucial.'[125] Barber realised his comment was 'bold, given the Blair/Brown differences'.[126] On the Home Office, Brown said 'by far his main concern was the budget rather than delivery'; Barber said that on 'asylum only getting the number of applicants under control would help reduce costs', and this was the focus of the PMDU's work.[127] The meeting had gone very well; Brown had listened to Blair's chief adviser on delivery and 'asked questions for almost an hour'.[128] Macpherson told the Chancellor that 'working relations were good' and the PMDU was planning to move into the recently refurbished Treasury building, 'which seemed to please' Brown.[129]

As the meeting ended, Brown and Barber began to talk about recent books they had read on Labour Chancellors of the past, which led Brown to ask Barber, 'Are you a historian?'[130] Barber confirmed that he was and that he had 'specialised in American history'; they proceeded to discuss their mutual interest in the topic.[131] Barber was delighted with the 'real personal connection' they had made.[132] In early November, Barber considered the progress of the PMDU: 'We, the Delivery Unit, have played a major part in creating an entirely new climate in Whitehall characterised by … a new enthusiasm for learning how to deliver.'[133] He also had 'the humility to recognise that "you're only as good as your last game"'. The PMDU had 'to constantly re-earn' its reputation.[134]

By chance, Barber saw Milburn in Whitehall, who explained that he had had some 'tough words' with his health civil servants and that he had conveyed 'in no uncertain terms that the PM was not happy with the progress on the DTC programme'.[135] Barber said that he would 'urge them to consider what bold execution actually meant' and in response Milburn said, 'That's good, that's clever.'[136] Regular dialogue was important and showed the positive relationship developing between Barber and Milburn. Indeed, as time went on, Milburn saw the value in the PMDU. Reflecting on the stocktake process in particular, he saw how the process also helped him to hold his own officials to account and allow for closer alignment with the Prime Minister:

In practice, what happened is that the Delivery Unit and the department – they're in a complex relationship, the Delivery Unit are holding to account, and at the same time seeking to assist. So, it's quite an interesting relationship. And from my point of view, by and large, as it turned out, it was super beneficial. I can remember very well, when I'd have a stocktake with Tony [Blair]. He would sit on one side of the Cabinet table, I'd sit on the other side of the Cabinet table, he'd have his phalanx of people on his side, including … the health policy adviser. And I'd have my senior civil servants and people charged with delivery and Tony would then ask a question and say, 'So, why is it that the waiting time target is behind where it [should be]?' Which allowed me to then pivot to my guys and say, 'Why is it, guys?' So, we were both aligned, because we were both as anxious to secure the delivery of the progress and targets as anyone was and it allowed us to almost to form a stronger political bridge between the Prime Minister and the Secretary of State, to ensure the system was aligned behind the policy objectives.[137]

The Permanent Secretary at the Department of Health, Nigel Crisp, also recognised the benefits of the Delivery Unit approach. Looking back, Crisp said, 'It was enormously helpful to me to know that Michael [Barber] was briefing the Prime Minister before our meetings with the same information as I had. It not only helped me to 'manage up' … but undoubtedly also helped to build confidence in me and the Department.'[138]

Clarke's first stocktake as Secretary of State for Education took place in early November. Barber gave an overview of the education agenda and then a discussion mostly on primary and secondary schools took place. He felt his own 'constant point about prioritising literacy and numeracy had been understood' by the education ministers.[139] From Clarke's perspective, his most important connection in government was with the Prime Minister, with whom he had a 'good relationship' and that meant that Blair 'could always say what he thought and change my view if necessary … I would always accept his authority.'[140] In this way, Clarke never viewed the PMDU as a challenge to individual ministerial responsibility.[141]

A TIDE FOR DELIVERY

In mid-November, Barber attended and presented at the Cabinet and Permanent Secretaries awayday. Barber emphasised 'Ambition, Focus, Clarity, Urgency, Irreversibility – and what they mean for departmental leadership'.[142] He went through 'the crucial relationship between reform and execution' and created a simple diagram to show how bold reform without effective execution created 'controversy without impact' whereas bold reform with effective execution created 'transformation'.[143] The street crime initiative of 2002 was regarded as an example of successful delivery. During the course of the day, Blair said he 'thought it was possible to get the right collaboration and for the centre to get "buy-in" from departments, as "Michael has managed to do" with the Delivery Unit'.[144] The Chancellor also said 'Well done' to Barber 'but then asked the question on which he was really focused' – 'At some point, you've got to think through the question of the role of markets in the delivery of public services.'[145] Barber told Brown that he 'thought we needed to really think it through from first principles rather than deal with the issue in an ad hoc way as different specific cases arose'.[146] The event showed the drive for delivery within the wider Cabinet, not just in the priority areas. Barber felt that the PMDU had 'reached a new level of authority and influence across government'; he noticed 'a tide flowing across Whitehall for delivery'.[147]

There were two stocktakes on 14 November, on drugs and the criminal justice system. Both involved 'an array of senior politicians, rather than being dealt with' as they had been in the previous year 'through the Home Office alone'.[148] This demonstrated the

PMDU's ability to examine cross-cutting issues. Relations between the PMDU and the Treasury were growing ever closer by the end of November, but within No. 10 Barber noted 'dark mutterings' from some of the Prime Minister's senior advisers 'about how bad relations' between Blair and Brown had become.[149] Meanwhile within the Treasury, Permanent Secretary Gus O'Donnell told Treasury staff that 'delivery was their priority [and] they were working closely' with the PMDU.[150] Barber subsequently reflected, 'There are real challenges ahead in … this relationship. It's one of the biggest risks for me.'[151]

On 19 November, a health stocktake took place. Milburn 'strongly' advocated the recommendations of the PMDU Accident & Emergency priority review (from September) and Barber was 'pleased to see how influential' their proposals had been.[152] Blair used the forum as it had been intended, to hold his ministers to account for progress. 'Looking at Michael's presentation, it seems to me, you are plateauing,' he said robustly. Milburn agreed and then there was discussion of what might be done. In concluding, Blair said, 'I expect to see real progress on these outcomes in the next six months.' Milburn 'signed up to that'.[153]

AN ENGAGED PRIME MINISTER

In early December, Barber had one of his 'relatively rare one-to-one meetings with Blair' (up to this date he had had about five), though Jeremy Heywood was also present.[154] They discussed the stocktake with the newly added departments: the process 'was working for the new departments', they took it seriously.[155] He briefed Blair on PMDU 'relations with the Treasury and told him that the Delivery Unit staff would be moving in there'; for Barber, 'given that relations between TB and GB are at an all-time low, it was important that he knew about this and approved'.[156] Blair said, 'That's fine. It's very important work. You should carry on.'[157]

Referring to the Delivery Unit's four-level intensity scale, they agreed that where they had utilised 'the Level 4 focus (street crime and asylum) it had a huge impact but on the Level 3 issues (e.g. education in London) we'd been less effective'.[158] The Prime Minister said he would like to 'focus on more issues at that Level 4. He knew he had lots of other things in the diary but what could be more important than driving delivery of key priorities.'[159] Blair's enthusiasm for the mechanism that Barber had developed – the four levels of intensity – was evident. Heywood and Barber 'began to protest that it would be hard to find more time in an already crowded diary'; yet Barber believed Blair's instinct was 'right in leadership terms – focus on the priorities'.[160] The Prime Minister began to go through 'his appointments and indicate things that didn't matter as much'; Heywood and Barber agreed 'to come up with a list of possible additional Level 4 issues for him to focus on'.[161] Candidate areas included 'drugs and either primary literacy/numeracy or Accident and Emergency'.[162] This example showed the Prime Minister's firm commitment to devoting his (finite) time and attention to delivery. But would such an increase in granular prime ministerial involvement prove to be sustainable?

Blair also asked Barber to start attending the weekly Monday morning meeting of his closest No. 10 advisers and civil servants; Barber was interested to see what difference it would make being in a new 'loop'.[163] Sally Morgan noted that Barber's inclusion in these meetings indicated that he had become 'a core team member'.[164] In the week before the next delivery report was finalised, Barber began to call Permanent Secretaries to discuss the contrast between their self-assessments and that of the PMDU. The departments were generally 'more positive' than the PMDU.[165] Rachel Lomax said she was 'closer' to the PMDU judgements; John Gieve 'debated' the difference in judgements and Barber made 'a couple of changes as a result of learning more'.[166] The delivery report and league table were finalised and disseminated to the four departments and to the Prime Minister in mid-December. Barber signalled the next phase in delivery to the Permanent Secretaries – 'we would shift the emphasis from plans, capacity and process to delivering results'.[167] On 10 December, a transport stocktake took place. Barber worked hard to establish a good working relationship with the new Permanent Secretary, Lomax. The reason for doing so, in Barber's view, was to create 'the space for my teams to do what they needed'.[168] This creation of space is a critical function of leadership. In the stocktake, Darling set out some of his upcoming announcements and revealed 'that congestion targets set in 2000 were unachievable and the government was giving up on them'.[169] Barber described Darling as 'relentlessly cautious ... clever and well-informed and sees his role in politics as to reduce expectations ... the ultimate technocrat. And, in a frontbench team you need some like him.'[170]

A CAPACITY TO LEARN

Barber presented at the PSX Cabinet committee on 18 December, going through departmental progress on each PSA target. Brown wanted Barber's opinion on targets, which he duly explained.[171]

In any department's portfolio, there needed to be a mix of ambitious and less ambitious ones [targets]; ... those who would have to deliver them should be involved and consulted in designing them; and ... for some areas where the goal was continuous improvement rather than step change, we could insist on good data collection and effective performance management and dispense with targets altogether.[172]

The Chancellor asked Barber and Nicholas Macpherson to produce a paper on targets for the next meeting of PSX.

In his penultimate diary entry of 2002, Barber reflected on relations with the Treasury: 'I ended the year with a real sense of having built a strong resilient relationship with the Treasury ... I set myself the goal, earlier in the year, of changing the culture of the Treasury. I see signs of it beginning to happen.'[173] The past year had been momentous for Barber and the Delivery Unit, and he listed his highs and lows of 2002.

The highs included:

- My ten-minute presentation to the Cabinet and Permanent Secretaries away day.
- Getting going and seeing through the stocktake presentation idea.
- The consistently strengthening reputation of the Delivery Unit.
- My meetings with Gordon Brown.
- My roundup meeting with Blair.
- The DU impact on data and its use.
- Priority reviews, especially on street crime and A&E.
- The July press conference with Blair.
- The entire Street Crime Initiative, especially my early contribution to it.
- The last phase of SR [spending review] 2002 and the negotiations.

Some of the low points:

- Estelle [Morris] and her resignation.

- The demise of Steve Byers and the press on the day he resigned.
- Moments of exhaustion.[174]

The year ended with a *Financial Times* front-page article which carried the story about the PMDU moving into the Treasury building and sought to turn it 'into another chapter in the TB–GB saga'.[175] It said that the Chancellor was 'set to grab' part of the Prime Minister's 'ever-expanding empire' – the PMDU, which had been 'regarded as a success'.[176] As Barber recorded in his diary, 'only later did the story clarify that reporting lines – mine to the PM – were unchanged'.[177] He told the Cabinet Office and No. 10 press offices to emphasise this and 'that the move was a sign of the strong collaboration between Tony and Gordon on the issue of delivery'.[178]

JANUARY TO APRIL 2003

MR TARGETS

The year began with Barber outlining his focus for the twelve months ahead – 'humility' was the essential word – and in doing so he gave an insight into the basis on which the PMDU was developing.[179] The opportunity to put this into practice came early on in the New Year when an internal PMDU delivery report on health, not intended for public consumption, was leaked to the media. The Department of Health had circulated the document to 300 chief executives of NHS trusts.[180] At the time, Barber was in Sydney to speak at a conference about his approach to delivery and was alerted to the article by the No. 10 press office.[181] The article, again on the front page of the *Financial Times*, quoted the delivery report: there was an 'immense risk' that the NHS would not take advantage of the unprecedented investment by government; the 'weakness' of new primary care trusts and strategic health authorities set up by Alan Milburn posed 'very significant challenges'; and the department needed 'to get the right people into the right jobs faster' to guarantee delivery.[182] Barber spoke with Milburn, who was 'unhappy but restrained'; Barber knew that the 'leak was a major problem for him [Milburn], not least because he had a debate coming up in Parliament the next day'.[183] In retrospect, Milburn's recollections indicate a sharper tone, and allude to Barber's capacity to absorb such frustration.

> I think that's a very, very kind interpretation of that conversation … I remember swearing at him, along the lines of, 'What the fuck is this? Why have you created this problem?' And I think not unreasonably, he would say, 'Well, you know, I've got to be able to present the facts as I see them.' And I not unreasonably would have said, 'Well, sure, but present them in private, ensure that they don't leak in public.'[184]

Barber spoke to his PMDU team and Jeremy Heywood, who informed him that it had not been raised at Prime Minister's Questions, so No. 10 was 'relaxed now', suggesting that it had not been earlier.[185] As a result Barber decided that the PMDU would review all information-sharing procedures. He was 'encouraged' to hear that No. 10 had told lobby journalists that the content of the leaked report 'was evidence that the feedback from Downing Street was robust and vigorous – not just shallow warm words'.[186] On returning from Australia, Barber checked in with the crucial people in Downing Street. In the days following the leak, the PMDU and the health reforms gained wider coverage in the media and Barber himself was the subject of a profile in *The Independent* entitled 'Mr

Targets'.[187] Barber noticed the caption under a photo of himself: 'Michael Barber keeps out of the limelight but his influence is recognised by every minister.'[188]

The first health stocktake since the leak took place on 14 January. In setting the tone for the meeting, Barber began by saying that 'none of the data I was about to show had appeared in public *yet*. There was some uneasy laughter from Blair and Milburn, but the joke helped.'[189] The data showed 'good progress on inpatients and modest progress on outpatients' waiting times.[190] Blair was on 'very good form throughout making the case for choice with real panache'.[191] At the end of the meeting, Barber went immediately to talk to Milburn about the leak. The Secretary of State 'said it was pretty bad – "I can't have that again," he said repeatedly'.[192] The aftermath of the leak showed the resilience of the relationships Barber actively nurtured.

In mid-January, Brown requested a meeting to discuss the issue Barber raised at PSX in December about 'replacing some targets with an effective performance management system'.[193] The following day, Barber met Brown, along with Ed Balls and Macpherson. For the Chancellor, 'the central problem … was how to arrive at a non-market, non-command-and-control model of delivery'.[194] Barber ran through the paper that he had 'hastily' put together; they took health as an example.[195]

A given [primary care] trust might be required to meet certain national minimum standards (which are crucial to equity, apart from anything else). In consultation with its local community, it would then establish other performance indicators. Data on the national and local indicators would be published regularly … Finally we agreed that government would need to intervene in cases where there was underperformance or a failure to meet the national standards. Here perhaps was the non-market, non-command-and-control means of delivery … it insists on results, not particular methods.[196]

An NHS trust would receive more devolved power over decision-making in return for transparency; it would be held to account by local citizens – consumer pressure – and central government. Despite Barber's suggestion that government would regulate national standards, the nature of the British political system would still lead to a demand for results and accountability from the Prime Minister for more micro-standards. The political imperative to exercise command and control from the centre would therefore perhaps remain unchanged. The extent to which NHS 'consumers' could reasonably hold hospitals to account, if they were presumably unwell and in need of urgent care, is questionable. For Barber, the dialogue with Brown had been 'a rapid fire, intellectual challenge'.[197] The strong relationship that he, a representative of the Prime Minister, was developing with the Chancellor was notable.

A QUESTION OF LOYALTY

Later that week Barber attended a dinner event in Versailles at which Ed Balls was present. The two 'analysed the issues – the future of public service reform, the role of targets and the relationship between purchaser, provider, consumer and price'.[198] In conversing with Balls, Barber reflected that 'you have to be struck by his speed and insight. The words torrent out but always very lucidly. He's less good at listening – he leaps immediately to a grasp of what you're saying – without necessarily waiting for any refinement or deep explanation.'[199] The relationship was of fundamental importance to

Barber's ability to do his job effectively, yet the closeness could be interpreted in more than one way. The day following the Versailles event, Barber came across Peter Mandelson.

> He [Mandelson] said, curiously I thought, 'I hope you're going to stay by the Prime Minister's side.' I guess he was referring to the *FT* story about the Delivery Unit moving to the Treasury, so I explained. Then ... he said, 'I saw you in a very animated conversation with Ed Balls.' The perception that my conversation the evening before was an act of disloyalty to the Blairites had never crossed my mind. I told Peter he needn't worry. I thought he was rather cool towards me throughout, though he said, 'I was only joking.'[200]

This was perhaps symptomatic of the growing rivalry and sensitivity between the Blair and Brown courts. Sally Morgan, however, believed that Mandelson's comment did not 'represent the No. 10 view' at the time.[201] There was a clear necessity to have a close working relationship with the Treasury. Barber met with the Prime Minister to talk about his emerging approach to targets, and he described the ideas that he had been discussing with the Chancellor. Blair looked 'tired but took an interest and strongly encouraged' Barber to continue to work up thoughts.[202] Barber told him 'that apart from wanting his view of the policy I also wanted to be sure that he was aware of any conversation' with Brown.[203] He informed the Prime Minister that the *Financial Times* story about the PMDU moving into the Treasury had given him 'some problems, even with ministers thinking that I was working for' Brown.[204] He 'wanted to remind him ... that all that was happening was that my staff are moving into the Treasury building'.[205] 'I thought it was something like that,' Blair said 'rather unconvincingly', as though he had forgotten that Barber had explained this to him before Christmas.[206] Barber thought that for the moment his relationship with Blair was 'strong and trusting'.[207] He had evidently made the decision to move the PMDU to the refurbished Treasury building himself; it therefore demonstrated the relative independence that the Prime Minister afforded him – Blair's leadership style was not micromanagement. Being physically based in the Treasury represented a move by Barber to strengthen relations as the Treasury's work was important to the PMDU, and a symbolically strong base for the PMDU team, who were then housed in a comparatively nondescript building in Whitehall.

PART OF THE INNER CORE

Barber and his wife attended a dinner at Home Secretary David Blunkett's house along with Tony and Cherie Blair, Sally Morgan and her husband, and Alastair Campbell and his partner Fiona Millar (who was an adviser to Cherie Blair). During the course of the evening, Blair asked Barber what they could expect on delivery in the next few months. Barber went through the 'key indicators' in the four main areas.[208] Blair said, 'So Michael, you really think we will have some positive evidence of delivery by the summer?' He wanted 'reassurance'; Barber said he thought they would.[209] Comparing that evening to a similar dinner with a smaller group in January 2002, Barber 'felt much more confidently part of the inner core'.[210] He recognised, however, that 'in politics these relationship questions shift all the time; who's in the loop, who's out changes too; failures of delivery, some entanglement with Gordon and it could all slip'.[211] This statement illustrates why creating the art of delivery to accompany the science was of fundamental importance. The emerging science of delivery (the consistent monitoring process) was crucial, but the application of this innovation would arguably have been ineffective without the art of delivery (the relentless relationship-building). For civil servants within the Delivery Unit, Barber's focus on building effective working relationships created the space and security for the team to be able get on with the job.

In the same week, the question of Barber's allegiance in the Blair–Brown saga came up again during a phone conversation with Blunkett. Referring to the *Financial Times* story of 31 December, Blunkett said, 'What's this about you moving to the Treasury?'[212] Barber told him the story 'had missed the point; that I certainly wasn't working for Gordon'. Blunkett said, 'Good ... because I'd have to cut off relations.'[213] Even established working relationships were fragile because of the growing political and personal divisions within New Labour. Blunkett and Barber discussed reform in the Home Office. The PMDU had been involved in improving the capacity to deliver within the four delivery departments. In late January, the situation in the Home Office was coming to a head, and Barber was due to present at the department's ministers and board awayday. In their telephone conversation, Blunkett and Barber agreed to explain that 'the Home Office had two options: reform itself urgently and thoroughly; alternatively a crisis from somewhere would impose reform upon them with unpredictable consequences'.[214] After the awayday, John Gieve called Barber 'in a state of significant anxiety': 'Everybody here is interpreting what you said as an ultimatum from the Prime Minister.'[215] Barber explained that he had not 'cleared' what he said with the Prime Minister but 'thought he'd agree with my message'.[216]

THE MAXIMUM AMOUNT OF DIVERSITY
CONSISTENT WITH EQUALITY

Barber attended a meeting with Brown, Balls and Macpherson to discuss public service reform and the forthcoming spending review. The Chancellor made a significant comment in response to Barber's paper on targets of the previous week: 'I think it solves the problem … Its proposals should form the basis for the next spending review.'[217] They moved on to discuss a major area of contention within New Labour, the limitations of markets in the delivery of public services. The focus was on an extract on 'equality and diversity' from Barber's book *The Learning Game*, published in 1996.[218] Balls read a few lines of an anecdote about Barber meeting a Treasury official in the 1980s 'who had said that whatever the problem they always knew under Thatcher that the question they had to answer was, "How do you make a market?"'[219] Barber asked, 'What would the equivalent question be under Labour? Ed stopped reading and Gordon said, "Well what would it be?"'[220] Barber quoted from his book: 'What is the maximum amount of diversity [of provider] consistent with equality?' Brown became animated and said, 'That's it!'[221] It was a 'sensational' moment for Barber; he felt this provided the 'way into Gordon's concept of "non-market, non-command-and-control models" of public service reform'.[222]

Balls recalled this episode and noted that it showed that Barber was not an 'outsider'; in fact he, Brown and Balls shared a 'similar understanding' of the limitations of market reforms to the NHS.[223] Barber wrote, 'This was a case of contributing to strategic policy-making of a major kind, which my present job rarely involves.'[224] Nicholas Macpherson observed that this was reciprocated: 'Brown always held Michael in very high regard, which is actually quite unusual for someone who so obviously had been put in there to sort of pursue Tony Blair's agenda.'[225] From a No. 10 perspective, Sally Morgan later commented that 'very few people were able to have relationships' with Brown and the Treasury and Barber was one of them.[226] Brown asked Barber to look at the text of a speech he was giving the following week. In what turned out to be a seminal speech, delivered to the Social Market Foundation on 3 February 2003, Brown expanded on Barber's principle from *The Learning Game*. The relevant excerpt from the speech, which was entitled 'A Modern Agenda for Prosperity and Social Reform', is as follows: 'In each area the questions are, at root, whether the public interest – that is opportunity and security for all – and the equity, efficiency and diversity necessary to achieve it, is best advanced by more or less reliance on markets.'[227] Macpherson commented that the pre-speech discussion was 'very good' and explained that Brown 'used speeches as a way of developing his own thinking and as a way of wrestling with the problem'.[228] Brown's conversation with Barber gave him the opportunity to do this. Interestingly, Blair wrote in his memoir that he felt Balls had created a 'strategy' for Brown whereby there was a 'trade-off between equity and markets; Blair is pushing us too far towards marketisation' and 'thus away from equity'.[229]

THE TRANSMISSION BELT

As a senior Cabinet minister in a delivery department, David Blunkett regularly dealt with the Delivery Unit. In an interview with the author, he detailed the benefits of the PMDU to departments.

> It's a two-way street. I didn't see the Delivery Unit as one-way and top-down, I saw it as a transmission belt. If we could persuade the Delivery Unit that there were … problems elsewhere that needed to be resolved before we could do what we wanted to

do – immigration was classic and the removal of people who we wanted to get out of the country, but if the Foreign Office didn't cooperate we couldn't do it … Michael was brilliant at persuading Tony when he was around him that they had to assist in acting.[230]

Blunkett's perspective that Barber and the Delivery Unit acted as a 'transmission belt' between departments and the Prime Minister gives an insight into the power that the Unit afforded departments too. The PMDU was principally designed as a tool for the Prime Minister, indeed it had been resisted by some ministers at first, thus it is notable that its collaborative approach allowed it to become mutually beneficial.

IRAQ AND THE VALUE OF A DELIVERY UNIT

The PMDU was gaining traction across Whitehall but in No. 10 the growing focus was on foreign policy and specifically Iraq, and it was starting to impact the Prime Minister's ability to concentrate on delivery. As Sally Morgan later observed, 'Tony was really engaged, it was easier pre-Iraq, with the best will in the world he became slightly more distracted.'[231] Morgan, however, concurred that it was the PMDU's responsibility to sustain momentum on delivery even when the Prime Minister's attention was elsewhere.[232] In early February, 'it became clear that' Blair only wanted to focus on asylum and the international situation.[233] Jeremy Heywood said that the 'diary explosion' had caused the cancellation of the drugs and Home Office stocktakes due to take place in early February.[234] The previous week's transport stocktake had also been cancelled, though the upcoming 'spot check meetings' for education in London and A&E were 'preserved from the clearances'.[235] The spot check meetings on the top ten priorities with Blair were additional opportunities for him and Barber to check in and challenge the ministerial teams and Permanent Secretary.[236] In light of the Prime Minister's focus on the volatile foreign agenda, Barber's initial reaction was to adapt: 'This means we need to develop something like the virtual stocktake; a means of driving the agenda forward even if Blair can't find the time. If there's a war this will be essential.'[237] For the immediate cancelled meetings, the PMDU turned the stocktake briefings into notes for the Prime Minister, in which they listed the actions they wanted to take anyway following the stocktake.[238] Nevertheless face-to-face stocktakes were important.

> My plan for future 'cancellations' is for them not to be cancelled. If Blair needs to pull out, he can. We should proceed anyway. Gus [Macdonald] can chair. Alternatively, we can go to the relevant department and let the Secretary of State chair while we make our case, with Blair's backing.[239]

This was a major moment in the PMDU's evolution. It marked the first sign of Blair altering his priorities in light of the foreign policy focus – but would this be temporary or lasting? The PMDU would aim to keep up the momentum but the remedial action was not a permanent fix; the Prime Minister's time and capital remained fundamental to success. Meanwhile in the Home Office the reform plans came to fruition including the appointment of two posts at 'Additional Permanent Secretary' level (often known as 'Second Permanent Secretary') – a commissioner for correctional services in England and Wales, with responsibility for penal policy, probation and youth justice, and a Second Permanent Secretary for crime, policing and counter-terrorism.'[240] Blunkett and Barber had been involved in planning these changes since the autumn. Barber felt John Gieve now had a 'team that has authority and weight'.[241] For Gieve 'it did relieve some of the pressure' on him.[242] Barber found it 'amazing how much effort it took to shift the system'.[243] Gieve reflected on the changes when interviewed – 'I warmed to Michael and his troops because what they were offering was not just another monitoring stick to beat me with, they actually got involved to help you sort things out. They worked on the whole pretty productively.'[244] Gieve was also very aware of the established relationship between the Home Secretary and Barber. The way in which Barber conducted himself made a difference as to whether Gieve saw this as a hindrance or a help.

> [Barber] was very adept at managing the official and the political. The fact that David Blunkett trusted him and had worked really closely with him on education was a huge plus for him in working in the Home Office because otherwise he would have been seen as an intruder. Instead of that David Blunkett, I'm sure, talked to him a lot one-to-one but Michael dealt very well with that. He didn't use it, as others might have, to undermine me either with the rest of the department or undermine my authority by saying 'Well, I've agreed with David that we'll do this' or 'We'll move so and so to such and such'.[245]

This was a revealing assessment from a Permanent Secretary with a vast delivery department in seemingly perpetual crisis. In

---

* In spring 2003, Martin Narey became the first commissioner for correctional services. In 2004, the National Offender Management Service was created and he became its first chief executive. Leigh Lewis was a Second Permanent Secretary in the Home Office, with responsibility for crime, policing and counter-terrorism (2003–05).

mid-February, despite the build-up to war, the centre continued to pursue domestic progress. Barber wrote:

> You might think in the circumstances that No. 10 would sink into a bunker mentality but it absolutely doesn't feel like that to me. We are all very practical, and determined to get things done. In these circumstances the value of a Delivery Unit is very clear indeed.[246]

A TAPESTRY THAT DRIVES IMPROVEMENT

During the period covered in this chapter, Barber started to become a recognisable figure in the media, beginning with his presentation at Blair's July 2002 press conference. The leak at the beginning of 2003 further propelled him into the spotlight, and at the end of February 2003 a new watershed was marked when Barber gave evidence to the Public Administration Select Committee (PASC). PASC, a relatively powerful select committee, was chaired by Labour MP Tony Wright and played a proactive role in monitoring and holding the government to account on issues judged as pertinent by its membership. Barber appeared alongside Macpherson on 27 February; their evidence formed part of the committee's report entitled 'On Target? Government by Measurement'.[247] The committee started its investigation from a number of basic assumptions:

> That the public wants and expects sustained improvements in the delivery of public services, which is also a Government priority; that service providers in receipt of public funds ought to be publicly accountable for their performance; and that setting targets can be one means of stimulating better performance by those who deliver services.[248]

Barber found the committee session itself enjoyable and 'challenging', he felt he 'kept calm under pressure, avoided being defensive and gave true answers'.[249] He thought Macpherson was 'good in emphasising that if we met all our targets, we'd have failed to set targets of sufficient ambition'.[250] Barber began by setting out what he thought was a clear exposition of the concept of how the government was seeking to implement public service reform.

> Targets and league tables and what you call 'government by measurement' are essential parts of an overall approach to achieving that vision. As John Browne put it in his evidence to you, they are part of a 'tapestry' that drives improvement.[251] They cannot be understood in isolation from that wider overall approach.

> 1. Clear national standards and clear targets are what we want to achieve … The national standards are set out in documents like the National Health Service Frameworks … It is up to you at the frontline how to achieve it.
> 2. Devolved funding and responsibility.
> 3. Good bench marking data and measurement of progress against performance indicators …
> 4. Best practice transfer.
> 5. Services should be held to account … Through inspection arrangements … and through published data.
> 6. On the basis of accountability, there are rewards for those who succeed, whether it is earned autonomy [or] foundation status.

> This overall framework of challenge and support is already delivering results. Crime is down significantly; secondary school standards are improved; primary school standards are improved;

mortality rates in cancer and coronary heart disease are greatly improved; waiting times are down.[252]

They were asked about the unintended consequences of targets. Macpherson considered: 'You can sometimes have a good target which may, over time, result in perverse incentives ... the key thing is that you need to learn as you go along.' Barber shared his appreciation of this issue:

The targets are representations of real world outcomes that we want to achieve. I am very familiar with the National Literacy Strategy target of 80 per cent of children getting level four in literacy. The real world outcome you want is children moving to secondary school able to read and write well ... You need to monitor for those perverse consequences as well as what is actually happening on the target and take all that data into account when making judgments about how to go forward.[253]

Macpherson went on to say, 'It is perfectly respectable to fail to hit a target so long as you are bringing about real change in that service.'[254] Barber was asked about the issue of asylum and Blair's commitment on *Newsnight* (7 February 2003) that the government would halve asylum applications by September 2003. Barber had not been consulted on this; he told the committee that it was an aspiration not a target. He added that the Prime Minister 'clearly judged that he wanted to be held to account publicly' for this.[255]

At the end of February, the Blair government faced a significant rebellion in Parliament when 121 Labour MPs broke the three-line whip to support a rebel amendment, which stated that the case for war with Iraq was unproven. The government won the vote, with the support of Conservative MPs. Earlier in the month, on 15 February, there had been a major anti-war march in London as part of coordinated protests around the world.[256] The focus on Iraq was to an extent beginning to drain Blair's time and, critically, his political capital. As Sally Morgan observed, 'Bluntly, after that [Iraq], his position was weaker and that made it more difficult.'[257]

BOLDNESS OF EXECUTION

Over the first weekend in March, the PMDU moved out of 53 Parliament Street and into the newly refurbished Treasury building on Horse Guards Road.[258] While the PMDU was drawing closer to the Chancellor's domain, the Prime Minister's growing attention on Iraq was beginning to create distance between him and his Unit. Barber and Heywood discussed the state of international affairs. Heywood said, 'We won't do anything except Iraq next week'; Barber believed that the 'diplomatic crisis' was reaching its climax.[259] Blair cancelled his attendance at two upcoming stocktakes.[260] The partial withdrawal of Blair's time and attention from PMDU mechanisms was potentially problematic. Yet the picture is complex, as crime and asylum remained domestic priorities for the Prime Minister during this high-intensity period, and the PMDU priority areas were still showing signs of progress. Blair asked Barber what the most recent asylum figures showed. Barber told him they were 'very good'.[261]

Barber met with Alistair Darling and Rachel Lomax, at their request. There had recently been an announcement that Lomax would be leaving the DfT to join the Bank of England. In response to a paper Barber had circulated on Blair's (refined) top ten priorities, Darling complained 'in a calm, modest tone as ever – about the excessive demands the centre made on his department'.[262] In communicating the Prime Minister's writ, the PMDU was evidently being critiqued as part of Blair's centralised style of governing, which affected ministerial autonomy. Barber gave his view that 'where there was a problem, the first responsibility for solving it lay with the department'.[263] Lomax was very positive about the PMDU and Barber believed that it had 'made a major contribution to changing both behaviours and beliefs in the department'.[264] Darling agreed to a PMDU priority review into rail delays.[265]

The issue of Iraq continued to grow in significance and attract further protest. Pressure on Blair from the left was mounting, 'many MPs had resolutions from their local party which would make their room for manoeuvre very limited', there was discussion of a leadership challenge, but the Parliamentary Labour Party was 'very cool' about it.[266] Barber continued to drive delivery, but he understood that for the moment the Prime Minister's 'agenda is Iraq, not delivery'.[267] Though Blair was focused on the international scene there continued to be battles about the scope and nature of the choice agenda. A 'major row' was caused because the Treasury still objected to Blair's announcement, in January, about 'the national roll out of choice at six months in the NHS'.[268] The Treasury team were frustrated 'because there had been an agreement that the London pilot ... should be evaluated by the Delivery Unit before its extension'.[269] Blair's health adviser, Simon Stevens, claimed that the 'decision to roll out choice was taken at the January health stocktake'; Barber pondered whether this was 'a calculated bounce' by No. 10.[270] Barber's view was that 'in the end if the Prime Minister wants to do something he should do it'; moreover the move was 'consistent' with the manifesto commitment and the April 2002 health strategy paper.[271] Nevertheless, at a meeting on the issue Balls was 'clearly furious'; Stevens outlined the No. 10 case, Heywood said it 'was done and it was all about the process from now on'.[272] Barber's contribution brought some consensus (or at least deferred further arguments): 'Everyone was agreed that the Delivery Unit should assess both the deliverability and affordability of the national rollout of the pilot … It leaves me with the problem (which I relish) of reporting in a way which wins the approval of two irreconcilable positions.'[273] To remain on the tightrope Barber would have to continue to hone his acrobatic skills.

THE ENGINE ROOM OF DELIVERY

The international crisis on Iraq continued to escalate and on 18 March the government put forward an emergency motion allowing for military action there. A nine-and-a-half-hour debate in the House of Commons followed and the motion was passed by 412 votes to 149.[274] This was a divisive and historic time for the country and the world. For Barber 'it meant a week in the engine room of delivery'.[275] The PMDU was doing exactly what it had been created to do: 'It was our job to sustain progress; it was a challenge to rise to, not a barrier to run into.'[276] Part of its ability to do that was the Prime Minister's commitment, and so despite Blair's present focus being elsewhere Barber sought to motivate PMDU staff and their departmental colleagues.

> [I told them that] the Prime Minister was no less interested in delivery at the moment – he just had less time for it and when his focus returns to it, I want to be able to demonstrate that we've solved this problem … I don't want him to come back to it all and have the overwhelming sense that nothing has changed.[277]

Blair would no longer attend the next health stocktake; instead, a meeting of the relevant civil servants, chaired by Barber, would take place in Permanent Secretary Nigel Crisp's office.[278] Importantly, the substitute stocktake, albeit without Blair, enabled the PMDU to 'keep the pressure on'.[279] On 19 March, the day after the Iraq vote, Barber attended PSX, with Alan Milburn 'as it were, in the dock'.[280] To Barber's surprise, the 'interrogations didn't involve a row over choice'.[281] There was a debate on waiting times, in which Brown brought Barber in on two occasions to explain what the 'major anxieties were'.[282] Barber's knowledge of the state of delivery was evidently of value to the Chancellor.

Barber met with Crisp for an informal evening meeting to discuss the PMDU's relationship with the Department of Health. The meeting proved to be an opportunity for honest, open conversation, to share 'worries' and 'reassure' one another to an extent.[283] This was fundamentally important to maintain the application of deliverology. Barber mused after the meeting that 'it's easy in the intense world we live in to become paranoid – but the only thing you can do in fact is get on with the job and work away at maintaining relationships'.[284] As part of his delivery brief and his own concern, Barber maintained a deep interest in education policy. In March, he met with the education team responsible for planning the implementation of the new leadership incentive grant; Barber found their plans 'utterly traditional' in method, and he noted the lack of 'institutional memory'.[285] Meanwhile this was a critical turning point on the impending question of military action in Iraq.

On 17 March, a 'special' meeting of the Cabinet was held; Blair told his ministers that the 'diplomatic process was now at an end'; the Cabinet 'endorsed the decision to give Saddam Hussein an ultimatum to leave Iraq and to ask the House of Commons to endorse the use of military action, if necessary, against Iraq'.[286] Later that day, President Bush issued an 'ultimatum giving Saddam Hussein 48 hours to leave Iraq'.[287] Robin Cook resigned from the Cabinet. The following day, the House of Commons approved a government motion seeking support for the decision that Britain 'should use all necessary means to ensure the disarmament of Iraq's weapons of mass destruction'.[288] On 20 March, the invasion of Iraq began.[289] US forces seized Baghdad International Airport by early April and on 1 May, Bush made his 'Mission Accomplished' speech and declared: 'Major combat operations in Iraq have ended. In the battle of Iraq, the United States and our allies have prevailed. And now our Coalition is engaged in securing and reconstructing that country.'[290] In late March, Barber described the impact of the conflict on the centre. 'It feels like business as usual to be honest except that there's a War Cabinet meeting every day.'[291] Barber was 'optimistic ... that delivery was beginning to become apparent and the influence of the Delivery Unit [was] a key part of that'.[292] In education, Barber's relationship with Charles Clarke continued to grow. He attended a dinner with Clarke and others including Permanent Secretary David Normington and minister of state David Miliband, where they debated the testing regime in schools; the next day Barber chaired the education stocktake.[293]

During the following week, Blair showed that he had entrusted the pursuit of the delivery agenda to Barber and was reassured in this knowledge. Barber saw Blair in Downing Street. Blair asked, 'How's the Home Front?' Barber replied, 'There's been no loss of momentum.' 'Glad to hear it,' the Prime Minister said.[294] Barber was pleased to record, in early April, that 'most of the indicators of progress pointed in the right direction – perhaps the start of a decisive shift in favour of delivery?'[295] The Prime Minister seemed to be personally re-engaging with the delivery agenda. Blair's confidence in the Delivery Unit may not have been as resolute if there had not already been early progress on street crime and asylum. Barber felt that 'if the [Iraq] war had been a year earlier it might have been more of a struggle'.[296] On 9 April, which was also Budget Day, Blair chaired the asylum round-up – 'the only meeting of its kind' that he had done in the last six weeks.[297] There was 'good news to report', and Blair recognised the progress that had been made but remained 'authoritative and demanding'.[298] The 2003 Budget was not one of the prominent Budgets during the period covered in this book: 2002 had been the major Budget of the parliament. In his 2003 Budget speech, Brown emphasised his commitment to maintain the investment in public services, and he discussed the progress made so far as well as the comparative economic strength of the country.[299]

CONCLUSION: ENTRENCHING THE DELIVERY UNIT

During this period – from April 2002 to the 2003 Budget – the PMDU arguably became entrenched in some of the most important processes and machinery of government. Barber formed stable working relationships with the new Secretaries of State for education and transport. There were worries over duplication and friction between Barber and the new Cabinet Secretary but they did not materialise. Richard Wilson had set a positive tone for engaging with Barber and Andrew Turnbull maintained this; their relationship was largely predicated on a shared focus of best practice on delivery matters. At the end of this period, Barber faced getting to know another new Permanent Secretary in the DfT.

The inclusion of the PMDU in the planning of the 2002 spending review was not pre-destined, though Barber had secured the trust of the Treasury and it saw value in the PMDU machinery. John Gieve, Permanent Secretary to the Home Office and former managing director of public services in the Treasury, commented that 'the PMDU improved the discussion over public services within government massively'.[300] The head of a prime ministerial unit that was just twelve months old was at the top table of decision-making along with the other most senior policy advisers to the Prime Minister and Chancellor, negotiating the next spending review.

As a result of the preparation for war and eventual invasion of Iraq, Barber and the PMDU had to adapt the art of delivery. To their credit, departments continued to collaborate. Blair started to re-engage in the delivery routines in early April 2003. In the intervening period, the Delivery Unit had persisted with the 'optical illusion' of an engaged Prime Minister.[301] The crisis had shown the value of a Delivery Unit.

A striking feature of this period was the deepening of Barber's relationship with Brown, yet this was a balancing act. Barber had to consider the political intrigue of the time, which could interpret a closeness to the Chancellor as tantamount to a distancing from the Prime Minister. With hindsight, Barber characterised the end of this period, spring 2003, as the time when deliverology reached a tipping point, though they did not know it at the time.[302]

CHAPTER SIX

APRIL 2003 TO THE 2004 BUDGET: MAKING PROGRESS, SACRIFICING POLITICAL CAPITAL

In early April 2003, the invasion of Iraq reached a turning point, when US forces seized Baghdad International Airport. Some in the media spoke of a 'Baghdad bounce' for the Prime Minister:

> Seven days ago, most commentators insisted that he was on the verge of another 'Vietnam War', today they are absorbed with the domestic aftermath of military victory. How big, they are asking, will Mr Blair's 'Baghdad bounce' be; how long will it last and what will he do with it?[1]

The progress achieved on public services while the media and the Prime Minister were focused on foreign policy was also noted: 'The coldest winter in most parts of Britain for more than a decade did not bring the NHS to its knees as a milder snap did three years ago.'[2] Inside government, Blair's re-engagement with the Delivery Unit in early April 2003 was a promising sign but things had not gone back to normal. Prime ministerial involvement had been critical to the PMDU's success and questions remained over the extent to which Blair would continue to commit to mechanisms such as stocktakes. How would he balance his foreign agenda with his ambitious public service reforms? How committed would he be to the existing domestic agenda, which had been set out but not yet fully implemented? During this time of flux, how would Barber bolster the relationships, routines and reputation of the Delivery Unit?

APRIL TO SEPTEMBER 2003

THE DISCIPLINE OF DELIVERY: THE END OF THE BEGINNING

Over the Easter break, Barber wrote notes for both the Prime Minister and the Chancellor, the former a series of 'Easter Reflections' and the latter a 'draft framework' for a speech Brown was to give at a PMDU conference at the end of April. In doing so he reflected on his relatively uncommon position: 'I'm one of the few people with the trust of both Blair and Brown, and with the capacity to communicate directly without undue deference' to both.[3] In writing to Blair, Barber posited his growing sense that 'the discipline of delivery is beginning to work.'[4] He quoted Churchill: 'This is not the end. It is not even the beginning of the end. But it may be the end of the beginning.'[5] There had been early progress on the crime, asylum and health targets and Barber concluded that 'if we kept up the drive for delivery, early progress now could turn into decisive progress a year from now and irreversible progress by early 2005'.[6] This was arguably a call from Barber to the Prime Minister to re-engage fully and trust the process. Improvements in the quality of public services were being recognised in the media. Journalist Will Hutton wrote that 'things are getting better in health, education and the fight against crime', though transport was 'notably excepted'.[7]

The Progress in International Reading Survey involving 140,000 10-year-old children in 35 countries, reported that England came third ... and for reading fiction joint top ...

The National Crime Survey ... in 2002 overall crime fell by 9% – an 11% fall in domestic burglary [and] a 17% fall in vehicle theft ... The risk of being a victim was at a 20-year low ...

For the first time in 10 years the numbers of people waiting to be admitted to hospital in England has fallen below a million; only 63 patients waited more than twelve months while 80% of patients spent less than four hours in A&E departments. Deaths from heart disease have fallen by 14% and deaths from cancer have fallen by 6% since 1997.[8]

The article also namechecked the PMDU as a contributor to progress and explained the Unit's role in adapting the culture of the Civil Service.

The ultimate sanction ... for Permanent Secretaries, is to be grilled by the Prime Minister about why their department is not performing. What this has generated is the first beginnings of a notable change in culture. Permanent Secretaries are transmuting from administrators and policy advisers into chief executives whose role is to raise their organisation's performance and meet delivery targets; they talk the managerial language of organisational change processes [and] performance management.[9]

Blair's refocusing on delivery was evident when on Easter Sunday he called Barber to check the progress of his delivery priorities and to discuss the integration of delivery back into his diary in the coming months. He said, 'I want to re-enter on these [issues] pretty strongly.'[10] The Prime Minister's attention was also beginning to be drawn to another perspective. Sally Morgan, then director of government relations in No. 10, explained that Blair 'was starting to focus on … [his] legacy: "What are the next big issues I ought to be doing?"'[11] The tension between Blair's tendency to focus on searching for new policy ideas rather than to concentrate on delivering the existing agenda was one that Barber had noticed. It was a feature of Blair's governing style which Barber periodically questioned. But this is arguably the nature of politics; an astute leader needs to simultaneously ensure the delivery of their current agenda while planning the next stage of reform.

Though the focus of this book is how the Prime Minister's Delivery Unit helped to transform the quality of public services, this endeavour did not happen in a vacuum. The matter of whether Britain should join the single currency, the euro, was a major debate between No. 10 and the Treasury, and undoubtedly a historic decision. At the time the new currency was used by twelve of the fifteen EU member states. The Treasury developed five key economic tests which the British economy would have to pass before joining the euro. In October 1997, the Chancellor ruled out Britain joining the EU's Economic and Monetary Union before 1999, as the government's five tests had not all been met. In 2001, Brown said the tests would be repeated and the results would be published within two years. By this point, the Prime Minister was pro-euro, his enthusiasm having grown during the second term, whereas the Chancellor had been keen to join in 1997 but by 2003 he was 'ambivalent' (at best).[12] On 9 June 2003, Brown announced that after another assessment the conditions for Britain's entrance to the Eurozone had not yet been met.[13] Britain would not join the euro. This major decision affected the climate in which the Delivery Unit operated, not least because it was a divisive issue for Blair and Brown.

In April 2003, Barber had an encouraging conversation about delivery in the Home Office with David Blunkett. They were both relieved that there was progress on asylum. Blunkett spoke of his desire to accomplish the levels of progress that they had achieved together in the first term.[14] Indeed, Barber reflected, 'I felt we were comrades-in-arms and indeed I feel our collaboration has been hugely influential in relation to the Home Office as more obviously it was in education.'[15] Meanwhile, in health Blair wanted to 'shift from the command-and-control state to the enabling state'.[16] As Secretary of State for Health, Alan Milburn echoed this view. He saw the developing public service reform agenda as

> emblematic of a big change for the Labour Party, which is a change really in how we saw the role of the state. I worked out that it wasn't really going to work if I was trying to run everything [in Health]. The people who needed to run everything were the local managers, the local doctors, the local nurses with [as much] input from local communities and local patients as possible. We were trying to change what the state did and how it did it. From one that was a controlling, to (in the shorthand) a more enabling state.[17]

Blair had used the 'enabling state' concept in his 2002 party conference speech and Barber had built his subsequent presentation to the Cabinet on delivery around this. In his 2002 speech, Blair outlined his vision for the enabling state.

> People want an individual service for them ... They want government to empower them, not control them. And they want

equality of both opportunity and responsibility. They want to know the same rules that apply to them apply to all. Out goes the Big State. In comes the Enabling State.'[18]

Barber felt that this language was now in the 'bloodstream of government'.[19] In his view, this had 'reinforced the sense of Blair returning vigorously to the domestic policy agenda'.[20] It certainly signalled Blair's continued ambition to reinvigorate Britain's public services. Milburn saw Blair's shift as a strategic change that was 'about making Labour relevant, not in terms of its values or its principles but the way it went about prosecuting them'.[21] In retrospect, he saw this as the most important of Blair's strategic changes.

[It] was about distinguishing between means and ends. That's the thing where political parties tend to get entangled. The ends are consistent, Labour is and has always been, and I hope always will be, a party that believes in redistributing opportunity and a party of social justice and fairness. But honestly values are the cheapest currency in politics, we can all make a speech about how we are a fair party, and we believe in social justice. What counts is whether you can actually do anything about it, and whether you have got the means to bring them about. And the means change because the world changes. It just does. So, you are continually having to recalibrate. And, of course, people are looking at you and thinking, 'Well you're selling it all out because you are changing your means.' But actually you remain unrelentingly focused on the ends.

---

* Labour leader Neil Kinnock used this phrase, 'the enabling state', in his 1985 party conference speech. 'An enabling state, which is at the disposal of the people instead of being dominant over the people … properly funding the system of justice and opportunity and care.'

A THREAT TO THE DELIVERY UNIT

At the end of April, the impact of Blair's absence from the PMDU mechanisms manifested itself in a way which deeply worried Barber. During the invasion of Iraq and the run-up to it, Blair had withdrawn from chairing stocktakes; instead of the stocktake a replacement meeting would go ahead with Lord Macdonald or Barber in the chair. After the conflict ended one would expect Blair to resume chairing stocktakes. But Jeremy Heywood informed Barber that Sally Morgan had 'advised the Prime Minister that the stocktakes went so well' with Barber and Macdonald 'running them during the war, that he doesn't need to do them anymore'.[22] This would enable Blair 'to do what he hankered after which is freeing up more of his diary to think'; he had found 'that freedom from routine meetings during the war had been very liberating'.[23] Heywood did not agree with Morgan's view but was worried that the decision had been taken.[24] Barber put the arguments to Heywood about the signals that such a move could send. The message of 'giving up on the stocktakes to Whitehall would be that either the PM had lost interest or he had become complacent.'[25] Though Barber recognised the Prime Minister's desire to have more time and had 'anticipated that the war would change his perceptions', he believed that such a decision 'threatened to destroy the capacity of the Delivery Unit to do the job he set it up to do'.[26]

A pragmatic Barber aimed to adapt. An options paper was submitted to the Prime Minister, which he shared with Heywood and Morgan. He suggested that they could get 'most of the leverage [in Whitehall], if not all, provided by the stocktakes while saving Blair 60–70% of his time'.[27] They could do this by

[Blair] chairing three stocktakes a year instead of six [per delivery department], with the other three being chaired by me [Barber] and the permanent secretary leading for the department; by dropping the Blair led stocktakes outside the main four departments; and reorganising the way we do drugs and CJS [criminal justice system] – using the Cabinet committees better; and having two wider meetings a year at which Blair can drive change not just with the ministers present but with frontline managers present too.[28]

Barber also pointed out in the paper that if Blair 'pulls out of the stocktakes, he would in effect cede all control over delivery to PSX, in other words, to Gordon. Can this possibly be in his personal interest?'[29] It was canny to highlight the practical implications of the decision on the power balance within the New Labour duopoly. Barber felt confident that he could 'convince Blair of the need to sustain, in the new slimline form, the stocktake programme' because 'it was he, not I who told the electorate the day after the last election, that they had issued him an instruction to deliver'.[30] Barber secured Cabinet Secretary Andrew Turnbull's support.[31] He awaited the Prime Minister's decision.

A Delivery Unit conference for 400 analysts took place on 30 April, which had been planned jointly with the Treasury. Barber and the PMDU's chief analyst, Tony O'Connor, opened the event. The Permanent Secretary to the Treasury, Gus O'Donnell, led the afternoon portion of the event and Brown 'delivered a message to the participants in a brief video clip, which included ... advocacy of "maximum choice possible"'.[32] Such events were important in disseminating and promoting the PMDU methodology – particularly the value of data.

REASSESSING DELIVEROLOGY

Barber received an email to say that Blair's weekly Monday morning meeting 'would no longer take place – it would be a diary meeting' and Barber 'wouldn't be required'. He read this as 'a setback' for him.[33] This meeting had become a central way for Barber to stay in the loop. On 6 May, Barber met with Blair in his office to discuss the future of stocktakes. Prior to the meeting he had checked Morgan's views and she had been 'supportive' of Barber's proposal.[34] Blair said he was 'happy' with what had been proposed and 'was obviously glad to gain the time that would come with only chairing three stocktakes a year with the big four departments' and with no others, as he had been doing during autumn 2002 and until early 2003.[35] This was a major decision in the Delivery Unit's favour; a crisis had been averted. As Barber said during an interview reflecting on this episode, 'being flexible' about how you work with the Prime Minister 'is fundamentally important'.[36] Moreover, from Barber's perspective it made the PMDU 'more steely, more focused, less distracted'.[37] This acknowledgement by Barber is significant. Barber had gone against his original design principles in widening the priorities that the PMDU surveyed, and thus the Prime Minister focused on. It was a problem of success. Prudence had to be reinstated when the larger portfolio began to jeopardise the core work of the PMDU.

Jonathan Powell commented that 'engaging the Prime Minister on a regular, but not persistent, basis' was an essential part of what made the Delivery Unit work.[38] In Powell's view, the stocktakes brought value because they allowed 'the Prime Minister to really get his teeth into the subject and sort out problems there and then at the table, rather than [by] endless correspondence between departments'.[39] Barber further cemented his own position by excluding Macdonald from chairing stocktakes in the updated proposals. He wanted to 'enhance' his own 'influence' and as a precaution against Macdonald being replaced in a ministerial reshuffle, which was due shortly; though none of this was explicitly discussed with Blair.[40] Barber's inclination about Macdonald's position proved to be correct when soon after this episode, the minister of state for the Cabinet Office announced his intention to stand down at the next reshuffle.[41]

At a meeting with the Home Office on drugs strategy, Barber discussed the impact of the Delivery Unit with Martin Narey, the commissioner for correctional services. Narey said that 'the disciplines the Delivery Unit had advocated were beginning to work and that it now seemed incredible that we managed for so long without them'.[42] This was a notable comment by a senior civil servant; it reflected how well embedded the PMDU now was in Whitehall. By mid-May, Blair having re-established his focus on 'driving the delivery agenda' through PMDU mechanisms, there were five stocktakes and Barber was working with the Prime Minister and his close advisers on the reform agenda in education and health.[43] Nevertheless he personally felt 'the classic paranoia of being at court. Was I in or was I out?'[44] He recognised that the 'increasing success on delivery will make it less interesting to Blair whose focus is inevitably on problems'.[45] This was a perceptive observation and arguably partially explained Blair's fluctuating focus on PMDU routines.

Barber chaired an official-level health stocktake (without Blair), while Permanent Secretary Nigel Crisp led for the department. The meeting took place in the No. 10 State Dining Room rather than in the Cabinet Room.[46] It was a productive meeting. Barber felt that he and his PMDU team were 'well-prepared' and asked 'challenging questions'; in response Crisp and his team were 'well-informed too and refreshingly open, all defensiveness apparently gone'.[47] Later that day, Blair chaired a drugs stocktake.[48]

ROLLING OUT THE CHOICE AGENDA IN HEALTH

Barber contributed to a meeting Blair held with his close No. 10 advisers – Adonis, Heywood, Morgan and Stevens – on the expansion of the choice agenda in health into wider areas of primary and secondary care. Primary care (GP service) is the first point of contact with the NHS for many people, but at the time most GPs' surgeries only operated during normal working hours (9 a.m.–5 p.m.). This caused issues for working people who needed appointments outside that time frame. Secondary care is largely defined as hospital care for planned (elective) and urgent operations, or emergency care. The New Labour reforms brought a higher expectation of the quality and speed of care provided by the NHS than ever before; such centrally set targets for services such as A&E waiting times and elective surgery waiting times did not previously exist. In part, the choice agenda was focused on the outcomes, such as the quality and speed of care, rather than maintaining the state as a monopoly provider. The plan was to offer consumers a choice of provider, for example to offer the choice to travel further to a private sector provider but to be treated more quickly. In the first stage, Blair's reforms aimed to use alternative providers (private and third sector) to bring down waiting times for routine elective operations, which would create more capacity. This sounded straightforward but the complexity came because it would require costing, piloting, evaluating and developing a national plan (with PMDU stress-testing), then the introduction of a choice and diversity of providers for each part of the NHS, like different types of elective surgery. Such a process was necessary because once the government committed publicly to providing this type of service nationally, the NHS would need to deliver to meet heightened public expectations.

The PMDU played a role in reconciling the differences between No. 10, Health and the Treasury on the deliverability of the national implementation of choice for patients. Commenting on this, Ed Balls later noted, 'The reality was that we would genuinely want the Delivery Unit's view.'[49] He added that additional motives within the Treasury were 'partly to slow things down a little bit and partly to sort of throw back at them, that if you've got this Delivery Unit you'd better make sure they've looked at it.'[50] The Treasury had insisted that the PMDU test the deliverability before national implementation. The PMDU's report said that the policy plan was 'deliverable but there are risks that have to be managed; and that the work so far suggests it's affordable but the analysis is not yet complete'.[51] Brown stated in his memoir that he 'was not against the use of the private sector when it was in the interests of patients to secure services'.[52] A tripartite agreement was reached on process – Barber would write to Crisp the following day, 'consulting No. 10 and Treasury on the draft', and the Chief Secretary to the Treasury, Paul Boateng, would write to Milburn to endorse Barber's conclusions and state the need to keep 'within existing resources'.[53] A Treasury official commented on how well Barber and the PMDU 'handled things'; for Barber the lesson was that 'if you build the trust and concentrate on the evidence and analysis you can avoid a Blair–Brown fight'.[54]

A NEW STAGE

Throughout May, Barber played an active role in the planning and presentation of the proposed changes to education funding – to recentralise funding powers, which at the time were controlled by local education authorities (LEAs). He had advocated this since 1999. The Prime Minister along with Adonis and Heywood in No. 10, Clarke and Miliband in the DfES, and the Treasury were involved in this debate. It gave Barber the opportunity to strengthen his personal relations with Blair.

At the end of May, David Rowlands was appointed as the new Permanent Secretary in the Department for Transport to replace Rachel Lomax. Rowlands had been director general for railways in the department. Barber thought he was knowledgeable and experienced but believed his 'attitude' to delivery was 'too passive'.[55] He met with Rowlands and Richard Bowker, the chairman and chief executive of the Strategic Rail Authority,* to discuss the 'static' progress of average rail reliability for the past twelve months.[56] Barber felt that Bowker was defensive and sought to resist the Delivery Unit's 'attempts to get involved in assisting on the grounds' that it was micromanagement.[57] In Barber's view, this along with 'departmental weakness' made tackling the issue difficult; it was one of Blair's top issues and progress was slow. In the two years since the PMDU had been created, there had been a lot of disruption and change in the DfT: major crises – the collapse of Railtrack and the fallout, and the political scandal of the Jo Moore and Martin Sixsmith affairs – two Secretaries of State and three Permanent Secretaries; and the splitting of the department in May 2002. This had been destabilising and progress on delivery had slowed. To Bowker's worries about micromanagement and caution over getting back on trajectory, Barber said, 'It's about you as Chief Executive convincing

---

*   The SRA set the strategic direction for the rail industry's planning service delivery and the development of the railway network and had sizeable funding powers.

your major shareholder (the PM) that the industry is really moving forward.'[58] He continued:

> Too often it seems as if improvements in performance are always promised next year but never actually arrive ... I can only give a strong account in the [next] Delivery Report if you give me the evidence ... When I compare this relationship to those in other [policy] areas it's still too distant ... We need to move the relationship on to the next stage.[59]

Barber's attitude was firm but conciliatory. Bowker agreed to a joint piece of work on how they could create extra 'indicators' for tracking change on a more regular basis.[60] Barber met with the Secretary of State for Transport, Alistair Darling, for a stocktake the following week; he approved the joint piece of work and concurred with Barber's approach.[61]

UNSATISFACTORY ACCESS AND USING UP SOCIAL AND POLITICAL CAPITAL

In early June, a one-to-one meeting Barber had scheduled with the Prime Minister was cancelled. Barber was unhappy with this and wrote to Blair's diary secretary, copying Heywood and Powell, to say that 'opportunities to talk to the PM about delivery were being steadily eroded – Monday briefings, stocktakes and now this meeting, which we had agreed to have in order to save the Prime Minister's time'.[62] He finished by saying that he 'was doing a pretty good job of maintaining the "optical illusion" of a Prime Minister constantly interested in delivery but for how long?'[63] A meeting was scheduled for the following week. Although the invasion of Iraq was completed in a relatively short period of time the fallout would last far longer. In early June, Barber reflected on the fact that evidence of weapons of mass destruction (WMDs) had still not been found in Iraq. This was a major topic of debate in the media, along with questions over the validity of a government dossier from September 2002 that had said Iraq had WMDs which could be launched within forty-five minutes.[64] Both assessments had been used as a basis for the invasion. Barber believed that the Prime Minister's 'trust factor' would be 'permanently tarnished', though he accepted that 'politics is a messy brutal business in which decisions have to be made on the basis of incomplete information'.[65]

The Cabinet Secretary, Andrew Turnbull, appraised Barber's progress in his performance management meeting in early June. He spoke of the PMDU's success and asked Barber, 'Why do you think the Treasury didn't develop a serious approach to delivery before you did?'

'I think perhaps I should ask you that question, Andrew,' Barber responded.[66]

When reflecting on this in an interview, Ed Balls commented that 'that's what we thought the Treasury was and that's what we thought the Treasury was being changed to … This was a very evolutionary process, we were learning as we went along.'[67] Indeed performance-monitoring and progress-chasing were largely part of the Treasury's role prior to the creation of the Delivery Unit.

On 12 June, there was a ministerial reshuffle instigated because Alan Milburn wanted to resign as Secretary of State for Health to spend more time with his young family.[68] This in itself could have had a significant impact on the bold direction and delivery of the health reforms. Milburn had been resolute in propelling the reforms that he and Blair had advocated, even at the cost of tense disagreements with Brown and the Treasury. Barber believed

Milburn had been 'the best' in the role since Aneurin Bevan, who had served as minister of health from 1945 to 1951 and presided over the creation of the NHS in 1948.[69] Reflecting on his tenure, Milburn sought to explain the balance between the supply side and demand side reforms he had pursued, and the underpinning values of equality that shaped his vision.

> The critical choice wasn't really about the supply side. People conflate these different levers. The truth is, the supply side changes, i.e. bringing in more competition and more capability from the private sector, more capacity from the private sector, those were supply side changes. What you were trying to also do is change the demand side. And the demand side changes were about empowering the patient to make the choices that they wanted to make ... My vision was, I wanted the individual NHS patient to have as much choice as the individual private sector patient, who could use the cash nexus to pay for treatment. We didn't want to use the cash nexus, we wanted to use the choice nexus to make it egalitarian and equal for people. The biggest change, I think, that I would have loved to have seen followed through, after my time, was about how you expanded patient choice as the principal driver [of reform], and not really how you expanded the role of the private sector. People have fixated about the role of the private sector, because it's ideological, right? But really what you want is the demand side from individual patients to make the system much more attuned to the needs of the consumer, rather than its own.[70]

Milburn's replacement, John Reid, was a formidable Cabinet minister and a Blairite, though health was a new brief for him. Reid had handled various policy areas since 1997 and most recently he had replaced Robin Cook (who had resigned two months earlier) as leader of the House of Commons and Lord President of the Council. Gus Macdonald stood down as planned and Douglas Alexander became minister for the Cabinet Office, though Alexander's role did not include ministerial oversight of the PMDU as Macdonald's had. According to Heywood, Blair trusted Barber to 'deputise for him on delivery'; this was a significant indication of trust.[71] Barber met Reid in mid-June to review the state of the health reforms. Reid was 'honest about his ignorance' of health policy but said, 'Tony wants me to do it, I'll give it my best shot.'[72] Helpfully the longstanding special adviser in DH Paul Corrigan remained in post and informed Reid that the PMDU was 'an ally in helping the Secretary of State to get the Department to do its job'.[73] This commendation was of great value to Barber in establishing good relations with the new Secretary of State. Barber left the meeting 'impressed with Reid's sharpness', and they agreed to meet every two weeks.[74] Reid said that when he had been in the DfT he had employed Bechtel* as project manager for the Channel Tunnel Rail Link (HS1) and he wanted Barber and the PMDU 'to be his Bechtel for the Health Service'.[75] As a Cabinet minister of a delivery department, Reid evidently saw the value in using the PMDU as a tool to achieve his goals.

Barber had a meeting with Blair on the Top Ten delivery priorities:

1. Rail
2. Congestion

---

* Bechtel, founded in the US in 1898, is a major construction and civil engineering company.

3. A&E
4. Waiting, booking and choice in health
5. Secondary education in London
6. Key Stage 2
7. Volume crime
8. Street crime
9. Asylum
10. Drugs[76]

They discussed options for an updated set of priorities and the non-core areas which the PMDU spent 20 per cent of its time on, such as the Department of Trade and Industry, the Department for Work and Pensions, the Department for Environment, Food and Rural Affairs and the Office of the Deputy Prime Minister.[77] Blair was engaged and agreed that Barber should give an updated delivery presentation to Cabinet. He was 'happy with progress on health and worried about transport and drugs'.[78] Around this time Barber was considering the next phase for the Delivery Unit.

> It became clear to me ... that we have as a Unit experienced the tipping point in the last few months. Until last year we had a system, good relations, priorities and a few good stories of delivery. Now though we've got delivery across the board. We demonstrated that our theories – based of course on practice elsewhere – work in practice in government.[79]

But as they pursued progress on delivery more intensively, Barber knew that presently solid working relationships would be tested: 'In some areas, for example, crime or [pupil] attendance and behaviour we should not fear to use up social capital in Whitehall to get the delivery we believe is necessary.'[80]

BRIDGING THE GAP, AN INDICATION OF TRUST

At the end of an asylum round-up meeting on 19 June, Blair said to Barber: 'Gordon and I have been talking about the reform agenda. We'd like you to pull together a series of meetings with people from here and the Treasury to thrash the issues out.'[81] This potentially significant role was a recognition of Barber's skill in being able to bridge the gap between Brown and Blair (and their respective courts) on some contentious aspects of public service reform. Indeed, Nicholas Macpherson characterised Barber as 'someone who helped deflate rows rather than create them'.[82] Jeremy Heywood drafted a letter for Brown's office which stated:

> The Prime Minister and the Chancellor of the Exchequer have had a number of discussions in recent weeks about the Government's forthcoming policy agenda ... The Prime Minister is now keen to reach detailed agreement with the Chancellor on key [domestic] policy issues ... Given the importance of these issues for the delivery agenda ... the Prime Minister has suggested that Michael Barber might convene a series of meetings with the key No. 10/Treasury staff.[83]

The meetings of what became known as the Reform Agenda Group would be chaired by Barber and attended by Heywood and Andrew Adonis from No. 10, and Ed Balls, Gus O'Donnell or Macpherson and Mark Bowman (Brown's principal private secretary) from the Treasury.[84] Barber recognised that this would be a 'critical phase' for him: after 'all the distraction' Blair had reconnected with delivery and trusted Barber; he felt he was 'in the centre of things again, perhaps more so than ever'.[85] Sally Morgan recognised that the idea of such a forum was 'absolutely what was needed' because 'you can't in the end move a reform agenda forward if the Treasury aren't engaged'.[86]

Ahead of the first meeting of the Reform Agenda Group, Barber met with Balls. Barber wanted to 'deal with the issues directly and try to reduce the tension'.[87] He gave clear messages – he would see if he could add value and if he did not Balls should tell him. Barber would seek to bring his 'expertise to bear and be prepared, if necessary, to go back to the PM, to tell him about delivery or affordability issues which blocked announcements'.[88] In response, Balls cautioned Barber against damaging his relationship with Macpherson and said it was a 'huge risk' to get involved because it could 'undermine' Barber's 'objectivity'.[89] Revealingly Balls warned Barber against 'coming between the "official" Treasury and the "political" Treasury'.[90] He also emailed Heywood 'to complain about an "official" chairing these meetings'.[91] Balls was keen to establish that Barber's 'equivalent' was Macpherson, not him, and referred to Barber as a 'Cabinet Office official'.[92] Balls had, however, been content for several years to broker Blair–Brown compromises with Heywood, who was also an official. He was seemingly dissatisfied with the creation of this new forum. Concluding the pre-meeting Balls said, 'It's a brave man who puts himself between the Prime Minister and the Chancellor.'[93] Barber replied, 'That's not the task ... it's to serve both of them,' but Balls disagreed with this as Barber left.[94] The challenge and risk involved for Barber were significant.

A FORUM FOR RESOLUTION?

The first official meeting of the Reform Agenda Group took place on 26 June. Macpherson could not attend but met with Barber afterwards.[95] Blair called Barber at the end of the week and received an update: the meeting had gone well; they went 'through the issues and made some progress'; they had 'opened up longer term issues including wider choice in health'.[96] On the use of the private sector in health, there seemed to Barber 'to be a meeting of minds'; Balls said the Treasury 'weren't ideologically opposed', Heywood said 'Blair wasn't ideologically in favour' of using the private sector in the Health Service.[97] This was indicative of the nuanced divisions over public service reform between Blair and Brown – deliverability and affordability were important but so were the ideological differences (and suspicions) on both sides. That they discussed these at this first meeting marked a degree of validation for this group as a forum for collective discussion and potentially resolution.

Barber joined a meeting convened by Blair in No. 10 on the topic of how to regain momentum; those present included Adonis, Campbell, Heywood, Morgan, Powell, Peter Mandelson and Philip Gould.[98] Campbell's recollection of the meeting, as recorded in his diary, was that 'TB wanted desperately for us to get back on the domestic agenda'.[99] The message from the Prime Minister's perspective was 'that we were doing things that would make us unpopular in the short term but deliver results in the long term'.[100]

A THREAT TO PROGRESS

In early July, the PMDU's relationship with the Treasury stalled over the former's involvement in the implementation of the next stage of the choice agenda in health. In late May, the PMDU had 'calmly' signed the Treasury up to their analysis of the 'affordability and deliverability' of choice for patients who had been on the waiting list for six months. They had then taken it through a meeting with Balls and others, and exchanged ministerial letters between the Treasury, Health and the PMDU.[101] Barber thought they would 'do the same' with their assessment of choice at the point of GP referral but this did not prove to be the case.[102] The PMDU team working on this informed Barber that the Treasury was 'in retreat': they did not want to sign up to the PMDU report as they thought '"Treasury ministers [*sic*]" (which is a euphemism for Ed Balls) would want to include in the letter a requirement that there be no more announcements on this subject until they had agreed the policy'.[103] The Treasury was evidently delaying this specific policy until it felt sufficiently consulted on the overall strategy for health reform. Barber intervened; he would not allow the Treasury to be officially recognised (with a logo) on the PMDU's deliverability and affordability analysis report unless it shared a draft of the letter from the Chief Secretary to the Department of Health and allowed him to clear the 'proposed changes' (to stop new announcements).[104] Balls was 'outraged' by Barber's stance – 'Who was I to dictate what Treasury ministers said in a letter?' Barber said he had misunderstood.

> Treasury ministers can say whatever they like in a letter but my responsibility was to manage the DU and its brand – and I wouldn't associate it with the imposition of new conditions. So, if I didn't support the Treasury minister's letter, the pack would be ours and not joint and I'd send it to Nigel [Crisp] without negotiating any further changes.[105]

It seemed that No. 10 and the departments' main tool against the Treasury was to make announcements on new policies, which often bounced the Treasury into accepting decisions and associated costs. The PMDU's delivery and affordability analysis report had become an important tool both for departments and for the Treasury, and Barber recognised its power. He advised Balls that he was 'making a mistake in obsessively fighting past battles'; Milburn had gone, the PMDU with the Treasury and Health 'had developed an excellent new model of partnership working – why throw all this away'? This was a bold approach by Barber; Balls was an 'unprecedentedly powerful figure' in the Treasury, nicknamed the 'deputy Chancellor'.[106] The result was that Macpherson and Barber agreed to negotiate the report and the letters. Barber was 'glad to have taken a firm line', which he had based on 'the sense that I probably had more leverage in the negotiation than one might think – Head of Delivery Unit acting alone versus Chief Economic Adviser acting for the Chancellor'.[107] It was a big gamble and might yet have consequences.

In the second week of July, the next round of delivery reports was finalised. The process had taken three months, and they were sent to the four departments, the Prime Minister and the Cabinet Secretary as well as a select few in No. 10 and the Cabinet Office.[108] The 'basic message' was that the following six months would be crucial: 'The blockages have to be brutally understood and the action taken, comprehensive and decisive.'[109] Barber met with David Normington and his top DfES team to discuss the delivery report. The report had been 'tough', Barber's covering letter emphasising the 'need to manage through to a result and be unapologetic about' standards.[110] Normington told Barber that the report had been 'demoralising'; it told them what they already knew and the 'lists of specified actions had been examples of micromanagement'.[111] Barber said that the lists of suggested actions had been 'arrived at and agreed' through 'constant interaction' with the department and there were 'no surprises'.[112] The report 'reflected the views of the Prime Minister and there was no point pretending he had confidence in the Department when he didn't'; in Barber's view it was better to be 'plain speaking'.[113] This interaction showed that though deliverology was well established and strong relationships with stakeholders were important, the PMDU remained firmly independent in expressing the state of affairs as they saw it. Nevertheless it is a notable and rare example of Barber and the PMDU being directly accused of attempting to micromanage a department.

Barber was glad that the PMDU report had been challenging for the DfES but noted that 'this was the edgiest meeting with a Permanent Secretary for some time'. The other delivery Permanent Secretaries had accepted their reports or even welcomed them (such as Leigh Lewis, Second Permanent Secretary in the Home Office).[114] Though Barber was focused on delivery, he noted the growing impact of the political climate because WMDs had still not been found in Iraq: 'Confidence in Blair personally is ebbing away, on the backbenches and out in the country. The Prime Minister's own personal confidence that they will be found has never appeared to waver, but he looks increasingly alone.'[115] During that week, despite a huge majority, the government only narrowly avoided defeat on a vote on foundation hospitals in England when MPs voted 286 to 251 in favour.[116] In mid-July, Barber updated Blair on the progress of the Reform Agenda Group from his perspective: 'It was hard work' and Balls 'was being uncooperative'. Blair urged Barber to 'press ahead'.[117] These were incredibly thorny issues for the parties involved, and there were genuine differences of opinion on the best policy to proceed with.

Barber chaired the second meeting of the Reform Agenda Group, which 'debated choice at the point of [GP] referral', and the Treasury seemed 'more engaged'.[118] Balls said that he did not want anything announced on this because it would 'raise expectations and in any case, he saw it as just a step to much more open forms of choice'.[119] Barber, on the other hand, argued that choice at the point of GP referral would help in meeting the six-month waiting times target and 'that it would be good to explain it publicly, as long as the announcement didn't go beyond the assumptions' agreed in the PMDU report.[120] The meeting ended with the tension 'unresolved'. Barber was informed by Macpherson that, contrary to their agreement, the letter from the Chief Secretary to the Treasury had been sent without consulting Barber and it included a ban on new announcements by departments.[121] John Reid had asked Brown about what he could say publicly, Brown 'had expressed his fears about where choice would go beyond the managed choice version we had evaluated', and so the letter included the ban as a preventative measure.[122]

Barber checked in with special adviser Paul Corrigan in Health at the end of the week. Reid and his team had decided to use Brown's speech of the previous week as a hinge for a speech Reid was due to give in mid-July. Barber had been unable to balance the competing stakeholders in the way that he had intended but managed to maintain cordial relations with DH. Barber 'apologised' for not being able to make the deal he had hoped to; Corrigan was 'abrupt' but said, 'There are historical forces at work, comrade.'[123] It seems that the creative tension exposed in the Reform Agenda Group was making established relationships more combustible. The art of delivery was being tested.

A DANGEROUS TIME, FALLING OUT WITH ED BALLS

A disagreement between Barber and Balls was instigated by a speech John Reid delivered on 16 July. The day before, Barber had received an email from Heywood to say that Balls was unhappy about the choice agenda and Reid's forthcoming speech, feeling it put at risk the PMDU–Treasury relationship.[124] Barber called Balls and agreed to advise Reid's office to emphasise an 'element of conditionality in the way choice was described (rollout would depend on the success of the pilots)'; it was a 'surprisingly amicable' conversation from Barber's perspective.[125] In the speech, Reid quoted Brown's earlier speech and contrary to Balls's desire for no new announcements, the Secretary of State for Health said, 'Through careful rollout and implementation we expect we will be able to expand choice at the point of referral … We want to extend choice in further directions within the NHS … into services such as chronic diseases, primary care and maternity services.'[126] This was unhelpful for relationships, but you cannot take the politics out of government. The next day a terse email exchange took place between Balls and Barber. Barber told Balls that he understood that Balls viewed Reid's speech as a risk to the PMDU–Treasury relationship. He had done as they agreed, and communicated to Health how he 'thought managed choice should be discussed' but he was 'not in a position (and wouldn't want to be) to decide what any minister says in a speech'.[127] Barber went on, 'We did our best throughout the process of assessing deliverability and affordability to be objective and analytical. Everyone agrees the process was exemplary and based on high levels of trust and collaboration between HMT/DH/PMDU people.'[128] He said he believed that 'between us we are having a major impact on government's capacity to deliver its key goals ... It would be a tragedy to blow it because of a disagreement between yourself and DH.'[129] Barber stated that he was 'proud of the strong alliance between HMT and PMDU on delivery' and admitted that though 'difficult issues' would arise they 'should deal with them by being as straight as possible with each other recognising that we have different jobs and lines of accountability which are bound to cause tensions occasionally'.[130] Balls, however, was not reassured.

This cannot simply be dismissed in this way as an HMT–DH disagreement. The Chx [Chancellor] is very upset that DH have misrepresented joint PMDU/HMT work in this way – especially as John Reid made it clear to the Chx that the pressure to make the announcement on choice in this way came from PMDU. As you know, we wanted to take more time bilaterally to bottom out the disagreements but you decided that you had to move more quickly to meet a particular announcement timetable ... I understand that you are trying to wear two hats and that that is causing very real difficulties.[131]

In response Barber said:

This is not an accurate account of what happened and if the Chx has been misinformed it would be important to correct that. The DU does not drive timetables for announcements in Health or anywhere else. It is not our job. The timetable for decisions on choice was, as you know, agreed with you months ago ... I will of course talk to Nick [Macpherson]. I also intend to get on with the central task which involves continuing the excellent relations with you and colleagues here.[132]

He went on to offer to talk the issues through with Balls in person. This exchange threatened to derail the pivotal constructive PMDU–Treasury relationship, which by this time was critical to Barber's art of delivery and the overall application of deliverology. Barber discussed the issue with Macpherson, whom he found to be 'reasonably sympathetic'.[133]

On the same day as the email exchange, 17 July, Barber gave a presentation to the Cabinet which he admitted was made all the more 'daunting' because he did so in 'the middle of my first major row with Ed Balls – and by proxy Gordon Brown'.[134] After Barber's presentation there was thirty minutes of discussion. The Foreign Secretary, Jack Straw, 'pointed out that the public didn't trust politicians but did trust public service workers – so we had to bring them with us'.[135] Reid agreed with Straw but also pointed out that 'public servants would often be defenders of the status quo and the government could not be in the pocket of the producer interest'.[136] A theme was picked up 'about the gap between the objective data and local perception' on health and police numbers.[137] Brown said, 'No amount of figures will do if trust in government is low.'[138] He also warned that they needed to find 'high standards of delivery in a period of slower growth in public expenditure'.[139] Blair summed up: 'We shall return to this in September.'[140] The wider reputation of the government was impacting the public perception of improvements in public services, thus showing how complex delivering public service reform can be.

THE ANTITHESIS OF SPIN

On 30 July, Barber presented for the second year at the Prime Minister's televised monthly press conference. He gave a fifteen-minute end-of-year report, on the progress of key public service indicators on health, asylum, crime, transport and education.[141] But he did not want it to be seen as a whitewash and so included the 'painstakingly honest' problems with schools funding, 'the plateau on primary tests, the rise in gun crime and the lack of progress on transport'.[142] The presentation incorporated a comprehensive series of PowerPoint slides showing the aims and progress made.[143] Barber was not subject to questioning after his presentation, but the Prime Minister was asked about the impact Iraq had on the progress of domestic reform.

Question from press: I was going to ask you about momentum you were just talking about then. Do you think there is any way in which the focus on international events has actually retarded your progress towards these targets that we have been looking at today?

Prime Minister: I think again, to be frank about it, there is no doubt at all that in the last year Iraq has formed a very large part of the agenda. There is no point in standing here and disputing that ... The bulk of my time is still being taken up, apart from in the very intense moments just before and just after the conflict started, with the public service agenda. And all the way through there have been things happening and progress made ... we have a real reform programme underway and we are pushing it forward.[144]

In the days following, the media coverage including *The Times* and

The Guardian focused on what the government had and had not achieved, which for Barber was a 'major success'.[145] Barber felt that the central message of his presentation, 'demonstrable progress but not yet irreversible', had 'struck home'.[146] There was also some mocking of Barber's style, use of graphs and jargon.[147] He had in fact 'wanted to be monotonous and deadpan; to read clearly but not to try to persuade and let the facts speak for themselves'; for his own 'credibility' he wanted 'to be the antithesis of spin'.[148]

In late July, Peter Mandelson discreetly rejoined Blair's team in an advisory role which 'was kept secret from all but the key political staff' inside No. 10.[149] Alastair Campbell was due to leave at the end of August, so perhaps it was no surprise that Blair wanted his most trusted advisers around him. What is more, Blair confided in Mandelson that the turmoil over Iraq felt like 'an albatross around my neck' and he saw 'his hopes for making a success of the second term draining away'.[150] In early September, Campbell introduced Barber to his successor, David Hill: 'This is Michael Barber, who runs the one bit of the central operation that actually works.'[151]

SEPTEMBER TO DECEMBER 2003

'SO LET US NOT TALK FALSELY NOW, THE HOUR IS GETTING LATE'

The first task for September in the PMDU was to finish the planning for and implement the reorganisation of the Unit in preparation for 'Year Three of the Parliament'.[152] The three guiding principles were: 'ruthless prioritisation, deeper collaboration and more vigorous challenge'.[153] The 'basic premise' for Barber was a lyric from Bob Dylan's 'All Along The Watchtower' (1967): 'So let us not talk falsely now, the hour is getting late.'[154] Indeed the government would switch to election campaigning mode within the next year. The PMDU narrowed its focus, which meant withdrawing some support from departments which it had begun to assist the previous autumn. It was reverting to the principles which had underpinned its original design. In early October, Barber and his PMDU team met with civil servants from the main four delivery departments to explain the new phase. There was some 'trepidation' about Barber's phrase 'We're prepared to use up social and political capital if necessary to get delivery'.[155] Barber told them that 'it wasn't that we wanted to use it up, indeed, what we like best is for them to challenge themselves as vigorously as we intend to. But delivery is important and we will do what it takes.'[156]

There was also a reorganisation going on within No. 10. David Hill succeeded Alastair Campbell as director of communications. He would not have the same authority as Campbell to direct civil servants, granted by an Order in Council in 1997 (for up to three people, of which two had been utilised by Campbell and Jonathan Powell). Geoff Mulgan retained his position as head of the Strategy Unit and succeeded Andrew Adonis as head of policy, who remained within No. 10 as a special adviser focused on education. Matthew Taylor, who had been director of the Institute for Public Policy Research (IPPR) think tank, joined as chief adviser to the Prime Minister on political strategy to work on the planning of the next manifesto.[157] There was no mention in the media of the fact that Adonis and Jeremy Heywood had jointly headed the Policy Directorate.[158] The 2001 No. 10 organogram had shown that technically Heywood was one level above Adonis.[159] Within No. 10, it was known that Heywood would be departing from the Civil Service in the coming months. Moreover, Peter Mandelson and John Birt, former director general of the BBC and Blair's unpaid adviser on strategy and blue skies thinking, were becoming increasingly dominant within No. 10.[160] Birt and Mandelson were 'close' friends and Mandelson described Birt as the 'main partner in the reorganisation project' designed to bolster Blair's position.[161]

Heywood briefed Barber on these changes and informed him that he had been reinvited to Blair's Monday morning meetings. There would also be an overall move to increase the formality of meetings; for example, more meetings would be minuted.[162] There was a new 'Birtian' proposal for each department to create five-year plans, 'each with a five-year financial strategy'; and that the PMDU's role should be 'widened to check implementation of the full plan – not just progress towards the PSA targets'.[163] This was seemingly designed to strengthen Blair's influence over the future of domestic reform, and would thus exacerbate tensions with the Treasury under Brown. In early September, Adonis, Barber, Heywood and Mulgan began to have discussions on the 'five-year planning process' with Health and Education.[164] Mulgan, also a special adviser turned civil servant, was someone whom Barber had 'known and admired for some time'. He observed with interest the new 'system, order and collective thinking' which Mulgan sought to bring to policymaking in No. 10.[165] Meanwhile Barber's relationship with David Hill seemed to be progressing well. In mid-October, they met as a double act with editors of major newspapers to discuss delivery.[166]

CONTEXT: A POWER STRUGGLE

This period was a watershed in relations between Blair and Brown. Between July and October, a group including Birt, Mandelson and Powell planned various ways to reduce the perceived threat of Gordon Brown. Such plans had been considered at various junctures during Blair's premiership. This plan was covertly named Operation Teddy Bear, and chiefly proposed dividing the Treasury in two. First, 'a new Ministry of Finance', led by Brown, 'would handle the macro-economics'.[167] Second, 'a separate US-style Office of the Budget and Delivery would be split off from the Treasury and placed either in the Cabinet Office or made a standalone department', led by someone who was trusted by Blair.[168] Blair eventually proposed the plan to Brown, who said no – 'it was a fateful moment'.[169] As Prime Minister Blair had the power to force through such a plan but ultimately he decided not to implement it. The threat to split the Treasury left Brown and his colleagues more alert to attempts to undermine his power, as the proposals were revived in the following two years.[170] The Prime Minister perhaps feared that if Brown were to go to the backbenches he would form a rival power base, at a time when trust in Blair within the Labour Party and the country was low. According to Mandelson, in early November, a deal was done between Blair and Brown whereby if Brown supported Blair in pursuing his domestic reforms then Blair would leave before the 2005 general election.[171] Blair reportedly told Mandelson to 'play along' with this because he did not believe Brown would support his domestic reforms and therefore the 'situation won't arise' where he would leave before the next election.[172] The contrast between Blair going from planning the 'equivalent of a nuclear strike' against Brown to apparently 'talking terms of surrender' was noted by Mandelson.[173] This provides context for understanding the increasingly challenging environment in which Barber was trying to reconcile the differences between Blair and Brown, to deliver the domestic reform priorities.

In mid-September, Barber attended a meeting at Chequers on Civil Service reform. Birt had proposed new plans for structural changes within departments.[174] The PMDU had not contributed directly to Birt's template but the Unit's work had shown what was and was not working in several departments. In the meeting, Blair credited Barber with keeping up momentum: 'If it hadn't been for Michael ... over the last few months, the whole delivery thing would have gone off the rails.'[175] On 11 September, the third meeting of the Reform Agenda Group took place on education funding; Adonis no longer attended and Mulgan was invited but could not attend. Ed Balls wanted to discuss 'the process for developing policy on funding more than the policy itself'; intervening in the process of policy development meant influencing whether it happened or not.[176] Balls wanted to understand why Barber was chairing these meetings, and what the status of Mulgan and Taylor would be. Heywood said Barber been asked to chair the meetings 'not as Head of the Delivery Unit but as "a person"'.[177] To both Blair and Brown, Barber was seen as a relatively neutral figure who could act as a bridge. In reality, the dam was threatening to burst. In summarising the meeting, Barber believed it 'represented the renewal of the war of attrition' which had begun in the summer.[178] Two weeks later, another meeting of the Reform Agenda Group took place. Barber called it 'the most relaxed meeting yet' and on this occasion there was no questioning of Barber's role as chair.[179] On the basis of a Treasury presentation, the group reached a 'shared analysis' of where they were on police reform and 'produced something like a shared agenda for change – more devolution, clarify funding and accountability, open up the higher echelons to outsiders'.[180] Evidently the Reform Agenda Group were able to build limited consensus on some areas of domestic reform.

In early October, Barber had a monthly round-up meeting with Blair at which Heywood, Mulgan and Powell were also present.

Barber gave Blair an update on the progress of the Reform Agenda Group – on education funding they had 'a good debate and the Treasury were "sceptical" but hadn't ruled anything out', they had 'broad agreement' for police reform but Barber expected health reforms to be 'the flashpoint'.[181] He added that the 'process was beginning to roll through' but he was unsure how the Labour Party conference of the previous week would impact relations.[182] This showed that perceived progress on policy could not be separated from the politics. Blair felt that progress on delivery was 'plateauing' and was particularly worried about asylum and crime, which in his view had a major impact on social cohesion in communities.[183] Barber discussed what was being done and took the Prime Minister's message back to his team. Tensions between Blair and Brown had been apparent at the Labour Party conference. Brown had declared in his speech that the Party was 'best when we are boldest, best when we are united, best when we are Labour'.[184] This was seen as a criticism of the Prime Minister, as it echoed Blair's 'best at our boldest' speech at the previous year's conference but reinforced the need to stay true to Labour Party values while pursuing a bold agenda. While Blair, now the longest continuously serving Labour Prime Minister since Clement Attlee, outlined in his conference speech the progress made during the past six years and confronted the divisive issue of Iraq,[185] he said that his job was not done and he intended to fight the next election.

On one of the seemingly intractable areas of delivery, rail performance, progress was being made. After several meetings between Blair, Barber, Alistair Darling, DfT Permanent Secretary David Rowlands and the chair of the Strategic Rail Authority (SRA), Richard Bowker, a work programme was set for the next six months.[186] Network Rail would have a new performance director and much of the contracted-out workforce would be contracted back in. The SRA was creating a performance plan for each train operating company which it would manage against. Darling committed to an internal target of improving rail performance from 80 per cent to 85 per cent PPM (Public Performance Measure). The PPM was used to monitor performance via train cancellations and lateness. The DfT also asked the Delivery Unit to 'help as much as you can' and to take an 'active' role in the Network Rail relationship.[187] Barber said it sounded 'simple and obvious' but had taken 'two very tough years' to put in place because 'since privatisation until now no one had managed the railway at all'.[188] The privatisation of British Rail in the 1990s, by John Major's Conservative government, had led to the fragmentation of the rail industry and a lack of levers for comprehensive planning and oversight within government. Blair was pleased with the stocktake and commented 'plaintively' to Darling, 'All I ever wanted was a properly managed railway.'[189]

There was a health stocktake on A&E waiting times on 7 October, chaired by Blair. Barber noted that the Prime Minister was effective in communicating the message, 'You've done well since January but there's much more to do to get this "shop window" right.'[190] Barber thought John Reid saw 'the influence' of the PMDU and valued its impact.[191] However, he found that the senior civil servants responsible for delivery within Health, including the Permanent Secretary, were still not at ease with the Unit.

In spite of the progress they've made and the mutual respect between us and them, they are always edgy as if worried we're out to undermine them. In fact, we're desperate for them to succeed and where we've worked most closely, as on A&E and choice, there has been remarkable progress. Even so, unlike the DfT or

Home Office, they always seem reluctant to accept genuine collaboration. In part, it's this fear but in part it's also a sense that
they think they can deliver on their own.[192]

A ROW REIGNITED

At the end of October, Barber received an email from Balls which
stemmed from an incident earlier in the year. According to Balls,
Heywood had told him that in July Barber had said the decision on
the rollout of choice (which 'the PMDU and Treasury had agreed
at official level') was then 'scuppered politically' by Balls,[193] but that
this was not true. Barber responded by saying 'there was no point
reopening the issue but the good news was that the policy we'd
hammered out was beginning to work, and this was the important
thing'.[194] But he did not deny the comment and Balls emailed back
saying he was 'personally offended'. In response Barber said that
he 'had not intended offence and was happy to talk to him but
not keep emailing'.[195] Barber was worried that this could affect his
relations with Brown.[196]

Later that day, Nicholas Macpherson sought to explain to Barber
the wider context that was heightening tensions. Balls was frustrated 'with the exclusion of the Treasury from the five-year strategy
discussions which Blair and the Policy Directorate' were taking forward and, compared to this, Barber's chairing of the Reform Agenda
Group was seen as 'a sideshow or a sop'.[197] The development of the
five-year strategies was viewed as a direct challenge to the policy
programme which the Treasury would lead and negotiate in the
forthcoming spending review. If there was no alignment, there was
a danger of duplication and increased friction. As No. 10 was leading the five-year strategy process it controlled the level and depth of
consultation with departments, including the Treasury. The Reform

Agenda Group did, however, pre-date the five-year strategies and was focused on reconciling short-term policy and implementation issues, rather than Birt's longer-term strategy planning. Charles Clarke explained that it was a symptom of 'different power centres in government, No. 11, Cabinet Office, No. 10 all doing their different things' and a 'dysfunctional relationship between No. 10 and No. 11'.[198] Barber discussed with Macpherson the issue of his standing with the Chancellor; Macpherson told him that he 'shouldn't worry too much'.[199] The outcome of these meetings reflected the largely resilient relationship that Barber and the PMDU had built with the Treasury. It was valued and not concentrated in a single individual. Nevertheless, Balls was a very powerful force within the Treasury and relations would need to be repaired.

The saga, however, continued. In early December, Barber secured a commitment from Heywood and Simon Stevens in No. 10 that an overview of the five-year health strategy would be shared with the Reform Agenda Group. Balls had refused to attend another meeting unless this happened.[200] Barber emailed this news to the group but shortly afterwards he received a call from Balls, who said that the paper he was due to receive was not what 'we had commissioned' and he was not prepared to attend the meeting.[201] Barber said this was the requested paper. Balls said, 'No it isn't … I can't believe this.' Though Balls was evidently angry and perhaps not used to being challenged by Barber in this way, Barber stayed 'calm' and tried to reassure Balls that the paper would not be 'waffle'.[202] Balls then said, 'I'm still very angry about what you said to Jeremy about my political interference in the decisions on choice in July.'[203] Barber said, 'There's nothing I can do if you choose to be angry … I've said consistently I'm happy to sort out the issue with you, I've been trying to fix to meet you for a coffee to discuss it.'[204]

Balls felt his 'integrity' had been questioned; Barber said he had not done this.[205] Barber agreed to circulate the paper in advance and asked Balls to contact him before the meeting if he 'didn't like it'.[206] This is an example of how personal relations can have a significant impact on the conduct of government. Relationships represent a fundamental part of the art of delivery; without the art, the science of delivery cannot be applied effectively.

On 11 December, the scheduled meeting of the Reform Agenda Group took place, Barber having circulated the health strategy paper two days prior. Macpherson said it was 'genuinely interesting' but not 'what we'd asked for'; he attached a set of questions to discuss in the meeting.[207] Balls emailed after this and suggested that the meeting be postponed until there was a 'proper paper'.[208] Heywood and Barber then emailed Balls stating the meeting should go ahead but it was unclear whether Balls would attend. Just before the meeting Barber was asked to meet with Balls in his office. Balls expressed his confusion over why the meeting was happening – 'he thought it was a strange way to proceed and that he had made his view clear that the meeting should have been cancelled'.[209] He said that Macpherson and his team had 'expressed their views without any prompting from him and that he agreed with them'.[210] This was fifteen minutes before the full meeting was due to begin. Barber replied:

> I knew he had a different view about holding the meeting but I had made the decision. I didn't know whether it would work but I had taken the decision out of a genuine desire to move the dialogue on – I knew he was unhappy with the paper but that was a reason to have the meeting and express his views. If we never met, we'd never make progress ... I told him I wanted him to trust me to try out the meeting.[211]

This was both a bold and conciliatory response from Barber, whose motivation was to find a way through. Balls agreed to come to the meeting but said, 'You're taking on huge risk, you know ... You're putting at risk your whole relationship with the Treasury.'[212] 'Life's full of risks,' said Barber.[213]

Barber cited this episode as an example where his conflict resolution approach was put into practice, to good effect. For Barber, the aim for meetings like this, whether undertaken by him or the PMDU team, was as follows: 'How do you go to the meeting, deliver the really tough message, make sure it's understood and they are going to do something about it, and leave with the relationship stronger than when you walked in?'[214] Barber and senior PMDU staff spent a great deal of time preparing other team members for meetings with senior civil servants: 'We were very thorough and very meticulous. It wasn't just about getting our head down on the data and being technical, it was thinking about these relationships.'[215] Jonathan Powell commented on Barber's 'very mild mannered' nature – 'even Ed Balls couldn't start an argument with him'.[216] He continued that Barber 'was very focused on results ... he did not let himself get distracted by nonsense'.[217] Clara Swinson, a civil servant who worked in the Delivery Unit, reflected on this trait of Barber's and its impact on the culture of the Unit.

I think his Quaker background makes a huge difference. His values, how he goes about it. He's a big personality, but he doesn't do it in a way – that, as you say, kind of stereotypical way – of making your point and being kind of semi-aggressive or wanting to be the first and last person to have spoken, he doesn't use his influence in that way. But you want to hear from him. So, it is humility. I think there's a confidence there as well, he definitely wouldn't have turned up and not said anything [in a meeting]. But it is a very particular style that is really, really effective ... You do have to give credit away. That was one of his phrases as well. As time went on, lots of people said, 'Michael's approach has done this,' but for a permanent secretary or a lead director in certain areas, he would say, 'You've done this, and you present it.'[218]

Barber's careful handling of what could have been a relationship-ending encounter meant that the planned Reform Agenda Group meeting went ahead, chaired by him. A Health civil servant presented the plans and he, along with Paul Corrigan, responded to questions from Macpherson.[219] Balls raised concerns but was told by the attendees from No. 10 and Health that these were unfounded. For example, Balls said 'he couldn't understand why anyone wanted the price mechanism to allocate healthcare among patients'.[220] A price mechanism would match supply and demand, which, unlike in the private sector, had not been used because the NHS is free at the point of use and thus demand is only limited by how quickly the NHS can provide treatment. Barber thought this was an 'extraordinary moment for a simple reason: no one has ever proposed this'; Stevens and Corrigan confirmed this to Balls and said Reid had 'ruled this out'.[221] There was discussion about the use of the private sector; Corrigan pointed out that the private sector would have to deliver at 'the standard national tariff' which the NHS used.[222] The debate 'raged but positively'.[223] Barber summed up and said that they needed a statement soon on the agreed issues. Balls said to Heywood the following week, 'The meeting on health [that] Michael chaired was very good. I don't know why we didn't do it long ago.'[224] When interviewed, Balls recalled the Reform Agenda Group and this meeting, and he stated that though this consultation process may have appeared to provide reassurance it is unlikely that he truly 'believed a word of it' because the Treasury was being kept at a distance from the planning process.[225] Macpherson, however, observed that the meetings 'did encourage a bit more of a dialogue'.[226]

The Chancellor's Pre-Budget Report announced the abolition of service delivery agreements (SDAs), to be replaced by delivery plans. These secondary-level targets detailed the outputs associated with the outcomes that were stipulated in broader public service agreements (PSAs). SDAs had been introduced as part of the 2000 spending review, and their abolition removed 500 secondary process and input targets.[227] Arguably this showed that the Treasury recognised the excessive bureaucratic demands of the original PSA framework. The delivery plans were designed by the PMDU and would now be scaled up and utilised across Whitehall as part of the Treasury's new framework. This was a significant impact of the Delivery Unit on the Treasury, which affected the way in which the whole Civil Service was expected to deliver domestic priorities.

In preparing the education delivery report, Barber met with a team from the DfES to discuss his thinking on their strategy. In the course of the meeting, the Permanent Secretary, David Normington, referred to Barber as 'our most passionate ally and our fiercest critic'.[228] This was a notable statement on how Barber was viewed. The next round of delivery reports was finalised and in advance of publication, Barber spoke with each of the four key Permanent Secretaries. They all accepted the PMDU judgements 'without defensiveness'.[229] On 15 December, Barber met with Blair to provide a delivery update; also present were Heywood, his successor Ivan Rogers (who would begin in the New Year), Mulgan and Powell.[230] The Prime Minister was keen to 'spend serious time' discussing Barber's paper on where they were on 'key outcomes'.[231] Blair was 'broadly happy' with the progress on health; on asylum he was 'more relaxed than for months'; on crime he was 'worried by the recent recorded crime figures which showed overall recorded crime and violent crime up from October 2002'.[232] Barber explained that David Blunkett was 'seriously exercised' by the figures and the PMDU were 'thoroughly reviewing how the Home Office is organised on crime'.[233] On education, Blair agreed with Barber that 'large sums of money appeared to be having minimal impact' on Key Stage 4 (ages fourteen to sixteen) results.[234] Barber reported that the Reform Agenda Group had made 'progress' and 'after months of resistance' Balls had 'come round'.[235] His and Balls's relationship seemed to improve; Balls told Barber that the delivery reports he had seen 'were excellent – so clear'.[236]

JANUARY TO MARCH 2004

DEPARTURES

The year began with two major departures from No. 10. Jeremy Heywood left the Civil Service at the end of 2003, to join Morgan Stanley as a managing director. Heywood had played a pivotal role for the Prime Minister and the government. In brokering compromises with Balls (on behalf of the Treasury under Brown), he had kept government business moving. He had been one of the most trusted advisers to Blair on policy and institutional reorganisations, and he had provided economic ballast in No. 10. He had been critical to the establishment of the PMDU and had worked closely with Barber to ensure the Unit had favourable conditions for success. Heywood's replacement as principal private secretary to the Prime Minister was Ivan Rogers.[237] Rogers was a career civil servant and was to move from the Treasury, where he had been director of budget and tax policy since 2002. Another trusted figure who was supportive of the Delivery Unit in No. 10, Peter Hyman, left in the New Year. During the first term, Hyman had identified several issues related to the government's capacity to deliver. At this late stage of the second term, with the PMDU well established, neither departure presented a threat to the stability of the Unit.

On 8 January 2004, Macpherson and Barber presented to the Public Service Reform Cabinet Committee. Blair, Brown, Blunkett, Reid and Prescott were in attendance and the topic was the future of targets. Barber and Macpherson had been conducting 'serious work together in the context of devolving decision-making about how targets could evolve into standards'.[238] Barber's main point was about power.

> In the great rush to devolve we need to remember, I said, that in future government will still be held to account and, secondly, devolution needs to empower consumers or citizens, not the professions who failed so miserably when they did control our public services. Hence the need for transparency, sharp accountability etc.[239]

The discussion that followed was a 'tough but good-natured debate about the next stage of public service reform'.[240] Brown said, 'Targets were never a substitute for strategy.'[241] He was also 'enthusiastic about local transparency and real-time data, "Transparency is the new discipline."'[242] He stated that there were 'real dangers' in the proposal to reduce the number of targets.[243] Reid echoed Barber's point about power – 'Who drives the system?' He said that 'you could have choice, and government had a role as "the equaliser"'.[244] Blair came in 'forcefully and with great clarity' to agree with Reid;

he said the Macpherson–Barber report was 'absolutely right'.[245] He agreed there was more to do 'to separate hard, published targets from management targets'.[246] Blair said it was the politician's job to ensure 'political realism', educate the public but be clear that 'no business would operate without' targets.[247] Blair agreed with Brown that targets were not a substitute for strategy; 'the key was to analyse how we wanted the system to work', 'structural change was necessary'; and they needed to decide 'how to distribute power between the centre, the "local delivery agent" and the consumer'.[248] He concluded, 'We will not deliver lasting change in the public services, simply by driving it from the centre.'[249] Brown went on to say to Blair, 'I agree with everything you just said ... We need to follow the logic through for the health service [and get] the balance between choice and national commitments.'[250] Blair summed up the meeting: 'This is a very important debate, make no mistake,' adding that they 'needed to find a language to express it for the ordinary person'.[251] To Barber and Macpherson the Prime Minister said, 'We are all in agreement about where you're going on targets.'[252] This episode showed a Prime Minister, Chancellor and key Cabinet ministers deeply engaged in considering the intellectual and practical strategies for the next stage of delivering public service reform.

Barber attended Blair's awayday at Chequers for his No. 10 team. He noted that it was 'striking how much the team had changed since those heady away days, after the 2001 election but before September 11th, no Anji [Hunter], no Alastair [Campbell], no Fiona [Millar], no Jeremy [Heywood]'.[253] Geoff Mulgan and Matthew Taylor were now the 'dominant contributors' along with Blair.[254] In the wide-ranging discussion on political strategy, Blair referred 'to the errors of the past', mentioning 'inexperience in government', 'excessive attacks on Tory ideas which might be useful' and 'the

Treasury pulling in a different direction'.[255] These admissions were striking, and Blair apportioned much of the blame to himself; in doing so he indicated the maturity and experience which he had gained after almost seven years as Prime Minister. Before Barber departed from the meeting Blair asked him to pursue a new activity – he wanted Barber and the PMDU to gather 'delivery facts' and develop a communications strategy. Barber said he would discuss this with Philip Gould and David Hill but also emphasised that he was 'focused on the boring, relentless grind of actually bringing delivery about'.[256] Privately, Barber felt that he needed to keep telling Blair this, because the Prime Minister 'didn't seem to appreciate what still needed to be done to ensure there were some "delivery facts" to get across'.[257]

In early January, Barber met with Blair to prepare for the up-coming education and Home Office stocktakes, to discuss how to proceed with Treasury relations and to 'clarify the future agenda' of the PMDU.[258] They agreed 'that now there was a way forward on the principles of health reform, the Reform Agenda Group could be wound up'.[259] No tenure was set when it had been created six months earlier; some clarification and progress had been made but it had been a struggle. Arguably the tension between No. 10 and the Treasury regarding the five-year strategies had hindered the progress of the Reform Agenda Group. Sally Morgan confirmed that they 'became part of the tussle with the Treasury'.[260] Macpherson expanded on this:

> Part of the problem was on the face of it we were all trying to work more closely together [but] on the other hand … we'd just had a spending review and if you wanted to develop five-year plans they should be in that context … Then the Treasury objected to

it. Blair's solution was 'Well, just go and do it and don't talk to the Treasury'. This made progress quite difficult.[261]

Barber had 'mixed feelings'; he had 'enjoyed the challenge' but it had been 'an enormous hassle' and he had a sizeable brief already.[262] Barber's firm but conciliatory approach had been notably different to the combative style with which No. 10 and the Treasury often engaged one another. Yet using this mode in a highly divisive political context had proved difficult and posed a risk to the relationships on which the Delivery Unit depended. An education stocktake chaired by Blair took place, in which Barber emphasised the need to focus on 'the tests at frontline level'; he was 'critical of the attendance and behaviour strategy' and on Key Stage 4 emphasised 'the need to focus on underperformance'.[263] David Miliband responded from the DfES, he was 'positive' about most of the activity on Key Stage 2 (ages seven to eleven) but said he was 'worried' about the PMDU evidence from Essex which found 'a lack of focus among the LEA's strategy' team.[264] Blair pressed the department 'to strengthen the focus on the results'; Barber thought it was a 'good performance' by Blair.[265] It gave him cause to reflect on the purpose of the PMDU: 'The meeting revealed exactly why a Delivery Unit was worth having. Without us and our processes, any meeting between the PM and the Secretary of State for Education would surely have focused on the tuition fees controversy [on the introduction of top-up fees]. Instead, it was barely mentioned.'[266]

The Secretary of State for Education, Charles Clarke, shared his view of the Delivery Unit and his department:

The whole [PMDU] process of illuminating the way the department operated was extremely positive and very helpful. And something, by the way, that wasn't done without the Delivery Unit being there ... It is the case that I recall conversations with the Prime Minister as the most significant part of the process.[267]

Barber had an 'instructive' conversation with Treasury civil servant Ray Shostak afterwards; it had been Shostak's first stocktake and he commented 'that the DfES agenda was very largely being driven by the Delivery Unit, to an unhealthy extent'.[268] Barber agreed: 'Everything that came up, Miliband or someone was referring to our view or reviews. We were really on top of things but they were too passive.'[269] Barber's involvement in education, particularly schools policy, was increasing. He was acting as head of the PMDU responsible for hastening delivery but also as an education expert who had spent four years crafting and implementing schools policy in that very department. He now saw much of the current regime as complacent and sought to rectify that. He was arguably working beyond his brief but the Prime Minister and the DfES valued his expertise and experience. Relationships may not have been as resilient had Barber not already had a strong, tested working relationship with David Normington.

The Home Office stocktake, which took place the following day, marked a contrast. Barber was able to report that there had been 'remarkable improvement in the Home Office over the last two years – lots of red had turned to green'.[270] He highlighted 'the successes (police reform and asylum) but also the major challenges – aspects of crime (violent, anti-social behaviour) and drugs'.[271] Blair was 'clear and forceful', urging them 'to drive forward with real energy and urgency'.[272] Looking back, John Gieve's view is that Blair's commitment to stocktakes was pivotal to success.

The effectiveness of the Delivery Unit depended also on the fact that the Prime Minister was willing to put in the hours, and that he was consistent. He was a good delegator. He was always clear on the direction he wanted us to go but reasonable in listening to the difficulties and obstacles. Typically, his questions would have been on the lines, 'I want you to go further, why can't you go further? Have you considered doing x, y and z?' ... In a sense that consistent set of questioning from the Prime Minister was very significant in orienting the department and it would not have come from David Blunkett [or other Cabinet ministers].[273]

This is an astute assessment of Blair, Barber and the Delivery Unit's approach. According to Gieve, 'the accountability went straight to the officials, they were answering and explaining directly to the Prime Minister what was going on'.[274] In contrast to the education stocktake, there was 'no defensiveness from ministers or officials'; Blunkett and Hazel Blears, minister of state in the Home Office, were 'engaging and positive, the Home Office officials confident'; the stocktake had been 'challenging, focused and encouraging'.[275] It certainly helped that Barber and Blunkett had worked together in government for seven years (by this point) and their relationship was strong and trusting. Since the autumn of 2001, Blunkett had also asked Barber to help bolster his department's capacity to deliver, whereas successive Secretaries of State for education had not done so.

DELIVERY IS POLITICAL

Blair asked Barber to give a presentation on delivery at the upcoming ministerial meeting at Chequers on the five-year plans. The presentation included the traffic light judgements on each department. This was the first time the three Secretaries of State and their Permanent Secretaries had seen the judgements on departments beyond their own – it was a 'symbolic step forward'.[276] Blair told his ministers that their opponents were undermining their claims. Cabinet ministers were reforming huge systems and would not get them perfect; but being clear about the next phase of reform was 'critical to their credibility', which was why the strategies were important.[277] Reid followed up with a presentation of his own. 'Delivery is political. We three and you, Tony, are in the crucible of whether social democracy will succeed in the next 30 years.'[278] He outlined the health strategy and emphasised that this was 'reform from the Left' – 'choice for all as opposed to a few'.[279] The group discussed how to reconcile moving from top-down decision-making to devolved, local decision-making; 'default' powers would be needed, making central government almost akin to a regulator.[280] Reid said, 'We will still be held accountable'; this echoed the message Barber had given at the previous week's Cabinet committee meeting.[281] Blunkett commented that 'the Delivery Unit model of a collaborative approach is crucial ... Why can't the other units around you [Blair] adopt a similar approach?'[282] He went on, 'We in the Home Office can't do it without a collaborative approach.'[283]

The development of 'The Plan', Blair's communications plan to gather 'delivery facts' and explain the progress to the public, was a project which saw Barber and the PMDU's Adrian Brown collaborate with the Prime Minister's senior advisers in No. 10. This included Gould, Hill, Mandelson, Powell and Taylor, who were all focused on different aspects of political strategy for the 2005 general election. At one meeting, Mandelson remarked, 'Michael Barber – just seeing you gives me confidence.'[284] Barber met with

Gould to discuss the perception gap between the progress being made and the public perception of progress. Barber emphasised that 'the NHS was becoming a major success story, which could be a real asset in the campaign'; Gould said that his recent polling confirmed this – 'people were beginning to notice'.[285] Gould also had 'strong data showing that people thought the services they used locally were getting better – but were not convinced about the same services nationally'.[286] The sense that the government was gearing up for an election in the following year was palpable. Indeed, in his memoirs Gould defined this period as the time in which he began planning the 'war book' – 'a summary of public opinion ... to sum up where we were'.[287] According to Gould's polling, at this point Labour were ahead on the economy, education and the NHS by margins of 5–8 per cent while the Conservatives were significantly ahead on asylum (17 per cent), crime and Europe.[288]

At the end of January 2004, the government faced a test of confidence. It narrowly won a vote on the introduction of top-up fees for university students, the Higher Education Bill being passed by just five votes, as there had been a significant rebellion within the Parliamentary Labour Party.[289] During this period Barber and the PMDU performed one of its 'core functions', that whenever Blair and the Downing Street machine were 'distracted', the Prime Minister could 'be sure we are still firmly focused on grinding out delivery'.[290] Around this time, Barber's relationship with Gordon Brown continued to thaw. The Chancellor's speechwriter, Beth Russell, got in touch, and through various emails Barber shared his thoughts on post-sixteen education with Brown; a topic explored in Barber's book *The Learning Game*.[291] Barber commented on the interaction with the Chancellor: 'When he engages intellectually, he's awesome.'[292]

John Reid launched a consultative paper which announced twenty-four core standards against which the NHS would be judged from April 2005, such as patient safety, cost effectiveness, accessible and responsive care and public health; these would replace the existing sixty-two standards targets for the NHS which determined star ratings for hospitals.[293] The star ratings system had been brought in by Alan Milburn in September 2001; Reid said he did not intend to abolish it but the chairman of the Health-care Commission, Sir Ian Kennedy, disliked it.[294] The subsequent reporting of Reid's announcement in the media was mixed: some newspapers took the opportunity to criticise the government for the use of centrally driven targets and others were more balanced and interrogated the potential impact of the reporting changes. *The Times*'s leader article commented on the 'excessive' number of targets but recognised that 'in the absence of a market mechanism … they did allow some discipline to be imposed on an institution that is the largest employer in Western Europe'.[295] *The Guardian*'s leader article stated:

> Nurses, doctors and health managers all welcomed yesterday's pledge from the health secretary to reduce the number of NHS performance targets and place a stronger emphasis on quality of care … But then they all would, wouldn't they? All of them are producers. The people whose reaction matters most are the patients … Criticism of targets is fashionable. But it risks forgetting what went before. Prior to Labour's public service agreements, some patients had to wait 18 months for treatments for which the wait will have fallen to six months by next year … The numbers of targets have been drastically cut – from 400 to 62 in health

– which is roughly one target for every billion pounds spent by the NHS. Is that really such an onerous system of accountability?[296]

Barber recorded in his diary that in the week of Reid's consultation announcement, he had a conversation with Brown and Macpherson about a forthcoming Treasury–PMDU joint paper on the future of targets which was due to be published publicly.

> Nick [Macpherson] set out the problem, John Reid's speech had been okay but the reporting on it suggested a complete U-turn on targets. Gordon said it was all down to the [media] briefing. He was clearly angry, thought the whole episode lacked discipline. Not only was the message wrong – but it came across as a defeat … Political to the core.
>
> We discussed what the implications of the reporting were for the publication of the joint Delivery Unit/Treasury document on the future of targets, which we had been due to put out in the next week or two. Gordon thought it would now look like a hastily put together reaction to the Reid speech and its reporting. I said it would have been much better if we'd put out our document first to establish the strategy and then the health announcement afterwards. Gordon nodded in agreement.[297]

Within government, Barber had been at the forefront of considering the future of targets since early 2002. Part of the issue was the vast number of initial PSAs that had been set in the first term. The PMDU was the semi-public face of the government's target regime; few recognised the Treasury's overarching PSA framework that accounted for the majority of targets. Barber reflected, 'We were the spearhead of the target culture so if the target culture came under criticism, we did.'[298] In mid-February, Barber was asked by the Prime Minister to assist in redrafting a speech he was to give on Civil Service reform. After working on it over the course of a week he joined Blair on the day of the speech, 24 February. In the speech, Blair outlined the lessons of his time in government so far:

> When I made my first speech on the Civil Service in October 1998, I relied necessarily on a lot of theory; my experience of government was limited. Now in February 2004, I can base my, necessarily subjective, views on almost seven years of experience ... The principal challenge is to shift focus from policy advice to delivery. Delivery means outcomes ... Sometimes, things will be tried and will fail. That shouldn't denote a major political crisis ...
>
> The success factors are ... a sense of ambition, including crucially the belief that apparently intractable problems can be solved; a relentless focus on outcomes; clarity including the application of the programme and project management techniques that have transformed business; urgency including finding out quickly what's working and what isn't and adapting accordingly; and finally seeing things through until change is irreversible ... My Delivery Unit, focusing on delivery of some of the government's most important public service objectives, has helped to spread this good practice and deepen its impact ... Rigour about performance must be at the heart of a leaner more effective Civil Service.[299]

Though the Delivery Unit was set up with a specific task of pursuing the delivery of the Prime Minister's priorities, it was evidently also having an impact on what the functions of the Civil Service should be. The Cabinet Secretary, Andrew Turnbull, launched a

White Paper entitled 'Civil Service Reform: Delivery and Values'. Many of Blair's themes were reflected in it. Turnbull contrasted the past features of success in the Civil Service alongside the expected future equivalent; the core values now included 'delivery' and the description of a Permanent Secretary's role went from 'the Minister's senior policy adviser' to 'the Minister's senior delivery agent and policy adviser'.[300] Turnbull described the Prime Minister's focus on delivery and his expectations:

> Week by week, in my meetings with the Prime Minister I am challenged, quite rightly, to deliver a more effective Civil Service, one that is capable of delivering the government's ambitions for better public services. The Prime Minister is himself engaged directly through his work with the major departments and through delivery stocktakes in pushing the agenda forward.[301]

The government and the Civil Service's advocacy of delivery was reaching its apex both internally and publicly.

There was an education stocktake in early March. The DfES 'gave a good account of themselves'; and on Key Stage 2 schools policy it accepted the PMDU's recommendations.[302] Blair 'pressed for more reform', perhaps because the forthcoming Budget was to focus on investment in education.[303] The Secretary of State, Charles Clarke, later commented on the value he saw in the PMDU's science and art of delivery.

> I certainly found the stocktakes useful ... I think the whole process was useful, the concept of having a set of stages that you are trying to achieve, having some kind of measurement of what your progress was in those stages. Michael is a very flexible man and

he understood that this process shouldn't be too rigid ... It was the right way to run things.[304]

In mid-March, during a health stocktake Barber was able to show that the data was improving 'on all aspects of waiting lists and times' and A&E waiting times were advancing after a six-month plateau.[305] Blair was 'relaxed' and 'reassured' by the progress; he wanted to 'debate future strategy rather than current delivery' – which demonstrated where the Prime Minister's attention increasingly was. Blair and Reid agreed that they should be looking for a new simplified target for 2008 which brought together the existing separate targets; the PMDU was doing 'modelling work' on this.[306]

THE 2004 BUDGET – PRUDENCE FOR A PURPOSE

The 2004 Budget, entitled 'Prudence for a Purpose', was a departure from its predecessors. It was informed by the upcoming Gershon Efficiency Review into the efficiency of Britain's public sector. Brown announced 'a stretching but realistic target for the whole public sector to deliver efficiencies of 2.5 per cent a year over the three years of the 2004 Spending Review period, which would deliver gains equivalent to £20 billion a year by 2007–08' and a cut of 40,000 in the number of civil servants.[307] As a result of the Lyons review on the relocation of public sector activities, which was published in advance of the Budget, the Chancellor also confirmed the relocation of 20,000 Civil Service jobs out of London and the South East. An increase in education spending was the centrepiece of the Budget: 'Education spending in England will grow by an annual average of 4.4% in real terms across the 2004 Spending Review period ... By 2007–08, education spending in the UK will be 5.6% of GDP, up from 5.4% in 2004–05.'[308] The joint Treasury–PMDU review of the future of targets was also released with the Budget, entitled 'Devolving Decision-Making: Refining Targets and Performance Management'.[309] The review had the following terms of reference: 'To explore how best to achieve decentralised delivery and responsive local and regional services in a way that is consistent with equity and efficiency, against a clear framework of national standards.'[310] It included an introduction from Brown which rationalised the transition in approach to reforming public services:

> Setting a modernisation agenda matched by ambitious targets to provide the necessary focus and discipline was the initial stage of the public service reform agenda. Without this discipline and focus, our objectives – from improving literacy and numeracy performance in primary schools to substantially reducing waiting times and cancer and heart care improvements in the NHS – could not have been achieved ... But our long-term objective has always been to match ambitious national standards with a vigorous local autonomy and flexibility whereby we maximise efficiency, equity and a personalised service for the patient, the pupil and the citizen generally.[311]

This was, essentially, Brown's version of a choice agenda. The review indicated that the refinement of PSAs, along with the abolition of SDAs, meant that on average each department had seven PSA targets.[312] It also emphasised the importance of building strong working relationships: 'Good working relationships are a strong determinant of success in public service delivery, where hierarchical levers are often lacking.'[313] The key recommendations were:

- Performance management should evolve by: refining PSAs

through increased consultation in target setting; within the framework of national PSAs, substantially reducing all input, output and process targets and controls; releasing high performers from further targets [i.e. intervention in inverse proportion to success].

- It is crucial that accountability both to the public and along delivery chains and incentives to improve are strengthened by: publishing regular and robust data; sharpening rewards and sanctions; identifying the appropriate organisation in local government or the intermediate tier to performance manage frontline delivery with central government becoming more strategic and only intervening as a last resort.
- Local performance management capacity needs to be strengthened.[314]

The review signified Macpherson's perspective that 'there was very good joint working between the PMDU and the Treasury.'[315]

CONCLUSION: THE HARD GRIND IN THE ENGINE ROOM

The period from April 2003 to the Budget in March 2004 was a critical phase for Barber and the Delivery Unit. It began with Blair beginning to refocus on the delivery of his domestic agenda after the invasion of Iraq. The Delivery Unit faced a potential threat as senior people in No. 10 considered whether the Prime Minister still needed to be so closely involved in delivery through stocktakes. Barber was responsive in adapting delivery mechanisms to this potential threat and secured his preferred outcome. The perception in government that Blair remained engaged in delivery was important and this was renewed by the Barber deal – the art of delivery in action. This episode showed the fragile reality of working for a Prime Minister. The lesson was that political commitment could not be taken for granted and ultimately, though the techniques of delivery were of fundamental importance, they could not be successfully applied without the hidden wiring being in place.

During this stage, the Prime Minister was repositioning himself in the face of growing unpopularity due to Iraq. He was becoming more focused on his own legacy and indeed battling with Brown. With the Delivery Unit now in its third year, and with progress emerging across the board, Barber wanted to make it irreversible. This was most pronounced in his interactions with the Treasury in the Reform Agenda Group and with the DfES. He did not fear using up political capital in the pursuit of delivery but it was a slow, hard grind in the engine room of delivery.

CHAPTER SEVEN

MARCH 2004 TO JULY 2005: THE FINAL CHARGE TO DELIVER

INTRODUCTION

The Prime Minister's Delivery Unit was put to the final test during the period from March 2004 to July 2005; it was time to prove whether deliverology could achieve the intended goals first set out in 2001 ahead of the 2005 general election. During this period, Blair's preparation for that election would intensify – would this impede the Delivery Unit's ability to secure progress? There would be an increasing necessity to ensure that the improvements were being communicated effectively to the public – what role would the Unit play in this? There would also be a growing focus on the public service reform agenda for a third term – how would the PMDU feature in this post-election planning? Key figures were leaving and reshuffles were being planned – how would the Delivery Unit be impacted? Meanwhile, perhaps most importantly, Barber had said from the outset that he saw his role as a four-year commitment – how would his impending departure as head of the PMDU affect the work of the Unit?

MARCH TO SEPTEMBER 2004

The day after the Budget, 18 March 2004, Blair held a meeting at Chequers on the five-year strategies. In the ministerial meeting, Barber noted the specific areas of concern which were discussed between Blair and Cabinet ministers. For example, the Secretary of State for Health, John Reid, 'accepted Blair's challenge' and agreed 'that in primary care some central role [for government] would be necessary through to 2008'.[1] Blair commented that the health plan was 'too technocratic' and that he needed Reid 'to encapsulate the nature of the health reform crisply and clearly'.[2] Barber observed that 'a growing obsession of Blair's, no doubt with the forthcoming election in mind, is to be able to explain his reform ideas to the public'.[3] On transport, Blair said to Alistair Darling, the Secretary of State, 'The problem is simple ... different from other departments ... you know what you want to do but you don't have the resources.'[4] Though transport had always been within the Delivery Unit's purview, it had undoubtedly received less attention in terms of ambitious policy innovation and investment. Policy had tended to focus on improving standards and problem-solving, including on rail privatisation legacy issues.

In late March, Barber reflected on the unintended (or perhaps intended) consequences of PSAs, as he saw them. PSA targets meant 'new secretaries of state couldn't so easily change the agenda – see John Reid after Alan Milburn or even Charles Clarke and Estelle Morris after David Blunkett'.[5] As Barber himself admitted, his own wrangles with the DfES and Clarke were perhaps 'about keeping him focused on the [existing] PSA targets for primary education, without them, I'd have had no chance'.[6] PSAs enabled Barber to hold successive Secretaries of State to account for targets set under their predecessors, many years after the targets were first published, even when a Secretary of State seemed to be seeking to shift the agenda towards their personal priorities. Secretaries of state therefore had to contend with all the usual pressures of party, Parliament, constituency and the wider public in addition to an ambitious Prime Minister and Chancellor (who were often at odds politically as well as on policy) and advisers like Barber, who were holding them to account using a Treasury tool for targets that pre-dated their tenure.

A stocktake on asylum and immigration took place at the end of March. There was notable progress – two consecutive months of asylum applications below 3,000 and the rest of the system, with the exception of the removal of failed asylum seekers, was improving.[7] They discussed the problem the government had with negative media coverage on the issue. Blair gave an 'impressive performance'; he said, 'Underneath asylum and immigration it's a race issue but we are stuck on dealing with it as long as there is abuse in the system … There will come a point when we can accuse them (the Tories) of playing a dangerous game' but they were not there yet.[8] Blair went on to outline the action he believed needed to be taken. The Home Secretary said he agreed with the Prime Minister's points and added a critique of the organisation in charge, the Immigration and Nationality Directorate (IND), whose representative had presented during the stocktake and remained present during this critique.[9]

Stocktakes evidently provided an opportunity for ministers to hold civil servants to account too. Both the director of the IND, Bill Jeffrey, and the Permanent Secretary to the Home Office, John Gieve, accepted that though progress had been made on asylum they needed to give more attention to immigration. Blair acknowledged their progress on many aspects and added, 'I've always said the Home Office is the toughest department.'[10] Home Secretary David Blunkett was particularly exercised because of a media furore over alleged manipulation of immigration and asylum figures. First, an ex-Home Office immigration official, Steve Moxon, claimed that officials in Sheffield were told to waive key checks on visa applications from countries which were due to join the EU on 1 May 2004. An internal inquiry found decisions had been taken by junior local officials, not ministers. Secondly, the Conservative shadow Home Secretary, David Davis, received leaked information from a diplomat in the British Consulate in Romania which disclosed a visa scam whereby migrants using forged documents were being granted visas to Britain from potential EU accession states, despite concerns of officials. Beverley Hughes, the minister of state for immigration, citizenship and counter-terrorism, said she had not known about this but after evidence to the contrary emerged, she resigned on 1 April 2004. Thirdly, further reported leaks from the Home Office stated that Hughes's office had allowed staff to reduce raids on companies thought to employ illegal immigrants, so that they would not be arrested and then opt to claim asylum, thus increasing the asylum figures, which could impact the meeting of the target.[11] In response the Home Office issued a statement:

The priority has certainly been to remove failed asylum seekers. But ministers have never asked the immigration service to hold back on other operations in order to prevent asylum claims. If they had, we would not have removed 12,000 non-asylum illegals and overstayers last year, a record figure. Asylum claims have fallen because of the closure of Sangatte (the refugee camp near Calais), the moving of border controls to France and stopping people coming through the Channel Tunnel.[12]

Barber considered whether the PMDU could become implicated in the crisis given the Unit's work on the asylum target with the Home Office and the IND.[13] The media, however, focused attention on the Home Office and its ministers. Barber, with the Prime Minister's approval, agreed to review the delivery plans on immigration.[14]

Elections often accelerate the planning for reforms to the machinery of government. Barber contributed to conversations on what a reformed centre of government should look like after the 2005 election. In early April, he attended the Cabinet Secretary's Delivery and Reform team awayday where he considered the implications of implementing the choice agenda.* Barber said that as they 'devolved' power to the frontline they 'had to avoid losing the capacity to deliver' and to consider whether professionals would be motivated to continually improve services.[15] During the event, the managing director of public services in the Treasury, Nicholas Macpherson, suggested considering the idea of a US-inspired Office of Management and Budget (OMB), which would control spending and priorities of departments, if there were changes in No. 10 and No. 11.[16] As we have seen, an OMB was unlikely to be accepted by Gordon Brown as Chancellor, who would have viewed it as an attempt to dilute his power (indeed it had been part of the Blairite Operation Teddy Bear in 2003) – but he would later revisit the idea as Prime Minister.[17]

On 6 April, a transport stocktake took place; 'uniquely for a stocktake' the Chancellor attended in place of the lower-ranking Chief Secretary to the Treasury.[18] Part of the meeting centred on the PMDU's priority review on how to improve rail performance in the short term. Barber noted Darling's enthusiasm for the review

---

* The Delivery and Reform team was a Cabinet Office group of a selection of heads of central units including the Strategy Unit, the Office of Public Service Reform and the PMDU.

and that 'for the first time there was a shared understanding of the short-term objective and clarity about who was responsible for what in terms of delay minutes'.[19] The major debate, in which Barber did not participate, was on the long-term 'future structure and funding of the railway'.[20] At Darling's request, Barber had been briefed on the structure debate; the 'major problem' was funding, which was why Brown attended the stocktake.[21] Darling and Brown set out the state of affairs – there was a £2 billion funding gap (the budget was £4 billion but the cost was £6 billion) and a rail fare increase of RPI + 2 per cent would bring in only £100 million, plus there would be a political cost.[22]

The government therefore needed to allocate a significant amount of funding or close down parts of the railway, as the governments of Harold Macmillan and Harold Wilson had in the 1960s, as result of the Beeching reports.* The forthcoming spending review provided an impetus for finding solutions as it would make the 'state of affairs transparent'.†[23] Barber reflected that Darling and Brown, oddly, had presented the problem to Blair and 'wanted to see if he had some kind of solution when what you'd expect was that they would set out a number of options, however unpalatable, and then discuss the merits and demerits of them with the PM'.[24] Though the discussion was 'good-humoured' Blair 'refused to flap or to attempt to propose solutions'; he left it to the Chancellor and Secretary of State for Transport to solve the problem.[25]

In this meeting, the core issues on transport policy during the second term were clear – the PMDU had focused on short-term

---

* Railways were closed across the country for the sake of efficiency, as recommended by two reports published in 1963 and 1965, authored by Dr Richard Beeching.

† The 2004 spending review provided annual average growth of 4.5 per cent in real terms over the three-year period; the expenditure of the DfT in 2007/8 would be £2.4 billion higher than in 2004/5.

improvements in standards. The DfT, No. 10 and the Treasury had identified new areas for improvement and some options on how to do this but there was a funding gap and seemingly an unwillingness from all parties to seriously resolve the issue, as this 'inconclusive discussion' illustrated.[26] Furthermore, resources and capacity were already being consumed by the delivery of two major rail infrastructure projects which the New Labour government had inherited from the previous Conservative administration, namely the West Coast Main Line upgrade and the Channel Tunnel Rail Link (known subsequently as High Speed 1 or HS1).

On education, Barber and the PMDU had been doggedly pursuing progress in the DfES on reforms to Key Stage 2, particularly since December 2003. This unrelenting approach could have damaged relations with the department. Barber met the director general for schools, Peter Housden, for a round-up meeting where they discussed the 'difficulties of the Key Stage 2 debate', namely the continued commitment to and effective implementation of the numeracy and literacy strategies.[27] Housden stated that the PMDU's 'action had in no way damaged' the relationship with the DfES.[28] The PMDU approach to challenging departments on their policy solutions was a balancing act, between interfering and justifiably questioning a department in order to meet targets. This was most pronounced in education where Barber was an expert himself and had crafted and implemented the schools policies in the first term. Now he was acting from his position as head of the PMDU in response to critical feedback on the UK's position from the education sector and PMDU analysis.

By early May, the PMDU was also exerting pressure on Home Office civil servants working on delivering the drugs strategy (which aimed to reduce harm to users and communities caused by drugs).[29]

Barber telephoned the senior civil servant in charge, Leigh Lewis, Second Permanent Secretary for crime, policing and counter-terrorism, to discuss the issues identified by the PMDU team and the dissatisfaction expressed by the Prime Minister.[30] Barber privately admitted that his intention was to unsettle Lewis, mainly because he saw it as 'beneficial to delivering the key outcomes', but Lewis 'welcomed this tip-off' because he was due to present to Blair the following week.[31] Barber informed Lewis that ahead of the meeting, the PMDU briefing would 'support the view that real progress had been made but there was much more to do'.[32] Relations between the Home Office and PMDU drugs teams were 'tense' at that point, as the PMDU was worried that a drugs crisis could arise.[33] It was not clear enough to Barber that they were 'sufficiently rigorous in seeing things through to a result'.[34] Barber suggested to Lewis (who agreed) that 'one way to reassure Blair' would be for the PMDU to conduct two frontline visits and report back.[35] Barber was using the Prime Minister's concern to accelerate progress while also encouraging the department to connect with the frontline – both were signatures of the PMDU approach under Barber.

Meanwhile in the Department of Health, the PMDU was facing pressure from the Secretary of State, John Reid. Reid had asked the PMDU to assess whether what he called a 'no-bullshit' target was deliverable; for patients it would mean 'four months from seeing the GP to the operation being done' whereas the existing target was 'three months from the appointment with the consultant to the operation occurring'.[36] Arguably, this was Reid appealing to the Prime Minister's priority for clear communication with the public in the run-up to the general election. The government was seeking to address 'the perception gap' – the emerging disparity between the delivery facts and public perception of lower public service standards. Barber told Reid that PMDU work suggested 'that a no-bullshit target of four months was deliverable by December 2008' and it would cost £2 billion, which would need to come out of Health's 'unallocated reserve of about £4 billion'.[37] Reid welcomed this work, though they both agreed that they would need to carefully consider how to approach the Treasury. They had had 'clear signals' from Brown and his close advisers that they were 'deeply suspicious of the proposed new target' and as a result, the Treasury wanted 'strong assurance' from the PMDU that it was genuinely 'deliverable'.[38] The PMDU would carefully have to navigate the established convention that it would not support departmental demands for more money in order to deliver a target. There was also a 'purely political risk' that in promoting a new target, the government would be effectively 'rubbishing' the existing 2005 six-month target, which could (and did) prove to be a 'major achievement in delivery terms' of that parliament.[39]

EXPECTED TO FAIL

In early May, Barber drafted a note on 'The Future of the Delivery Unit' to the Cabinet Secretary, Andrew Turnbull, after consulting three Permanent Secretaries, David Normington in Education, David Rowlands in Transport and John Gieve in the Home Office. Their 'basic message' was that they respected and valued the PMDU and wanted more.[40] Normington, however, said 'very frankly' that when it was set up he 'expected it to fail but it hadn't'.[41] They did not want the Unit to be abolished after four years, which had been Barber's 'stated ambition' at the outset, though by this point he 'hoped the PMDU would only continue by popular demand'.[42] The three delivery Permanent Secretaries provided their explanation for the Unit's success: 'clear priorities, which we stick to; excellent people; good processes/products; strong backing from the PM; effective problem-solving; real investment in relationship-building'.[43] This insight into how Permanent Secretaries viewed the PMDU is valuable. The human side of the PMDU was of considerable importance – particularly the Prime Minister's political sponsorship, the consistent and attentive focus on relationship-building and the Unit's pragmatic approach. At an earlier meeting, the Permanent Secretary to the Treasury, Gus O'Donnell, listed similar reasons.[44] Barber and the PMDU management team were planning for the period after the current set of targets were due to be delivered; as part of this they were preparing to take on new priorities with 2008 deadlines. The plans were presented to Turnbull and received 'broad endorsement for the direction of change.'[45]

During this period, Barber continued to be involved in the consideration and refinement of the five-year strategies, which had been in development since autumn 2003.[46] His operational knowledge of delivery in major policy areas and expertise in education were useful to the Prime Minister. Prior to a Cabinet committee meeting, Barber and Blair discussed the current progress on key delivery areas. Promisingly Barber informed him that there was a strong possibility of meeting the waiting times target early. Blair asked why this was and Barber explained that it was due to the building up of capacity including the introduction of choice (of providers) after six months of being on the waiting list.[47] On the perception gap, Blair said he thought the public was 'really beginning to notice that the NHS was improving'.[48] Polling by the British Social Attitudes survey showed that NHS satisfaction was increasing steadily during the second term with a marked upward trend during 2004.[49] Barber was 'upbeat' about the state of delivery overall and thought there was a 'good chance that people would see it and believe it'.[50]

He reflected, as he had done a year earlier, that if necessary, the Unit should expend this capital to ensure delivery – 'We should not fear to use up social capital in Whitehall to get the delivery we believe is necessary.'[51]

DISPENSING WITH THE ART OF DELIVERY

In June, Barber attended a spending review meeting with Treasury and DfES civil servants which aimed to settle the education public service agreements. Barber's frustration with the DfES boiled over and resulted in a regrettable clash with Clarke's special adviser, Robert Hill. Initially Barber aimed to help the DfES 'against the Treasury' on schools standards but on the issue of school attendance he used the meeting to challenge what he viewed as the department's 'lack of ambition'.[52] A DfES civil servant defended the department's position in part by stating that the 'data had proved so hard to shift'. Barber replied, 'The reason the data hasn't shifted is that you haven't had a strategy.'[53] Hill responded angrily, 'You can't talk like that, Michael ... we do have a strategy ... it may be an inadequate one but we do have a strategy.'[54] Barber's point may have been proved but at an unseemly expense which Barber himself admitted left him 'embarrassed' for being 'so blunt'; he recognised that 'it was the wrong place' to critique the strategy.[55] This was not a fine example of the art of delivery and was uncharacteristic of Barber's approach. Barber later explained the tension when it came to the DfES, a policy area in which he had a legacy:

> [Education was] the most difficult one because Health started tense but I worked on that and I didn't have history. But in Education, they thought that in the second term I was trying to get them to do what I would have done if I had stayed. There was part

of me that was trying to get them to do what I would have done if I'd stayed. I probably would have been director general of schools if I'd stayed there. So that was more difficult.[56]

On 23 June, Blair gave a speech on public service reform. Several people in No. 10 had assisted in drafting the text, including Barber.[57] The Prime Minister spoke of planning the agenda for a third term and described his government's reforms as 'the recasting of the 1945 welfare state to end entirely the era of "one size fits all" services and put in their place modern services which maintain at their core the values of equality of access and opportunity for all'.[58] This summed up Blair's approach – a commitment to the principles and outcomes but a rejection of the state as a monopoly provider. Blair went on to emphasise that the 'user' would drive the quality of public services and believed his vision combined 'choice, excellence and equality in a modern universal welfare state'.[59] The following day the first of the five-year strategies was published by the Department of Health, driven by the Prime Minister. The departments had created the strategies but they had been monitored and shaped by No. 10 (including the PMDU) and the Treasury. The health strategy, entitled 'The NHS Improvement Plan: Putting People at the Heart of Public Services', outlined the progress so far, the plan going forward and how they would make it happen. The Secretary of State for Health's preface included the following section highlighting areas of progress since 1997:

The maximum waiting time for an operation fell from eighteen months to less than nine months; 94 per cent of patients were seen, diagnosed and treated within four hours of arrival in A&E, the maximum waiting time for an outpatient appointment had fallen from twenty-six weeks to seventeen weeks; 97 per cent of patients were able to see a GP within two days; and there was a 22 per cent increase in doctors and a 21 per cent rise in the total number of nurses.[60]

Despite Blair's rejection of monopoly state providers in his speech, the health five-year strategy put the NHS at the heart of healthcare provision, but there would be choice and diversity. This demonstrated that though the Blair government could diversify the providers, universal healthcare fundamentally required an overarching public sector provider. Barber's involvement in the planning of the health five-year strategy was evident when he met Reid on the day of publication. Reid said to Barber, 'I'll hold you personally responsible if this doesn't work,' especially the centrepiece, which was a new start-to-treatment target of four months. Barber said, 'That's fine by me because it will work.'[61]

On 1 July, Barber gave a presentation to the Cabinet about the state of delivery. All Prime Ministers have to carry the confidence of Cabinet with them and a Cabinet always retains the ability to make a Prime Minister's position untenable. It was therefore important for Barber to give a convincing presentation as it would impact the Cabinet's conviction in the progress being made. Barber finished his presentation with a declaration, 'It's time for results.'[62] Blair made a significant remark in response: 'Some changes in government work and some don't … The Delivery Unit and your leadership of it have been exceptional.'[63] This was followed by a debate on the education strategy and a summing up by Blair; Blunkett approved of the fact that the strategy had been brought to Cabinet for discussion.[64] The result was positive, though no explicit vote had taken place.[65]

THE 2004 SPENDING REVIEW

The spending review negotiations culminated in early July and Barber noted that it was striking how little involved he was.[66] He attributed this to the fact that the education and health settlements were already complete and because the PMDU's target monitoring routines were now integrated and so the Treasury, the relevant department and the PMDU were aware of any issues.[67] This corresponds with Ed Balls's account of the 2004 spending review: 'By the time you got to 2004 the Treasury and the Delivery Unit were working so closely together that it would become much more of a sort of collective view.'[68] It was around this time that Balls left government as chief economic adviser (since 1999), to prepare for the next general election in which he sought to be elected as MP for Normanton. He used an interview soon after his candidacy was announced to outline his views on the role of markets in public services.

> You cannot drive efficiency or equity through individual purchase and decision. Health [the NHS] only works effectively when you have collective purchase, which is an important role of primary care trusts. Our health policy recognises the limits of markets and individual budgets and prices ... There can be contestability. Primary care trusts are using their collective purchasing role to drive prices down. It is not being driven by individuals buying in the marketplace.[69]

Nicholas Macpherson, meanwhile, was appointed managing director of budget and public finances in the Treasury in July 2004. Aside from the Chancellor, the most important Treasury relationships for Barber and the PMDU to get right had been those with Balls and Macpherson. Both had been in established positions when the

PMDU was created in June 2001, whereas the people occupying the senior posts of Permanent Secretary and Chief Secretary to the Treasury had changed during this period. When interviewed, Balls and Macpherson reflected on Barber's relationship with the Treasury. Balls later explained how it evolved:

> So, stage one, they had to agree to being cooperative rather than shifting the responsibility and that succeeded. Two, we came to see that prime ministerial challenge for non-delivery was empowering for all of us. Thirdly, they were very competent and very good. So, the reality was it ended up with a deep cooperative relationship between the Treasury and the Delivery Unit. We got way beyond 'this is a precursor to the Treasury losing the responsibility'.[70]

Macpherson recalled the value which Barber and the PMDU provided:

> Michael was really respected by the Treasury because he wasn't of the Treasury but he brought expertise and experience to the party which was genuinely lacking at that time; and anybody sensible in the Treasury recognised [that] would be necessary if performance was going to be improved. There was distrust at the beginning but the Treasury ended up valuing the fact that the PMDU was around.[71]

Macpherson also described the importance of his personal relationship with Barber:

> I just thought Michael was a very interesting person. I thought

he brought some real analytical rigour to the party. At a personal level, I think we just got on well and were interested in achieving the same objectives. Neither of us were terribly interested in massive turf disputes and equally we were working with people who for understandable political reasons weren't quite as trusting as we were.[72]

The departure of Balls and Macpherson did not significantly jeopardise the PMDU's relationship with the Treasury during the final year of the parliament, largely because the spending review, which set departmental budgets and PSAs for three years, had been finalised. It was published on 12 July 2004. The 2000 and 2002 spending reviews had seen major increases in spending to improve and reform public services, especially health. In 2004, the increases continued, but efficiencies and other areas such as defence and policing were also prioritised. Barber described Brown's statement in the House of Commons as 'relentless and powerful as ever'.[73] The major announcements were:

- Gross cuts of 84,150 Civil Service posts by 2008 to allow for more frontline investment.
- Overall spending on national security to more than double.
- 20,000 community police officers by 2008.
- Health spending to rise by 7.1 per cent over the next three years.
- Education spending to increase from £63 billion to £77 billion.[74]

The 'Better Public Services' section of the spending review referred to the joint PMDU–Treasury 'Devolving Decision Making Review', which had been published with the 2004 Budget. It advocated measures related to the choice and devolution agenda:

'strengthen further the achievement of national objectives; increase devolution and flexibility for frontline professionals and communities; achieve more personalised public services'.[75] Around this time, Gieve spoke publicly about the way in which the Civil Service culture had adapted to delivery: 'Hitherto, targets were seen as something we set for executive agencies of government, not for main policy-making central departments, but I think that has been almost entirely a force for the good. It's made central departments think whether the policymaking they are doing is contributing to generally good outcomes.'[76] This is an illuminating comment from a Permanent Secretary who had been a civil servant under Thatcher and Major. It illustrates the way in which Blair's government built on the Next Steps agencies (created in the 1990s and concentrating on operational delivery). By 1997, much of the delivery capability was outside of Whitehall; Blair's reforms brought culture change and an enhanced capacity to deliver *within* Whitehall.

A STEP CHANGE IN DELIVERY

On 22 July, Blair held his monthly press conference. Since 2002, the July press conference had included a presentation on delivery by Barber, akin to an end of term review prior to the summer recess. Blair started the session. 'There has without doubt been a step change in delivery across our public services in the last year. Waiting times for treatment are falling fast. Deaths from cancer and heart disease are down.'[77] Barber explained the progress in health:

The waiting list hovered above a million until early 2003, but in the last year has fallen very significantly, and in May of this year it was below 900,000 for the second consecutive month ... There is an explanation for this progress, it is not just about the build-up of capacity, it is about the introduction of choice [of provider] at six months for patients, the introduction of competition through treatment centres, and indeed the introduction of three-year funding for primary care trusts which improves planning and accountability.[78]

On education, Barber referenced the reduction in the number of low-performing schools: 'In 1997 there were 616 secondary schools where fewer than 25 per cent of pupils achieved five higher grades at GCSE, by last year that had reduced to 224.'[79] Other areas of success included the teacher shortage problem, which had been 'tackled very effectively', and the literacy hour, which independent research confirmed was not only affecting the eleven-year-olds' test results, but five years later was having an effect on pupils' GCSE results.[80] He identified two challenges: one, 'to get off the plateau for 11-year-olds' literacy and numeracy, and we will know whether that has happened in August'; two, the problem of truancy, which had 'remained intractable over a ten-year period, and it doesn't matter whether you look at secondary or primary education, no progress has been made there'.[81] Barber finished by summarising: 'There is widespread and significant progress across the public services which is becoming irreversible. The foundations have been laid for further radical reform. The task is far from complete.'[82]

The media articles on the press conference recognised the impact of Barber and the PMDU. Peter Riddell in *The Times* gave his assessment:

The most important words at the end of term Downing Street press conference came not from Tony Blair, but from Michael Barber, the Head of the Delivery Unit ... Mr Barber's presentation, repeating what he recently told the Cabinet, addressed the central question of how the Government's record should be judged and the choice for voters at the next election. Has the additional spending made a difference to the quality of services?

A year ago, Mr Barber's verdict was 'demonstrable progress in most areas but not yet irreversible'. Now, the assessment is more positive: 'widespread and significant progress across the public services, becoming irreversible.'[83]

The media reportage also showed the importance of this domestic progress for the government's reputation. James Blitz in the *Financial Times* wrote:

A few weeks ago, it looked as if Tony Blair was on his last legs politically, a man crushed by the consequences of the Iraq war. Yesterday, however, the Prime Minister's tone was confident … The tide is beginning to turn for the government on the reform of public services, as Michael Barber, the Head of the Prime Minister's Delivery Unit, told reporters.[84]

SEPTEMBER TO DECEMBER 2004

THE END GAME

The period from September to December marked the last phase in which the PMDU could seriously push for delivery before the build-up to the 2005 general election. On 13 September, at a regular Monday morning meeting in No. 10 the Prime Minister reinforced the need to be attentive in this phase, and this verbal commitment was important for Barber and the PMDU: 'Blair said … that he wanted to ensure the stocktake programme was adhered to through to Christmas because he thought there was some "slippage" around … I was very encouraged by Blair's comment.'[85]

Barber met with civil servants from the Department of Health where he 'challenged and cajoled them' on the progress of key targets.[86] On access to primary care (that is, access to a GP) Barber said it was 'a question of finishing the job' as the target was due to be met in December.[87] He urged them 'to sharpen their capacity to act in November if the data revealed a few remaining laggards but was thoroughly reassured that they were on top of things'.[88] This was not the case on 'choose and book', whereby patients would be able to choose and book the date and location of hospital appointments (due by December 2005). The meeting revealed that there were problems with the huge IT programme that underpinned the service, 'slippage in meeting deadlines and tensions at the top of the Department'.[89] Barber acknowledged that perhaps the PMDU had 'been slow to pick all this up but it set alarm bells ringing' in his mind and he took this up afterwards with the PMDU health team.[90]

A new internal Delivery Unit product, quarterly monitoring reports,* gave a snapshot of the progress made since the last delivery report in July. Barber was alarmed to see that on several priorities his team were predicting marginal progress if any between July and December. In both 'planning and capacity', people were still predicting some priority areas would be red or amber-red, even though back in July, Barber had insisted that these areas were turned to at least amber-green.[91] At a subsequent awayday, Barber told his team that either the delivery report actions 'weren't being implemented

---

* Quarterly monitoring reports were designed by Peter Thomas, a director in the PMDU.

as they should or we had drafted the Delivery Reports wrongly. Either way we had to question our own performance in each of these cases.'[92] The PMDU team were responsive and 'began to think hard about how they could strengthen what was planned and, if necessary, shift their priorities'.[93] Barber also discussed the moral dimension to their work:

> I emphasised the importance of our mission and the ethical basis of our work. Our techniques were morally neutral but our approach to relationships and above all our mission were over-whelmingly moral. The question arose later in the day about how this squared with Civil Service neutrality, which I dealt with by saying that the neutrality applied to political parties – it did not mean you couldn't have passion for a cause.[94]

The following week, Blair and Barber had a one-to-one meeting on the 'state of play on delivery'; they also discussed a 'radical agenda' for a third term and Barber's future.[95] Blair said firmly, 'I am going to stay a full term by the way … I'm going to go for broke.'[96] They agreed that Barber should be involved in the discussions about the reform of the centre of government ahead of the next election and Barber advised Blair on what he thought he should do.

> I said he needed to get the whole plan for the first year sorted out in advance. 'The moral of the last few years is you really have to exploit the first year.' I said he should line up a whole sequence: new structure at the centre, new machinery of government, the revolutionaries both political and official lined up to take key positions, the delivery plans for the five-year strategies in place, an overall strategy for year one and a decisive stance in relation

to Spending Review 2006, which would be Blair's last chance to influence resource allocation.[97]

This interaction demonstrated Barber's understanding of the machinery of government at macro and micro levels as well as the imperative for a Prime Minister to make progress quickly, even in a third term. Blair reflected on his own understanding of how to govern and the impact of Iraq on trust: 'I feel oddly that this is the first term and the next one the second ... I really understand better than ever now how to do the job ... Though for reasons we understand I'm less trusted than before.'[98] He invited Barber to that week's Cabinet meeting to hear him tell his colleagues that they needed to 'turn everything amber to green' by Christmas.[99]

Blair chaired a stocktake on asylum and immigration. He was frustrated that the number of asylum seekers was rising and removal numbers had plateaued; he expressed this 'frustration' to those present, including the Home Secretary and the relevant minister of state in the Home Office, Des Browne.[100] It was an issue on which Blair felt the Conservatives would challenge the government in the upcoming election and he wanted a strong policy to counter them. Ahead of the stocktake, Barber relayed the Prime Minister's frustration to Bill Jeffrey, the head of the IND. In the meeting, Jeffrey outlined the action they were going to take and explained the problems. Barber told the Prime Minister that the PMDU had reviewed the IND plans and had been 'impressed'.[101] Barber's management of people and information, the art of delivery, produced the result he hoped for. Blair listened to Jeffrey and 'said exactly what a Delivery Unit would want him to say – that's all fine ... as long as we get back on track by Christmas'.[102] Blair's commitment to delivery evidently remained strong; the work of the PMDU was critical to the success of his second term and in securing a third mandate.

A health stocktake demonstrated the Prime Minister's continued deep engagement with public service reform but also the strong, standardised approach to delivery developed in the Department of Health. Blair allocated one and a half hours to the meeting and opened up the discussion with John Reid. Barber described the relationship between the Prime Minister and the Secretary of State for Health: 'They are able to have a genuine interaction – differences of emphasis, a rounded discussion but also complete agreement about the goals and the politics surrounding them.'[103] Barber began the meeting with a presentation on delivery, in which he was positive but also 'hard-hitting about the plateau' in certain areas and explained the 'clear agreement' with Health about how the PMDU would work with them on system reform.[104] He explained the change he had noticed in the Department of Health's delivery capability:

What impresses me about DH nowadays is that they have a standard approach to delivery which works. Published data, focus on the Trusts with a problem, put in teams to help them – and rely on clear standards to do the trick for the rest. Largely, they learned this with us, as for example on A&E.[105]

In retrospect, Nigel Crisp, Permanent Secretary at the Department of Health and chief executive of the NHS, saw that though there were downsides to targets – too many, some poorly designed, some people gamed the system, and some individuals focused too narrowly on a given target – there were still huge benefits.

We could have done better at managing all of these things but the upside of targets was also enormous. In the pre-target NHS that I took over in 2000 about 4% of heart patients died whilst on the waiting list for surgery. We therefore targeted heart waiting lists ... and reduced mortality on the waiting list to zero – more than 5,500 [people] waited more than three months for heart surgery in 2000, but no one did in 2005. In 2000 only 24% of patients received 'clot busting' drugs within an hour of a heart attack despite the evidence of their effectiveness being available for almost 20 years. The use of targets together with management action and service redesign increased that to 55% by March 2005. Delivery of these two cardiac targets helped save many lives.[106]

DELIVERY FACTS AND THE PERCEPTION GAP

In early December, the delivery league table was finalised; it came out 'greener than ever' and Barber was 'proud' of what the PMDU had achieved:[107] 'We really have made progress in the last twelve months across a wide spectrum – though as I shall say to the Cabinet on Thursday, while this progress is impressive it's from a low base and transformation still lies ahead.'[108]

Barber gave a presentation to the Cabinet on 9 December and told four brief stories of success on operation waiting times, A&E waiting times, London secondary schools and the criminal justice system. He drew out lessons about 'data, delivery chains, account-ability ... and about choice and contestability'.[109] Then he showed the progress made across the delivery agenda including, for the first time, putting the delivery league table in front of the Cabinet. Though the progress in the past twelve months had been marked, Barber discussed the gap between what had been achieved and the public perception of progress.[110] He used popular culture to show that the message was starting to get through; an episode of the BBC soap opera *EastEnders* showed a character, Ian Beale, complaining that 'people spend at least five hours in A&E', to which his wife Jane responded, 'It's a lot better nowadays.'[111] One Cabinet minister joked that this was worth several ministerial speeches in terms of impact.[112] Barber identified the lessons they had learnt about how to bring about transformation – 'the right mindset, powerful performance management and bold reform'.[113] He explained the importance of 'the guiding coalition ... where there was shared understanding among the seven key people [in government] rapid progress could be made – where this was missing it was much more difficult'.[114] He also addressed the importance of targets: 'There is no way that the maximum [A&E] wait would be down to four hours now, if there hadn't been a target ... Or that those five LEAs (in London) would be where they are without that floor target.'[115]

Barber received strong endorsements for this presentation from the Prime Minister and other Cabinet ministers. After Cabinet, Barber briefed Andrew Grice, a journalist from *The Independent*, on the perception gap data which the government was publishing the following day. The resulting article had the headline 'Things have only got better. But will Blair benefit?'

One of the trends that most perplexes him [Blair] is the 'perception gap' between people's view of their local services – which is getting better, particularly among regular users of them – and their less favourable impression of the nation's services generally.

But there are some cautious grounds for optimism that the gap is closing. Professor Barber's charts had 26 green lights, showing that the public thinks services are improving, and only three red ones indicating the opposite. The number of 'delivery facts' that the Government would love us to believe has risen from six to eight since the spring.[116]

The data which Barber used was based on independent polling by MORI on 'Public Attitudes to Public Services' conducted in 2004, commissioned by the Cabinet Office. In his briefing, Barber explained to Grice the reasons for the perception gap as he saw them:

1. A 'time lag' before people notice service improvements …
2. The improvements in some services have been from a low base, with the quality provided moving from 'not good' to 'adequate'. So people are not going to dance in the streets when twelve-hour waits in A&E are cut to a maximum of four hours, as they will be this month …
3. People's expectations are rising all the time. As consumers, they expect supermarkets to get better, so why not schools and hospitals? So, the Government finds itself running to catch up.[117]

What Barber did not mention, perhaps through tact, but which Blair had mentioned back in October, was that the Prime Minister and therefore to an extent the government 'is less trusted than before' the conflict in Iraq and the subsequent political fallout.[118] The foreign affected the domestic.

END OF AN ERA

On 15 December, the Home Secretary, David Blunkett, resigned over accusations that he had used his position to fast-track a visa application for his former partner's nanny. A report on his conduct by Sir Alan Budd was published on 21 December; he found a 'chain of events' linking Blunkett to a faster-than-average issuing of a visa but Budd was unable to determine whether Blunkett had sought special treatment for the nanny or had only highlighted an example of poor performance by the Immigration Directorate.[119] For Barber, the loss of Blunkett was 'the saddest day' of his professional life.[120] The shared experience of crafting and delivering reform first in education from 1997 to 2001, and then in the Home Office from 2001 to 2004, had fostered a deep, trusting relationship between Blunkett and Barber. Blunkett believed that the Delivery Unit approach not only worked, but also brought more formality and data to the conduct of government.

> It had a matrix for identifying problems but also with ideas about solutions because any fool can monitor and identify that you're doing badly, we all knew where we were doing badly, the real challenge is bringing expertise to bear and cooperation ... in the system to help you do it.[121]

Blunkett also singled out Barber's personal approach as critical to delivery.

> Michael was extremely good – personally good because of his manner, because of his quiet way of listening and persuading and getting people to do things, his steeliness inside ... his willingness to acknowledge when he thought he'd got it wrong and hold himself to account ... And [his] knowledge that in the end if the buck stops with you, you've got to do something about it.[122]

Blunkett's resignation prompted a reshuffle which resulted in

Charles Clarke moving from Education to the Home Office, Ruth Kelly replacing him in Education, and David Miliband, who had been minister of state for schools, taking over from Kelly as minister of state for the Cabinet Office. Given the friction between himself and Clarke, Barber briefed his Home Office team on this 'new challenge' and said they 'had to secure' their relationships with John Gieve and Leigh Lewis, as they would be 'more important' now.[123] Fortunately for Barber and the PMDU, much of the progress on delivery for this parliament had been achieved.

Furthermore, in Gieve, Barber had a Permanent Secretary who saw delivery as part of his role. In an interview in 2004, Gieve stated, 'I see my key role as building a machine that really does deliver and which has the levers and the partnerships that influence what happens on the ground.'[124]

On 20 December, Barber met with Ruth Kelly where he discussed the short-term delivery issues, including the next stocktake scheduled for January. Barber was impressed with Kelly's 'quickness of mind' and 'thoughtfulness' and 'sensed that she had real strength too'.[125] In his end of year highlights Barber included 'best piece of Delivery Unit business ... the overwhelming sense of the results going in the right way was tremendously satisfying'; 'the Cabinet presentations in July and December were really satisfying'; and 'biggest worry – at the start of the year KS2 [Key Stage 2]; at the end of the year asylum, both applications and removals'.[126]

JANUARY TO MAY 2005

THE LAST STAND

The period from January to May 2005 marked a switch, with the Prime Minister and government becoming increasingly focused on the forthcoming election. Meanwhile the PMDU continued to pursue delivery of 2005 targets with less political involvement and began to focus on targets for a third term. In early January, Barber attended a meeting chaired by Blair at Chequers to establish further clarity on policy. The election was at the forefront of the Prime Minister's mind and his domestic agenda for a third term was key.[127] Members of the Policy Directorate presented their papers and Blair asked 'operational questions' about how the policies would be delivered in practice.[128] Barber reflected, 'It struck me that I've often underestimated in my account of Blair the degree to which he really does think operationally. Or perhaps this is an example of how he's becoming a more effective Prime Minister.'[129] They then discussed Blair's 'real passion: the opening up of the supply-side; he wanted all the five-year plan measures – expansion of good schools, academies, foundation status – accelerated'.[130] Blair, eight years in as Prime Minister, was evidently not losing any of his zeal for reform; his drive for change was palpable. He wanted to be convinced that for policies on which he would have to spend political capital, he received 'bangs for buck'.[131] On education, Barber emphasised 'the need to see through some key programmes which would deliver short-term results' while the reforms they had been discussing would impact on the medium and long term.[132]

The Prime Minister was becoming increasingly focused on the upcoming general election. The Monday morning meeting on 10 January was 'extremely brief' and the 'striking aspect' of it from Barber's point of view was that it was 'all about election preparation, the whole focus' being on a May election.[133] This was 'not a surprise' to Barber but it had 'important implications for the Delivery Unit' which he relayed to the PMDU management team.[134] He identified two key tasks, short-term progress-chasing and medium-term planning, which the PMDU had 'to pursue probably without much attention from the PM or the politicians'.[135] Barber met Blair for a one-to-one meeting on 17 January. He advised the Prime Minister at length on the preparations he thought were necessary ahead of a potential third term – what the specific priorities were and how they would be delivered.

> 'You're a man in a hurry … You need to get the people in place, the organisation sorted out and plans for the first three months sorted out before the election.' … He needed to distinguish between the perfect centre of government and the perfect centre for a Prime Minister with a time limit.[136]

They discussed the Delivery Unit, about which Blair said he had never had negative feedback.[137] In the same week, Barber had productive follow-up meetings on the December delivery reports with Permanent Secretaries David Normington (Education) and David Rowlands (Transport).[138] He noted that relations with the DfES, which had been 'difficult' in 2004, were now 'excellent'.[139] He attributed this to the department's acceptance of PMDU recommendations and to a new Secretary of State with a 'similar agenda to Blair' and particularly 'good relations' with No. 10.[140] Relations with Rowlands were 'good' even though a recent PMDU priority review had 'caused some tension' with DfT civil servants.[141] As a result of the priority review on rail performance, Network Rail would begin to performance-manage both the tracks and the train operating companies 'region-by-region against trajectory'.[142] Moreover, rail performance through the autumn and winter had been 'relatively good'.[143] At the political level, Barber met with Alistair Darling to explain the priority review; he felt Darling trusted the

PMDU's judgement.[144] Darling 'strongly endorsed' the PMDU recommendations.[145]

In late January, an education stocktake took place, Kelly's first as Secretary of State for Education.[146] Barber commented that she was 'very impressive' and 'displayed no sense of anxiety – on the contrary what was most noticeable was her mastery of the detail, her clarity about both politics and substance, her overwhelming competence and determination and a degree of insight and assurance which was remarkable'.[147] Barber featured in a *Guardian* article on Blair's inner circle: 'Behind the scenes his role is to track whether the government delivers the public sector improvements it promises. His findings are important in the political battle with the Tories over inefficiency and waste.'[148] By early February, the four-hour waiting time A&E figure was 97.7 per cent, which was the best yet but still just below the target level of 98 per cent.[149]

A stocktake on the criminal justice system took place on 31 January. It was the first with Charles Clarke as Home Secretary. Blair was well prepared, taking 'every opportunity' to ask the representatives from the police whether there were any powers they needed to tackle the issues; they were 'stumped' and this meant that they were running out of reasons for 'failing to deliver'.[150] Afterwards Clarke complained that the meeting 'had been a waste of time'.[151] On this occasion the stocktake seemed more useful for the Prime Minister than the Secretary of State.

What remained of the existing delivery agenda was being encroached on by election preparations. Blair would no longer chair the pre-election stocktakes scheduled to take place in March, which would become official-level stocktakes. This frustrated Barber but he understood. Barber asked the Prime Minister, 'How much did he care if we just missed the A&E target? Answer – not really at all, but he was happy for the PMDU to keep the pressure on and understood that we had to be more religious about targets than he did.'[152] There were times when the Prime Minister would choose to step back to focus on other priorities but the point of the Delivery Unit was that it could drive delivery even when the Prime Minister could not personally commit as much time. The PMDU's agility was crucial to its effectiveness. Two weeks later, election mode had intensified further. Barber noted, 'It's all about the election now. I hardly see Blair these days.'[153] Yet his meetings with Secretaries of State continued.

By mid-March, Barber was privately considering life after the Delivery Unit: whether he stayed in government or not was up for question but from the outset he had said that he saw being head of the PMDU as a four-year task for him and this remained true. He ruminated, 'Who will do this silent but massively influential job for the Delivery Unit after I leave?'[154] He met with Paul Corrigan, special adviser to the Health Secretary, and noted the significance of Corrigan's longstanding role as well as their relationship and shared perspective: 'I realised how much my understanding with Paul had meant in our collaboration on health policy … Together he and I, without having to talk that often, knew we were on the same agenda, pushing in the same direction. Classic guiding coalition stuff.'[155] Similarly, Clara Swinson who was a civil servant in the PMDU working on the health brief, reflected on the importance of relationships: 'It was completely fundamental, to build trust. The "guiding coalition" was really big. It was drummed into us. But then we did it in departments, it wasn't about a single person. We had to really think who else was around, how to build [relationships].'[156] Tony O'Connor, a civil servant and chief analyst in the PMDU, similarly commented that within the Unit staff 'would use the same kind of model about building the trust, understanding what was going on, making sure that they [departments] could trust us and bounce things off of us if they wanted ... So that model became important for us but at a different level of the organisation.'[157] This underlines the necessity of deep, strong working relationships in achieving delivery.

The February rail performance results were the best performance in a single month since before the Hatfield rail crash in October 2000; Barber felt the PMDU's 'persistence against the odds' had paid off.[158] The march to delivery continued. Barber chaired two stocktakes, sitting in the Prime Minister's chair at the Cabinet table; 'holding the meetings in that room gave them much greater authority and formality and as a result they had real impact'.[159] The stocktakes triggered in Barber's mind recognition of the 'mindset shift' that Nigel Crisp had achieved at Health:[160]

> Nigel Crisp's leadership has been simply demonstrated by his personal commitment to a document ... looking at the reform of the NHS, acknowledging that it is moving to a new stage in which they don't yet know how to manage the NHS and anticipating the risks ahead. As a result, there is a strong commitment now to reform in his top team and a determination to get on with it.[161]

The 2005 Budget was focused on the election, rather than a landmark in terms of new investment. It contained announcements with a short-term impact including a rise in the threshold of inheritance tax, postponement of petrol duty inflation, freezing of several taxes, council tax refunds for pensioners and a rise in child tax credit. The Chancellor declared that the country had now experienced 'the longest period of economic growth since records began in 1701'.[162]

APRIL TO JULY 2005

CLOSE OF PLAY

In early April, Barber wrote to the Prime Minister's chief of staff, Jonathan Powell, and his principal private secretary, Ivan Rogers, to tell them that after much consideration he was 'minded' to leave government to take up a position at the management consultancy McKinsey.[163] He explained to Blair that one of the main reasons for his decision was so that he could better financially support his adult daughter after she had suffered a serious, life-changing accident; Blair was 'consistently supportive'.[164] Barber had spent two terms in government working tirelessly under huge pressure which affected family life; he was 'mentally tired'.[165] He was also keen to work on delivery issues in other countries.[166] Nevertheless, the Prime Minister would have liked Barber to stay. Powell said he hoped Blair would be able to persuade Barber to change his mind because he would be a 'huge loss', and he thanked him for his 'remarkable' contribution.[167]

Around this same time the PMDU received good news on key priorities – 'rail performance improved again', removal of failed asylum seekers 'turned the corner' and the A&E 98 per cent target was 'finally hit'.[168] Illegal asylum and immigration proved to be a prominent issue in the Conservative Party's election campaign. Blair's insistence that the issue be a priority throughout his second term had proved to be politically sound. In late April, Barber told his team that he would be leaving government in July.[169] He also spoke with Rogers about who should be his successor. 'How will they combine the managerial impact with the "political" confidence required in No. 10? Perhaps then a combination of a good Civil Service manager with an effective Cabinet Office minister?'[170]

Meanwhile the PMDU began providing a series of 'top team' delivery training sessions, facilitated by Barber, for several departments including the Department of Constitutional Affairs, DfES and Health. In these sessions, the 'first half was about their record, aimed at drawing out the lessons of delivery from their experience' and the PMDU's; 'the second half was about identifying their priorities for the next Parliament, working out which needed the most attention and then applying the lessons to them'.[171] In the training event for the Department of Health, Barber highlighted the strength of the team: 'The team is the most sophisticated and talented we've seen and their track record gives them confidence. Even so, the challenge ahead is huge.'[172]

A THIRD TERM

On 5 May 2005, the general election took place, and Labour won a third term, though with a parliamentary majority reduced from 166 to 66. In his memoir, Tony Blair described what the process had been like from his perspective:

> The 2005 election was ugly: fraught in its build-up; marred in its running by internal disputes; vicious in the nature of the campaign; and precarious in its aftermath …
>
> We had won despite all the drawbacks, despite the war, the length of time I had been Prime Minister, tuition fees, the internal wrangle with Gordon … This was an election we were never destined to win with enthusiasm, but … we were never going to lose.[173]

The reduced majority 'dampened' Blair's 'spirits' but he had felt the campaign had 'hardened' him and he had 'grown up as a leader'.[174] The contrast between Blair's confidence before winning the

2001 election and the 2005 election was stark. He outlined the task as he saw it: 'Now I was prepared to manage what I knew would be a continual fight with Gordon. I had to get the reform programme embedded.'[175] After the election, there was a Cabinet reshuffle, though most key positions were unchanged: John Reid was moved from Health to become Secretary of State for Defence, Patricia Hewitt succeeded Reid at Health and David Blunkett was brought back into government as Secretary of State for Work and Pensions. Barber's overall impression was that Blair did not seem like 'a triumphant PM returning to embark on a bold third term, on the contrary, Blair seem[ed] beleaguered and, as ever, short of revolutionaries'.[176]

Barber continued to contribute to the transition team for the third-term planning. There was a revival of the Cabinet committee system, a 'set of proposed cabinet committees which Blair would chair – these included his wishes for committees on health reform, school reform, drugs and organised crime etc.'[177] These committees would 'be crucial' for the PMDU because they would 'replace stocktakes', which had been the cornerstone of the PMDU process in the second term.[178] Stocktakes had been a pivotal accountability method for the Prime Minister, and it remained to be seen how the replacement Cabinet committees would work in practice. The key difference between the Cabinet committees and the PMDU stocktakes was the attendance list. The Cabinet committee membership was far wider than a stocktake, including the Deputy Prime Minister, John Prescott, and the Chancellor of the Exchequer. Barber was privately sceptical; he did not think they suited Blair's style of working. For example, he believed Blair would never have an argument with an individual Secretary of State in front of Prescott and Brown, which meant he would need to do deals with them bilaterally in advance, which would put 'enormous pressure on his time'.[179] One would think that the New Labour government had learnt in the first term, with PSX, that using a Cabinet committee to monitor and hasten delivery was of limited use. Barber's nuanced understanding of the art of delivery was evidenced in one of the lessons he sought to impart to his senior management team in the PMDU:

> It's important to recognise a strong political impulse when you see one – and then respond to it. If you ignore it or hope it'll go away you can find yourself being either run over or, worse still, marginalised. This is the kind of thing that PMDU leadership after me will need to understand.[180]

Barber continued to attend the weekly Monday morning meetings. At the first one after the election, Blair wanted 'preparation for a series of meetings in June on key policy areas' including health and education; Barber and the head of the Policy Unit, Matthew Taylor, agreed to jointly plan these.[181] On 20 May, Barber attended the Prime Minister's awayday at Chequers. He and Blair had a conversation about the Delivery Unit's priorities for the new parliament. Blair asked Barber who would succeed him and when he was actually leaving. 'We're going to miss you … We're going to miss you terribly,' he said.[182] Blair identified that Barber's successor 'needed the intellect and the organisational skill but also the politics'; he said Barber had 'mastered the politics and this was very important'.[183] The Prime Minister revealed that in the recent interviews that he had conducted with the candidates for the next Cabinet Secretary they had all spoken about the effectiveness of the Delivery Unit: 'They had the feeling that you were on their side.'[184] Four candidates were Permanent Secretaries whom Barber had worked with as head of the PMDU.

On 9 June, the Cabinet committee meeting on health took place. It began as a stocktake would, with Barber presenting a delivery update. The new Secretary of State for Health, Patricia Hewitt, was in attendance with Permanent Secretary Nigel Crisp and others.[185] Barber raised various issues in his presentation and Hewitt responded to these challenges saying that 'they were aware of them and set out the actions they were taking'.[186] For Barber, this was 'the purpose of the stocktakes – using the data to hold a Secretary of State to account in front of the Prime Minister and in this case, the DPM and Chancellor'.[187] Brown asked whether in future Barber could provide an update on all PSAs in his presentation. 'Blair looked doubtful – on obesity and smoking the data didn't change as fast as the other stuff in my charts.' Barber said they could do a 'one-page status report covering everything'.[188] This demonstrated the value that the Chancellor saw in the PMDU but also raised the issue of an ever-expanding brief.

Blair challenged Hewitt 'on why payment-by-results should adversely affect productivity, she began to answer but then stumbled' and said, 'I don't pretend to be an expert on this, after four weeks, Tony...'[189] This caused Barber to ruminate that 'the longer he stays as PM so the more he understands areas of policy better than his own secretaries of state, especially of course when they are new'.[190] The Chancellor proposed that Health and the Treasury do a joint study on expenditure. Blair neither assented to nor rejected it. Brown said he was 'not wanting to reopen whether we should do this but we need to do this study'.[191] Blair's interventions were about pressing ahead.

My very strong steer … Pushing reform is the key … People are very nearly prepared to accept the link between reform and improvement … This is the point to accelerate reform … The danger is that reform in some areas reveals problems all the more clearly where they are unreformed.[192]

During a discussion about hospital closures Prescott said 'he didn't believe the NHS would close hospitals, that he was sceptical about the whole programme and that management mattered more than reform'.[193]

Later that day, Julian Le Grand, the influential academic and senior policy adviser to the Prime Minister, called Barber. He said that at the end of the meeting Blair had been 'apoplectic … he hated the meeting and wanted to go back to the stocktakes we'd had before.'[194] Charles Clarke concurred: 'The stocktake process was far more effective in doing what we were doing than any Cabinet sub-committee.'[195] Le Grand acknowledged that this was exactly what Barber had predicted. 'Blair doesn't want to have to defend himself from' Brown and Prescott, 'he wants to drive his programme through'.[196] Later on Barber found out that there was now a suggestion that 'an informal stocktake' should take place before each Cabinet committee meeting.[197]

On 11 June, Michael Barber received a knighthood in the Queen's Birthday Honours. *The Guardian* reported that 'figures who have helped to shape and push through Tony Blair's vision for reform in the public services get their reward today' and added that Barber was also 'famed for the statistically dense presentations' he delivered at Blair's press conferences.[198] In mid-June, the Permanent Secretary to the Treasury, Sir Gus O'Donnell, was appointed as the next Cabinet Secretary, succeeding Sir Andrew Turnbull. Nicholas Macpherson succeeded O'Donnell as Permanent Secretary to the Treasury; he had been 'crucial to the success of the Delivery Unit'.[199]

Blair's commitment to his domestic priorities continued. At the regular Monday meeting on 20 June, he spoke with 'real energy, passion and direction' on health and education; he relayed the areas on which he wanted more focus.[200] Strikingly Blair commented in 'despair', 'It's incredible how the system slows down change at every stage … Awesome.'[201] In his third term, eight years in as Prime Minister, Blair was still grappling with the pace at which the Civil Service machine moved in response to his agenda. Interestingly, a Cabinet committee meeting on education was postponed and in its place a 'traditional stocktake' was scheduled with the 'minor modification' that representatives from the Treasury would not attend.[202] The return of the stocktake was celebrated by Barber as a 'triumph of common sense over technocracy'; he believed that 'the system should be organised around the Prime Minister not the other way about'.[203] After the meeting Blair said the stocktake had been 'exactly what he wanted'.[204] Barber asked Blair how he compared the education stocktake to the recent Cabinet committee on health.

'I must have been out of my mind; I don't know how on earth I agreed to that; Jonathan says I did.'

'It came up at that Chequers meeting on 21 March,' Barber said. 'But you were in pre-election mode … I personally never thought they would work.'

'I don't want to spend meetings educating JP [Prescott] and arguing with GB [Brown],' Blair said.[205]

STREET FIGHTERS
After the education stocktake, Barber's final one as head of the

PMDU, Blair visited the Delivery Unit team at their office in the Treasury building. He told them that 'of all the changes in the government machine he'd made, this was the best and the most successful'.[206] The Prime Minister said he and they knew 'how good a leader' Barber had been and 'how sad he was' that Barber was leaving but he asserted that 'the PMDU role was no less necessary'.[207] He said the PMDU had 'not just monitored progress but pitched in and helped', praising the way in which the Unit had 'built relationships with departments'.[208] At one point Barber said to Blair, 'These people are your street fighters.'[209] He said, 'Yes, but they do it with such charm.'[210] The PMDU staff were 'delighted'.[211] Blair was asked about Barber's successor; one team member said it was obvious there could not be 'another Michael', but what qualities did he think were necessary?[212] Blair said 'obviously the intelligence and the ability but also the small "p" political skills' which Barber had mastered.[213] Afterwards, Blair and Barber had their final one-to-one meeting; it was 'a rare moment of reflection and reflective conversation' between the Prime Minister and his outgoing chief adviser on delivery.[214] After four years in post and eight working for the New Labour government, Sir Michael Barber's tenure as head of the Prime Minister's Delivery Unit came to an end on 8 July 2005.

Just over a year later, on 7 September 2006, Blair announced his intention to stand down within twelve months. After ten transformative years in government and three successive election victories, he departed as Prime Minister on 27 June 2007. The intervening two years between the 2005 election and his resignation saw Blair continue to fervently pursue reform though his political capital waned. The high point for the delivery of public service reform during the Blair years was undoubtedly the second term from 2001 to 2005.

CONCLUSION: THE ALCHEMY OF DELIVERY

This final period in the story of the Prime Minister's Delivery Unit under Barber was crucial: deliverology was shown to work. Progress had been delivered on the vast majority of the Prime Minister's public service priorities.[215] The blend of art and science, routines and relationships, steeliness and humility, discipline and dynamism formed the alchemy of delivery. For four years, the PMDU was not just focused on improving the delivery departments' ability to deliver but it was also able to advance the centre's understanding of what it took to do this. In doing so, it created space for departments to deliver and defined what success looked like in clear, measurable terms.

Barber and the Delivery Unit, as a prime ministerial unit, had a uniquely deep and effective relationship with the Treasury under Brown. Tony O'Connor, chief analyst in the Delivery Unit, saw the Treasury–PMDU relationship as the 'strongest' (outside No. 10) and 'that was made even stronger when we physically moved into the Treasury Building'.[216] Within No. 10, Barber's relationships were solid and trusting, and he believed rare – 'It was really important that they trusted me politically, even though I was a civil servant. I was able to move between spheres more easily than nearly anybody.'[217] Barber concluded, 'A lot of it is about the way you invest in the relationships, the nature of your interactions on a personal level.'[218]

CHAPTER EIGHT

CONCLUSION: THE ART OF DELIVERY REVEALED

THE ART AND THE SCIENCE OF DELIVERY

We have unearthed the story of how a seemingly common-sense yet transformative mechanism to improve public services, the Prime Minister's Delivery Unit, worked in practice during Tony Blair's pivotal second term. By the time of the 2005 general election, the quality of public services in health had been improved across all targets, in education the target areas had almost all improved upon 2001 standards, in the Home Office and criminal justice system all targets had improved on 2001 standards, and though road congestion had not improved rail punctuality had.[1] Charles Clarke, former Secretary of State for Education and Home Secretary, stated that the Delivery Unit 'was probably the biggest single contributor' to the delivery of public service reform in the Blair government.[2] John Gieve, Permanent Secretary to the Home Office, said, 'It was transformational.'[3] But the Unit's success was not inevitable.

Much has been written about the science of delivery but little has been written about what the present author has identified as the 'art of delivery'. This book has benefited from an unrivalled resource, the unpublished, private diaries of Michael Barber. They were cross-referenced with new interviews with prominent Cabinet ministers, senior civil servants and special advisers who worked closely with and within the PMDU, as well as other media articles and some government papers. Together these sources have formed a jigsaw that reveals how the art of delivery was crafted during the implementation of Britain's most ambitious public service reform agenda since the creation of the welfare state during the Attlee government.

THE DOWNSIDES OF THE DELIVERY UNIT

Deliverology did not emerge without mistakes and critique, and in assessing the Delivery Unit it is important to recognise where problems arose. When the Unit was created, it quickly became an added source of pressure for Cabinet ministers and senior civil servants in delivery departments. Alan Milburn as Secretary of State for Health was initially frustrated with the dual accountability that the PMDU would create in addition to Chancellor Gordon Brown's PSX Cabinet committee. David Normington, Permanent Secretary at the Department for Education and Skills, expressed worries about micromanagement, though he also saw Barber as the department's most passionate ally.

What's more, Barber and the Delivery Unit were learning on the job and this did result in errors of judgement being made, and then rectified. For example, Barber did not consult Permanent Secretaries before releasing the first delivery report that assessed departments' capacity to deliver and progress on meeting targets. This process was amended after that first report. In asserting his own position, there were tensions between Barber and Cabinet ministers. Secretary of State for Education Estelle Morris initially saw Barber's presentations during stocktakes as an intrusion on her time with the Prime Minister. Soon after the Unit was created, the minister for the Cabinet Office, Gus Macdonald, who had ministerial oversight of the PMDU, clashed with Barber for not sufficiently consulting him in negotiations with the Treasury.

With Transport, in comparison to other delivery departments, Barber was unable to form a strong relationship with Permanent Secretary Sir Richard Mottram, who led the department until 2002. He also found it hard to form effective working relationships with the DfT's associated public bodies such as the Strategic Rail Authority, which as holders of the purse strings and deciders of strategy were very powerful. Though significant progress was made on targets, there was tension between Barber and the Permanent Secretary in Health, Nigel Crisp, especially during the first couple of years of the second term. John Gieve, Permanent Secretary to the Home Office, got on well with Barber; however, he too felt that during the 2002 spending review, the Delivery Unit contributed to the centre's tendency to take control of policymaking to the detriment of departmental autonomy. Barber himself challenged departmental autonomy on education, by taking a very proactive and critical stance on the implementation of schools policy, which he had been responsible for in the first term. In early 2003, the Secretary of State for Transport, Alistair Darling, complained of the excessive demands of the centre, in response to Barber sharing the Prime Minister's top priorities. In distributing the Prime Minister's writ, however, Barber did not seek to exacerbate divisions; it was often his job to build consensus between irreconcilable positions. Barber's relationships with the Prime Minister and important individuals in No. 10 were consistently strong; nevertheless, he was a relative outsider and he was often insecure about whether he was in the loop or not.

The performance management framework of the Delivery Unit and the devolution of accountability through the choice agenda at times looked to be on opposing paths. Tensions emerged around Blair's desire to reduce the number of overall targets in government, as well as in the introduction of policies aligned with the choice agenda, such as foundation hospitals. The tensions between the Delivery Unit and the implementation of the burgeoning choice agenda did not, in the end, result in any significant divisions. In retrospect, when asked whether there was conflict between the choice agenda and the Delivery Unit approach, Milburn explained how he saw both as levers of the same machine:

> Sort of yes and no. In terms of the spectrum of levers that you have at your disposal to shift things and improve things – you have performance management at one end of the spectrum, and you have market mechanisms at the other end of the spectrum, broadly. And broadly, clearly, the Delivery Unit were going to be on the performance management end of the spectrum, because guess what, that's what they were doing. They were performance-managing the system, by report cards: how well is it doing, what does the trajectory and timeline look like? Meanwhile, I was constructing a new set of levers over here. But no one for a moment, certainly in the system, believed that I wasn't also quite a tough performance management guy, because I was. The truth is, when you're doing these types of changes, and you're trying to make these types of improvements, you need every lever

you can get your hands on. And it's only a combination of these things that really work.[4]

When the Delivery Unit was established in 2001, there were clear principles on keeping the Unit focused on a limited number of prime ministerial priorities. But, as the early shoots of success emerged and other departments sought to gain access to deliverology, these principles were relaxed and the priorities widened considerably during 2002–03. Indeed, two PMDU civil servants I interviewed felt this expansion blunted the previously sharp focus of the Unit. Tony O'Connor, a civil servant in the PMDU, remarked, 'Our focus was diluted having to cover a wider range of measures. While we had built up an established relationship with the officials in the four core departments, our stakeholder group had expanded.'[5] Not only was this unsustainable for a small unit, which Barber was determined to keep to forty members of staff; Barber should also have recognised the inevitability that the Prime Minister would have to withdraw, at his own request, from the burgeoning areas in which he was personally involved. If Barber had been more careful, perhaps the Unit would not have faced the potential threat of Blair no longer chairing stocktakes in the summer of 2003. If this had happened it would have signalled to the rest of Whitehall a downgrading in the PMDU's importance to the Prime Minister. Lastly, as a political appointee turned civil servant, Barber's desire to be trusted on a political level by No. 10 and the Treasury as a New Labour supporter was somewhat incompatible with being an impartial civil servant. As discussed, there are many challenges and critiques of Barber and the PMDU, yet in the interviews conducted for this book there was remarkably little criticism. This is arguably due to Barber's style and the manner in which he and the Unit engaged with No. 10, the Treasury and delivery departments at the political and official level.

THE ART DEFINED

Prime Ministers and their governments typically spend a great deal of time on policy – developing ideas, building support and then securing the safe passage of reforms through Parliament. This process is a huge task. Governments often spend less time monitoring the implementation of reforms and problem-solving where gaps in capacity to deliver emerge. The disparity between a focus on generating activities and examining outcomes can become a problem for a Prime Minister, yet Britain lacked a framework for delivery until 2001. In his second term, Blair managed to combine ambitious policy and effective delivery. He was helped, in large part, by the Delivery Unit under the leadership of Barber. There were extraordinary conditions for success: a second massive election win, with the likelihood of a third; an emboldened and engaged Prime Minister holding himself publicly accountable; committed delivery ministers; a bold reform programme; an excellent economic climate; and unprecedented government investment. There were also real challenges.

The PMDU kept Blair focused on his short-to-medium-term priorities throughout the Iraq operation and an ever-evolving ambitious reform programme. When his time and attention were directed towards these other aspects of governing, the Delivery Unit continued to work in his name to maintain momentum. Though the relations between the Prime Minister and Chancellor were in a constant state of flux, Barber managed to form a bridge between the two that held for the duration of the second term. It was a bridge that brought together the technocratic processes with the political nous, tenacity and self-effacing personality needed to make the methods operational in such a highly charged environment. As this book has illustrated, the art of delivery consisted of a collection of elements that, along with the science of delivery, enabled effective implementation.

PRIME MINISTERIAL RESPONSIBILITY

Individual ministerial responsibility is a well-established convention of British government whereby a minister is responsible to Parliament for the actions of their department. Through consistent commitment of time and political capital, both publicly and within government, as well as a desire to be publicly held personally accountable for the delivery of his public service reform agenda, one could argue that Blair introduced the concept of prime ministerial responsibility. In any case, the media held Blair accountable for the government's track record. As one of Blair's key reforming partners, Milburn saw first-hand how Blair grew and defined new responsibilities for himself as Prime Minister.

> First of all, his [Blair's] appetite for understanding grew, his appetite for engagement grew, and his appetite for solution-based decision-making grew as well. I think he increasingly recognised that he had an instrumental role to play as Prime Minister. In … what I was trying to do, which is to both, at one and the same time, improve delivery and change the system, he had an important role to play. And not just as a supporting actor. What you're doing is you're flying the machine, and you're building it at the same

time, or … rebuilding [it] … That's quite hard. I think he came to understand that the role of Prime Minister was more than just saying, one, this should happen, or two, why hasn't that happened, or three, I'm going to issue an instruction that it should happen. And that's great … [Blair's] eye was absolutely on it continually.[6]

During an event of the Strand Group at King's College London in 2015, Blair was asked what advice he would give to the then Prime Minister. He remarked, 'If the Prime Minister wants to ensure successful delivery, he personally will have to pay attention to it.'[7] Nicholas Macpherson concurred with this. 'Prime ministerial delivery units are only as good as the Prime Minister … a Prime Minister can wish to have lots of structures but unless they are prepared to give some time to it they're just not going to get the traction.'[8]

Blair saw the 2001 general election result as an 'instruction to deliver' and, on an annual basis, Blair and Barber reported on the progress of delivery to the media. Normington observed the forensic way in which Blair operated in stocktakes. 'The Prime Minister was invariably on top of the detail and knew the answers better than the officials in front of him.'[9] While Blair characteristically created multiple central units which all vied for his time and attention, Barber was savvy enough to secure a commitment from the Prime Minister that first, he, Barber, would report directly to Blair, and second, Blair would chair stocktakes on a regular basis. The Prime Minister's Delivery Unit would not have been successful without these components, especially during the first two formative years of its life.

Blair's willingness to be explicitly and personally accountable also resulted in an enhanced role for No. 10 as an institution. Indeed, Milburn reflected that 'what the Delivery Unit helped to do was to make No. 10 the primary accountability mechanism for delivery departments. In the old days that would have been the Treasury.'[10] Arguably, the Treasury maintained an accountability role through the spending review framework, and as it collaborated more closely with the PMDU. Blair's commitment to the PMDU's work was managed alongside the myriad responsibilities of being Prime Minister and leader of the Labour Party, with a focus on delivering his last mandate and winning the next election. Milburn expanded on the multitude of functions Blair sought to fulfil.

> We campaign in poetry and we govern in prose?[*] Well, that is just true, it just is all the stuff that we're now talking about. There's a lot of prose and not much poetry. There is hard grind, data, analysis, levers, systems. Now, as a politician, you have got to be able to tell stories, construct narratives, provide frameworks, provide understanding, secure buy-in, all of those things as well, but it's underpinned by all the boring stuff.

THE VALUE OF RELATIONSHIPS

Relationships were the lifeblood of the Delivery Unit. Just six months in, Jeremy Heywood, principal private secretary to the Prime Minister and experienced Whitehall power broker, told Barber that he had significantly increased the power of the Prime Minister and, critically, he had done so without harming relationships.[11] In practice, Barber had to simultaneously leverage established relationships with an existing shared history, build new relationships that worked quickly, and be incredibly attentive to

---

[*]   Milburn quoting Mario Cuomo, governor of New York 1983–94.

THE ART OF DELIVERY

the shifting geography of power within No. 10, the Treasury and delivery departments. Simon Rea, who worked for the Delivery Unit under Barber, reflected, 'With the right relationships we could achieve almost anything (and often did) and without [them] we could achieve nothing.'[12]

RELATIONSHIPS WITH DELIVERY DEPARTMENTS

Though Barber had a shared history and good relationships with numerous ministers, advisers and civil servants, that did not mean it was straightforward to refocus them on delivery. Barber was now performance-managing people whom he had worked with or for. Moreover, every individual in government is subject to competing pressures. That said, the experience of working together in the first term or prior to government meant that in many cases there was a foundation to build on. This was most keenly observed in the relationship between Barber and David Blunkett. As Home Secretary, Blunkett trusted Barber from the outset. He asked Barber to assist him with Home Office delivery issues and on occasion Barber also supported Blunkett's policy proposals in debates at the centre. On the other hand, Barber had worked closely with Normington in the first term, yet this did not result in a frictionless relationship between his department and the Delivery Unit. Nevertheless, progress was achieved and relationships were productive, if at times bumpy.

There were many relationships where Barber had to start from scratch to foster trust and work in partnership. In the Department of Health, he eventually managed to form productive working relationships with Alan Milburn, his successor John Reid, and the Permanent Secretary, Nigel Crisp. There were tensions early on but they were overcome, in part, by Barber's diplomacy. In the Home Office, John Gieve did not know Barber prior to the Delivery Unit, but they were able to form a solid working relationship. This was partly due to the alignment between their agendas for the Home Office. Gieve had moved from the Treasury as an outsider to the Home Office with a view to reforming the department. Blunkett, as Home Secretary, was also forthright in pursuing internal reform. Barber, Blunkett and Gieve worked in sync during a time when the pressure on the Home Office was immense. In both Health and the Home Office, there was, to an extent, a guiding coalition of key individuals working in unison to achieve agreed outcomes.

Each appointment, resignation and reshuffle in Cabinet and at Permanent Secretary level had to be navigated by the Delivery Unit. Relationships are the lynchpin of the art of delivery. Each new appointment presented an opportunity as well as a risk. Too many changes at the highest political and official level did disrupt delivery. Each new Secretary of State and Permanent Secretary had their own agenda and way of working and needed time to adjust to the new role. This, however, was not seen as an acceptable reason for non-delivery within or outside government. From mid-2003, with relationships at every level well established but the time for delivery growing short, Barber was willing to risk the relationships the Unit had formed and expend political capital to push harder for progress.

RELATIONSHIPS WITH THE TWO CENTRES OF POWER – NO. 10 AND THE TREASURY

To be effective, the Delivery Unit had to form strong foundations with the two centres of power within the Blair government – No. 10 and the Treasury. Barber himself explained:

The two dominant institutions on which I had to rely to defend my corner were firstly No. 10, especially the Policy Directorate, and secondly the Treasury. Though the Delivery Unit was widely seen in both of these revered institutions to have made a good start, I was constantly insecure about both relationships and therefore constantly investing in them.[13]

Neither relationship was guaranteed but both were pivotal. Barber revealed the purpose behind this. 'I had to ensure at all times that the Delivery Unit understood where policy was going and was aligned.'[14] The most important relationship for the Delivery Unit was undoubtedly with the Prime Minister. His confidence in the Unit and willingness to commit his time to its routines was imperative and had this been lost, the Unit would have ceased to succeed. Once Blair had decided to proceed with setting up a Delivery Unit, with Barber at the helm, they set about shaping the agenda. Barber already had a clear design and principles for the Unit, as planned with Heywood and Jonathan Powell prior to the 2001 general election. Blair supported these and encouraged the Unit to have a sharp focus on a small number of priorities. The Prime Minister demonstrated his mettle almost immediately in response to opposition from the Chancellor. Brown challenged the autonomy of the Unit during the negotiation of the protocol on how the PMDU would engage with the Treasury and departments. Blair was resolute and would not concede easily, though the Treasury did secure attendance at stocktakes. This was the only major challenge of this kind from Brown to Blair against the Delivery Unit.

There are several occasions in Barber's diaries where he expresses frustration with the degree of focus that Blair was giving to the Delivery Unit routines. One critique of Barber in the early phase was his lack of consideration of the multitude of areas which a Prime Minister needs to give attention to. Blair's commitment to delivery never wavered, though the time he could dedicate to it altered. Indeed, Powell explained that Blair 'grew to trust' the Delivery Unit 'more and more as it produced results and now he goes around the world advocating for the idea with leaders that he meets'.[15] Barber would often receive unscheduled telephone calls from the Prime Minister, sometimes at the weekend, to check the state of delivery. Late 2002 was a high point in the Prime Minister's desire to commit more time to delivery and expand the areas which he gave personal attention to. Blair had been buoyed by the success of the street crime initiative in the spring of 2002 and the idea that his personal involvement resolved issues and accelerated progress.

Yet arguably the high point in terms of Blair's confidence in the PMDU was 2003, after the invasion of Iraq when his continued chairing of stocktakes was being questioned by his No. 10 team. Barber, though initially perturbed, was responsive to Blair's changing time constraints and adapted the stocktakes. Barber would chair official-level stocktakes, while Blair would chair a reduced number of standard stocktakes. These adjustments sustained Blair's commitment while making more efficient use of his time. During this period, Gus Macdonald stepped down as minister for the Cabinet Office and his successor did not have the same involvement as Macdonald initially had in the PMDU. If Blair had not had confidence in the Unit and its leadership, he would not have allowed Barber to have an enhanced role. Barber became a resource for the Prime Minister to objectively understand his public service reform priorities, how they were progressing, what issues arose, and how they were being addressed. Barber's position was strengthened by his involvement in numerous activities beyond the delivery of existing policy: he attended Chequers awaydays where new strategy and policy was debated and he often presented on progress; he contributed to debates on the direction of policy with the Prime Minister, Chancellor and Cabinet ministers; and he assisted Blair and Brown with speeches on public service reform and the Civil Service.

The relationships between the Delivery Unit and Blair's team in No. 10, including Heywood, Powell, Anji Hunter, Sally Morgan, Alastair Campbell, Andrew Adonis and Peter Hyman, were crucial. These individuals spent the most time with Blair and thus their views mattered. Heywood and Powell had formed good initial relations with Barber prior to the 2001 election, and these were strengthened as soon as Barber started the delivery role. Across-the-board relationships with the No. 10 team were strong from the outset. Heywood, as principal private secretary to the Prime Minister and joint head of the Policy Directorate, played a major role in establishing the Delivery Unit. That he too saw the necessity of a delivery unit prior to the election was significant. Sally Morgan reflected on the importance of Barber's skill in building relationships.

> It is about relationships actually. It's about being somebody that nobody disliked. That sounds sort of a bit wet but actually that's very, very important. A lot of people actively liked him. He got on with people. People knew he had integrity. They knew he was trying to do it for the right reasons. And as far as anybody could do it, he also had a decent relationship with the Treasury.[16]

Furthermore, Barber formed good working relationships with each successive Cabinet Secretary during Blair's second term. Sir Richard Wilson saw value in the PMDU and supported Barber in launching the Unit in a crowded centre. Sir Andrew Turnbull came in with an enhanced delivery function compared to his predecessors. Though this brought a potential challenge to the PMDU's monopoly on delivery at the centre, in fact Barber shared his knowledge with Turnbull, and Turnbull welcomed this expertise as part of his Delivery and Reform Team within the Cabinet Office. The Cabinet Secretaries of the day sought to reorientate the function of Civil Service towards delivery.

Conversely, the relationship with the Treasury was tough to get right in the beginning. It began with suspicion, tension and bullish behaviour from the Chancellor of the Exchequer, Gordon Brown, and his chief economic adviser, Ed Balls, who viewed the PMDU as a threat to the Treasury's power over the domestic agenda. The first couple of months after the 2001 election were spent agreeing a protocol, Heywood having a central role in negotiating this on behalf of Blair. Barber established an effective partnership with Nicholas Macpherson, managing director of public services in the Treasury. Within a year, the Delivery Unit began working closely with the Treasury on the 2002 spending review to assess public service agreements and the deliverability of departmental plans. This would not have happened without the trusting relationships and valuable mechanisms developed by Barber. By spring 2003, Barber had cultivated relationships with Brown and Balls that were based on trust and shared conversations about the values that underpinned New Labour's public service reform. The Treasury came to see Barber and the Delivery Unit as an ally.

The Delivery Unit under Barber exceeded expectations in this aspect and improved the institutional relationship between No. 10 and the Treasury on delivery. Relations between the two centres of power were broadened, new interactions and important information flows were formalised through stocktakes and delivery routines. Barber's decision to move the Delivery Unit into the newly refurbished Treasury building in March 2003 also had a positive impact on improving relations. Clara Swinson, a civil servant in the PMDU, reflected on how the Unit's relationship with the Treasury developed: 'There weren't phases that changed overnight, but it was definitely a bit uncomfortable, a bit scratchy at the beginning. There was a time when we came a lot closer together, partly because we were also co-located just around the corner from the [Treasury] spending teams.'[17] The move signalled Barber's commitment to working with the Treasury and in a practical sense made formal and informal contact easier. These activities did not happen to this degree in the first term and probably would not otherwise have happened in the second term. Though Heywood remained the most important official broker of government business with Balls, Barber brought a degree of harmony, formality and collective discussion between the Treasury and No. 10 on delivery matters. Macpherson observed the value of the PMDU to the Treasury.

I do think the PMDU's involvement allowed the Treasury to get involved and see things which it probably wouldn't have seen otherwise ... There was a high degree of trust and we were co-located and we ran into each other the whole time. Michael always made the point that he liked the Delivery Unit being in the Treasury and I think the sort of visibility of it helped cross-departmental working ... And it was also in the Treasury's interest to have a Prime Minister interested in this stuff, it actually worked in the Treasury's favour ... It did result in public services being delivered better than they otherwise would have been.[18]

Prime ministerial responsibility aided the Treasury, though there were some examples of friction, for instance with the Reform Agenda Group, which Blair and Brown asked Barber to form in the summer of 2003. The context in which it operated changed quickly; dysfunctional interactions between No. 10 and the Treasury over the Prime Minister's five-year strategy planning constrained Barber's ability to build consensus. The PMDU was not immune to these hostilities and the rivalry between Blair and Brown had serious flashpoints throughout the second term. Barber's relationships and the shared value that the mechanism offered largely protected the PMDU from being pulled into these battles.

BARBER THE MAN: THE IRON FIST IN THE SOFTEST OF VELVET GLOVES

Barber possessed a rare blend of inner steeliness, integrity, humility and a sense of mission which fundamentally shaped the Delivery Unit and contributed to its success. Professor Jon Davis has described his style as 'the iron fist in the softest of velvet gloves'.[19] This description of Barber's character was put to the Cabinet ministers, civil servants and special advisers interviewed for this book. David Blunkett said, 'Michael was extremely good, personally good because of his manner, because of his quiet way of listening and persuading and getting people to do things ... His absolute steeliness inside, his willingness to acknowledge when he thought he had got it wrong and hold himself to account ... A nice mix of personal empathy and ability to persuade.'[20] Vanessa Nicholls, a civil servant in the PMDU, noted the integrity Barber exemplified: 'He never played games. And it was really clear that we were not to play games either.'[21] Macpherson explained that 'the reason why the PMDU worked was very much down to him. He is someone who is very difficult to dislike. He gets on with people ... But equally he was prepared to be very tough. Generally, he worked through the right channels and created trust.'[22] Sally Morgan, a close political adviser to Blair throughout this period, said, 'Yes, I think in the end most people who are in the centre and were in any way successful probably had that ... You end up with an inner steeliness but you've got to get on with everybody otherwise you can't get anything done ... And I think people didn't question Michael's motives.'[23] Alan Milburn lights on the link between Barber's personality and the Delivery Unit's success:

> I think the thing about him is that, one, great personality, nice style, soft delivery, all of that sort of stuff, is quite important because it's all about building relationships of trust. Because here you are in what is potentially quite a conflictual relationship. The guy's writing your report card, that's a bit uncomfortable. Now, he just happens to be a really nice writer, and a nice guy. So that all helps in terms of building a relationship with trust. And two, he was and is a guy of very high integrity. Even when it was uncomfortable for him to be shouted at by the likes of me, nonetheless, he maintained an integrity position.[24]

A TOOL FOR CABINET MINISTERS AND DEPARTMENTS

The Delivery Unit was created fundamentally as a tool for the Prime Minister. It had also arguably been formed to act as a buffer to the Treasury under Brown. Remarkably, Barber was able to cast the Delivery Unit as an instrument that provided mutual benefits for No. 10, the Treasury and delivery departments. It became more than a mechanism for the Prime Minister to monitor and hasten short-term outcomes. It helped those it worked with to learn how to govern better. For departments, it performed a variety of functions, all with the aim of facilitating delivery: problem-solving – priority reviews for intractable issues and communicating blocks to No. 10; assessing deliverability – for Treasury spending reviews, new policy pilots and informing five-year strategies; enhancing capacity to deliver – the PMDU advised on the reorganisation and creation of new departmental units; and disseminating best practice – using deliverology methods through training and events. After initial scepticism, Milburn soon saw the benefit of the PMDU in allowing for 'a stronger political bridge between the Prime Minister and the secretary of state, to ensure the system was aligned'.[25] He continued:

> For it to be aligned between the Prime Minister and the secretary of state was an enormous source of strength because then we were fighting the same battle, rather than fighting each other. The problem with the stocktake format is clearly that he's posing questions, and I'm trying to deflect answers, but actually, when you've got aligned data, you're both aligned around problem-solving, which is pretty powerful.[26]

Blunkett described the Delivery Unit as a 'continuing transmission belt' for communicating blocks to delivery directly to the Prime Minister.[27] Barber lighted on this description when interviewed:

> That's a big point, we were able to unblock for individual departments some other department … In a way, if the Home Secretary

goes to the Foreign Secretary it can just become a stand-off. This way you could get much more departmental cooperation ... So-called 'joined-up government', we were doing it.[28]

By making the Delivery Unit work for Cabinet ministers and Permanent Secretaries, Barber was able to gain additional buy-in from them because they valued the usefulness of the PMDU for their own purposes. But the PMDU was an added source of pressure for departments. John Gieve commented on this: 'I felt under acute pressure' because of the demands from across the centre of government, various units and the Treasury.[29] But he continued, 'What I found with the Delivery Unit was uniquely that they actually helped me to respond to pressures.'[30]

CONSISTENT PRIORITISATION AND ROUTINES

The science of delivery is the second half of the deliverology whole. It is the ostensibly straightforward performance management methods, adapted and applied thoughtfully, rigorously and consistently. At the heart of this was the need to keep the government focused on the need to deliver what it had already announced. This consistent prioritisation was maintained through Barber's personal interactions with the Prime Minister and through the PMDU routines, primarily stocktakes and the delivery report (which contained a league table of targets, with traffic light indications of progress). Macpherson revealed the impact of this: 'It forced people to have plans, measures and indicators. And in No. 10 the delivery meetings provided a framework by which things happened.'[31] Sir Andrew Turnbull, the Cabinet Secretary from 2002 to 2005, and an initial sceptic when the Unit was first mooted, said that the Delivery Unit made a 'lasting impact' and the methods became 'so familiar ... that it is easy to forget how much intellectual capital they embody'.[32] Macpherson saw the routines and the analytical expertise of the Unit as powerful and respected. He contrasted the often young, very intelligent but inexperienced Treasury civil servants to an experienced Barber, 'saying "Let's deconstruct a hospital's waiting time process" ... The expertise ... made quite a big difference.'[33] Gieve stated that the production of a 'semi-independent' report 'brought a completely different quality of data to the discussion'.[34] This, combined with stocktakes, allowed for 'a serious discussion about delivery which we wouldn't have had inside the department ... That consistent set of questioning from the Prime Minister was very significant in orienting the department.'[35] Milburn echoed this. 'The quality of what was produced was enormously high, and was founded in high-quality data and high-quality analysis.'[36] Normington explained that 'the message' on what the priorities were was 'consistent and unchanging' and the Prime Minister 'never let up'.[37]

Charles Clarke characterised the progress-chasing dimension of the Delivery Unit and stocktakes as 'extremely important and extremely positive'.[38] He did not see the Delivery Unit as a challenge to individual ministerial responsibility.[39] Clarke went on, 'I don't think the Civil Service if left to do it without the Michael Barber Delivery Unit would have succeeded in doing it. There simply wasn't that culture in place.'[40] Clarke critiqued the 'poor' Cabinet committee structure during Blair's government and explained how 'the collective nature of Cabinet government was essentially done through writing round'.[41] In a government where the traditional formal decision-making processes were not always utilised, the PMDU's introduction of a new formal routine that was consistently used for a whole parliament was significant. Sally Morgan, who attended stocktakes, observed that they 'became really quite important, pivotal moments of holding people to account ... Out of those a lot of things would happen.'[42] The PMDU brought more formality to the conduct of the Blair government than is hitherto recognised. Alan Milburn agrees that the Unit brought more formality as well as a 'data-driven format' on a 'common basis', which channelled the government to focus on solutions that from Milburn's perspective 'was just invaluable'.[43] When asked whether he saw the Delivery Unit as encroaching on individual ministerial responsibility, he said, 'No, absolutely not. I'm sure I was sceptical about the establishment of it ... But by the time I left, it was clear that the Delivery Unit was an ally, rather than an enemy.'[44]

LEGACY – THE QUIET REVOLUTIONARY

The exploration of the Delivery Unit under Michael Barber has illustrated how delivery disciplines were initially constructed and how they were adapted to ensure that they remained relevant and resilient as the geography of power shifted. The art of delivery that Barber developed had, at its heart, the cultivation and maintenance of strategic power relationships. The Delivery Unit was arguably able to make so much progress in just four years because it was led by a quiet revolutionary, who took seemingly technocratic methods and used them to help the Blair government transform the quality of public services. Morgan said, 'It drove a different view of what government was there to do – that it wasn't just about policy, it was about getting something done.'[45]

In the writing of this book, deeper insights about how the

Delivery Unit worked under Barber have emerged: throughout the second term the Delivery Unit adapted to allow Blair to maintain personal involvement in delivery routines; 9/11 and the invasion of Iraq did not result in a loss of momentum or focus on delivery for the PMDU; Barber felt persistent paranoia in the early phase about not being 'in the loop'; a comparatively deep, trusting partnership between Barber and the Treasury under Gordon Brown was forged; Cabinet ministers, Permanent Secretaries and special advisers saw value in the PMDU for their own departmental purposes; Barber's personality demonstrably shaped the PMDU's institutional culture and reputation; Barber encountered difficulties at times in working with the DfES and the Department of Health; a significant amount of Barber's time was spent on relationship-building; the PMDU team were learning on the job, not from a pre-determined playbook; and Barber's flexibility and diplomacy proved pivotal to the PMDU's success post-Iraq, with a Prime Minister who had been changed by war. Macpherson summed up Barber and the Delivery Unit's impact: 'It just improved the effectiveness of the centre of government.'[46]

After Barber left government in 2005, the Delivery Unit continued to make a difference and be of value to Tony Blair and then from 2007 Prime Minister Gordon Brown but it did not command the same gravitas. There is a difference between a Prime Minister's Delivery Unit as a unit at the heart of No. 10, compared to a unit that provides a coordinating delivery service to the government. When problems with delivery arose during Brown's premiership, the Prime Minister could be heard exclaiming, 'Where's my Michael Barber? Where's my Delivery Unit?'[47] By the 2010 general election, the Delivery Unit had been absorbed into the Treasury and its purview expanded – but it had ceased to be as effective. That it did not continue to be successful in the long term could perhaps indicate the necessity to have someone politically in the loop as its head.

Nevertheless, the Delivery Unit had a lasting impact on the Civil Service by helping to embed delivery as an explicit and valued skill in Whitehall. David Normington assessed the impact from his viewpoint: 'This focus on delivery and outcomes was more significant in changing the way the Service thought and acted than any individual reform measure.'[48] After the formation of a coalition government in 2010, Prime Minister David Cameron abolished the Delivery Unit.[49] Cameron quickly encountered the impact of this. In retrospect he said:

> You need a delivery unit because you have got to be able to be permanently checking up on whether the things you think are being done, are actually being done. I did have experiences as Prime Minister of sometimes chairing a meeting, and saying right we have decided to do 'x' and six months later you would say how is 'x' coming along and then you would find out that literally nothing had happened.[50]

Making delivery a priority is a political choice. Indeed, both John Reid and Ed Balls have commented on the Blair government's approach to delivery. Reid stated that 'delivery is political'[51] and Balls said that 'you only have a Delivery Unit and PSAs if you believe in government and think delivery is important'.[52] Normington observed that though the Blair government's approach to delivery was 'too centralist', the leadership from No. 10 'was the single most important reason why public services improved … It made the Blair premiership unique.'[53] For many years the Prime Minister's Delivery

Unit no longer existed in name but many government departments created their own delivery units. The vast majority of Prime Ministers since have sought to recreate delivery units of sorts, though the names may have differed. Twenty years after the first PMDU was set up, Conservative Prime Minister Boris Johnson commissioned a review from Barber on his government's capacity to deliver. A new Prime Minister's Delivery Unit was set up in early 2021 to manage the domestic priorities of the government following the Covid pandemic.[54] It continued to operate under Prime Ministers Liz Truss and Rishi Sunak. In 2024, with the election of the first Labour government since 2010, we have in Keir Starmer a Prime Minister with a vision for mission-driven government and a landslide majority to get on with the job. If the renewal envisioned is to be achieved, 'delivery' will need to be consistently hardwired in. The new Mission Delivery Unit has a huge challenge ahead to improve public services and deliver on the wider missions. But if the Prime Minister's speed in setting up a new delivery unit is an indicator of how serious he personally is about delivering then the keystone component of the art of delivery is in place. It seems there is much mileage left in the Delivery Unit model yet, not least in demonstrating competency and ultimately delivering modern, high-quality public services for citizens and taxpayers.

As set out at the beginning of this book, whether you are a citizen, policymaker, public servant or politician, we all use the NHS and schools, rely on crime prevention, and travel on public transport systems. To understand something of how they were transformed by the Blair government is to gain a deeper knowledge of our own shared history. There is another angle worth considering: as governing becomes ever more complex, governments not just in Britain but around the world are being held to account more than ever by the media, citizens, legislatures and judiciaries. The expectations of citizens as consumers are higher than ever before and thus governments that want to be effective and re-elected need to understand how to deliver. As successive leaders around the world have recognised, delivery disciplines of one form or another are central to success. Though to be successful, they cannot be delivery units in name only.[55] In retrospect Blair commented, 'Delivery, making the change which works, is the only real test of government ... it is also the only way to protect democracy.'[56]

What's more, since Tony Blair left office in 2007, his public service reform legacy has not featured strongly in the collective memory of the country. Perhaps this book will contribute to understanding this lost narrative, by illustrating how he, Michael Barber and the New Labour government worked relentlessly to transform the quality of Britain's public services.

NOTES

CHAPTER ONE: AN INSTRUCTION TO DELIVER

1   T. Blair, Institute for Government, 28 June 2010, https://www.instituteforgovernment.org.uk/blog/evening-tony-blair accessed 28 May 2019.

2   Quoted in M. Barber, *Instruction to Deliver* (London: Methuen, 2008), p. 46.

3   Barber (2008), p. 47.

4   Ibid., p. xvi.

5   Ibid., p. 30.

6   Ibid.

7   Ibid., p. 39.

8   A. Seldon, *Blair Unbound* (London: Simon and Schuster, 2007), p. 40.

9   Barber (2008), p. 48.

10 House of Lords Constitution Committee, 'The Cabinet Office and the Centre of Government', January 2010, p. 15.

11 P. Hyman, *1 out of 10: From Downing Street Vision to School Reality* (London: Vintage, 2005), p. 171.

12 Hyman (2005), pp. 171–2.

13 Ibid., p. 175.

14 Ibid.

15 Barber (2008), p. 70.

16 J. Y. Kim, 'As Prepared for Delivery' speech, World Bank, 12 October 2012, http://www.worldbank.org/en/news/speech/2012/10/12/remarks-world-bank-group-president-jim-yong-kim-annual-meeting-plenary-session accessed 19 June 2015.

17 M. Barber, 'The Science of Delivery', Mile End Group, Queen Mary University of London, 29 January 2014, https://www.youtube.com/watch?v=xaF84du_zUE accessed 29 May 2019.

18 Michael Barber and Tony Blair briefly referred to 'the art of delivery' in 2013 at an event at the World Bank. There has been no detailed explanation or historical study published by Barber, Blair or any academic to date on how Barber and the Prime Minister's Delivery Unit created an 'art of delivery' from 2001 to 2005. Barber et al, 'Delivering Results – A Conversation with Jim Yong Kim, Tony Blair and Michael Barber', 10 April 2013, https://www.worldbank.org/en/news/speech/2013/04/10/delivering-results-conversation-jim-yong-kim-tony-blair-michael-barber accessed 16 April 2020.

19 J. Nye, *Soft Power: The Means to Success in World Politics* (New York: Public Affairs, 2004), preface.

20 G. Osborne, E. Balls and D. Cameron, 'Inside Number 10: David Cameron – The First Six Months', *Political Currency* podcast, 2 January 2025.

21 J. Rentoul, 'Gove (fails to) recruit another Blairite', *The Independent*, 24 March 2011, https://

web.archive.org/web/20110326053551/http://blogs.independent.co.uk/2011/03/24/gove-recruits-another-blairite/ accessed 6 June 2016.

22   M. Clement, 'The new No10 Delivery Unit has the potential to turn Boris Johnson's rhetoric into real world outcomes', *The Independent*, 29 June 2021.

23   M. Barber and T. Blair, 'How to Run a Government', Strand Group, King's College London, 11 June 2015, https://www.youtube.com/watch?v=a5GuPdD2cOk accessed 24 August 2015.

24   M. Barber, *How to Run a Government* (London: Allen Lane, 2015) Kindle Edition, Loc 42.

25   Leader, 'Chris Barber Obituary', *The Times*, 20 August 2012.

26   Ibid.

27   M. Barber Diary, 3 August 2005.

28   Barber (2008), p. 4.

29   Barber Diary, 26 June 2004.

30   Barber (2008), p. 6.

31   Ibid., p. 5.

32   Ibid., p. 7.

33   Ibid., p. 9.

34   M. Barber Curriculum Vitae, 2009, https://www.hse.ru/data/2009/11/20/1227763095/Michael-Barber-CV.pdf accessed 8 May 2019.

35   Barber (2008), p. 11.

36   M. Barber, Interview with author, 2018.

37   Barber (2008), p. 22.

38   Ibid., p. 23.

39   Ibid.

40   Ibid., p. 26.

41   Ibid., p. 23.

42   Ibid., p. 25.

43   A. Adonis, *Education, Education, Education: Reforming England's Schools* (London: Biteback, 2012), p. 27.

44   C. Swinson, Interview with author, 2023. In September 2024, Clara Swinson was appointed head of the Mission Delivery Unit in Keir Starmer's Labour government.

45   M. Barber, *The Learning Game: Arguments for an Education Revolution* (London: Indigo, 1997), p. 11.

46   G. Mulgan and A. Lee, 'Better Policy Delivery and Design: A Discussion Paper', Performance and Innovation Unit, January 2001, http://www.civilservant.org.uk/library/policy/2001_piu_better_policy_delivery_and_design.pdf accessed 3 February 2016.

47   Barber (2008), p. 33.

48   Ibid.

49   Ibid., p. 38.

50   Barber Diary, 18 March 2001.

51   M. Barber, 'The Very Big Picture', *Improving Schools* 3 (2000), p. 5.

52   Barber (2000), p. 14.

53   Ibid., p. 17.

54   A. Blick and G. Jones, *At Power's Elbow: Aides to the Prime Minister from Robert Walpole to David Cameron* (London: Biteback, 2013), p. 82.

55   P. Hennessy, *Cabinet* (Oxford: Basil Blackwell, 1986), p. 17.

56   J. Turner, *Lloyd George's Secretariat* (Cambridge: Cambridge University Press, 1980), p. 193.

57   Parliamentary Archives, Lloyd George Papers, LG/F/74/2/3, Cited in, A. Blick and G. Jones, 'A century of policy advice in No. 10', No. 10 History Blog, 5 January 2017, https://history.blog.gov.uk/2017/01/05/a-century-of-policy-advice-at-no-10-part-one/#_ftn1 accessed 10 August 2018.

58   Parliamentary Archives, Lloyd George Papers, LG/F/74/10/4, Cited in, Blick and Jones, 'A century of policy advice in No. 10', No. 10 History Blog, 5 January 2017, https://history.

blog.gov.uk/2017/01/05/a-century-of-policy-advice-at-no-10-part-one/#_ftn1 accessed 10 August 2018.

59 Parliamentary Archives, Lloyd George Papers, LG/F/74/10/4, Cited in, Blick and Jones (2017).

60 G. Best, *Churchill: A Study in Greatness* (Oxford: Oxford University Press, 2003), p. 200.

61 Best (2003), p. 201.

62 Blick and Jones (2013), p. 181.

63 J. Davis, *Prime Ministers and Whitehall 1960–74* (London: Hambledon Continuum, 2007), p. 121.

64 Davis (2007), p. 120.

65 Ibid., p. 113 and p. 131.

66 Ibid., p. 128.

67 Ibid., p. 129.

68 Barber Diary, 17 November 2001.

69 J. Campbell, *Edward Heath: A Biography* (London: Random House, 1993), p. 315.

70 Davis (2007), p. 162.

71 P. Hennessy, *The Prime Minister: The Office and its Holders since 1945* (London: Penguin, 2001), p. 369.

72 C. Haddon, 'Reforming the Civil Service – The Efficiency Unit', Institute for Government, 2012.

73 Haddon (2012), p. 8.

74 Ibid., p. 7.

75 Hennessy (1990), p. 625.

76 House of Commons Public Administration Select Committee, 'From Citizen's Charter to Public Service Guarantees', July 2008.

77 Hennessy (2001), p. 515.

78 P. Hennessy, *Distilling the Frenzy: Writing the History of One's Own Times* (London: Biteback, 2012), p. 19.

79 See full list of interviews in Bibliography.

80 T. Blair, *A Journey* (London: Hutchinson, 2010) Kindle edition, Loc 6838.

81 Blair (2010), Loc 6838.

82 Ibid., Loc 6824.

83 Ibid., Loc 1112.

84 Ibid., Loc 4441.

CHAPTER TWO: BLAIR'S FIRST TERM, 1997 TO 2001

1 UK Polling Report, 1992–97, http://ukpollingreport.co.uk/historical-polls/voting-intention-1992-1997 accessed 11 June 2019.

2 T. Blair, 'Leader's Speech, Blackpool 1996', British Political Speech, 1 October 1996, http://www.britishpoliticalspeech.org/speech-archive.htm?speech=202 accessed 22 November 2015.

3 M. Everett and E. Faulkner, 'House of Commons Briefing Paper: Special Advisers', House of Commons Library, 28 January 2015, www.parliament.uk/briefing-papers/SN03813.pdf accessed 22 June 2016, p. 4.

4 Everett and Faulkner (2015), p. 14.

5 Memorandum of Conversation, 'Private meeting with Prime Minister Blair and British Cabinet', The White House, 29 May 1997, http://clinton.presidentiallibraries.us/files/original/5aa4876f138a60330e869d23b372880d.pdf accessed 23 June 2016.

6 BBC News, 'Labour Leader John Smith dies at 55', BBC News, 12 May 1994, http://news.bbc.co.uk/onthisday/hi/dates/stories/may/12/newsid_2550000/2550803.stm accessed 12 January 2016.

7 P. Mandelson, *The Third Man* (London: Harper Press, 2010), pp. 169–71. And E. Balls, 'The Blair Years' Seminar, King's College London, 25 January 2016.

8   Blair (2010), Loc 2012.
9   Ibid., Loc 1955.
10   Ibid., Loc 2056.
11   Ibid., Loc 1078 and 2091.
12   T. Blair, 'The Agenda for a Generation', Ruskin College Oxford, 16 December 1996, http://www.educationengland.org.uk/documents/speeches/1996ruskin.html accessed 5 May 2015.
13   Blair (2010), Loc 840.
14   Ibid.
15   Ibid., Loc 854.
16   Ibid., Loc 879.
17   J. Powell, *The New Machiavelli: How to Wield Power in the Modern World* (London: Bodley Head, 2010) Kindle edition, Loc 1414.
18   E. Balls, 'Treasury and Economic History since 1945' Seminar, King's College London, 13 November 2015.
19   A. Campbell, *The Alastair Campbell Diaries Volume 2: Power and the People 1997–1999* (London: Hutchinson, 2011) Kindle edition, Loc 443.
20   D. Coyle, 'Brown names economic advisers to the Treasury', *The Independent*, 4 August 1997, http://www.independent.co.uk/news/business/brown-names-economic-advisers-to-the-treasury-1243908.html accessed 7 January 2016.
21   Campbell (2011), Loc 197.
22   P. Gould, *The Unfinished Revolution: How New Labour Changed British Politics Forever* (London: Hachette Digital, 2011), p. 415.
23   Campbell (2011), Loc 502.
24   Ibid., Loc 504.
25   A. Bevins, 'New sleaze row knocks at door of No. 10', *The Independent*, 1 June 1997, http://www.independent.co.uk/news/new-sleaze-row-knocks-at-door-of-no10-1253774.html accessed 1 February 2016.
26   Campbell (2011), Loc 4885.
27   Ibid., Loc 4875.
28   T. Blair, 'Bringing Britain Together' Speech, London, 1997.
29   Office of the Deputy Prime Minister, 'The Social Exclusion Unit', Office of the Deputy Prime Minister, April 2004, http://webarchive.nationalarchives.gov.uk/+/http://www.cabinetoffice.gov.uk/media/cabinetoffice/social_exclusion_task_force/assets/publications_1997_to_2006/seu_leaflet.pdf accessed 3 February 2016.
30   Blair (2010), Loc 1071.
31   Ibid., Loc 1072.
32   Powell (2010), Loc 404.
33   Hennessy (1986), p. 17.
34   Blair (2010), Loc 1073.
35   R. Butler, Interview with author, 2011.
36   Blair (2010), Loc 1110.
37   J. Davis and J. Rentoul, *Heroes or Villains?: The Blair Government Reconsidered* (Oxford: OUP, 2019), p. 84.
38   Ibid., pp. 82–3.
39   Blair (2010), Loc 1075.
40   Ibid., Loc 1091.
41   R. Wilson, Interview with author, 2011.
42   Wilson Interview (2011).
43   Ibid.
44   Blair (2010), Loc 4449.
45   J. Heywood, 'Men of Secrets, The Cabinet Secretaries: Interview with Sir Jeremy Heywood', Mile End Group, Queen Mary University of London, 2013, http://www.cabinetsecretaries.

com/_lib/pdf/Former%20Cabinet%20Secretary%20Jeremy%20Heywood%20 Interview%20with%20Anthony%20Seldon.pdf accessed 20 January 2016.

46   Campbell (2011), Loc 5703.

47   Blair (2010), Loc 5515.

48   Ibid., Loc 4453.

49   Ibid., Loc 4454.

50   Ibid., Loc 1092.

51   Campbell (2011), Loc 4876.

52   P. Riddell and P. Webster, 'Farewell No. 11, Hello Normanton', *The Times*, 3 July 2004.

53   T. Jarvis, 'Welfare-to-Work: The New Deal Research Paper' (London: House of Commons Library, 12 November 1997).

54   Blair (2010), Loc 4515.

55   N. Panchamia and P. Thomas, *Civil Service Reform in the Real World* (London: Institute for Government, March 2014), p. 46.

56   G. Brown, 'Speech on the 1998 Comprehensive Spending Review', House of Commons, 14 July 1998, http://www.ukpol.co.uk/2015/09/19/gordon-brown-1998-speech-on-the-comprehensive-spending-review/ accessed 20 October 2015.

57   J. Gieve, Interview with author, 2018.

58   HM Treasury, 'Comprehensive Spending Review: Public Service Agreements 1999 – 2002', HM Treasury, December 1998, https://www.gov.uk/government/uploads/system/uploads/attachment_data/file/260759/4181.pdf accessed 20 October 2015.

59   Cabinet Office, 'Modernising Government White Paper', Cabinet Office, March 1999, https://www.wbginvestmentclimate.org/uploads/modgov.pdf accessed 8 January 2016, p. 36.

60   HM Treasury, 'Comprehensive Spending Review: Public Service Agreements 1999 – 2002', HM Treasury, December 1998, https://www.gov.uk/government/uploads/system/uploads/attachment_data/file/260759/4181.pdf accessed 20 October 2015.

61   C. Clarke, Interview with author, 2018.

62   Blair (2010), Loc 4534.

63   M. Ivens, 'There's a big silver lining on that Tory cloud', *Sunday Times*, 17 June 2001.

64   HM Treasury, 'Public Sector Finances Databank: B2 Public Expenditure (% GDP)', December 2012.

65   R. Chote et al, 'Public Finances 1997 – 2010: 2010 Election Briefing Note', Institute for Fiscal Studies, March 2010, http://www.ifs.org.uk/bns/bn93.pdf accessed 16 November 2015, p. 4.

66   HM Treasury, 'The Treasury and Economic History since 1945' Seminar, King's College London, 13 November 2015.

67   Chote et al (2010), p. 4.

68   Ibid.

69   J. Rentoul 'Daily Catch-Up: Professor Balls on the "catastrophe" of running a surplus', *The Independent*, 16 November 2015, http://www.independent.co.uk/voices/comment/daily-catch-up-professor-balls-on-the-catastrophe-of-running-a-surplus-a6735796.html accessed 16 November 2015.

70   G. Brown, 'Modernising the British Economy: The New Mission for the Treasury' Speech, HM Treasury, 27 May 1999, http://webarchive.nationalarchives.gov.uk/20130129110402/http://www.hm-treasury.gov.uk/newsroom_and_speeches/speeches/chancellorexchequer/speech_chex_270599.cfm accessed 4 February 2016.

71   Powell (2010), Loc 1953.

72   Ibid., Loc 1953.

73   A. Browne, 'NHS faces another winter crisis', *The Observer*, 28 October 2001.

74   Blair (2010), Loc 5444.

75   Ibid., Loc 5455.

76   Leader, 'Bygone Budgets: March 2000', *The Guardian*, 14 February 2001, http://www.theguardian.com/uk/2001/feb/14/budget2001.budget accessed 5 February 2016.

77 Wilson Interview (2011).

78 Blair (2010), Loc 5517.

79 T. Blair, 'Touchstone Issues', 29 April 2000, https://www.theguardian.com/politics/2000/jul/17/labour.politicalnews1 accessed 13 June 2019.

80 Blair (2000).

81 Ibid., Loc 5921.

82 Ibid., Loc 5925.

83 Ibid., Loc 5921.

84 A. Milburn, 'The Blair Years' Seminar, King's College London, 13 February 2023.

85 Milburn, 'The Blair Years' (2023).

86 J. Le Grand, 'Knights, Knaves or Pawns? Human Behaviour and Social Policy', *Journal of Social Policy* 26 (1997).

87 Wilson Interview (2011).

88 Cabinet Office, 'Modernising Government White Paper', Cabinet Office, March 1999, https://www.wbginvestmentclimate.org/uploads/modgov.pdf accessed 8 January 2016, p. 37.

89 Cabinet Office (1999), p. 6.

90 Gould (2011), p. 431.

91 T. Blair, Speech and Q&A to Venture Capital Association, July 1999. Quoted in Barber (2008), p. 46.

92 Blair (2010), Loc 5444 – 5466.

93 S. Morgan, Interview with author, 2018.

94 Morgan Interview (2018).

95 Milburn, 'The Blair Years' (2023).

96 Ibid.

97 Ibid.

98 Ibid.

99 Wilson Interview (2011).

100 Ibid.

101 Campbell (2011), Loc 13244.

102 Butler Interview (2011).

103 Wilson Interview (2011).

104 J. Heywood, 'Men of Secrets, The Cabinet Secretaries: Interview with Sir Jeremy Heywood', Mile End Group, Queen Mary University of London, 2013, http://www.cabinetsecretaries.com/_lib/pdf/Former%20Cabinet%20Secretary%20Jeremy%20Heywood%20Interview%20with%20Anthony%20Seldon.pdf accessed 20 January 2016.

105 Wilson Interview (2011).

106 Ibid.

107 Powell (2010), Loc 1926.

108 Ibid., Loc 1919.

109 Ibid., Loc 1926.

110 Blair (2010), Loc 1154.

111 Hyman (2005), p. 171.

112 Ibid., p. 172.

113 Ibid., p. 173.

114 Ibid.

115 Ibid.

116 Ibid., p. 174.

117 Blick and Jones (2013), p. 289.

118 Cabinet Office, 'Modernising Government White Paper', Cabinet Office, March 1999, https://www.wbginvestmentclimate.org/uploads/modgov.pdf accessed 8 January 2016, p. 18.

119 Mulgan and Lee (2001).

120 Ibid.

121 House of Commons Public Administration Select Committee, 'Special Advisers: Boon or Bane?', 28 February 2001, http://www.publications.parliament.uk/pa/cm200001/cmselect/cmpubadm/293/29302.htm accessed 4 February 2016.

122 PASC (2001), para 18.

123 Ibid., para 35.

124 Ibid., para 81.

125 A. Milburn, Interview with author, 2023.

126 Blair (2010), Loc 5439.

127 N. Crisp, *24 Hours to Save the NHS* (Oxford: OUP, 2011), p. 1.

128 BBC News, 'Countdown to Crisis: Eight days that shook Britain', BBC News, 14 September 2000, http://news.bbc.co.uk/1/hi/uk/924574.stm accessed 5 February 2016.

129 Powell (2010), Loc 819.

130 Blair (2010), Loc 6029.

131 Ibid., Loc 6045.

132 Wilson Interview (2011).

133 Ibid.

134 Ibid.

135 BBC News, 'Blair confirms election delay', BBC News, 2 April 2001, http://news.bbc.co.uk/1/hi/uk_politics/1255703.stm accessed 4 February 2016.

136 Wilson Interview (2011).

137 Blair (2010), Loc 6359.

138 Ibid., Loc 6368.

139 Barber Diary, 25 March 2001.

140 Ibid.

141 Ibid., 14 March 2001.

142 D. Normington, 'The Blair Years' Seminar, King's College London, 8 February 2016.

143 Barber Diary, 14 March 2001.

144 Barber (2008), p. 5

145 Barber Diary, 25 March 2001.

146 Ibid., 7 May 2001.

147 Ibid.

148 Ibid.

149 Ibid.

150 Ibid.

151 Ibid.

152 Ibid.

153 Ibid.

154 Ibid., 19 May 2001.

155 Quoted in A. Evans, *The Intimacy of Power: An Insight into Private Office, Whitehall's Most Sensitive Network* (London: Biteback, 2024), p. 360.

156 Barber Diary, 19 May 2001.

157 J. Powell, Interview with author, 2019.

158 Barber Diary, 19 May 2001.

159 Ibid.

160 Ibid.

161 Ibid.

162 S. Heywood, *What Does Jeremy Think? Jeremy Heywood and the Making of Modern* Britain (London: William Collins, 2020), p. 108.

163 Ibid.

164 Barber Diary, 19 May 2001.

165 Barber Interview (2018).

166 Barber Diary, 19 May 2001.

167 Ibid.
168 Ibid.
169 Ibid.
170 Heywood (2020), p. 127.
171 Barber Diary, 19 May 2001.
172 Ibid.
173 Ibid.
174 Ibid.
175 Ibid.
176 Ibid.
177 Ibid.
178 Ibid.
179 Ibid.
180 P. Riddell, 'Blair looks to business for Whitehall fix', *The Times*, 1 June 2001.
181 Barber Diary, 2 June 2001.
182 Barber (2008), p. 37.

CHAPTER THREE: 2001 GENERAL ELECTION TO 9/11

1   Labour Manifesto 2001, May 2001, http://www.politicsresources.net/area/uk/e01/man/lab/ENG1.pdf accessed 3 August 2016.
2   Hyman (2005), p. 173.
3   T. Blair, *On Leadership: Lessons for the 21st Century* (London: Hutchinson Heinemann, 2024) Kindle edition, p. 7.
4   T. Blair, 'Tony Blair's Victory Speech', *The Guardian*, 8 June 2001.
5   Morgan Interview (2018).
6   Barber Diary, 9 June 2001.
7   Ibid.
8   Ibid.
9   Ibid.
10 Ibid.
11 D. Wastell, 'BP executive to become Labour business adviser', *Sunday Telegraph*, 3 June 2001.
12 Barber Diary, 9 June 2001.
13 Ibid.
14 Blunkett Interview (2018).
15 Ibid.
16 Barber Diary, 16 June 2001.
17 Ibid., 17 June 2001.
18 Ibid.
19 J. Sherman, 'Brown protects power base from expanded No. 10', *The Times*, 15 June 2001.
20 Barber Diary, 17 June 2001. Part of quote in Barber (2008), p. 63.
21 Ibid.
22 Ibid., 23 June 2001.
23 Ibid.
24 Ibid.
25 Ibid.
26 Morgan Interview (2018).
27 Barber Diary, 23 June 2001.
28 Ibid.
29 A. Campbell, *The Alastair Campbell Diaries Volume 3: Power and Responsibility 1999–2001* (London: Hutchinson, 2011) Kindle Edition, Loc 13680.
30 Campbell (2011), Loc 13655.
31 Barber Diary, 23 June 2001.

32   Ibid.
33   Ibid.
34   Ibid.
35   Ibid.
36   Ibid.
37   Ibid.
38   Ibid., 24 June 2001.
39   Ibid.
40   Ibid.
41   No. 10 Organogram, 2001, http://www.publications.parliament.uk/pa/cm200102/cmselect/cmpubadm/262/1110101.pdf accessed 9 August 2016.
42   Barber Diary, 24 June 2001.
43   Ibid.
44   Ibid.
45   Ibid.
46   Ibid.
47   M. Ivens, 'There's a big silver lining on that Tory cloud', *Sunday Times*, 17 June 2001.
48   Barber Diary, 24 June 2001.
49   Ibid.
50   Powell Interview (2019).
51   Ibid.
52   Ibid.
53   E. Balls, Interview with author, 2016.
54   Balls Interview (2016).
55   Blair's Strategy Adviser on 'blue skies' thinking. Mandelson (2011), Loc 6338.
56   Balls Interview (2016).
57   Ibid.
58   N. Macpherson, Interview with author, 2018.
59   Macpherson Interview (2018).
60   BBC News, 'More Power for Downing Street', BBC News, 22 June 2001, http://news.bbc.co.uk/1/hi/uk_politics/1402492.stm accessed 8 August 2016.
61   House of Commons Written Answers from the Prime Minister, 19 October 2001, http://www.publications.parliament.uk/pa/cm200102/cmhansrd/vo011019/text/11019w01.htm accessed 8 August 2016.
62   Barber Diary, 24 June 2001.
63   Ibid.
64   Ibid., 30 June 2001.
65   Ibid.
66   Barber Diary, 30 June and 1 July 2001.
67   Blunkett Interview (2018).
68   Ibid.
69   Ibid., 30 June and 1 July 2001.
70   Ibid., 1 July 2001.
71   Ibid.
72   Ibid.
73   Ibid.
74   Ibid., 7 July 2001.
75   Ibid.
76   Ibid.
77   Ibid.
78   Ibid.
79   Ibid.

80   Ibid.
81   Ibid.
82   Ibid.
83   Ibid., 8 July 2001.
84   Morgan Interview (2018).
85   Powell Interview (2019).
86   Barber Diary, 8 July 2001.
87   Ibid.
88   Ibid.
89   Ibid.
90   Milburn Interview (2023).
91   Ibid., 14 July 2001.
92   Ibid.
93   Ibid.
94   Ibid.
95   Ibid.
96   Ibid.
97   Ibid.
98   Ibid.
99   Ibid., 15 July 2001.
100   Ibid.
101   Ibid.
102   Ibid.
103   Ibid.
104   Ibid.
105   Ibid.
106   Ibid.
107   Ibid.
108   Balls Interview (2016).
109   Barber Diary, 15 July 2001.
110   Ibid.
111   Ibid., 21 July 2001.
112   Ibid.
113   Ibid.
114   Ibid.
115   Ibid.
116   Balls Interview (2016).
117   Barber Diary, 21 July 2001.
118   Ibid.
119   Ibid., 22 July 2001.
120   Ibid.
121   Ibid., 21 July 2001.
122   Ibid.
123   Ibid., 22 July 2001.
124   Ibid.
125   Ibid.
126   Ibid., 29 July 2001.
127   Cabinet Office, Ministerial Committee on Public Services and Public Expenditure (PSX), http://webarchive.nationalarchives.gov.uk/20040722024905/http://www.cabinet-office.gov.uk/cabsec/2003/cabcom/psx.htm accessed 18 July 2018.
128   Barber Diary, 29 July 2001.
129   Ibid.

130 Ibid., 30 July 2001.
131 Ibid.
132 Ibid.
133 Ibid., 31 July 2001.
134 Ibid.
135 Ibid.
136 Campbell (2011), Loc 14343.
137 Barber Diary, 31 July 2001.
138 Campbell (2011), Loc 14353.
139 Barber Diary, 31 July 2001.
140 Ibid.
141 Ibid.
142 Ibid.
143 Ibid.
144 Campbell (2011), Loc 14376.
145 J. Rentoul, 'The whole point of setting a target is to distort activity', *The Independent*, 16 February 2016, https://www.independent.co.uk/voices/comment/daily-catch-up-the-whole-point-of-setting-a-target-is-to-distort-activity-sir-michael-barber-a6875681.html accessed 13 June 2019.
146 Barber Diary, 31 July 2001.
147 Ibid.
148 Campbell (2011), Loc 14386.
149 Barber Diary, 1 August 2001.
150 Ibid.
151 Ibid.
152 Ibid.
153 Ibid.
154 Clarke Interview (2018).
155 Barber Diary, 2 August 2001.
156 Ibid.
157 Ibid.
158 Ibid., 24 August 2001.
159 Ibid., 25 August 2001.
160 Ibid.
161 Ibid.
162 Ibid.
163 Ibid.
164 Ibid.
165 Ibid., 7 September 2001.
166 Campbell (2011), Loc 14568.
167 Barber Diary, 9 September 2001.
168 Ibid.
169 Campbell (2011), Loc 14576.
170 Barber Diary, 24 June 2001.
171 V. Nicholls, Interview with author, 2023.
172 Barber Interview (2018).

CHAPTER FOUR: 9/11 TO THE 2002 BUDGET

1 T. Blair, '9/11 Statement', BBC News, 11 September 2001, http://news.bbc.co.uk/1/hi/uk_politics/1538551.stm accessed 11 January 2017.
2 S. Lander (former Director General of MI5) quoted, Seldon (2007), p. 62.
3 Barber Diary, 15 September 2001.

4   Blunkett Interview (2018).
5   Gieve Interview (2018).
6   Barber Diary, 15 September 2001.
7   Ibid.
8   Ibid.
9   Ibid.
10 Ibid., 22 September 2001.
11 Ibid.
12 G. W. Bush, 'Address to Congress', 20 September 2001.
13 Barber Diary, 23 September 2001.
14 Ibid., 22 September 2001.
15 Ibid.
16 Ibid.
17 Ibid.
18 Ibid., 29 September 2001.
19 Ibid.
20 Ibid.
21 Ibid.
22 Ibid.
23 Ibid.
24 Ibid.
25 Ibid.
26 Ibid.
27 Ibid.
28 Ibid.
29 Ibid.
30 Ibid.
31 Ibid.
32 Campbell (2013), Loc 811.
33 Barber Diary, 29 September 2001.
34 Blunkett (2006), p. 297.
35 Barber Diary, 29 September 2001.
36 Ibid.
37 Ibid.
38 Ibid.
39 Ibid., 30 September 2001.
40 Ibid.
41 Ibid.
42 Ibid.
43 Barber Diary, 6 October 2001.
44 Ibid.
45 Ibid.
46 Ibid.
47 Ibid.
48 Ibid.
49 Ibid.
50 Ibid.
51 Ibid.
52 Ibid.
53 Ibid.
54 T. Blair, Labour Conference Speech, 2 October 2001.
55 Ibid.

56   J. Le Grand, *Motivation, Agency and Public Policy: Of Knights and Knaves, Pawns and Queens* (Oxford: OUP, 2003), p. 11.

57   Quoted, Barber (2008), p. 337.

58   Barber Diary, 6 October 2001.

59   Ibid.

60   Ibid.

61   Blunkett (2006), p. 305.

62   Barber Diary, 13 October 2001.

63   Ibid.

64   Barber (2008), p. 101.

65   Ibid., pp. 104–5.

66   Barber Diary, 13 October 2001.

67   Ibid.

68   Ibid.

69   Ibid.

70   Ibid.

71   Davis and Rentoul (2019), p. 163.

72   Barber Diary, 13 October 2001.

73   Ibid.

74   Ibid.

75   Ibid., 20 October 2001.

76   Milburn Interview (2023).

77   Barber Interview (2018).

78   Ibid.

79   Ibid.

80   S. Jenkins, 'The Treasury's own great train robbery', *The Times*, 12 October 2001.

81   A. Sparrow, 'Sept 11: A good day to bury bad news', *Daily Telegraph*, 10 October 2001.

82   Ibid.

83   Barber Diary, 13 October 2001.

84   Ibid.

85   Ibid.

86   Ibid.

87   T. Blair, 'Speech on Public Service Reform', 16 October 2001, http://webarchive.nationalarchives.gov.uk/20040621031906/ http://number10.gov.uk/page1632 accessed 10 January 2017.

88   Blair, 'Speech on Public Service Reform', 16 October 2001.

89   Barber Diary, 20 October 2001.

90   Ibid.

91   Ibid.

92   Ibid.

93   Ibid.

94   Ibid.

95   Milburn Interview (2023).

96   Ibid., 21 October 2001.

97   Ibid.

98   Ibid.

99   Ibid.

100   Ibid.

101   Ibid., 27 October 2001.

102   Ibid., 29 October 2001.

103   Blunkett (2006), p. 312.

104   Barber Diary, 29 October 2001.

105 Ibid.
106 Campbell (2013), Loc 1466.
107 Barber Diary, 29 October 2001.
108 Ibid.
109 Ibid., 10 November 2001.
110 Ibid.
111 Seldon (2007), p. 57.
112 Barber Diary, 10 November 2001.
113 Ibid.
114 Ibid.
115 Ibid.
116 Ibid.
117 Davis and Rentoul (2019), p. 163.
118 Barber Diary, 10 November 2001.
119 Ibid.
120 Blunkett (2006), pp. 291–2.
121 Barber Diary, 10 November 2001.
122 Ibid., 11 November 2001.
123 Ibid.
124 Ibid.
125 Ibid., 17 November 2001.
126 Ibid.
127 Milburn Interview (2023).
128 Ibid.
129 Ibid.
130 Barber Diary, 17 November 2001.
131 Ibid.
132 Ibid.
133 Morgan Interview (2018).
134 Barber Diary, 24 November 2001.
135 Ibid.
136 Balls Interview (2016).
137 Barber Diary, 25 November 2001.
138 Ibid.
139 Ibid.
140 Ibid.
141 Ibid.
142 Macpherson Interview (2018).
143 Wanless Review: Interim Report, November 2001, http://webarchive.nationalarchives.gov.uk/20130107105354/http:/www.hm-treasury.gov.uk/consult_wanless_index.htm accessed 20 January 2017.
144 Barber Diary, 1 December 2001.
145 Ibid.
146 Ibid.
147 Ibid.
148 Ibid.
149 Ibid.
150 Ibid.
151 Ibid.
152 Ibid., 2 December 2001.
153 Ibid.
154 Ibid.

155 Ibid.
156 Ibid.
157 Balls Interview (2016).
158 Barber Diary, 2 December 2001.
159 Ibid., 8 December 2001.
160 G. Brown, 'Health Service Resources' Letter from the Chancellor to the Health Secretary, 6 December 2001.
161 Brown (2001).
162 Barber Diary, 8 December 2001.
163 Ibid.
164 Barber Diary, 15 December 2001.
165 Ibid.
166 Ibid.
167 Gieve Interview (2018).
168 Ibid.
169 Powell Interview (2019).
170 Barber Diary, 15 December 2001.
171 Ibid.
172 Ibid.
173 Ibid., 29 December 2001.
174 Balls Interview (2016).
175 Barber Diary, 29 December 2001.
176 Ibid.
177 Ibid.
178 Ibid.
179 Ibid.
180 Ibid.
181 Ibid.
182 Ibid.
183 Ibid.
184 Ibid.
185 Barber (2008), p. 119.
186 Barber Diary, 29 December 2001.
187 Ibid.
188 Ibid., 19 January 2002.
189 Ibid.
190 Ibid.
191 Ibid.
192 Ibid.
193 Ibid.
194 Ibid.
195 Ibid.
196 Barber Diary, 19 January 2002. Quoted, Barber (2008), p. 115.
197 Ibid., 2 February 2002.
198 Ibid., 26 January 2002.
199 Ibid.
200 Ibid., 9 February 2002.
201 Ibid., 10 February 2002.
202 T. Blair, Speech and Q&A to Venture Capital Association, July 1999. Quoted, Barber (2008), p. 46.
203 Barber Diary, 10 February 2002.
204 Ibid.

205 Ibid.
206 Ibid.
207 Ibid.
208 Ibid.
209 Ibid.
210 Ibid.
211 Ibid.
212 Ibid.
213 Ibid., 17 February 2002.
214 Ibid.
215 Ibid., 16 February 2002.
216 Ibid.
217 Ibid.
218 Ibid.
219 Ibid.
220 Ibid., 17 February 2002.
221 Ibid.
222 Ibid.
223 Ibid.
224 Ibid.
225 Ibid., 16 February 2002.
226 Ibid., 17 February 2002.
227 Gieve Interview (2018).
228 Barber Diary, 17 February 2002.
229 Ibid.
230 Ibid.
231 Ibid., 23 February 2002.
232 Ibid., 2 March 2002.
233 N. Watt and P. Wintour, 'Spinners, fixers and the prince of wonks – Blair's reforms have created a new breed in Whitehall', *The Guardian*, 23 February 2002.
234 Watt and Wintour (23 February 2002).
235 Barber Diary, 2 March 2002.
236 T. Roosevelt, 'Speak softly and carry a big stick; you will go far.'
237 Barber Diary, 4 March 2002.
238 Ibid., 10 March 2002.
239 Ibid.
240 Ibid.
241 Ibid.
242 Ibid., 10 March 2002. Quoted, Barber (2008), p. 141.
243 Ibid., 16 March 2002.
244 Ibid.
245 Ibid.
246 Ibid.
247 Ibid., 2 March 2002.
248 Barber (2008), p. 152 and 391.
249 Ibid., p. 392.
250 Ibid., p. 152.
251 Barber Diary, 16 March 2002.
252 Ibid.
253 Ibid.
254 Ibid.
255 Ibid.

256 Ibid.
257 Ibid.
258 Campbell (2013), Loc 3919.
259 Barber Diary, 16 March 2002.
260 Ibid.
261 Ibid., 23 March 2002.
262 Ibid.
263 Ibid.
264 Ibid.
265 Ibid.
266 Ibid.
267 Ibid.
268 Ibid.
269 Ibid.
270 Ibid., 29 March 2002.
271 Ibid.
272 Ibid.
273 Ibid.
274 Ibid.
275 Ibid. Quoted, Barber (2008), p. 160.
276 Ibid.
277 Ibid.
278 Ibid.
279 Ibid.
280 Ibid.
281 Ibid.
282 Ibid.
283 Ibid.
284 Ibid.
285 Ibid.
286 Ibid.
287 Ibid., 31 March 2002.
288 Ibid.
289 Ibid.
290 Ibid., 7 April 2002.
291 Ibid.
292 Ibid., 13 April 2002.
293 Ibid.
294 Ibid.
295 Ibid.
296 Ibid.
297 Ibid.
298 Ibid.
299 Ibid.
300 Ibid.
301 Ibid.
302 Ibid.
303 Ibid.
304 Ibid.
305 Balls Interview (2016).
306 Barber Diary, 14 April 2002.
307 Ibid.

308 Ibid.
309 Ibid.
310 Campbell (2013), Loc 4211.
311 Ibid., Loc 4227.
312 Ibid.
313 Ibid., Loc 4256.
314 Barber Diary, 20 April 2002.
315 Ibid.
316 Ibid.
317 Ibid.
318 Ibid.
319 Ibid.
320 Ibid.
321 Ibid.
322 Ibid.
323 Ibid.
324 Ibid.
325 Ibid.
326 Ibid.
327 Ibid.
328 Barber (2008), p. 158.
329 Leader, 'Street Crime Pledge Met', BBC News, 12 September 2002.
330 Blunkett Interview (2018).
331 Gieve Interview (2018).
332 Barber Diary, 20 April 2002.
333 Ibid.
334 Ibid.
335 Ibid.
336 Ibid.
337 Ibid.
338 R. Chote et al, 'Public Spending under Labour', Institute for Fiscal Studies, March 2010, https://www.ifs.org.uk/bns/bn92.pdf accessed 15 April 2020, p. 4.
339 Ibid.
340 G. Brown, Budget Speech, 17 April 2002, http://webarchive.nationalarchives.gov.uk/20100407010852/http://www.hm-treasury.gov.uk/bud_budget02_speech.htm accessed 20 February 2017.
341 BBC, 'Budget 2002', BBC News, 17 April 2002, http://news.bbc.co.uk/1/hi/uk_politics/1933547.stm accessed 20 February 2017.
342 E. Balls, *Speaking Out* (London: Hutchinson, 2016), p. 103.
343 Ibid., p. 102.
344 Balls Interview (2016).
345 G. Brown, Budget Speech, 17 April 2002, http://webarchive.nationalarchives.gov.uk/20100407010852/http://www.hm-treasury.gov.uk/bud_budget02_speech.htm accessed 20 February 2017.
346 Wanless Review: Final Report, April 2002, http://webarchive.nationalarchives.gov.uk/20130107105354/http://www.hm-treasury.gov.uk/consult_wanless_final.htm accessed 21 February 2017.
347 Barber Diary, 20 April 2002.
348 Ibid.
349 Ibid.

CHAPTER FIVE: APRIL 2002 TO THE 2003 BUDGET

1 Balls (2016), p. 103.
2 Barber Diary, 21 April 2002.
3 L. Elliott et al, 'Inside the Treasury', *The Guardian*, 16 April 2002.
4 Barber (2008), p. 142.
5 For example: Leader, 'The disgraceful Stephen Byers', *The Economist*, 28 February 2002. G. Jones, '67% of people think Byers should quit', *Daily Telegraph*, 28 February 2002.
6 Described in Chapter Four of this book.
7 Barber Diary, 1 June 2002.
8 Handwritten letter from Stephen Byers MP to Michael Barber, 19 June 2002.
9 Barber Diary, 29 June 2002.
10 Ibid.
11 Barber Interview (2018).
12 Ibid.
13 Ibid.
14 Ibid.
15 L. Elliott et al, 'Inside the Treasury', *The Guardian*, 16 April 2002.
16 Barber Diary, 11 May 2002.
17 Ibid.
18 Ibid.
19 Ibid., 29 June 2002.
20 Ibid.
21 Ibid., 6 July 2002.
22 Referred to in Barber (2008), p. 132.
23 Macpherson Interview (2018).
24 Barber Diary, 6 July 2002.
25 Ibid.
26 Ibid.
27 Ibid.
28 Ibid.
29 Ibid.
30 Ibid.
31 Ibid.
32 Ibid.
33 Ibid.
34 Ibid.
35 Ibid.
36 Ibid.
37 Ibid.
38 Ibid.
39 Milburn Interview (2023).
40 Barber Diary, 13 July 2002.
41 Ibid.
42 Ibid.
43 Ibid.
44 Ibid.
45 Leader, 'Hitting the ceiling', *The Times*, 16 July 2002.
46 HM Treasury, '2002 Spending Review', July 2002, http://webarchive.nationalarchives. gov.uk/20071204144532/http://www.hm-treasury.gov.uk/media/5/7/SR2002%20leaflet.pdf accessed 12 August 2017.

47 Barber Diary, 20 July 2002.
48 Ibid.
49 HM Treasury (2002).
50 P. Wintour, 'Lack method of measurement', *The Guardian*, 15 July 2002.
51 Ibid.
52 Balls Interview (2016).
53 Ibid.
54 Balls (2016), p. 135.
55 Barber (2008), p. 57.
56 M. Barber, 'Presentation at Prime Minister's Press Conference', 25 July 2002, http://webarchive.nationalarchives.gov.uk/20020819055246/http://www.pm.gov.uk:80/output/Page5746.asp accessed 20 July 2017.
57 Barber Diary, 5 September 2002.
58 Ibid.
59 A. Campbell, *The Burden of Power: Countdown to Iraq* (London: Arrow, 2012) Kindle edition, Loc 5577.
60 Barber Diary, 5 September 2002.
61 P. Riddell, 'No. 10's remote control focuses vision for a short time only', *The Times*, 26 July 2002.
62 Nicholls Interview (2023).
63 Barber Diary, 5 September 2002.
64 Ibid., 8 September 2002.
65 Barber (2008), p. 143.
66 Ibid., p. 165.
67 Ibid.
68 Ibid.
69 Ibid.
70 Ibid., p. 166.
71 Milburn Interview (2023).
72 Milburn, 'The Blair Years' (2023).
73 Barber Diary, 28 September 2002.
74 Crisp (2011), p. 87.
75 Barber Diary, 28 September 2002.
76 Crisp (2011), p. 88.
77 Balls (2016), p. 105.
78 G. Brown, *My Life, Our Times* (London: Bodley Head, 2017), p. 169.
79 Milburn, 'The Blair Years' (2023).
80 Brown (2017), p. 170.
81 Milburn Interview (2023).
82 A. Milburn, 'We have to give the voters more than this', *The Times*, 7 August 2002.
83 Leader, 'Right Idea', *The Times*, 7 August 2002.
84 Barber Diary, 28 September 2002.
85 T. Blair, 2002 Party Conference Speech, 1 October 2002.
86 Balls Interview (2016).
87 Brown (2017), p. 169.
88 Milburn, 'The Blair Years' (2023).
89 Balls (2016), p. 105.
90 Barber Diary, 5 October 2002.
91 E. Balls, Interview with author, 2017.
92 P. Butler and S. Parker, 'Foundation Trusts', *The Guardian*, 13 November 2002.
93 Butler and Parker (2002).
94 Balls (2016), p. 106.

95   Barber Diary, 12 October 2002.

96   A. Rawnsley, *The End of the Party: The Rise and Fall of New Labour* (London: Penguin Group, 2010), p. 81.

97   Barber Diary, 5 October 2002.

98   Ibid., 12 October 2002.

99   Ibid.

100   Ibid.

101   Ibid.

102   Ibid.

103   Barber (2008), p. 198.

104   Barber Diary, 7 December 2002.

105   Ibid., 12 October 2002.

106   Ibid.

107   Ibid.

108   Barber Diary, 12 October 2002.

109   Leader, 'Education Secretary resigns', BBC News, 25 October 2002.

110   House of Commons Public Administration Select Committee, Minutes of Evidence, 24 March 2003, http://www.publications.parliament.uk/pa/cm200203/cmselect/cmpubadm/62-x/3032403.htm accessed 3 September 2015.

111   Barber Diary, 26 October 2002.

112   Ibid.

113   Blair (2010), Loc 9454.

114   Barber Diary, 26 October 2002.

115   Ibid.

116   Ibid. Referred to in Barber (2008), p. 88.

117   Ibid.

118   Ibid.

119   Ibid.

120   Ibid.

121   Ibid., 6 November 2002.

122   Ibid., 8 November 2002.

123   Ibid., 2 November 2002. That Macpherson coined the phrase (but not when) is quoted in Barber (2008), p. 70.

124   Ibid., 8 November 2002.

125   Ibid.

126   Ibid.

127   Ibid.

128   Ibid.

129   Ibid.

130   Ibid.

131   Ibid.

132   Ibid.

133   Ibid., 2 November 2002.

134   Ibid.

135   Ibid., 8 November 2002.

136   Ibid.

137   Milburn Interview (2023).

138   Crisp (2011), p. 156.

139   Barber Diary, 9 November 2002.

140   Clarke Interview (2018).

141   Ibid.

142   Barber Diary, 16 November 2002.

143 Ibid.
144 Ibid.
145 Ibid.
146 Ibid.
147 Ibid.
148 Ibid., 17 November 2002.
149 Ibid., 24 November 2002.
150 Ibid.
151 Ibid.
152 Ibid.
153 Ibid.
154 Barber Diary, 7 December 2002.
155 Ibid.
156 Ibid.
157 Ibid.
158 Ibid.
159 Ibid.
160 Ibid.
161 Ibid.
162 Ibid.
163 Ibid., 8 December 2002.
164 Morgan Interview (2018).
165 Barber Diary, 7 December 2002.
166 Ibid.
167 Ibid., 14 December 2002.
168 Barber Interview (2018).
169 Barber Diary, 14 December 2002.
170 Ibid.
171 Ibid., 22 December 2002.
172 Ibid., 26 December 2002.
173 Ibid.
174 Ibid.
175 Ibid., 1 January 2003.
176 C. Newman, 'Whitehall watchers read much into removals', *Financial Times*, 31 December 2002.
177 Barber Diary, 1 January 2003.
178 Ibid.
179 Ibid.
180 Barber (2008), p. 174.
181 Ibid., p. 173.
182 N. Timmins, 'Extra NHS cash may be squandered', *Financial Times*, 8 January 2003.
183 Barber Diary, 8 January 2003.
184 Milburn Interview (2023).
185 Ibid.
186 Ibid.
187 A. Grice, 'Mr Targets on a mission to reform Whitehall', *The Independent*, 9 January 2003.
188 Barber Diary, 14 January 2003.
189 Ibid., 19 January 2003.
190 Ibid.
191 Ibid.
192 Ibid.
193 Ibid.

194 Ibid.
195 Ibid.
196 Ibid.
197 Ibid.
198 Ibid.
199 Ibid.
200 Ibid.
201 Morgan Interview (2018).
202 Barber Diary, 25 January 2003.
203 Ibid.
204 Ibid.
205 Ibid.
206 Ibid.
207 Ibid.
208 Ibid., 26 January 2003.
209 Ibid. Quoted in Barber (2008), p. 176.
210 Ibid.
211 Ibid.
212 C. Newman, 'Whitehall watchers read much into removals', *Financial Times*, 31 December 2002. Barber Diary, 26 January 2003.
213 Ibid.
214 Ibid. Quoted in Barber (2008), p. 174.
215 Ibid.
216 Ibid.
217 Ibid., 1 February 2003.
218 Barber (1997), p. 163.
219 Barber Diary, 1 February 2003.
220 Ibid.
221 Ibid.
222 Ibid.
223 Balls Interview (2017).
224 Barber Diary, 1 February 2003.
225 Macpherson Interview (2018).
226 Morgan Interview (2018).
227 G. Brown, Speech to the Social Market Foundation, 3 February 2003.
228 Macpherson Interview (2018).
229 Blair (2010), Loc 9401.
230 Blunkett Interview (2018).
231 Morgan Interview (2018).
232 Ibid.
233 Barber Diary, 7 February 2003.
234 Ibid.
235 Ibid.
236 Ibid., 16 February 2003.
237 Ibid., 7 February 2003.
238 Ibid.
239 Ibid.
240 Ibid.
241 Ibid.
242 Gieve Interview (2018).
243 Barber Diary, 7 February 2003.
244 Gieve Interview (2018).

245 Ibid.

246 Barber Diary, 15 February 2003.

247 House of Commons Public Administration Select Committee, 'On Target? Government by Measurement', July 2003.

248 PASC (2003), p. 5.

249 Barber Diary, 3 March 2003.

250 Ibid.

251 House of Commons Public Administration Select Committee, Minutes of Evidence from Lord Browne of Madingley, 28 November 2002. 'Targets are but one part of the whole tapestry of things you have to do to get people motivated, to aspire to do things, as well as to comply to certain standards.' Lord Browne, then Chief Executive of BP.

252 House of Commons Public Administration Select Committee, Minutes of Evidence from Michael Barber and Nicholas Macpherson, 27 February 2003.

253 PASC, Minutes of Evidence, 27 February 2003.

254 Ibid.

255 Ibid.

256 Leader, 'Million march against Iraq War', BBC News, 16 February 2003.

257 Morgan Interview (2018).

258 Barber Diary, 8 March 2003.

259 Ibid.

260 Ibid.

261 Ibid.

262 Ibid., 9 March 2003.

263 Ibid.

264 Ibid.

265 Ibid.

266 Ibid., 15 March 2003.

267 Ibid., 16 March 2003.

268 Ibid.

269 Ibid.

270 Ibid.

271 Ibid.

272 Ibid.

273 Ibid.

274 M. Tempest, 'Parliament gives Blair go-ahead for war', *The Guardian*, 18 March 2003.

275 Barber Diary, 21 March 2003.

276 Barber (2008), p. 176.

277 Barber Diary, 21 March 2003.

278 Ibid.

279 Ibid.

280 Ibid.

281 Ibid.

282 Ibid.

283 Ibid.

284 Ibid.

285 Ibid.

286 Cabinet Conclusion, 17 March 2003. Quoted in The Report of the Iraq Inquiry: Volume 7, 6 July 2016, p. 15.

287 Iraq Inquiry: Volume 7, 6 July 2016, p. 15.

288 Ibid.

289 Ibid., p. 19.

290 Ibid., p. 175.

291 Barber Diary, 29 March 2003.
292 Ibid.
293 Ibid., 30 March 2003.
294 Ibid., 2 April 2003.
295 Ibid., 12 April 2003.
296 Barber Interview (2018).
297 Barber Diary, 18 April 2003.
298 Ibid.
299 G. Brown, Budget Speech, 9 April 2003.
300 Gieve Interview (2018).
301 Barber (2008), p. 177.
302 Ibid.

CHAPTER SIX: APRIL 2003 TO THE 2004 BUDGET

1 T. Hames, 'The Baghdad bounce makes Blair a winner on all fronts', *The Times*, 7 April 2003.
2 Hames (7 April 2003).
3 Barber Diary, 18 April 2003.
4 Ibid.
5 W. Churchill, 'The End of the Beginning' Speech, Mansion House, 10 November 1942. Quoted in Barber Diary, 18 April 2003.
6 Barber Diary, 18 April 2003.
7 W. Hutton, 'Three cheers for the public sector', *The Observer*, 13 April 2003.
8 Hutton (2003).
9 Ibid.
10 Barber Diary, 20 April 2003.
11 Morgan Interview (2018).
12 S. Cameron, 'Did Gordon Brown really keep us out of the Euro?', *Daily Telegraph*, 26 June 2013.
13 G. Brown, Statement on Economic and Monetary Union, Hansard, 9 June 2003.
14 Barber Diary, 26 April 2003.
15 Ibid.
16 Ibid., 27 April 2003.
17 Milburn, 'The Blair Years' (2023).
18 T. Blair, Labour Party Conference Speech, 1 October 2002.
19 Barber Diary, 27 April 2003.
20 Ibid.
21 Milburn, 'The Blair Years' (2023).
22 Ibid., 2 May 2003.
23 Ibid.
24 Ibid.
25 Ibid.
26 Ibid.
27 Ibid.
28 Ibid.
29 Ibid.
30 Ibid.
31 Ibid.
32 Ibid., 4 May 2003.
33 Ibid., 10 May 2003.
34 Ibid.
35 Ibid.
36 Barber Interview (2018).

37 Ibid.
38 Powell Interview (2019).
39 Ibid.
40 Barber Diary, 10 May 2003.
41 Ibid., 18 May 2003.
42 Ibid., 11 May 2003.
43 Ibid., 17 May 2003.
44 Ibid.
45 Ibid.
46 Ibid., 18 May 2003.
47 Ibid.
48 Ibid.
49 Balls Interview (2017).
50 Ibid.
51 Barber Diary, 18 May 2003.
52 Brown (2017), p. 170.
53 Barber Diary, 24 May 2003.
54 Ibid.
55 Ibid., 1 June 2003.
56 Ibid.
57 Ibid.
58 Ibid.
59 Ibid.
60 Ibid.
61 Ibid., 8 June 2003.
62 Ibid.
63 Ibid.
64 Leader, 'Weapons dossier sent back six times', BBC News, 6 June 2003.
65 Barber Diary, 8 June 2003.
66 Ibid.
67 Balls Interview (2017).
68 Happold, T., 'Milburn resigns from government', *The Guardian*, 12 June 2003.
69 Barber Diary, 21 June 2003.
70 Milburn Interview (2023).
71 Barber Diary, 21 June 2003.
72 Ibid.
73 Ibid.
74 Ibid.
75 Ibid.
76 Ibid., M. Barber, 'Agenda for Meeting with PM', June 2003. [Hardcopy in M. Barber Private Diary]
77 Ibid.
78 Ibid.
79 Ibid., 12 June 2003.
80 Ibid.
81 Ibid., 21 June 2003.
82 Macpherson Interview (2018).
83 Barber Diary, 21 June 2003. Letter from the Prime Minister's Principal Private Secretary Jeremy Heywood (Domestic Policy Reform), 19 June 2003. [Hardcopy in M. Barber Private Diary]
84 Ibid.
85 Ibid., 28 June 2003.

86   Morgan Interview (2018).
87   Barber Diary, 28 June 2003.
88   Ibid.
89   Ibid.
90   Ibid.
91   Ibid.
92   Ibid.
93   Ibid.
94   Ibid.
95   Ibid.
96   Ibid.
97   Ibid., 29 June 2003.
98   Ibid., 5 July 2003.
99   Campbell (2013), Loc 12154.
100   Ibid.
101   Barber Diary, 6 July 2003.
102   Ibid.
103   Ibid.
104   Ibid.
105   Ibid.
106   Davis and Rentoul (2019), pp. 171–2.
107   Barber Diary, 6 July 2003.
108   Ibid., 12 July 2003.
109   Ibid.
110   Ibid., 19 July 2003.
111   Ibid.
112   Ibid.
113   Ibid.
114   Ibid.
115   Ibid., 12 July 2003.
116   Leader, 'Hospital shake-up scrapes through', BBC News, 8 July 2003.
117   Barber Diary, 12 July 2003.
118   Ibid., 12 and 13 July 2003.
119   Ibid., 12 July 2003.
120   Ibid.
121   Ibid.
122   Ibid.
123   Ibid., 13 July 2003.
124   Ibid., 19 July 2003.
125   Ibid.
126   J. Reid, Choice Speech to the Health Network, 16 July 2003, https://webarchive.
      nationalarchives.gov.uk/ukgwa/+/http://www.dh.gov.uk/en/MediaCentre/Speeches/
      Speecheslist/DH_4071487 accessed 19 June 2018.
127   Barber Diary, 19 July 2003. Email exchange between Michael Barber and Ed Balls, 17 July
      2003. [Hardcopy in M. Barber Private Diary]
128   Ibid.
129   Ibid.
130   Ibid.
131   Ibid.
132   Ibid.
133   Ibid.
134   Ibid.

135 Ibid.
136 Ibid.
137 Ibid.
138 Ibid.
139 Ibid.
140 Ibid.
141 Barber Diary, 1 August 2003.
142 Ibid.
143 See key slides: T. Blair, Prime Minister's Press Conference, 30 July 2003, https://webarchive.nationalarchives.gov.uk/ukgwa/20030731053138/http://www.pm.gov.uk:80/output/Page4294.asp accessed 19 June 2018.
144 T. Blair, Prime Minister's Press Conference, 30 July 2003.
145 Barber Diary, 1 August 2003.
146 Ibid.
147 M.A. Sieghart, 'Stop boldly talking, it's time to boldly go for it', *The Times*, 31 July 2003. 'The Prime Minister loves punishing journalists at these events … Yesterday, we were treated to phrases such as: "implement workforce remodelling", "sustain impact of strategies and embed in whole school approach" and "extend diversity and collaboration".'
148 Barber Diary, 1 August 2003.
149 Mandelson (2010), p. 366.
150 Ibid.
151 Barber Diary, 13 September 2003.
152 Ibid., 7 September 2003.
153 Ibid.
154 Ibid.
155 Ibid., 12 October 2003.
156 Ibid.
157 B. Yong. and R. Hazell, *Special Advisers: Who they are, What they do, Why they matter* (London: Hart Publishing, 2014), p. 21.
158 T. Happold, 'Blair announces No. 10 shake-up', *The Guardian*, 3 September 2003.
159 No. 10 Organogram, 2001 http://www.publications.parliament.uk/pa/cm200102/cmselect/cmpubadm/262/1110101.pdf accessed 9 August 2016.
160 A. Campbell, *The Alastair Campbell Diaries Volume 5: Outside, Inside 2003–2005* (London: Biteback, 2016) Kindle edition, Loc 1322.
161 Mandelson (2010), p. 368.
162 Barber Diary, 7 September 2003.
163 Ibid.
164 Ibid.
165 Ibid., 12 October 2003.
166 Ibid., 18 October 2003.
167 Mandelson (2010), p. 369.
168 Ibid.
169 Ibid., p. 371.
170 Brown (2017), p. 186.
171 Mandelson (2010), p. 373.
172 Ibid.
173 Ibid.
174 Barber Diary, 14 September 2003.
175 Ibid., 13 September 2003.
176 Ibid., 14 September 2003.
177 Ibid.
178 Ibid.

179 Ibid., 27 September 2003.
180 Ibid.
181 Ibid., 11 October 2003.
182 Ibid.
183 Ibid.
184 G. Brown, Labour Party Conference Speech, 29 September 2003.
185 T. Blair, Labour Party Conference Speech, 30 September 2003.
186 Barber Diary, 12 October 2003.
187 Ibid.
188 Ibid.
189 Ibid.
190 Ibid.
191 Ibid.
192 Ibid., 18 October 2003.
193 Ibid., 31 October 2003.
194 Ibid.
195 Ibid.
196 Ibid.
197 Ibid., 2 November 2003.
198 Clarke Interview (2018).
199 Barber Diary, 2 November 2003.
200 Ibid., 6 December 2003.
201 Ibid.
202 Ibid.
203 Ibid.
204 Ibid.
205 Ibid.
206 Ibid.
207 Ibid., 14 December 2003.
208 Ibid.
209 Ibid.
210 Ibid.
211 Ibid.
212 Ibid.
213 Ibid.
214 Barber Interview (2018).
215 Ibid.
216 Powell Interview (2019).
217 Ibid.
218 Swinson Interview (2023).
219 Barber Diary, 14 December 2003.
220 Ibid.
221 Ibid.
222 Ibid.
223 Ibid.
224 Ibid., 21 December 2003.
225 Balls Interview (2017).
226 Macpherson Interview (2018).
227 G. Brown, Pre-Budget Report Statement, 10 December 2003.
228 Barber Diary, 6 December 2003.
229 Ibid., 13 December 2003.
230 Ibid., 21 December 2003.

231 Ibid.
232 Ibid.
233 Ibid.
234 Ibid.
235 Ibid.
236 Ibid.
237 T. Helm, 'Blair loses another aide', *Daily Telegraph*, 10 December 2003.
238 Macpherson Interview (2018).
239 Barber Diary, 10 January 2004.
240 Ibid.
241 Ibid., 10 and 11 January 2004.
242 Ibid.
243 Ibid.
244 Ibid.
245 Ibid.
246 Ibid.
247 Ibid.
248 Ibid.
249 Ibid.
250 Ibid., 11 January 2004.
251 Ibid.
252 Ibid.
253 Ibid.
254 Ibid.
255 Ibid.
256 Ibid.
257 Ibid.
258 Ibid., 17 January 2004.
259 Ibid.
260 Morgan Interview (2018).
261 Macpherson Interview (2018).
262 Barber Diary, 17 January 2004.
263 Ibid.
264 Ibid.
265 Ibid.
266 Ibid.
267 Clarke Interview (2018).
268 Barber Diary, 17 January 2004.
269 Ibid.
270 Ibid.
271 Ibid.
272 Ibid.
273 Gieve Interview (2018).
274 Ibid.
275 Barber Diary, 17 January 2004.
276 Ibid.
277 Ibid., 18 January 2004.
278 Ibid.
279 Ibid.
280 Ibid.
281 Ibid.
282 Ibid.

283 Ibid.
284 Ibid., 24 January 2004.
285 Ibid.
286 Ibid.
287 Gould (2011), p. 472.
288 Ibid.
289 Leader, 'Blair wins key top-up fees vote', BBC News, 27 January 2004.
290 Barber Diary, 1 February 2004.
291 Ibid.
292 Ibid., 7 February 2004.
293 Leader, 'NHS Targets: The art of aiming high', *The Guardian*, 11 February 2004.
294 Leader, *The Guardian* (11 February 2004).
295 Leader, 'Star struck: Unhealthy tendencies in the latest reform of NHS targets', *The Times*, 9 February 2004.
296 Leader, *The Guardian* (2004).
297 Barber Diary, 15 February 2004.
298 Barber Interview (2018).
299 T. Blair, Civil Service Reform Speech, 24 February 2004.
300 Cabinet Office, 'Civil Service Reform – Delivery and Values White Paper', 24 February 2004, p. 28.
301 A. Turnbull, Civil Service Reform Speech, 24 February 2004.
302 Barber Diary, 14 March 2004.
303 Ibid.
304 Clarke Interview (2018).
305 Barber Diary, 20 March 2004.
306 Ibid.
307 HM Treasury, 2004 Budget, 17 March 2004.
308 Ibid.
309 HM Treasury and PMDU, 'Devolving decision-making: Refining targets and performance management', March 2004.
310 HM Treasury and PMDU (2004).
311 Ibid.
312 Ibid., p. 6.
313 Ibid., p. 46.
314 Ibid., p. 51.
315 Macpherson Interview (2018).

CHAPTER SEVEN: MARCH 2004 TO JULY 2005
1 Barber Diary, 27 March 2004.
2 Ibid.
3 Ibid.
4 Ibid., 28 March 2004.
5 Ibid.
6 Ibid.
7 Ibid., 3 April 2004.
8 Ibid.
9 Ibid.
10 Ibid.
11 D. Leppard, 'New migrant crisis hits Blunkett', *Sunday Times*, 4 April 2004.
12 Ibid.
13 Barber Diary, 11 April 2004.
14 Ibid.

15   Barber Diary, 4 April 2004.
16   Ibid.
17   Davis and Rentoul (2019), p. 239.
18   Barber Diary, 12 April 2004.
19   Ibid.
20   Ibid.
21   Ibid.
22   Ibid.
23   Ibid.
24   Ibid.
25   Ibid.
26   Ibid.
27   Ibid., and Barber (2008), p. 190.
28   Ibid.
29   Barber (2008), p. 215.
30   Barber Diary, 8 May 2004.
31   Ibid.
32   Ibid.
33   Ibid.
34   Ibid.
35   Ibid.
36   Ibid.
37   Ibid.
38   Ibid.
39   Ibid.
40   Ibid.
41   Ibid.
42   Ibid.
43   Ibid.
44   Ibid.
45   Ibid., 16 May 2004.
46   Ibid.
47   Ibid., 23 May 2004.
48   Ibid.
49   J. Appleby et al, British Social Attitudes Report 32: Health, NatCen, 2015, p. 4.
50   Barber Diary, 23 May 2004.
51   Ibid., 12 June 2004.
52   Ibid., 19 June 2004.
53   Ibid.
54   Ibid.
55   Ibid.
56   Barber Interview (2018).
57   Barber Diary, 26 June 2004.
58   T. Blair, Public Service Reform speech, 23 June 2004.
59   Ibid.
60   Department of Health, The NHS Improvement Plan, 24 June 2004, p. 5.
61   Barber Diary, 26 June 2004.
62   Ibid., 4 July 2004.
63   Ibid.
64   Ibid.
65   Ibid.
66   Ibid., 10 July 2004.

67 Ibid.
68 Balls Interview (2016).
69 P. Riddell and P. Webster, 'Farewell No. 11, hello Normanton', *The Times*, 3 July 2004.
70 Balls Interview (2016).
71 Macpherson Interview (2018).
72 Ibid.
73 Barber Diary, 17 July 2004.
74 Leader, 'At-a-glance: Spending Review', BBC News, 12 July 2004.
75 HM Treasury, 2004 Spending Review, July 2004, p. 27.
76 A. Davidson, 'The MT Interview: John Gieve', *Management Today*, 1 July 2004.
77 T. Blair, Prime Minister's Press Conference, 22 July 2004.
78 M. Barber, Prime Minister's Press Conference, 22 July 2004.
79 Ibid.
80 Ibid.
81 Ibid.
82 Ibid.
83 P. Riddell, 'Headteacher's report: much work still to do', *The Times*, 23 July 2004.
84 J. Blitz, 'Luck and loyalty help sunny outlook', *Financial Times*, 23 July 2004.
85 Barber Diary, 19 September 2004.
86 Ibid., 9 October 2004.
87 Ibid.
88 Ibid.
89 Ibid.
90 Ibid.
91 Ibid.
92 Ibid.
93 Ibid.
94 Ibid.
95 Ibid.
96 Ibid.
97 Ibid.
98 Ibid.
99 Ibid.
100 Ibid., 23 October 2004.
101 Ibid.
102 Ibid.
103 Ibid., 30 October 2004.
104 Ibid.
105 Ibid.
106 Crisp (2011), p. 65.
107 Barber Diary, 4 December 2004.
108 Ibid.
109 Ibid., 11 December 2004.
110 Ibid.
111 Ibid.
112 Ibid.
113 Ibid.
114 Ibid. The guiding coalition concept is based on Professor John Kotter's book *Leading Change* (1996).
115 Barber Diary, 11 December 2004.
116 A. Grice, 'Things have only got better. But will Blair benefit?', *The Independent*, 11 December 2004.

117 Ibid.
118 Barber Diary, 16 October 2004.
119 Leader, 'Blunkett resigns over visa accusations', BBC News, 15 December 2004.
120 Barber Diary, 18 December 2004.
121 Blunkett Interview (2018).
122 Ibid.
123 Barber Diary, 18 December 2004.
124 A. Davidson, 'The MT Interview: John Gieve', *Management Today*, 1 July 2004.
125 Barber Diary, 27 December 2004.
126 Ibid.
127 Ibid., 8 January 2005.
128 Ibid., 9 January 2005.
129 Ibid.
130 Ibid.
131 Ibid.
132 Ibid.
133 Ibid., 15 January 2005.
134 Ibid.
135 Ibid.
136 Ibid., 22 January 2005.
137 Ibid.
138 Ibid., 23 January 2005.
139 Ibid.
140 Ibid.
141 Ibid.
142 Ibid.
143 Ibid.
144 Ibid.
145 Ibid.
146 Ibid., 29 January 2005.
147 Ibid.
148 Leader, 'Blair's inner circle', *The Guardian*, 27 January 2005.
149 Barber Diary, 6 February 2005.
150 Ibid.
151 Ibid.
152 Ibid., 27 February 2005.
153 Ibid., 5 March 2005.
154 Ibid., 19 March 2005.
155 Ibid., 12 March 2005.
156 Swinson Interview (2023).
157 T. O'Connor, Interview with author, 2023.
158 Barber Diary, 12 March 2005.
159 Ibid.
160 Ibid., 13 March 2005.
161 Ibid.
162 Leader, 'The Budget', BBC News, 16 March 2005.
163 M. Barber, Email to I. Rogers and J. Powell, 8 April 2005. [Hardcopy in M. Barber Private Diary]
164 Barber (2008), p. 257.
165 M. Barber and M. Clement, 'The Art of Delivery: The Prime Minister's Delivery Unit 2001–05', Institute of Historical Research Seminar, 26 March 2019.
166 Barber (2008), p. 257.

167 J. Powell, Email to M. Barber and I. Rogers, 8 April 2005. [Hardcopy in M. Barber Private Diary]

168 Barber Diary, 16 April 2005.

169 Ibid., 1 May 2005.

170 Ibid., 23 April 2005.

171 Ibid.

172 Ibid.

173 Blair (2010), Loc 9878.

174 Ibid., Loc 10187 and 10203.

175 Ibid., Loc 10219.

176 Barber Diary, 7 May 2005.

177 Ibid., 14 May 2005.

178 Ibid.

179 Ibid., 5 June 2005.

180 Ibid., 14 May 2005.

181 Ibid., 21 May 2005.

182 Ibid.

183 Ibid.

184 Ibid.

185 Ibid., 12 June 2005.

186 Ibid.

187 Ibid.

188 Ibid.

189 Ibid.

190 Ibid.

191 Ibid.

192 Ibid.

193 Ibid.

194 Ibid.

195 Clarke Interview (2018).

196 Barber Diary, 12 June 2005.

197 Ibid.

198 H. Muir, 'Politics Reformers' Rewards', *The Guardian*, 11 June 2005.

199 Barber Diary, 18 June 2005.

200 Ibid., 25 June 2005.

201 Ibid.

202 Ibid., 19 June 2005.

203 Ibid.

204 Ibid.

205 Ibid.

206 Ibid.

207 Ibid.

208 Ibid.

209 Ibid.

210 Ibid.

211 Ibid.

212 Ibid.

213 Ibid.

214 Ibid., 26 June 2005.

215 Barber (2008), pp. 428–9.

216 O'Connor Interview (2023).

217 Barber Interview (2018).

218 Ibid.

CHAPTER EIGHT: CONCLUSION

1   Barber (2008), pp. 428–9.
2   Clarke Interview (2018).
3   Gieve Interview (2018).
4   Milburn Interview (2023).
5   O'Connor Interview (2023).
6   Milburn Interview (2023).
7   M. Barber and T. Blair, 'How to Run a Government', Strand Group, King's College London, 11 June 2015, https://www.youtube.com/watch?v=a5GuPdD2cOk accessed 24 August 2015.
8   Macpherson Interview (2018).
9   Davis and Rentoul (2019), p. 163.
10   Milburn Interview (2023).
11   Barber Diary, 19 January 2002.
12   Barber (2008), p. 139.
13   Ibid., p. 114.
14   Ibid., p. 54.
15   Powell Interview (2019).
16   Morgan Interview (2018).
17   Swinson Interview (2023).
18   Macpherson Interview (2018).
19   J. Davis comment to M. Clement, 2018.
20   Blunkett Interview (2018).
21   Nicholls Interview (2023).
22   Macpherson Interview (2018).
23   Morgan Interview (2018).
24   Milburn Interview (2023).
25   Ibid.
26   Ibid.
27   Blunkett Interview (2018).
28   Barber Interview (2018).
29   Gieve Interview (2018).
30   Ibid.
31   Macpherson Interview (2018).
32   Barber (2008), p. 258.
33   Macpherson Interview (2018).
34   Gieve Interview (2018).
35   Ibid.
36   Milburn Interview (2023).
37   Davis and Rentoul (2019), p. 163.
38   Clarke Interview (2018).
39   Ibid.
40   Ibid.
41   Ibid.
42   Morgan Interview (2018).
43   Milburn Interview (2023).
44   Ibid.
45   Morgan Interview (2018).
46   Macpherson Interview (2018).
47   R. Page-Jones quoted, S. Cleary, *What impact did the machinery of government and leadership*

changes have to the PMDU 2005–2007? Undergraduate dissertation, Queen Mary University of London, 2011.

48 Davis and Rentoul (2019), p. 163.
49 M. Clement, 'How to run a government', The Policy Institute, King's College London, 3 August 2015, https://blogs.kcl.ac.uk/policywonkers/how-to-run-a-government/ accessed 11 March 2019.
50 Osborne, Balls and Cameron, 'Inside Number 10: David Cameron – The First Six Months', *Political Currency* podcast, 2 January 2025.
51 Barber Diary, 18 January 2004.
52 Balls Interview (2016).
53 Davis and Rentoul (2019), p. 163.
54 M. Clement, 'The new No10 Delivery Unit has the potential to turn Boris Johnson's rhetoric into real world outcomes', *The Independent*, 29 June 2021.
55 M. Barber, 'Success Delivered: How delivery units make a difference for governments and the citizens they serve', *Delivery Associates*, 2018.
56 Blair (2024), p. 51.

BIBLIOGRAPHY

PRIMARY SOURCES

Interviews

Balls, Ed, Interview with author, 2016.

Balls, Ed, Interview with author, 2017.

Barber, Michael, Interview with author, 2018.

Blunkett, David, Interview with author, 2018.

Butler, Robin, Interview with author, 2011.

Clarke, Charles, Interview with author, 2018.

Gieve, John, Interview with author, 2018.

Macpherson, Nicholas, Interview with author, 2018.

Milburn, Alan, Interview with author, 2023.

Morgan, Sally, Interview with author, 2018.

Nicholls, Vanessa, Interview with author, 2023.

O'Connor, Tony, Interview with author, 2023.

Powell, Jonathan, Interview with author, 2019.

Swinson, Clara, Interview with author, 2023.

Wilson, Richard, Interview with author, 2011.

Unpublished Sources

Balls, Ed, 'Treasury and Economic History since 1945' Seminar, King's College London, 13 November 2015.

Balls, Ed, 'The Blair Years' Seminar, King's College London, 25 January 2016.

Barber, Michael, Private Diary 2001 – 2005.

Barber, Michael, 'Delivery Update: Transport' for the Prime Minister, 16 November 2001. [Hardcopy in M. Barber Private Diary]

Barber, Michael 'Planning for Delivery: Next Steps' for the Prime Minister, 16 November 2001. [Hardcopy in M. Barber Private Diary]

Barber, Michael, 'Delivery Update: Health' for the Prime Minister, 7 December 2001. [Hardcopy in M. Barber Private Diary]

Barber, Michael, 'Agenda for Meeting with PM', June 2003. [Hardcopy in M. Barber Private Diary]

Barber, Michael, Email exchange between Michael Barber and Ed Balls, 17 July 2003. [Hardcopy in M. Barber Private Diary]

Barber, Michael, Email to I. Rogers and J. Powell, 8 April 2005. [Hardcopy in M. Barber Private Diary]

Barber, Michael and Michelle Clement, 'The Art of Delivery: The Prime Minister's Delivery Unit 2001–05', Institute of Historical Research Seminar, 26 March 2019.

Brown, Gordon, 'Health Service Resources' Letter from the Chancellor to the Health Secretary, 6 December 2001. [Hardcopy in M. Barber Private Diary]

Heywood, Jeremy, Letter from the Prime Minister's Principal Private Secretary (Domestic Policy Reform), 19 June 2003. [Hardcopy in M. Barber Private Diary]

Milburn, Alan, 'The Blair Years' Seminar, King's College London, 13 February 2023.

Normington, David, 'The Blair Years' Seminar, King's College London, 8 February 2016.

Powell, Jonathan, Email to M. Barber and I. Rogers, 8 April 2005. [Hardcopy in M. Barber Private Diary]

Published Sources

Adonis, Andrew, *Education, Education, Education: Reforming England's Schools* (London: Biteback, 2012).

Balls, Ed, *Speaking Out* (London: Hutchinson, 2016).

Barber, Michael, *The Learning Game: Arguments for an Education Revolution* (London: Indigo, 1997).

Barber, Michael, 'The Very Big Picture', *Improving Schools* 3 (2000), pp. 5–17.

Barber, Michael, 'Presentation at Prime Minister's Press Conference', 26 July 2002,

http://webarchive.nationalarchives.gov.uk/20020819055246/http://www.pm.gov.uk:80/output/Page5746.asp accessed 20 July 2017.

Barber, Michael, *Instruction to Deliver* (London: Methuen, 2008).

Barber, Michael, Curriculum Vitae, 2009,

https://www.hse.ru/data/2009/11/20/1227763095/Michael-Barber-CV.pdf accessed 8 May 2019.

Barber, Michael, *Deliverology 101: A Field Guide for Educational Leaders* (California: Corwin, 2010).

Barber, Michael, Tony Blair and Jim Yong Kim, 'Delivering Results – A Conversation with Jim Yong Kim, Tony Blair and Michael Barber', 10 April 2013,

https://www.worldbank.org/en/news/speech/2013/04/10/delivering-results-conversation-jim-yong-kim-tony-blair-michael-barber accessed 16 April 2020.

Barber, Michael, 'The Science of Delivery', Mile End Group, Queen Mary University of London, 29 January 2014, https://www.youtube.com/watch?v=xaF84du_zUE accessed 29 May 2019.

Barber, Michael, *How to Run a Government: So that Citizens Benefit and Taxpayers Don't Go Crazy* (London: Allen Lane, 2015).

Barber, Michael and Tony Blair, 'How to Run a Government', Strand Group, King's College London, 11 June 2015, https://www.youtube.com/watch?v=a5GuPdD2cOk accessed 24 August 2015.

Barber, Michael, 'Success Delivered: How delivery units make a difference for governments and the citizens they serve', *Delivery Associates*, 2018.

Blair, Tony, 'The Agenda for a Generation', Ruskin College Oxford, 16 December 1996, http://www.educationengland.org.uk/documents/speeches/1996ruskin.html accessed 5 May 2015.

Blair, Tony, Labour Party Conference Speech, 1 October 1996, http://www.britishpoliticalspeech.org/speech-archive.htm?speech=202 accessed 22 November 2015.

Blair, Tony, 'Bringing Britain Together' Speech, London, 1997.

Blair, Tony, 'Touchstone Issues', 29 April 2000, https://www.theguardian.com/politics/2000/jul/17/labour.politicalnews1 accessed 13 June 2019.

Blair, Tony, 'Tony Blair's Victory Speech', *The Guardian*, 8 June 2001, http://www.theguardian.com/politics/2001/jun/08/election2001.electionspast1 accessed 20 November 2015.

Blair, Tony, Labour Party Conference Speech, 1 October 2002.

Blair, Tony, Prime Minister's Press Conference, 30 July 2003, http://webarchive.nationalarchives.gov.uk/20031229070736/http://www.pm.gov.uk:80/output/Page4295.asp accessed 19 October 2017.

Blair, Tony, Labour Party Conference Speech, 30 September 2003.

Blair, Tony, Speech at *The Guardian* public services summit, 29 January 2004.

Blair, Tony, Civil Service Reform Speech, 24 February 2004.

Blair, Tony, Public Service Reform speech, 23 June 2004.

Blair, Tony, Prime Minister's Press Conference, 22 July 2004, http://webarchive.nationalarchives.gov.uk/20080909020430/http://www.number10.gov.uk/Page6153 accessed 8 February 2018.

Blair, Tony, Labour Party Conference Speech, 28 September 2004.

Blair, Tony, Institute for Government, 28 June 2010, https://www.instituteforgovernment.org.uk/blog/evening-tony-blair accessed 28 May 2019.

Blair, Tony, *A Journey* (London: Hutchinson, 2010).

Blair, Tony, *On Leadership: Lessons for the 21st Century* (London: Hutchinson Heinemann, 2024).

Blunkett, David, *The Blunkett Tapes: My Life in the Bear Pit* (London: Bloomsbury, 2006).

Brown, Gordon, 'Speech on the 1998 Comprehensive Spending Review', House of Commons, 14 July 1998, http://www.ukpol.co.uk/2015/09/19/gordon-brown-1998-speech-on-the-comprehensive-spending-review/ accessed 20 October 2015.

Brown, Gordon, 'Modernising the British Economy: The New Mission for the Treasury' Speech, HM Treasury, 27 May 1999, http://webarchive.nationalarchives.gov.uk/20130129110402/http://www.hm-treasury.gov.uk/newsroom_and_speeches/speeches/chancellorexchequer/speech_chex_270599.cfm accessed 4 February 2016.

Brown, Gordon, Budget Speech, 17 April 2002, http://webarchive. nationalarchives.gov.uk/20100407010852/http://www.hm-treasury.gov.uk/bud_budget02_speech.htm accessed 20 February 2017.

Brown, Gordon, Speech to the Social Market Foundation, 3 February 2003.

Brown, Gordon, Budget Speech, 9 April 2003, http://webarchive. nationalarchives.gov.uk/20100202140748/http://www.hmrc.gov. uk/budget2003/index.htm accessed 12 September 2017.

Brown, Gordon, Statement on Economic and Monetary Union, Hansard, 9 June 2003.

Brown, Gordon, Labour Party Conference Speech, 29 September 2003.

Brown, Gordon, *My Life, Our Times* (London: Vintage Detail, 2017).

Bush, George W., 'Address to Congress', 20 September 2001.

Cabinet Office, 'Modernising Government White Paper', Cabinet Office, March 1999, https://www.wbginvestmentclimate.org/ uploads/modgov.pdf accessed 8 January 2016.

Cabinet Office, 'Civil Service Reform – Delivery and Values White Paper', 24 February 2004.

Cabinet Office, Ministerial Committee on Public Services and Public Expenditure (PSX),

http://webarchive.nationalarchives.gov.uk/20040722024905/ http://www.cabinet-office.gov.uk/cabsec/2003/cabcom/psx.htm accessed 18 July 2018.

Callaghan, James, Ruskin Speech: 'A Rational Debate Based on Facts', 18 October 1976, http://www.educationengland.org.uk/ documents/speeches/1976ruskin.html accessed 21 May 2015.

Campbell, Alastair, *The Alastair Campbell Diaries Volume 1: Prelude to Power 1994–1997* (London: Hutchinson, 2010).

Campbell, Alastair, *The Alastair Campbell Diaries Volume 2: Power and the People 1997–1999* (London: Hutchinson, 2011).

Campbell, Alastair, *The Alastair Campbell Diaries Volume 3: Power and Responsibility 1999–2001* (London: Random House, 2011).

Campbell, Alastair, *The Burden of Power: Countdown to Iraq* (London: Arrow, 2012).

Campbell, Alastair, *The Alastair Campbell Diaries Volume 5: Outside, Inside 2003–2005* (London: Biteback, 2016).

Capability Reviews: The Findings of the First Four Reviews, July 2006, http://www.civilservice.gov.uk/wp-content/uploads/2011/09/FindingsFirst4_tcm6-6649.pdf accessed 1 June 2015.

Churchill, Winston, 'The End of the Beginning' Speech, Mansion House, 10 November 1942.

Colville, John, *The Fringes of Power: Downing Street Diaries 1939–1955* (London: Hodder and Stoughton, 1985).

Committee on Standards in Public Life, 'Reinforcing Standards', 1 January 2000, http://webarchive.nationalarchives.gov.uk/20140131031506/http://www.archive.official-documents.co.uk/document/cm45/4557/chap6.pdf accessed 22 June 2016.

Committee on Standards in Public Life, 'Government Response to the Sixth Report', 26 July 2000, https://www.gov.uk/government/uploads/system/uploads/attachment_data/file/260853/4817.pdf accessed 22 June 2016.

Crisp, Nigel, *24 Hours to Save the NHS* (Oxford: OUP, 2011).

Crossman, Richard, *The Crossman Diaries: Selections from the Diaries of a Cabinet Minister 1964–1970* (ed.) A. Howard (London: Jonathan Cape/Hamish Hamilton, 1979).

Darling, Alistair, *Back from the Brink* (London: Atlantic Books, 2011).

Department of Health, The NHS Improvement Plan, 24 June 2004.

Department for Education and Skills, Five Year Strategy for Children and Learners, 8 July 2004.

Fulton Committee on the Civil Service, Report of the Committee, June 1968.

Gould, Philip, *The Unfinished Revolution: How New Labour Changed British Politics Forever* (London: Hachette Digital, 2011).

Healey, Denis, *The Time of My Life* (London: Michael Joseph, 1989).

Heywood, Jeremy, 'Men of Secrets, The Cabinet Secretaries: Interview with Sir Jeremy Heywood', Mile End Group, Queen Mary University of London, 2013, http://www.cabinetsecretaries. com/_lib/pdf/Former%20Cabinet%20Secretary%20Jeremy%20 Heywood%20Interview%20with%20Anthony%20Seldon.pdf accessed 20 January 2016.

Heywood, Suzanne, *What Does Jeremy Think? Jeremy Heywood and the Making of Modern Britain* (London: William Collins, 2020).

HM Treasury, 'Comprehensive Spending Review: Public Service Agreements 1999 – 2002', HM Treasury, December 1998, https://www.gov.uk/government/uploads/system/uploads/ attachment_data/file/260759/4181.pdf accessed 20 October 2015.

HM Treasury, 'Analysing UK Fiscal Policy' Report, November 1999, http://webarchive.nationalarchives.gov.uk/20130129110402/ http://www.hm-treasury.gov.uk/d/anfiscalp99.pdf accessed 16 November 2015.

HM Treasury, 'Reconciliation of SR 2000 PSA targets to SR 2002 PSA targets', July 2002, http://webarchive.nationalarchives.gov. uk/20071204200807/http://www.hm-treasury.gov.uk/media/7/8/ PSA%20reconciliation.pdf accessed 15 August 2017.

HM Treasury, 2002 Spending Review, July 2002, http://webarchive. nationalarchives.gov.uk/20071204144532/http://www.

hm-treasury.gov.uk/media/5/7/SR2002%20leaflet.pdf accessed 12 August 2017.

HM Treasury, 2004 Budget, 17 March 2004.

HM Treasury, 2004 Spending Review, July 2004, http://webarchive. nationalarchives.gov.uk/20070305105700/http://www.hm-treasury.gov.uk/spending_review/spend_sr04/report/spend_ sr04_repindex.cfm accessed 10 January 2018.

HM Treasury and PMDU, 'Devolving decision-making: Refining targets and performance management', March 2004, http:// webarchive.nationalarchives.gov.uk/+/http:/www.hm-treasury. gov.uk/media/9B9/26/devolving_decision1_409.pdf accessed 17 September 2017.

House of Commons Liaison Committee, 'Minutes of Evidence from Tony Blair', 16 July 2002, http://www.publications. parliament.uk/pa/cm200102/cmselect/cmliaisn/1095/2071602. htm accessed 23 June 2015.

House of Commons Public Administration Select Committee, 'Special Advisers: Boon or Bane?', 28 February 2001, http:// www.publications.parliament.uk/pa/cm200001/cmselect/ cmpubadm/293/29302.htm accessed 4 February 2016.

House of Commons Written Answers from the Prime Minister, 19 October 2001, http://www.publications.parliament.uk/pa/ cm200102/cmhansrd/vo011019/text/11019w01.htm accessed 8 August 2016.

House of Commons Public Administration Select Committee, 'Minutes of Evidence from Lord Browne of Madingley', 28 November 2002.

House of Commons Public Administration Select Committee, 'Minutes of Evidence from Michael Barber and Nick Macpherson', 27 February 2003, https://www.publications.parliament.uk/pa/

cm200203/cmselect/cmpubadm/482-i/3022702.htm accessed 9 May 2025.

House of Commons Public Administration Select Committee, 'Minutes of Evidence from Sir Andrew Turnbull', 13 March 2003.

House of Commons Public Administration Select Committee, 'Minutes of Evidence from Estelle Morris MP', 24 March 2003, http://www.publications.parliament.uk/pa/cm200203/cmselect/cmpubadm/62-x/3032405.htm accessed 18 August 2015.

House of Commons Public Administration Select Committee, 'Minutes of Evidence, Memorandum by the Government (PST 60)', March 2003, http://www.publications.parliament.uk/pa/cm200203/cmselect/cmpubadm/62-x/3032406.htm accessed 9 March 2015.

House of Commons Public Administration Select Committee, 'On Target? Government by Measurement', July 2003, http://www.publications.parliament.uk/pa/cm200203/cmselect/cmpubadm/62/62.pdf accessed 18 August 2015.

House of Commons Public Administration Select Committee, 'From Citizen's Charter to Public Service Guarantees', July 2008, https://publications.parliament.uk/pa/cm200708/cmselect/cmpubadm/411/41102.htm accessed 7 March 2019.

House of Lords Constitution Committee, 'The Cabinet Office and the Centre of Government', January 2010, http://www.publications.parliament.uk/pa/ld200910/ldselect/ldconst/30/30.pdf accessed 9 March 2015.

Hyman, Peter, *1 out of 10: From Downing Street Vision to School Reality* (London: Vintage, 2005).

Kim, Jim Yong, 'As Prepared for Delivery' speech, World Bank, 12 October 2012, http://www.worldbank.org/en/news/speech/2012/10/12/remarks-world-bank-group-president-jim-yong-kim-annual-meeting-plenary-session accessed 19 June 2015.

Labour Party Manifesto, 1997.

Mandelson, Peter and Roger Liddle, *The Blair Revolution: Can New Labour Deliver?* (London: Faber, 1996).

Mandelson, Peter, 'On the Record' Interview Transcript, BBC, 11 May 1997, http://www.bbc.co.uk/otr/intext/Mandelson11.5.97.html accessed 27 July 2015.

Mandelson, Peter, *The Blair Revolution Revisited* (London: Politico's, 2002).

Mandelson, Peter, *The Third Man* (London: Harper Press, 2010).

Memorandum of Conversation, 'Private meeting with Prime Minister Blair and British Cabinet', The White House, 29 May 1997, http://clinton.presidentiallibraries.us/files/original/5aa4876f138a60330e869d23b372880d.pdf accessed 23 June 2016.

Mulgan, Geoff and Andrea Lee, 'Better Policy Delivery and Design: A Discussion Paper', Performance and Innovation Unit, January 2001, http://www.civilservant.org.uk/library/policy/2001_piu_better_policy_delivery_and_design.pdf accessed 3 February 2016.

No. 10 Downing Street, 'Prime Minister's Press Conferences' June 2002 – December 2003, http://webarchive.nationalarchives.gov.uk/20031229072725/http://www.pm.gov.uk:80/output/Page2991.asp accessed 21 August 2017.

Office of the Deputy Prime Minister, 'The Social Exclusion Unit', Office of the Deputy Prime Minister, April 2004, http://webarchive.nationalarchives.gov.uk/+/http:/www.cabinetoffice.gov.uk/media/cabinetoffice/social_exclusion_task_force/assets/publications_1997_to_2006/seu_leaflet.pdf accessed 3 February 2016.

Osborne, George, Ed Balls and David Cameron, 'Inside Number 10: David Cameron – The First Six Months', *Political Currency* podcast, 2 January 2025.

Powell, Jonathan, *The New Machiavelli: How to Wield Power in the Modern World* (London: Bodley Head, 2010).

Reid, John, Choice Speech to the Health Network, 16 July 2003, http://webarchive.nationalarchives.gov.uk/+/http://www.dh.gov.uk/en/MediaCentre/Speeches/Speecheslist/DH_4071487 accessed 19 June 2018.

Report of the Hutton Inquiry, 28 January 2004.

Report of the Iraq Inquiry, 6 July 2016.

Sherman, Jill, 'Brown protects power base from expanded No. 10', *The Times*, 15 June 2001.

Straw, Jack, *Last Man Standing: Memoirs of a Political Survivor* (London: Macmillan, 2012).

Turnbull, Andrew, 'Cabinet Office: Reform and Delivery in the Civil Service', June 2002.

Turnbull, Andrew, Civil Service Reform Speech, 24 February 2004.

UK Polling Report, 1992–97, http://ukpollingreport.co.uk/historical-polls/voting-intention-1992-1997 accessed 11 June 2019.

Wanless Review: Interim Report, November 2001, http://webarchive.nationalarchives.gov.uk/20130107105354/http:/www.hm-treasury.gov.uk/consult_wanless_index.htm accessed 20 January 2017.

SECONDARY LITERATURE

Behn, Robert, 'How scientific is the "science of delivery"?' *Canadian Public Administration*, 60 (2017), pp. 89–110.

Best, Geoffrey, *Churchill: A Study in Greatness* (Oxford: Oxford University Press, 2003).

Blick, Andrew and George Jones, *Premiership: The Development, Nature and Power of The Office of the British Prime Minister* (Exeter: Imprint Academic, 2010).

Blick, Andrew and George Jones, *At Power's Elbow: Aides to the Prime Minister from Robert Walpole to David Cameron* (London: Biteback, 2013).

Blick, Andrew and George Jones, 'A century of policy advice in No. 10', No. 10 History Blog, 5 January 2017, https://history.blog.gov.uk/2017/01/05/a-century-of-policy-advice-at-no-10-part-one/#_ftn1 accessed 10 August 2018.

Bogdanor, Vernon, *From New Jerusalem to New Labour: British Prime Ministers from Attlee to Blair* (Hampshire: Palgrave Macmillan, 2010).

Botsman, Peter and Mark Latham, *The Enabling State: People Before Bureaucracy* (Annandale, NSW: Pluto Press, 2001).

Bower, Tom, *Gordon Brown* (London: HarperCollins, 2004).

Cabinet Office, 'Sir Jeremy Heywood Biography', Cabinet Office, February 2016, https://www.gov.uk/government/people/jeremy-heywood accessed 3 February 2016.

Campbell, John, *Edward Heath: A Biography* (London: Random House, 1993).

Castellani, Lorenzo, *The Rise of Managerial Bureaucracy: Reforming the British Civil Service* (Hampshire: Palgrave Macmillan, 2018).

Chote, Robert, Rowena Crawford, Carl Emmerson and Gemma Tetlow, 'Public Finances 1997 – 2010: 2010 Election Briefing Note', Institute for Fiscal Studies, March 2010, http://www.ifs.org.uk/bns/bn93.pdf accessed 16 November 2015.

Chote, Robert, Rowena Crawford, Carl Emmerson and Gemma Tetlow, 'Public Spending under Labour', Institute for Fiscal Studies, March 2010, https://www.ifs.org.uk/bns/bn92.pdf accessed 15 April 2020.

Cleary, Sian, *Undergraduate Dissertation: What impact did the machinery of government and leadership changes have to the PMDU 2005–2007?* Queen Mary, University of London, 2011.

Clement, Michelle, 'How to run a government', The Policy Institute, King's College London, 3 August 2015, https://blogs.kcl.ac.uk/policywonkers/how-to-run-a-government/ accessed 11 March 2019.

Clement, Michelle, 'The Art of Delivery: The Prime Minister's Delivery Unit 2001 to 2005', *No. 10 History of Government*, 26 August 2022, https://history.blog.gov.uk/2022/08/26/the-art-of-delivery-the-prime-ministers-delivery-unit-2001-2005/ accessed 9 August 2023.

Collins, James and Jerry I. Porras, *Built to Last: Successful Habits of Visionary Companies* (New York: HarperBusiness, 1994).

Collins, James, *Good to Great: Why Some Companies Make the Leap – and Others Don't* (New York: HarperBusiness, 2001).

Davis, Jon, *Prime Ministers and Whitehall 1960–74* (London: Hambledon Continuum, 2007).

Davis, Jon and John Rentoul, *Heroes or Villains?: The Blair Government Reconsidered* (Oxford: OUP, 2019).

Diamond, Patrick, 'New Labour and the Politics of Depoliticisation: The Delivery Agenda in Britain's Public Services 1997 – 2007', Policy and Politics Conference Paper, September 2013.

Evans, Alun, *The Intimacy of Power: An Insight into Private Office, Whitehall's Most Sensitive Network* (London: Biteback, 2024).

Everett, Michael and Ed Faulkner, 'House of Commons Briefing Paper: Special Advisers', House of Commons Library, 28 January 2015, www.parliament.uk/briefing-papers/SN03813.pdf accessed 22 June 2016.

Fawcett, Paul and Oonagh Gay, House of Commons Library Research Paper, 'The Centre of Government – No. 10, the Cabinet Office and HM Treasury', December 2005, http://

researchbriefings.parliament.uk/ResearchBriefing/Summary/ RP05-92 accessed 18 August 2015.

Friedman, Benjamin M., *The Moral Consequences of Economic Growth* (New York: Alfred A. Knopf, 2005).

Haddon, Catherine, 'Reforming the Civil Service – The Efficiency Unit', Institute for Government, 2012, https://www. instituteforgovernment.org.uk/publications/reforming-civil-service-efficiency-unit accessed 18 August 2015.

Harris, Josh and Jill Rutter, 'Centre Forward: Effective Support for the Prime Minister at the Centre of Government', Institute for Government, 2014, http://www.instituteforgovernment.org. uk/sites/default/files/publications/Centre%20Forward%20-%20 Final.pdf accessed 16 February 2015.

Hennessy, Peter, *Cabinet* (Oxford: Basil Blackwell, 1986).

Hennessy, Peter, *Whitehall* (London: Pimlico, 1990).

Hennessy, Peter, *Hidden Wiring: Unearthing the British Constitution* (London: Victor Gollancz, 1995).

Hennessy, Peter, *Muddling Through: Power, Politics and the Quality of Government in Postwar Britain* (London: Gollancz, 1996).

Hennessy, Peter, *The Prime Minister: The Office and its Holders since 1945* (London: Penguin, 2001).

Hennessy, Peter, *Distilling the Frenzy: Writing the History of One's Own Times* (London: Biteback, 2012).

Holt, Richard, *Second Among Equals: Chancellors of the Exchequer and the British Economy* (London: Profile, 2001).

Hood, Christopher and Gwyn Bevan, 'What's measured is what matters: Targets and Gaming in the English Public Health Care System', *Public Administration* 3 (2006), pp. 517–38.

Jarvis, Tim, 'Welfare-to-Work: The New Deal Research Paper' (London: House of Commons Library, 12 November 1997).

Jenkins, Simon, *Thatcher and Sons: A Revolution in Three Acts* (London: Allen Lane, 2006).

Kaufman, Gerald, *How to be a Minister* (London: Faber & Faber, 1997).

Kavanagh, Dennis and Anthony Seldon, *The Powers Behind the Prime Minister: The Hidden Influence of Number Ten* (London: HarperCollins, 2000).

Kelman, Steven, 'Improving service delivery performance in the United Kingdom: Organization theory perspectives on central intervention strategies', *Journal of Comparative Policy Analysis* 8 (2006), pp. 393–419.

Kettle, Martin, 'Peter Mandelson and Roger Liddle: The Blair Revolution', *Renewal* 4 (1996), pp. 94–7.

Kotter, John P., *Leading Change* (USA: Harvard Business Review Press, 2012).

Le Grand, Julian, 'Knights, Knaves or Pawns? Human Behaviour and Social Policy', *Journal of Social Policy* 26 (1997), pp. 149–69.

Le Grand, Julian, *Motivation, Agency and Public Policy: Of Knights and Knaves, Pawns and Queens* (Oxford: Oxford University Press, 2003).

Le Grand, Julian, *The Other Invisible Hand: Delivering Public Services Through Choice and Competition* (Oxford: Princeton University Press, 2007).

Lodge, Guy and Ben Rogers, 'Whitehall's Black Box: Accountability and Performance in the Senior Civil Service', Institute for Public Policy Research, 2006.

Marsh, David, David Richards and Martin Smith, 'Re-assessing the Role of Departmental Ministers', *Public Administration* 78 (2000), pp. 305–26.

Marsh, Ian, 'The Blair Governments, Public Sector Reform and State Strategic Capacity', *Political Quarterly* 80 (2009), pp. 33–41.

Nye, Joseph, *Soft Power: The Means to Success in World Politics* (New York: Public Affairs, 2004).

Panchamia, Nehal and Peter Thomas, 'Civil Service Reform in the Real World', Institute for Government, 2014, http://www.instituteforgovernment.org.uk/sites/default/files/publications/260314%20CSRW%20-%20final.pdf accessed 17 January 2015.

Peston, Robert, *Brown's Britain* (London: Short Books, 2005).

Prabhakar, Rajiv, *Stakeholding and New Labour* (Hampshire: Palgrave Macmillan, 2003).

Prabhakar, Rajiv, *Rethinking Public Services* (Hampshire: Palgrave Macmillan, 2007).

Rawnsley, Andrew, *Servants of the People: The Inside Story of New Labour* (London: Penguin Group, 2000).

Rawnsley, Andrew, *The End of the Party: The Rise and Fall of New Labour* (London: Penguin Group, 2010).

Rentoul, John, *Tony Blair: Prime Minister* (London: Sphere, 2001).

Richards, David and Martin J. Smith, 'Power, Knowledge and the Core Executive: the Living Chimera of the Public Service Ethos and the Role of the British Civil Service', *West European Politics* 23 (2000), pp. 45–66.

Richards, David and Martin J. Smith, 'Central control and policy implementation in the UK: A case study of the Prime Minister's Delivery Unit', *Journal of Comparative Policy Analysis* 8 (2006), pp. 325–45.

Richards, David, David Blunkett and Helen Mathers, 'Old and New Labour Narratives of Whitehall: Radicals, Reactionaries and Defenders of the Westminster Model', *Political Quarterly* 79 (2008), pp. 488–98.

Richards, Steve, *Whatever It Takes: The Real Story of Gordon Brown and New Labour* (London: Fourth Estate, 2010).

Riddell, Peter, *The Unfulfilled Prime Minister: Tony Blair's Quest for a Legacy* (London: Politico's, 2006).

Seldon, Anthony, *Blair* (London: Free, 2004).

Seldon, Anthony and Dennis Kavanagh (eds), *The Blair Effect 2001–05* (Cambridge: Cambridge University Press, 2005).

Seldon, Anthony, *Blair Unbound* (London: Simon and Schuster, 2007).

Seldon, Anthony and Guy Lodge, *Brown at 10* (London: Biteback, 2010).

Smith, Martin J., *The Core Executive in Britain* (Hampshire: Palgrave Macmillan, 1999).

Stothard, Peter, *Thirty Days: Tony Blair and the Test of History* (New York: HarperCollins, 2003).

Timmins, Nicholas, *The Five Giants: A Biography of the Welfare State* (London: William Collins, 2017).

Toynbee, Polly and David Walker, *Better or Worse: Has Labour Delivered?* (London: Bloomsbury, 2005).

Toynbee, Polly and David Walker, *Did Things get better? An Audit of Labour's Successes and Failures* (London: Penguin, 2001).

Turner, John, *Lloyd George's Secretariat* (Cambridge: Cambridge University Press, 1980).

Yong, Ben and Robert Hazell, *Special Advisers: Who they are, What they do, Why they matter* (London: Hart Publishing, 2014).

NEWSPAPER ARTICLES

Barber, Michael, '"A Heaven-Sent Opportunity": James Callaghan and the Ruskin Speech', *Times Educational Supplement*, September 1996, https://www.tes.co.uk/article.aspx?storycode=19771 accessed 5 May 2015.

Bevins, Anthony, 'New sleaze row knocks at door of No. 10', *The Independent*, 1 June 1997, http://www.independent.co.uk/news/new-sleaze-row-knocks-at-door-of-no10-1253774.html accessed 1 February 2016.

Blair, Tony, 'A Battle Half Won', *The Guardian*, 14 April 2002, http://www.theguardian.com/society/2002/apr/14/futureforpublic services.comment accessed 27 July 2015.

Blitz, James, 'Luck and loyalty help sunny outlook', *Financial Times*, 23 July 2004.

Bowie, Jess, 'Interview: John Manzoni', *Civil Service World*, 20 February 2015, http://www.civilserviceworld.com/articles/interview/interview-john-manzoni accessed 5 May 2016.

Brown, Gordon, 'On the Record' Interview Transcript, *BBC*, 23 March 1997, http://www.bbc.co.uk/otr/intext/Brown23.3.97.html accessed 27 July 2015.

Browne, Anthony, 'NHS faces another winter crisis', *The Observer*, 28 October 2001.

Butler, Patrick and Simon Parker, 'Foundation Trusts', *The Guardian*, 13 November 2002.

Cameron, Sue, 'Did Gordon Brown really keep us out of the Euro?', *Daily Telegraph*, 26 June 2013.

Carvel, John, 'Reid baffles NHS with revised standards', *The Guardian*, 11 February 2004.

Clement, Michelle, 'The new No10 Delivery Unit has the potential to turn Boris Johnson's rhetoric into real world outcomes', *The Independent*, 29 June 2021.

Coyle, Diane, 'Brown names economic advisers to the Treasury', *The Independent*, 4 August 1997, http://www.independent.co.uk/

news/business/brown-names-economic-advisers-to-the-treasury-1243908.html accessed 7 January 2016.

Davidson, Andrew, 'The MT Interview: John Gieve', *Management Today*, 1 July 2004.

Foster, Matt, 'Downing Street moves to tighten grip on Whitehall with new "Implementation Taskforces"', *Civil Service World*, 2 June 2015, http://www.civilserviceworld.com/articles/news/downing-street-moves-tighten-grip-whitehall-new-implementation-taskforces accessed 9 June 2015.

Grice, Andrew, 'Mr Targets on a mission to reform Whitehall', *The Independent*, 9 January 2003.

Grice, Andrew, 'Things have only got better. But will Blair benefit?', *The Independent*, 11 December 2004.

Hames, Tim, 'The Baghdad bounce makes Blair a winner on all fronts', *The Times*, 7 April 2003.

Happold, Tom, 'Milburn resigns from government', *The Guardian*, 12 June 2003.

Happold, Tom, 'Blair announces No. 10 shake-up', *The Guardian*, 3 September 2003.

Helm, Toby, 'Blair loses another aide', *Daily Telegraph*, 10 December 2003.

Hutton, Will, 'Three cheers for the public sector', *The Observer*, 13 April 2003.

Ivens, Martin, 'There's a big silver lining on that Tory cloud', *Sunday Times*, 17 June 2001.

Jenkins, Simon, 'The Treasury's own great train robbery', *The Times*, 12 October 2001.

Jenkins, Simon, 'From Power to the People to PowerPoint', *The Times*, 1 August 2003.

Jones, George, '67% of people think Byers should quit', *Daily Telegraph*, 28 February 2002.

Jones, George, 'Blair pledge to curb muggings in months', *Daily Telegraph*, 25 April 2002, http://www.telegraph.co.uk/news/uknews/1392109/Blair-pledge-to-curb-muggings-in-months.html accessed 24 June 2015.

Jones, George, 'Fury erupts at Blair's botched reshuffle', *Daily Telegraph*, 14 June 2003.

Leader, 'Labour Leader John Smith dies at 55', BBC News, 12 May 1994, http://news.bbc.co.uk/onthisday/hi/dates/stories/may/12/newsid_2550000/2550803.stm accessed 12 January 2016.

Leader, 'Billions for the NHS', BBC News, 21 March 2000, http://news.bbc.co.uk/1/hi/in_depth/uk/2000/budget2000/684419.stm accessed 5 February 2016.

Leader, 'Countdown to Crisis: Eight days that shook Britain', BBC News, 14 September 2000, http://news.bbc.co.uk/1/hi/uk/924574.stm accessed 5 February 2016.

Leader, 'Blair confirms election delay', BBC News, 2 April 2001, http://news.bbc.co.uk/1/hi/uk_politics/1255703.stm accessed 4 February 2016.

Leader, 'Labour has met its target on waiting-lists, but it was the wrong target', *The Independent*, 12 May 2001.

Leader, 'Tony Blair's Speech on Public Services', *The Guardian*, 21 May 2001.

Leader, 'Tony Blair's Victory Speech', *The Guardian*, 8 June 2001.

Leader, 'More Power for Downing Street', BBC News, 22 June 2001, http://news.bbc.co.uk/1/hi/uk_politics/1402492.stm accessed 8 August 2016.

Leader, 'An Act of Leadership', *The Guardian*, 26 January 2002, http://

www.theguardian.com/society/2002/jan/26/futureforpublic services.comment accessed 27 July 2015.

Leader, 'The disgraceful Stephen Byers', *The Economist*, 28 February 2002.

Leader, 'Responses to the 2002 Budget', *The Guardian*, 17 April 2002.

Leader, 'Blair sets street crime deadline', BBC News, 24 April 2002, http://news.bbc.co.uk/1/hi/uk_politics/1949358.stm accessed 23 June 2015.

Leader, 'Sixsmith to quit government post', *Daily Telegraph*, 7 May 2002.

Leader, 'Education receives £15bn extra', BBC News, 15 July 2002.

Leader, 'Hitting the ceiling', *The Times*, 16 July 2002.

Leader, 'Blair's four-point plan for action', *The Guardian*, 26 July 2002.

Leader, 'Street Crime Pledge Met', BBC News, 12 September 2002.

Leader, 'Education Secretary Resigns', BBC News, 25 October 2002, http://news.bbc.co.uk/1/hi/education/2359695.stm accessed 18 August 2015.

Leader, 'Million march against Iraq War', BBC News, 16 February 2003.

Leader, 'Weapons dossier sent back six times', BBC News, 6 June 2003.

Leader, 'Hospital shake-up scrapes through', BBC News, 8 July 2003.

Leader, 'New Labour, New Britain', *The Guardian*, 31 July 2003.

Leader, 'Blair wins key top-up fees vote', BBC News, 27 January 2004.

Leader, 'Star struck: Unhealthy tendencies in the latest reform of NHS targets', *The Times*, 9 February 2004.

Leader, 'NHS Targets: The art of aiming high', *The Guardian*, 11 February 2004.

Leader, 'Blair to end immigration abuse', BBC News, 7 April 2004.

Leader, 'At-a-glance: Spending Review', BBC News, 12 July 2004.

Leader, 'Blunkett resigns over visa accusations', BBC News, 15 December 2004.

Leader, 'Blair's inner circle', *The Guardian*, 27 January 2005.

Leader, 'The Budget', BBC News, 16 March 2005.

Leader, 'Targets can Kill', *Daily Telegraph*, 10 April 2005.

Leader, 'Chris Barber Obituary', *The Times*, 20 August 2012.

Leppard, David, 'Street crime soaring by 26%, Home Office figures reveal', *Sunday Times*, 10 February 2002.

Leppard, David, 'New migrant crisis hits Blunkett', *Sunday Times*, 4 April 2004.

Mandelson, Peter, 'On the Record' Interview Transcript, BBC, 25 February 1996, http://www.bbc.co.uk/otr/intext95-96/Mandelson25.2.96.html accessed 27 July 2015.

Milburn, Alan, 'We have to give the voters more than this', *The Times*, 7 August 2002.

Muir, Hugh, 'Politics Reformers' Rewards', *The Guardian*, 11 June 2005.

Mulholland, Helene, 'Profile: Ed Balls', *The Guardian*, 28 June 2007.

Parker, Simon, 'Following from the front', *The Guardian*, 13 February 2002.

Parker, Simon, 'Attack on Labour's "appalling public services failures"', *The Guardian*, 19 June 2002, http://www.theguardian.com/society/2002/jun/19/conferences.politics accessed 27 July 2015.

Rentoul, John, 'Gove (fails to) recruit another Blairite', *The Independent*, 24 March 2011, https://web.archive.org/web/20110326053551/http://

blogs.independent.co.uk/2011/03/24/gove-recruits-another-blairite/ accessed 6 June 2016.

Rentoul, John, 'Professor Balls on the "catastrophe" of running a surplus', *The Independent*, 16 November 2015, http://www.independent.co.uk/voices/comment/daily-catch-up-professor-balls-on-the-catastrophe-of-running-a-surplus-a6735796.html accessed 16 November 2015.

Rentoul, John, 'The whole point of setting a target is to distort activity', *The Independent*, 16 February 2016, https://www.independent.co.uk/voices/comment/daily-catch-up-the-whole-point-of-setting-a-target-is-to-distort-activity-sir-michael-barber-a6875681.html accessed 13 June 2019.

Riddell, Peter, 'Blair looks to business for Whitehall fix', *The Times*, 1 June 2001.

Riddell, Peter, 'No. 10's remote control focuses vision for a short time only', *The Times*, 26 July 2002.

Riddell, Peter, 'The jury's out but it's not listening to you, Mr Blair', *The Times*, 6 August 2003, http://www.thetimes.co.uk/tto/law/columnists/article2042602.ece accessed 10 August 2015.

Riddell, Peter, and Philip Webster, 'Farewell No. 11, hello Normanton', *The Times*, 3 July 2004.

Riddell, Peter, 'Headteacher's report: much work still to do', *The Times*, 23 July 2004.

Russell, Bertrand, 'Queen's Birthday Honours: Labour's reform architect honoured', *The Independent*, 11 June 2005.

Sieghart, Mary A., 'Stop boldly talking, it's time to boldly go for it', *The Times*, 31 July 2003.

Sparrow, Andrew, 'Sept 11: A good day to bury bad news', *Daily Telegraph*, 10 October 2001.

Tempest, Matthew, 'Labour MPs revolt over Iraq', *The Guardian*, 26 February 2003.

Tempest, Matthew, 'Cook resigns from Cabinet over Iraq', *The Guardian*, 17 March 2003.

Tempest, Matthew, 'Parliament gives Blair go-ahead for war', *The Guardian*, 18 March 2003.

Timmins, Nicholas, 'Extra NHS cash may be squandered', *Financial Times*, 8 January 2003.

Walker, David, 'There's a new chief executive, but old Whitehall still rules', *The Guardian*, 16 January 2015.

Wastell, David, 'BP executive to become Labour business adviser', *Sunday Telegraph*, 3 June 2001.

Watt, Nicholas, 'Blair berates old Labour "snobs"', *The Guardian*, 7 July 1999.

Watt, Nicholas and David Hencke, 'MPs say PFI has had its day', *The Guardian*, 24 March 2000, http://www.theguardian.com/business/2000/mar/24/privatefinance.society accessed 27 July 2015.

Watt, Nicholas and Patrick Wintour, 'Blair's regrets over three wasted years', *The Guardian*, 30 April 2007, http://www.theguardian.com/society/2007/apr/30/publicservices.politics accessed 27 July 2015.

Waugh, Paul, 'Milburn fuels row with Treasury over reform of hospitals', *The Independent*, 1 October 2002.

White, Michael, 'PM's speechwriter quits to teach', *The Guardian*, 16 February 2004.

Willetts, David, 'They haven't thought it through', *The Guardian*, 3 August 2001, http://www.theguardian.com/society/2001/aug/03/futureforpublicservices.comment accessed 27 July 2015.

Wintour, Patrick, 'Brown aims at lone parents after hitting youth jobs target', *The Guardian*, 1 December 2000, http://www.theguardian.com/society/2000/dec/01/socialcare.politics1 accessed 27 July 2015.

Wintour, Patrick, 'Lack method of measurement', *The Guardian*, 15 July 2002.

Wintour, Patrick, 'Blair to Double Foundation Hospitals Scheme', *The Guardian*, 30 July 2003.

Wintour, Patrick, 'Counter terrorism strategy comes under fire', *The Guardian*, 24 October 2005, http://www.theguardian.com/politics/2005/oct/24/terrorism.immigrationpolicy accessed 27 July 2015.

ACKNOWLEDGEMENTS

Fourteen years ago, someone who had a transformative impact on the public services we use and deeply value offered an opportunity which would have a transformative impact on the life of a person they had never met. That someone was Sir Michael Barber, and that person was me.

Michael Barber, a historian by training, had kept a diary of his time in Tony Blair's government while he was head of the Prime Minister's Delivery Unit. Michael Barber approached Professor Jon Davis about using these diaries for wider benefit. They agreed to include the diaries as part of a remarkable PhD project. I was selected as the right person to pursue the project. After quite a journey, the PhD was completed in 2020. The next task was to turn a thesis into a book, and for that I sought advice from the godfather of contemporary British government history – Professor the Lord Peter Hennessy. Peter, who had taught me as an undergraduate back at Queen Mary University of London, saw value in the project being published. He along with my mentor and colleague Jon Davis offered invaluable advice on a book proposal.

The years of work this book required were fuelled by the purpose I saw in the project from the first time it was proposed. As a millennial, I was a beneficiary of Blair's public service reforms. At primary school in the late 1990s, I remember the introduction of numeracy and literacy hour to raise expectations and results. Then as a pupil at a large comprehensive school, I saw first-hand the sweeping renewal of the state. Not least the cold, dingy portacabins being replaced with extensive new school buildings and sports facilities. There was a fresh sense of pride and ambition in the school. I am also the daughter of a secondary school science teacher. When I was fifteen, a work experience placement in the flagship Sure Start programme showed me how policymakers and public servants make change happen. Fast forward to studying British government at university, where it became clear to me that public services were transformed across the board during Blair's decade as Prime Minister. Yet it was also stark that New Labour received very little acknowledgement for this achievement, both at the time and in the immediate aftermath. Indeed, it has taken decades for us to start to look back and see that period as a golden age for high-quality public services.

It is now more widely recognised that Blair's reforming zeal grew over time and that he, his Cabinet and his Chancellor Gordon Brown worked in their different ways to take the welfare state from the low ebb of 1997 to the high-water mark achieved in the first decade of the 2000s. By the time this book project came about, we had also begun to see the 'science of delivery' method being disseminated around the world. Yet, it seemed to me as a historian that there were still gaps in understanding what it *really* must have taken to achieve such transformative change. How were the lessons that appear to be common-sense today actually learnt back then? That is the story that fascinated me; it is the story that I have sought to unearth and share. Any mistakes in these pages are my own.

I would like to thank the many individuals who made this book possible. Sir Michael Barber for seeing the value of history and for his enduring trust and belief in the project. It is no small thing to give someone the only copy of your diaries for several years. The many ministers, civil servants and special advisers who granted me interviews and answered my questions: Ed Balls, Michael Barber, Tony Blair, David Blunkett, Robin Butler, Charles Clarke, John Gieve, Nick Macpherson, Alan Milburn, Sally Morgan, Vanessa Nicholls, David Normington, Tony O'Connor, Jonathan Powell, Clara Swinson and Richard Wilson. For many of these individuals, this was the first time they had spoken publicly about the inner workings of public service reform and delivery. Thanks also go to the special guests who have shared their reflections with my students on the 'New Labour Years' postgraduate class, which I lead at King's College London. The course is co-taught alongside the brilliant John Rentoul, chief political commentator at *The Independent*, biographer of Blair and someone whom I am grateful to have been able to exchange and sharpen ideas with.

My deep thanks go to the 'irrepressibly upbeat' Jon Davis for his incredible generosity, vision and friendship over almost two decades. To James Johns for making the PhD project possible. To my PhD supervisors (aforementioned) Jon Davis and the late Professor Richard Roberts for their guidance. To my examiners Professor Helen Parr and Dr Martin Farr for the rigorous viva and helpful comments. To Peter Hennessy for setting the standard and being a source of endless technicolour inspiration. To my colleagues Jack Brown, Martin Stolliday and Chetun Patel, whose humour and wisdom I have drawn on. To Eleanor Hallam and Ashley Sweetman: our PhD fellowship kept me upbeat and resilient through the inherently solitary PhD process. To Marie Kemplay and Sian Cleary, who were early pioneers (via their research dissertations) in examining the Delivery Unit. To my much-loved colleagues past and present at the Strand Group (and the Mile End Group before it) – under the entrepreneurial leadership of Jon Davis, our shared values and camaraderie underpin my professional life. Thank you also to Professor Bobby Duffy and the Policy Institute at King's for providing a supportive and energising environment. To my past and present students at King's College London, your interest and engagement refines my thinking and allows me to do what I love. To my family and friends, who saw this journey unfold over many years and willed me on. To my publishers at Biteback, Olivia Beattie and James Stephens, who believed in this project (and the next one) enough to take a chance on a new author. Thank you all!

Over several years, I collected many threads of perspective to weave together the inside story of how the Blair government transformed Britain's public services. My intention is that this book offers value for those who see the benefit in capturing and learning about how government works in practice. After all, new Prime Ministers and their governments do not arrive to a clean slate; they are deeply impacted (whether they know it or not) by what came before – and therefore so are all of us.

Michelle Clement
London
February 2025

ABOUT THE AUTHOR

Dr Michelle Clement is a historian of British government. She is a lecturer and researcher at the Strand Group, in the Policy Institute, King's College London. She is also researcher in residence at 10 Downing Street.

INDEX